OECD PROCEEDINGS

D0308766

Macroeconomic Policies and Structural Reform

ORGANISATION FOR ECONOMIC CO-OPERATION AND DEVELOPMENT

9000476

ORGANISATION FOR ECONOMIC CO-OPERATION AND DEVELOPMENT

Pursuant to Article 1 of the Convention signed in Paris on 14th December 1960, and which came into force on 30th September 1961, the Organisation for Economic Co-operation and Development (OECD) shall promote policies designed:

– to achieve the highest sustainable economic growth and employment and a rising standard of living in Member countries, while maintaining financial stability, and thus to contribute to the development of the world economy;
– to contribute to sound economic expansion in Member as well as non-member countries in the process of economic development; and
– to contribute to the expansion of world trade on a multilateral, non-discriminatory basis in accordance with international obligations.

The original Member countries of the OECD are Austria, Belgium, Canada, Denmark, France, Germany, Greece, Iceland, Ireland, Italy, Luxembourg, the Netherlands, Norway, Portugal, Spain, Sweden, Switzerland, Turkey, the United Kingdom and the United States. The following countries became Members subsequently through accession at the dates indicated hereafter: Japan (28th April 1964), Finland (28th January 1969), Australia (7th June 1971), New Zealand (29th May 1973), Mexico (18th May 1994), the Czech Republic (21st December 1995) and Hungary (7th May 1996). The Commission of the European Communities takes part in the work of the OECD (Article 13 of the OECD Convention).

FOREWORD

On 18-19 January 1996, the OECD Economics Department convened an international conference on "Interactions between Structural Reform, Macroeconomic Policies and Economic Performance", as part of the follow-up programme of work on the *OECD Jobs Study*. This volume of the conference proceedings contains the papers presented at the conference and summarises the discussions that took place.

Since the early 1980s, OECD Member countries have adopted a policy strategy that pursues macroeconomic stability and structural reforms designed to improve the functioning of markets. While inflation is now low, fiscal positions have deteriorated, prospects for long-run growth have not improved, unemployment has increased, particularly in Europe, and there are concerns about inequality and living standards. OECD countries thus face challenges to which the policy response has been insufficient. The conference sought to assess why this has been so, and to provide a wide spectrum of opinion about how to meet these challenges. In particular, it sought to identify and assess the cost and benefits of structural reform, the nature of the political resistance to it, and how macroeconomic policies interact with change in structures and institutions designed to promote trade and growth.

This proceedings volume, published on the responsibility of the Secretary-General of the OECD, is intended as a contribution to the ongoing, policy debate on how to achieve faster growth from which all sections of society benefit and to which they can contribute.

TABLE OF CONTENTS

Opening remarks   7

List of participants   11

Session I: The Benefits of Structural Reform for Economic Performance

Combatting Unemployment: Is Flexibility Enough?
  Richard Jackman, Richard Layard and Stephen Nickell   19

Comments by Werner Röger   51

General discussion   57

The Macroeconomic Effects of Financial Sector Reforms:
an Overview of Industrial Countries
  Palle Andersen and William White   59

Annex: The "Credit Channel" view   83

Comments by Alan Winters   99

General discussion   103

Trade Liberalisation and Economic Performance
  Jan Haaland and Victor Norman   105

Appendix: Model and Reference Case   119

Comments by Nicholas Vanston   123

General discussion   127

Session II: Interaction among Macroeconomic Policies and Structural Reform

Structural Reforms and their Implications for Macroeconomic Policies
Hans Gersbach and George Sheldon 131
Comments by Richard Jackman 169

Macroeconomic Policy in the Presence of Structural Maladjustment
Robert Gordon 173
Comments by Robert Ford 205

Substitutabilities vs Complementarities between Structural and
Macroeconomic Policies
Jean-Paul Fitoussi 209
Comments by Flemming Larsen 229

Long-run Macroeconomic Effects of Fiscal Consolidation and Increased
Competition in Europe
Werner Röger 237
Appendix: Selection of Parameter Values for European Wage Rule
and the Mark-up? 257
Comments by Palle Andersen 263
General discussion of session II 269

Session III: The Key Challenges and Priorities for the OECD
in Pursuit of Improved Structural Reform

Labour Market Implications of Changing Corporate Governance in Japan
Masaru Yoshitomi 273
Comments by Yutaka Imai 297

Tax Reform in the United States: Prospects and Potential Effects
Alan Auerbach 301
Appendix: The Auerbach-Kotlikoff Simulation Model? 315

Structural Reform in OECD Countries: Critical Interactions with the Rest
of the World
Alan Winters 317

Concluding discussion 341

OPENING REMARKS

by

Kumiharu Shigehara
Head of Economics Department, OECD

It is a great pleasure for me to welcome you all to this international conference on Interactions between Structural Reform, Macroeconomic Policies and Economic Performance. I would like to explain the background to this conference and to give some guidance on the arrangements.

Institutionally, this conference is part of the follow-up work, which Ministers asked the Organisation to carry out upon the completion of the 1994 OECD Jobs Study. This work proceeds on two tracks. One deals with the establishment of country-specific policy recommendations, aiming to adapt and flesh out the general policy recommendations contained in the Jobs Study so as to fit to the specific conditions that prevail in individual OECD countries. This work is beginning to see the light of day in the form of chapters dedicated to this issue in OECD country surveys.

The other track of the follow-up work to the Jobs Study consists of a number of so-called thematic reviews. These are in-depth studies of particular issues dealt with in the Jobs Study but where it was felt that analysis should be taken further. Let me just mention that thematic reviews are currently being prepared for the OECD Ministerial Meeting in May on active labour market policies; the role of and interaction between tax and transfer systems; and, the role of technology in affecting labour market outcomes. The fourth thematic review deals with the topic of this conference, that is the interactions between structural reform, macroeconomic policies and economic performance.

The issue of macro-structural interactions is not a new one to the OECD. To give but one example, this was something the Economics Department discussed in its publication "Assessing Structural Reform – Lessons for the Future" which was published in 1994. In addition to summarising OECD countries' experience with structural reform over the 1990-93 period, we drew out ten lessons for future structural reform. Time is short here, so let me mention just lesson 10 which in headline form read: There can be synergies between structural reform and the macroeconomic environment.

Despite much work on macro-structural interactions both at the OECD and elsewhere, our knowledge remains incomplete. For us to live up to our role as policy advisors, we need to be able to give better answers to the questions which policy makers are faced with when trying to implement and refine the OECD policy strategy which was adopted in the early 1980s. It will be recalled that this strategy had a medium-term focus and assigned to macroeconomic policies the primary role of providing a stable macroeconomic environment through price stability and sound fiscal positions. Structural policies, on the other hand, were to enhance the efficient working of economies and improve the allocation of resources.

Countries have made varying progress along this path. Most progress has been achieved in reforming financial markets, on the structural side, and on moving towards price stability, on the macroeconomic side. However, there has so far been little if any progress in restoring health to public finance, and structural reforms in labour and product markets have been insufficient to prevent a significant rise in unemployment, particularly in Europe. At the same time, financial markets have sometimes been characterised by highly volatile behaviour.

Against this background, I hope this conference will take us further in at least two areas of concern to policy makers. The first is the documentation that structural reform *is* useful. For policy makers, it is important to be able to demonstrate that appropriate reform can improve economic performance. This is so because reforms usually involve short-term costs and only bring benefits in the longer run. Moreover, the benefits are often spread thinly over large segments of the population whereas the costs are concentrated on more narrow groups who have a clear incentive to resist reform. As policy advisers, we are therefore in the business of having to supply the arguments needed to convince sceptical electorates of the need for reforms.

Secondly, the conference should take us further in the discussion of how to implement the policy strategy and, in particular, how policy interactions can help or hinder implementation. Several issues are of interest here. One relates to the appropriate sequencing of structural reforms. An intriguing aspect of this is that the optimal sequencing may be different from an economic and a political view. For example, the sequencing which may look economically efficient in the sense of reducing transition costs and achieving the benefits as quickly as possible may not be the sequencing which maximises the political momentum behind reform and gives the best chances of advancing reform on a broad front.

Another issue is what role macroeconomic policies should play in the implementation of structural reform. It can be argued – and is indeed argued in some of the papers we have in front of us – that macro policies should aim to smooth the way for structural reform. For example, in order to gain acceptance of reform, policy makers may promise that macro policy will react quickly to take up any slack developing as a result of reform. Alternatively, the view might be that only when the situation is really desperate and macro policies look absolutely un-yielding is it possible to gain sufficient political momentum for structural reform.

Finally, structural policies also have an important role to play in facilitating the conduct, and in improving the outcome, of macro policies. For example, the combination of financial de-regulation and lack of structural adjustment in European labour markets may sometimes have acted to increase interest rate premia and the cost of capital, discouraging business investment. Higher interest rates have also spilled over into budget balances. As another example, the costs of disinflation in the 1980s in terms of both the duration and the magnitude of the necessary increase in unemployment was higher in those countries which had not put in place the appropriate labour and product market reforms. As a third example, one might wonder whether the effectiveness of monetary policy in Japan has been undermined by the less developed state of capital markets, at a time when the transmission of monetary policy through the banking channel has been weakened by balance-sheet problems. People may well disagree on the relative importance of the three examples, but they illustrate the type of impacts that structural conditions may have on the macroeconomic environment and policies.

On the organisation of the conference, let me say the following. We have three half-day sessions to discuss ten papers and to draw up policy conclusions. This means we have a heavy programme in front of us. The three papers to be presented in this morning's session focus on the effects of structural reform on economic performance, on the time frame over which these effects occur and the factors which may accelerate the benefits and reduce the transitional costs. In the afternoon session, we will move on to discuss interactions between macro and structural policies on the basis of four papers which focus mainly on Europe and its unresolved structural unemployment and budgetary problems. In the session tomorrow morning, we will aim to identify the main challenges for the future by region and in the global context. Before wrapping up the discussion of the previous day, we shall consider reform issues that are of specific importance in Japan and the United States, and the last of the ten conference papers to be presented before the concluding debate will provide us a useful reminder that further liberalisation of international flows of goods, services and capital has to play an important role in the structural reform process. This process is far from being completed with many opportunities to the mutual benefit of trading nations still remaining unexploited.

LIST OF PARTICIPANTS

Palle S. Andersen, *Senior Economist, Bank for International Settlements*

Mr. Andersen has been with the BIS since 1982 and prior to that was Head of Division in the OECD. He has also been associated with the Reserve Bank of Australia, first as a visiting scholar and later as Head of the Research Department.

Alan J. Auerbach, *Professor and Director, Robert D. Burch Center for Tax Policy and Public Finance*

Mr. Auerbach is currently Robert D. Burch Professor of Economics and Law, and Director of the Burch Center at the University of California, Berkeley. Formerly Professor of Economics and Law at the University of Pennsylvania, and Chairman of the Economics Department at Penn from 1988 through 1990. He has served as Deputy Chief of Staff of the US Joint Committee on Taxation in 1992 and as a consultant to the US Treasury in the formulation of its 1984 tax reform proposals. He has also consulted the OMB, the Finance Ministry of Sweden, the New Zealand Treasury, the OECD, the IMF and the World Bank on issues of taxation, and appeared frequently as an invited witness before committees of the House and Senate on a variety of topics. His professional affiliations include Research Associate of the National Bureau of Economic Research since 1978, an elected Fellow of the Econometric Society in 1986, and he served as an elected member of the Executive Committee of the American Economic Association from 1992 through 1994.

Alan Budd, *Chief Economic Advisor, H.M. Treasury*

Mr. Budd has been Chief Economic Adviser to Her Majesty's Treasury since 1991. Before that he was Economic Adviser to Barclays Bank. Between 1974 and 1988 he was at the London Business School where he was Professor of Economics and Head of the Centre for Economic Forecasting. He started his professional career as a Lecturer in Economics at Southampton University. He followed that by a period in the early 1970s as an Economic Adviser at the Treasury. He has been a visiting Professor at Carnegie-Mellon University in Pittsburgh and at the University of New South Wales in Sydney. He is Deputy Chairman of the Economic Policy Committee of the OECD.

Jean-Paul Fitoussi, *University Professor at the Institut d'études politiques de Paris and Secretary general of the Association internationale des sciences économiques*

Mr. Fitoussi's research focuses on the theories of inflation, unemployment, foreign trade and the role of macroeconomic policies. He is author of a number of major books in these areas. As President of the Observatoire français des conjunctures économiques, and founder and member of an international economic policy group within this institution, he has made numerous written contributions to the current economic policy debate, notably on issues of European economic integration.

Robert Ford, *Counsellor for Macroeconomic Policy, OECD*

Mr. Ford joined the Bank of Canada Research Department in 1982. In 1988 he joined the OECD Economics Department as a Senior Economist. Between 1992 and 1995 he was a senior Economist and Deputy Division Head in the Research Department of the IMF before returning to the OECD Economics Department in his current post.

Hans Gersbach, *Professor, University of Heidelberg*

Mr. Gersbach has been Full Professor at the University of Heidelberg since August 1995 after having been Associate Professor at the University of Basel in Switzerland. In 1992 he was Research Project Manager in the McKinsey Global Institute in Washington DC. Before that he was Assistant Professor of economics at the University of Basel and visiting scholar at the University of California in Los Angeles. After he had completed his doctoral thesis he also worked with McKinsey & Co. in Switzerland.

Robert J. Gordon, *Stanley G. Harris Professor in the Social Sciences, Northwestern University*

Mr. Gordon has been at Northwestern University since 1973. His research focuses on differences in economic behaviour among Europe, Japan and the United States, and on changes in US economic performance over the past century. He is a Research Associate of the National Bureau of Economic Research and a Research Fellow of the Centre for Economic Policy Research (London). He is a Guggenheim Fellow, a Fellow and Treasurer of the Econometric Society, and a senior adviser to the Brookings Panel of Economic Activity. He is co-founder and from 1978 to 1994 co-organiser of the International Seminar on Macroeconomics. In 1995-96 he has served on a national commission to assess the accuracy of the US Consumer Price Index.

Yutaka Imai, *Head of Country Studies Division, OECD*

Mr. Imai joined the OECD Secretariat in 1975. Throughout his career at the OECD he has worked in different capacities in the Department of Economics, including as Counsellor to the Head of Department. Prior to joining the OECD he was Senior Consultant at the Boston Consulting Group and taught macroeconomics and corporate finance at the University of California, Los Angeles and the University of Southern California.

Richard Jackman, *Reader in Economics at the London School of Economics, and Programme Director for Human Resources at the Centre for Economic Performance*

Mr. Jackman has written extensively on unemployment policies and long-term unemployment, and on labour market problems in transitional economies. He has been a Consultant to the World Bank, and more recently to the International Labour Office in connection with the ILO/UNDP project on Economic Policy and Employment. He is joint author with Richard Layard and Stephen Nickell of *Unemployment: Macroeconomic Performance and the Labour Market* (Oxford University Press, 1991).

Flemming Larsen, *Deputy Director, Research Department, IMF*

Mr. Larsen joined the World Economic Studies Division of the IMF's Research Department in 1985, and became Chief of that Division in 1988. In 1992 he assumed the senior responsibility for the World Economic Outlook project. In 1990-91, on external assignment from the IMF, he served as Head of the International Monetary and Financial Matters Division in DGII of the European Commission. In 1984-85, he was Director of Forecasting of Wharton Econometrics. Earlier in his career, he spent ten years with the Economics Department of the OECD, where he worked as a country desk office and as a senior economist in the Economic Prospects Division.

Richard Layard, *Director of the London School of Economics' Centre for Economic Performance*

Mr. Layard has worked for many years on the problems of unemployment and inflation and is co-author of *Unemployment: Macroeconomic Performance and the Labour Market* (1991). During the 1970s he worked on income distribution, co-authoring *The Causes of Poverty* for the Royal Commission on that issue. He was also part-time consultant to the Treasury. During the mid-1980s he was Chairman of the Macroeconomic Policy Group set up by the European Commission, and later co-chairman of the World Economy Group set up by the UN University. In 1985 he founded the Employment Institute in the United Kingdom to press for action to prevent long-term unemployment. Since 1991 he has worked as a part-time adviser to the Russian government.

Thorvald Moe, *Chief Economic Adviser and Deputy Permanent Secretary at the Norwegian Ministry of Finance*

Before taking up his present position in 1989, Mr. Moe was Norwegian Ambassador to the OECD for three years. During this period he was on special leave from the Ministry of Finance where he started his career in 1970 and where, since 1978, he has been Director General of the Economic Policy Department. He has served on various commissions and committees, including as Chairman of Working Party No. 1 of the Economic Policy Committee of the OECD and Vice-Chairman of the Norwegian Green Tax Commission on Policy to Promote Sustainable Development. Since 1990 he has also held a teaching assignment as part-time professor of macroeconomics at the Bodø Graduate School of Business.

Philippe Nasse, *Managing Director for Economic Policy and Forecasts, ministère de l'Économie*

Mr. Nasse took up his present position in January 1994. Before that he was Head of École nationale de la statistique et de l'administration économique. Between 1982 and 1990 he was Deputy Director at the Direction de la prévision after having served for several years as Head of the Short-term Analysis Department at the Institut national de la statistique et des études économiques of which he is Inspecteur général.

Victor D. Norman, *Professor, Norwegian School of Economics, Bergen*

Mr. Norman started his academic career in 1971 as Assistant Professor of shipping economics at the Norwegian School of Economics, where four years later he was appointed Professor of International Economics, and where in 1990-92 he was Vice-rector. In 1993-94 he lectured international economics at the Agder University College. He was visiting fellow at the Universities of Warwick and Sussex, and he has recurrently been visiting professor at the Stockholm School of Economics. Since 1987 he has been Research Fellow at the Centre of Economic Policy Research in London and since 1993 also at the Centre for Economic Performance, London School of Economics.

Werner Röger, *Economist, European Commission*

Mr. Röger joined the European Commission in 1989, serving in the Economic Modelling Unit of the Directorate General for Economic and Financial Affairs. Before that he worked seven years as a research officer at the Institute for Applied Economics in Tübingen, Germany.

Kumiharu Shigehara, *Head of the Economics Department, OECD*

Mr. Shigehara was appointed Head of the Economics Department and Chief Economist at the Organisation for Economic Co-operation and Development in Paris in May 1992. He served in the OECD on three previous occasions. He first joined the OECD in 1970 and served as the Head of Monetary Division from 1972 to 1974; he was Deputy Director of the General Economics Branch from 1980 to 1982, and its Director from 1987 to 1989. Before and after his services in the OECD, he held various posts at the Bank of Japan, including that of Manager on International Finance and Domestic Policy Planning. Before taking up his present position, he was Director General of the Institute for Monetary and Economic Studies and Chief Economist at the Bank of Japan.

Nicholas J. Vanston, *Head of Research Allocation Division, OECD*

Originally from the private sector, where he helped start a consultancy company, Mr. Vanston joined the OECD in the mid-1970s. He has worked in several Divisions in the Economics Department, including as a senior economist on two Country Desks. He was also responsible during several years for the analysis and projections of foreign trade and current accounts of the OECD, involving a four-year assignment as OECD Secretary to the Group of Ten. Since September 1995, he is Head of the Resource Allocation Division of the Economics Department, which has responsibility for providing policy analysis and advice on labour and product markets in OECD countries.

William R. White, *Economic Adviser, Head of the Monetary and Economic Department, Bank for International Settlements*

Mr. White took up his present position in May 1995. He began work as an economist in the Bank of England in 1969 and from there he moved to the Bank of Canada in 1972. In 1979 he became Chief of the Bank of Canada's Research Department and was appointed Adviser to the Governor in 1984. In 1988 he was appointed Deputy Governor, where his responsibilities included the analysis of international economic and financial developments, and operational matters pertaining to the Bank 's activities in foreign exchange markets.

L. Alan Winters, *Chief of the International Trade Division of the World Bank*

Mr. Winters is on leave from his post as Professor of Economics at the University of Birmingham, UK and was for six years Co-Director of the International Trade Programme of the Centre for Economic Policy Research. His publications include numerous books and articles on topics such as non-tariff barriers, European Integration, East-West trade, agricultural protection and the GATT. He is currently working on the role of regional arrangements in development.

Masaru Yoshitomi, *Vice Chairman of the Research Institute of the Long-Term Credit Bank of Japan*

Mr. Yoshitomi is also Visiting Executive Professor at the Wharton School of the University of Pennsylvania and Chairman of the US-Japan Management Studies Center at Wharton. Before that he held various senior positions in the Japanese Government and the OECD: in 1991-1992 Director General of the Co-ordination Bureau of the Economic Research Institute of the Economic Planning Agency (EPA); from 1987 to 1991 Director General of the Economic Research Institute of the EPA and from 1984 to 1987 Director in the Economics and Statistics Department of the OECD. Earlier on he worked during six years as an economist for the United Nations in Bangkok and for the IMF in Washington DC.

Session I

THE BENEFITS OF STRUCTURAL REFORM
FOR ECONOMIC PERFORMANCE

COMBATTING UNEMPLOYMENT: IS FLEXIBILITY ENOUGH?

Richard Jackman, Richard Layard and Stephen Nickell[1]
London School of Economics and Political Science

What is the route to lower unemployment? Is it through greater labour market flexibility, involving deregulation and decentralisation? Or are there areas where more collective action, rather than less, is required?

To examine this issue we have tried to see how differences of policy and institutions affect the unemployment levels in the different OECD countries. (We are concerned not with cyclical fluctuations but with the average levels of unemployment over a run of years.) The factors whose possible influence we examine are:

- how unemployed people are treated (benefit levels and active help with job-finding);
- how wages are determined;
- how skills are formed;
- how far jobs are protected by redundancy legislation;
- how heavily employment is taxed; and
- how far labour supply is reduced through reductions in hours of work and through early retirement.

Our conclusions are that the most important influences on unemployment come from the first three factors.

- The longer *unemployment benefits* are available the longer unemployment lasts. Similarly, higher levels of benefits generate higher unemployment, with an elasticity of around one half. On the other hand *active help* in finding work can reduce unemployment. So more "flexibility" may need to be complemented by more intervention to provide active help.
- Union coverage and union power raise unemployment. But if *wage bargaining* is decentralised, wage bargainers have incentives to settle for more than

the "going rate", and only higher unemployment can prevent them leap-frogging. Although decentralisation makes it easier to vary *relative* wages, this advantage is more than offset by the extra upward pressure on the *general* level of wages. Thus, where union coverage is high, co-ordinated wage bargaining leads to lower unemployment.

– Conscious intervention to raise the *skill levels* of less able workers is an important component of any policy to combat unemployment. Pure wage flexibility may not be sufficient because it leads to growing inequality which in turn discourages labour supply from less able workers.

Thus in our first three areas it is clear what types of reform are needed. If well designed, such reforms might halve the level of unemployment in many countries.

But there are other proposed remedies some of which have been advocated either in the OECD Jobs Study or the Delors White Paper. These include: less employment protection, lower taxes on employment, and lower working hours. Our research does not suggest that lower employment taxes or lower hours would have any long term effects; while the effects of lower employment protection would be small.

– *Lower employment protection* has two effects. It increases hiring and thus reduces long-term unemployment. But it also increases firing and thus increases short-term unemployment. The first (good) effect is almost offset by the second (bad) one. The gains from flexibility are small.

– *Employment taxes* do not appear to have any long-term effect on unemployment and are borne entirely by labour. There may be some short-term effects, but it is not clear that there would be any fall in inflationary pressure if taxes on polluting products were raised at the same time as taxes on employment were lowered.

– *Hours of work* appear to have no long-term effect upon unemployment. Equally, if *early retirement* is used in order to reduce labour supply, it is necessary to reduce employment pari passu unless inflationary pressure is to increase. While flexible hours and participation can reduce the fluctuations in unemployment over the cycle, they cannot affect its average level.

We can now proceed to the evidence for these assertions. We begin by looking at the pattern of unemployment differences between countries and estimate an equation which explains it, using all the factors we find significant. We then discuss each factor in turn, drawing on other evidence where relevant. We end with policy conclusions.

COUNTRY DIFFERENCES

There are wide differences in unemployment rates across countries, but one feature of these differences has been little noticed: a large part of the variation is in long-term unemployment. This is shown in Table 1. It appears that countries can live with very different rates of long-term unemployment, whereas some short-term unemployment seems inevitable. The reason for this "optional" nature of long-term unemployment appears to be that long-term unemployment has a much lower effect on wage pressure than does short-term unemployment (OECD 1993, p. 94).

To explain unemployment it is therefore useful to explain separately not only the total of unemployment but also its two different parts (short-term and long-term). We shall explain unemployment rates in 1983-88 and 1989-94, using the following main explanatory variables:

– Replacement rate (per cent).

– Benefit duration (years; indefinite = 4 years).

– Active labour market policy per unemployed person as per cent of output per worker (ALMP).

– Union coverage (1 under 25 per cent, 2 middle, 3 over 75 per cent).

Table 1. **Unemployment rates, total, long-term and short-term**

Percentage

	1983-88			1989-94		
	Total	Long-term	Short-term	Total	Long-term	Short-term
Belgium	11.3	8.0	3.3	8.1	5.1	2.9
Denmark	9.0	3.0	6.0	10.8	3.0	7.9
France	9.8	4.4	5.4	10.4	3.9	6.5
Germany	6.8	3.1	3.7	5.4	2.2	3.2
Ireland	16.1	9.2	6.9	14.8	9.4	5.4
Italy	6.9	3.8	3.1	8.2	5.3	2.9
Netherlands	10.5	5.5	5.0	7.0	3.5	3.5
Portugal	7.6	4.2	3.5	5.0	2.0	3.0
Spain	19.6	11.3	8.4	18.9	9.7	9.1
United Kingdom	10.9	5.1	5.8	8.9	3.4	5.5
Australia	8.4	2.4	5.9	9.0	2.7	6.2
New Zealand	4.9	0.6	4.3	8.9	2.3	6.6
Canada	9.9	0.9	9.0	9.8	0.9	8.9
United States	7.1	0.7	6.4	6.2	0.6	5.6
Japan	2.7	0.4	2.2	2.3	0.4	1.9
Austria	3.6	n.k.	n.k.	3.7	n.k.	n.k.
Finland	5.1	1.0	4.0	10.5	1.7	8.9
Norway	2.7	0.2	2.5	5.5	1.2	4.3
Sweden	2.6	0.3	2.3	4.4	0.4	4.0
Switzerland	0.8	0.1	0.7	2.3	0.5	1.8

Note: Long-term means over one year.
Source: Total: OECD standardised rates except for Italy (which is the US BLS measure). Long-term: Total times share of long-term in total (as in OECD Employment Outlook, appendix).

- Co-ordination in wage bargaining (1 low, 2 middle, 3 high).
- Employment protection (ranking: 1 low, 20 high).
- Change in inflation (percentage points per annum).

The last variable is included because it is always possible to achieve a temporary fall in unemployment through allowing inflation to increase.[2] The value of the variables are in Table 2.

The explanatory regression was a pooled regression for the two sub-periods. (We checked that the two sets of coefficients in the two sub-periods were not as a set significantly different.) The results are in Table 3. In the equation for long-term unemployment we also include short-term unemployment as a regressor.

OECD countries do of course display quite severe persistence in unemployment, and our two six-year periods may not be long enough to eliminate these effects.[3] However, terms measuring lagged unemployment were either insignificant or incorrectly signed, and have therefore not been included. The pooled regression was however estimated by the random-effects method which to some extent discounts the effects of persistent country specific factors.

Turning to our results, we can first explain the cross-country variation of *long-term* unemployment. All the variables reflecting the treatment of unemployed people come in with the predicted sign. The system of wage bargaining is also important. Employment protection *raises* long-term unemployment.

However when we turn to *short-term* unemployment, things change. Not surprisingly, benefit duration and active labour market policy (ALMP) are unimportant. And, as expected, employment protection *reduces* short-term unemployment, by reducing the inflow to unemployment.

Turning to the effects on total unemployment, employment protection has an insignificant effect. But unemployment does respond to how unemployed people are treated and to how wages are determined.

To understand why all these variables might affect unemployment, we need to see how they fit into an integrated framework. This is provided by the system of wage and price equations. Assuming no price surprises, we have

Wage equation

$$\log W = \_\gamma \log(cu) + Z + \log(Y/L) \tag{1}$$

Price equation (simplified)

$$\log W = \beta + \log(Y/L) \tag{2}$$

where W is the real cost per worker, u the unemployment rate, c the "effectiveness" of the unemployed, Z the impact of other wage pressure variables, and Y/L is output per head of labour force.

Table 2. **Explanatory variables**[1]

	Replacement rate	Benefit duration	ALMP	Union coverage	Union coordination	Employer coordination	Employment protection	Change in inflation
Belgium	60	4	10.0 / 14.6	3	2	2	17	-0.76 / -0.52
Denmark	90	2.5	10.6 / 10.3	3	3	3	5	-0.86 / -0.46
France	57	3.75 / 3	7.2 / 8.8	3	2	2	14	-1.38 / -0.30
Germany	63	4	12.9 / 25.7	3	2	3	15	-0.34 / -0.04
Ireland	50 / 37	0.5	9.2 / 9.1	3	1	1	12	-1.52 / -0.54
Italy	2 / 20	4	10.1 / 10.3	3	2	2 / 2	20	-1.68 / -0.52
Netherlands	70	0.5 / 2	4.0 / 6.9	3	2	2	9	-0.14 / 0.14
Portugal	60 / 65	3.5 / 0.8	5.9 / 18.8	3	2	2	18	-2.74 / -1.28
Spain	80 / 70	4	3.2 / 4.7	3	1	1	19	-1.24 / -0.60
United Kingdom	36 / 38	4	7.8 / 6.4	3 / 2	2	1	7	0.16 / -1.02
Australia	39 / 36	0.5	4.1 / 3.2	2	2	1	4	0.02 / -1.24
New Zealand	38 / 30	0.5	15.4 / 6.8	2	2 / 1	1	2	0.36 / -1.22
Canada	60 / 59	0.5 / 1	6.3 / 5.9	1	1	1	3	-0.08 / -0.84
United States	50	0.5	3.9 / 3.0	2	1	1	1	-0.04 / -0.48
Japan	60	0.5	5.4 / 4.3	2	2	2	8	-0.20 / -0.36
Austria	60 / 50	4	8.7 / 8.3	3	3	3	16	-0.46 / 0.06
Finland	75 / 63	1.5 / 2	18.4 / 16.4	3	3 / 2	3	10	-0.26 / -0.72
Norway	65	1.5	9.5 / 14.7	3	3	3	11	-0.34 / -1.12
Sweden	80	1.2	59.5 / 59.3	3	3	3	13	-0.75 / -1.02
Switzerland	70	1	23.0 / 8.2	2	1	3	6	-0.12 / -0.50

1. When variable changes between the two sub-periods, the first number is for 1983-88 and the second for 1989-94.

Source: **Replacement rate and benefit duration**: Mainly US Department of Health and Social Services, *Social Security Programmes throughout the World*, 1985 and 1993. See LNJ Annex 1.3. **ALMP**: *OECD Employment Outlook*, 1988 and 1995. For the first sub-period the data relate to 1987 and for the second to 1991. We include all active spending, except on the disabled. **Union coverage – union co-ordination and employer co-ordination**: See LNJ Annex 1.4 and *OECD Employment Outlook* 1994 pp. 175-185. **Employment protection**: *OECD Jobs Study* (1994) Part II Table 6.7 Col. 5 p. 74. Country ranking with 20 as the most strictly regulated. **Inflation**: *OECD Economic Outlook*.

Table 3. **Regressions to explain log unemployment rate**

20 OECD countries, 1983-88 and 1989-94, percentage

	Total unemployment (1)		Long-term unemployment (2)		Short-term unemployment (3)	
Replacement rate (percentage)	0.011	(1.6)	0.004	(0.5)	0.009	(1.2)
Benefit duration (years)	0.09	(1.3)	0.16	(1.9)	0.04	(0.6)
ALMP (percentage)	−0.008	(0.7)	−0.03	(2.0)	−0.0008	(0.07)
Union coverage (1-3)	0.66	(2.7)	0.56	(1.7)	0.54	(2.2)
Co-ordination (1-3)	−0.68	(3.2)	−0.29	(0.9)	−0.57	(2.4)
Employment protection (1-20)	−0.005	(0.2)	0.09	(2.7)	−0.04	(1.6)
Change in inflation (percentage points per annum)	−0.17	(1.7)	−0.13	(1.1)	−0.15	(1.6)
Constant	−3.96	(7.3)	−3.28	(2.9)	−3.8	(7.0)
Dummy for 89-94	0.16	(1.9)	0.1	(0.9)	0.16	(2.1)
Log (short-term unemployment)		..	0.94	(4.0)		..
R^2	0.59		0.81		0.41	
s.e.	0.51		0.59		0.52	
N	40		38		38	

Dependent variables:
(1)   Total unemployed as percentage of labour force.
(2)   Long-term unemployed (over one year) as percentage of labour force.
(3)   Short-term unemployed (under one year) as percentage of labour force.
t-statistics in brackets. These are based on the method of "random effects".

Notes: ALMP is measured by current active labour market spending as percentage of GDP divided by current employment. To handle problems of endogeneity and measurement error this is instrumented by active labour market spending in 1987 as percentage of GDP divided by average unemployment rate 1977-79. The coefficients measure the proportional effect on unemployment of a unit change in an independent variable; where the unit is measured as in Table 2.

Thus the equilibrium unemployment rate is given by

$$\log(cu) = \frac{Z - \beta}{\gamma}.$$ (3)

The key variables affecting unemployment are those which affect "wage pressure" (namely c and the Zs) plus the effect of unemployment in offsetting wage pressure (γ). We can now examine each of the possible causes of unemployment for their effect on wage pressure.

POLICIES TO THE UNEMPLOYED

Benefits

Benefits work through two mechanisms. First, they reduce the fear of unemployment and thus directly increase wage pressure from the unions (a simple Z factor). But second, and more important, they reduce the "effectiveness" of unemployed people (c) as fillers of vacancies. This encourages *employers* to raise wages. It also reduces the competition which newly unemployed workers will face in their search for jobs, which again encourages the *unions* to push for higher wages.

Since any reduction in effectiveness (c) leads to an equiproportional increase in unemployment, one can obtain an estimate of the effects of benefits (working through c) from micro cross-sectional studies which explain exit rates by benefits, holding vacancies constant. These estimates typically give an elasticity of exit rates with respect to the replacement ratio of around one half, with a wide range on either side (Narendranathan *et al.*, 1985; Atkinson and Micklewright 1991).

A second key dimension of unemployment benefits is their potential duration. Long-term benefits increase long-term unemployment. There are two processes at work here. First benefits reduce exit rates in general. But the resulting long-term unemployment further reduces exit rates. For in those countries where long-term unemployment is common, the exit rates for the long-term unemployed are much lower than for the short-term unemployed – in other words they have lower c. At least in part this appears to reflect a state-dependence of exit rates on duration (Jackman and Layard, 1991). Thus the incidence of long-term unemployment shifts out the U/V curve in many European countries (Budd, Levine and Smith, 1988).

However when unemployment benefits run out quite quickly exit rates decline much less as duration lengthens. This is confirmed by Meyer and Katz (1991) and Carling *et al.*, (1995) for the US and Sweden, where benefits run out after 6 and 14 months respectively. By contrast in Britain and Australia, where benefits are long-lived, there is much more state dependence. (Jackman and Layard, 1991; Fahrer and Pease, 1993.)

Active labour market policies (ALMP)

If long-duration benefits have negative effects, one approach is simply to provide *no help* to unemployed people beyond some period. Given sufficient wage flexibility, this will increase employment. But the cost will be more unequal wages, and not all of long-term unemployment will be eliminated.

An alternative is to provide *some help* to all who do not get benefit, but to give it through activity rather than though benefits. This cuts off the flow of long-term unemployment at least for the period for which the active measures last, and gives all the unemployed at least a chance to prove themselves.

This latter alternative is the Swedish model: active labour market policy *replaces* benefits. It should be sharply distinguished from other systems of active labour market policy where the uptake of the help offered is voluntary, so that labour market activity is an *optional alternative* to benefits. While active labour market policies of the second kind do continue in many countries, there is an interesting shift towards the Swedish model in Switzerland, while Denmark which has always had a similar general approach to Sweden's has now shortened the "passive" period of benefit duration to two years (Schwanse, 1995). In our regression equation, we find that dropping Sweden eliminates the effect of active labour market policy spending on long-term unemployment, consistent with the view that only Swedish-style ALMPs make a real difference.

The case for active labour market policy comes of course from social cost-benefit analysis. But it is also important to note that in terms of costs and benefits to the Ministry of Finance, *optional* ALMP is quite costly per unit reduction in unemployment, since those helped by the subsidy will include a disproportionate number of people who would have exited anyway (the problem of "deadweight"). *Replacement* ALMP can more nearly break-even, since all of those still unemployed are helped; there is thus a known maximum for the proportion of those helped who would have exited otherwise (the problem of "deadweight" is reduced, through avoiding creaming).

The other problem with active labour market policy is "substitution and displacement" – if an employer employs someone who would not have exited otherwise, this may disemploy someone else who would otherwise have been employed. In normal discussions this problem is greatly exaggerated. For the aim of ALMP is to help people who would otherwise have had low exit probabilities. By positive discrimination in their favour, vacancies go to them rather than to others who had better exit probabilities (were more employable). The effect is to increase the total stock of employable workers who are still unemployed. So vacancies get filled faster and employment expands. By helping the hard to place, the total stock of employable labour expands. In response the total stock of jobs expands.

We can easily see this in the context of our model – equations (1) and (2). There is a certain required level of cu. Through the active labour market policy the average effectiveness of the unemployed (c) is increased. This decreases wage pressure at each level of unemployment (see Figure 1). In consequence there is an increase in the equilibrium employment rate. Assuming that when prices are set the mark-up of prices over wages is constant, as in Figure 1, unemployment falls by the same proportion that average effectiveness (c) rises.

But what about substitution and displacement? If for example action is taken to help the long-term unemployed, does this increase short-term unemployment? The logic of our model says No.

Suppose the short-term unemployed have effectiveness c_s and the long-term unemployed have effectiveness c_L. Equilibrium requires a given level of $(c_s u_s + c_L u_L)$ in order to restrain wage pressure. We now through ALMP improve c_L, while c_s remains unchanged. What happens? u_L falls and u_s remains unchanged. Why?

◆ Figure 1. *Effects of Active Labour Market Policies (ALMP)*

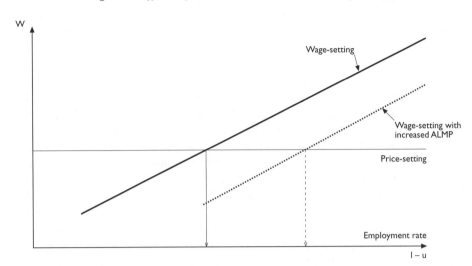

The stock of short-term unemployed depends on the total inflow into unemployment (S) and on the exit rate from short-term unemployment. This latter is equal to c_s times the exit rate for a person with effectiveness equal to unity, *i.e.*, it equals $c_s S/cu\ L$, where L is labour force. But cu is given. Thus if S/L and c_s remain unchanged, so does the exit rate from short-term unemployment and so does the stock of short-term unemployed.

The short-term unemployed get the same number of jobs per period because the long-term unemployed also get the same number of jobs per period. The only thing that has changed is that the *stock* of long-term unemployed has fallen since the exit rate from long-term unemployment has risen. Thus the long-term unemployed do not take jobs from the short-term unemployed.

There is no job-fund. Employment expands as the effective supply of labour expands. This should be obvious to anyone who contemplates the employment miracle which occurred when the Pilgrim Fathers landed at Cape Cod and found a sudden increase in the demand for labour on those inhospitable shores. But, as expressed so far, it is a medium term argument. In the short-run there may be some constraints on the demand side. For example, if nominal demand is fixed, an increase in the effective supply of labour will generate *some* new jobs, due to lower inflation, but the increase in jobs will be less than the increase in labour supply. If, however, the government has an inflation target, then even in the short-run employment will increase in line with the effective supply of labour.

This result provides important insights but may need modifying to suit the details of particular schemes. In any case it says nothing about the effectiveness of particular schemes. This depends on how well they do indeed improve the effectiveness of the individuals who are exposed to them.

Clearly schemes are more effective when they are not optional (see above) but then they are also more difficult to study – since there is no control group. Thus most studies of ALMP relate to optional schemes and compare people who were and were not exposed to such schemes. The microeconomic studies have been well summarised in OECD (1993) and Fay (1995). The general findings are i) a good return to assistance with job-finding; ii) a goodish return to subsidised self-employment; iii) some return to targeted recruitment subsidies; iv) a weaker return to public sector job creation and v) an often weak return to the training of unemployed people. In most cases heavy deadweight is the main factor reducing the return.

Our conclusion is that major expansions of ALMP can only be justified where the aim is to achieve universal coverage of some group (e.g., the long-term unemployed). This will greatly reduce deadweight, since in any disadvantaged group the overall outflow rates are generally low. It is also the only way to make any large dent in unemployment.

Going further, what is needed is in fact a change of regime. When people enter unemployment they need to understand that there will be no possibility of indefinite life on benefits. Instead it should be made clear that, after a period of say one year, public support will be provided only through participation on a programme. But access to the programme is guaranteed. This will have the twin effect of a) helping those who really need help and b) driving off the public purse those who only want help in the form of cash.

This is the Swedish model, which played a central role in holding down Swedish unemployment to around 2 per cent until the end of the 1980s.[4] The model has of course come under heavy pressure recently due to bad macroeconomic management: over-expansionary policy in the late 1980s followed by over-contraction. The Swedes have been right to continue with ALMP, since institutional/cultural arrangements of this kind cannot easily be re-established once they have been abandoned (Layard, 1995). But the experience makes it clear that ALMP is not primarily a counter-cyclical device – it needs to be a permanent feature of the economic and social system.[5]

WAGE BARGAINING

The next key factor affecting equilibrium unemployment is the system of wage determination. In systems where wages are settled in a decentralised way (either by employers' fiat or by bargaining) there is always a problem of leapfrogging. Even in the absence of bargaining, some employers may have an incentive to pay an "efficiency" wage above the supply price of labour, in order to motivate and retain staff. Indeed, unless unemployment is high enough, they will generally try to pay more than the going wage paid by other employers. Unions will also seek to raise their pay above that of other unions.

This problem of leapfrogging can be reduced when wages are centrally co-ordinated (namely by centralised positions adopted by the unions and the employers). A simple illustration will suffice, where unions can freely choose their pay so as to maximise the expected income of their members. If the choice is *decentralised*, the union chooses the firm-level wage (W_i) to maximise a function like (W_i-A)N_i where N_i is firm-level employment, and A is expected income outside the firm. A is then given by $(1 - u)W^e + uB$, where W^e is the expected outside wage and B benefits. (The price level is taken as exogenous.) This leads to a wage given by

$$\frac{W_i - A}{W_i} = \left(\frac{\partial N_i}{\partial W_i} \frac{W_i}{N_i} \right)^{-1}$$

So, for equilibrium (W_i equal to W^e), unemployment is given by

$$u = \left(\frac{\partial N_i}{\partial W_i} \frac{W_i}{N_i} \right)^{-1} \left(1 - \frac{B}{W} \right)^{-1}$$

By contrast a *centralised* union would be setting the wage for everybody and would choose it to maximise NW, recognising that workers disemployed by the wage settlement would have no alternative income opportunity (so that A = 0), unemployment benefits simply being a transfer from employed to unemployed union members. Unless an increase in employment required a more than proportionate fall in the real wage, the union would choose a wage consistent with full employment. A similar result can be obtained in a wage bargaining model. If by contrast employers set efficiency wages, there are also advantages from co-ordination to reduce leap-frogging, though employers would collectively choose non-zero unemployment as a worker-discipline device.

All this is on the assumption of homogenous labour. If labour is heterogenous, the arguments for decentralisation become more powerful. Under co-ordinated bargaining it is quite difficult to achieve the shifts in relative wages that may be required in response to differential shifts of relative demands and supplies. Thus co-ordinated bargaining reduces unemployment by cutting out leapfrogging, but increases it by worsening structural imbalances. The overall outcome is an empirical issue.

The issue appears to be quite clearly resolved in Table 2. Co-ordination has a powerful influence in reducing unemployment. An unco-ordinated economy will have, other things equal, an unemployment rate more than twice as high as an economy with highly co-ordinated wage-setting arrangements. Our results suggest, however, that a fully co-ordinated economy with a high degree of union coverage will have approximately the same unemployment rate as an economy with low union coverage and no co-ordination.

In this context we should perhaps refer to the view of Calmfors and Driffill (1988) that, while full centralisation has advantages, co-ordination at the industry level gives the worst of all worlds (due to the low demand elasticity for labour in one industry). The implication is that if full centralisation is too difficult, one should go for full decentralisation. We believe this argument is misleading. On the empirical level the finding is not robust (Soskice, 1990). Moreover it ignores the obvious point that, when comparing countries, it is not only the degree of centralisation which rises but the degree of union coverage. The United States does not have decentralised bargaining; it has hardly any unions. Other things equal, higher coverage is bad for employment but this effect can be offset by sufficient co-ordination. This is precisely what our equation shows.

With regard to the impact of relative wage flexibility, we tried introducing the degree of wage dispersion as a further independent variable in the Table 3 regressions. It turned out insignificant in relation to total unemployment (t = 0.6) and long-term unemployment (t = −0.9), but to have a significant positive effect (t = 4.2) in increasing short-term unemployment. These results suggest the complexity of the issues surrounding wage flexibility.

The truth is that co-ordination is a very subtle affair.[6] But the more there is, it appears, the better. Equally the task of achieving it appears to have become more difficult, possibly reflecting the greater exposure to international competition in both product and factor markets in recent years.

SKILLS IMBALANCE[7]

One possible reason why unemployment is higher than in the 1970s is the steady fall in the demand for unskilled workers. If this is not matched by an equal fall in supply, this can certainly cause an increase in unemployment.

To see this we can (for simplicity) divide the labour force into two categories, skilled and unskilled denoted 1 and 2 respectively. We shall assume that output is produced by a Cobb-Douglas production function

$$Y = A N_1^{\alpha_1} N_2^{\alpha_2} K^{\alpha_3} \qquad (\alpha_1 + \alpha_2 + \alpha_3 = 1)$$

Thus the demand for labour of type i is given by[8]

$$\ln W_i \_ \log \alpha_i + \log(Y / L) - \log l_i + u_i \tag{4}$$

where W is the cost per worker, L total labour force and $l_i = L_i/L$. It follows that, if the unemployment rate of a group is to remain constant when α_i rises or falls, wages must adjust in line. Equally, when the labour force composition changes, wages must also adjust.

The problem is that wages do not normally adjust as they "should". Usually it takes extra unemployment to get wages down. There is much evidence to support the following wage equation

$$\ln W_i = \_\gamma \log u_i + z_i + \log(Y/L) \tag{5}$$

where z_i measures a return of wage pressure effects. From (1) and (2) we can see that the unemployment of a group is determined by

$$u_i + \gamma \log u_i = \log l_i - \log \alpha_i + z_i \tag{6}$$

If the relative demand for a group (α_i) falls faster than the relative supply of people in that group (l_i), then $(\log l_i - \log \alpha_i)$ falls, and the unemployment rate in that group rises. There is thus a ceaseless race between shifts in demand and shifts in supply.

The change in unemployment of group i is

$$du_i = \phi_i (d \log l_i - d \log \alpha_i)$$

where $\phi_i = u_i/(u_i + \gamma)$. We can interpret this in terms of Figure 2. The demand for type i labour (relative to its supply) shifts to the left by the same amount if the labour supply (l_i) increases by 1 per cent or the labour demand (α_i) falls by 1 per cent. Both of the shifts in supply and demand have the same effect. The effect on unemployment is greater the more rigid are wages. The lower is g the more rigid are wages and the greater the rise in unemployment. Moreover the absolute rise in unemployment is greater the higher the existing level of unemployment (u_i) – due to the curved nature of the wage function.

In modern societies a race is in progress between the increase in the demand for skilled labour (measured by α_1) and the supply of skilled labour (measured by l_1). If the supply of skill fails to increase as fast as the demand, total unemployment will rise. To see this, note that the total change in unemployment is

$$du = d(u_1 l_1 + u_2 l_2) = u_1 dl_1 - u_2 dl_1 + l_1 du_1 + (1 - l_1) du_2$$
$$= \_(u_2 - u_1) dl_1 - (\phi_2 - \phi_1) dl_1 + (\theta_2 - \theta_1) d\alpha_1$$

where $\theta_i = \phi_i l_i/\alpha_i$.

The first of these terms is a pure composition effect – if the labour force becomes more concentrated in low-unemployment groups, unemployment will tend to fall. The second term reflects the problems which stem from wage rigidity. Since log wages depend on *log* unemployment, one extra point of unemployment reduces wages less for a group whose unemployment is high. Thus switching labour into the skilled group *reduces* overall unemployment – the downwards force on skilled

◆   Figure 2. **Effect of an upwards shift in the relative supply (l_i) and demand of labour (α_i)**

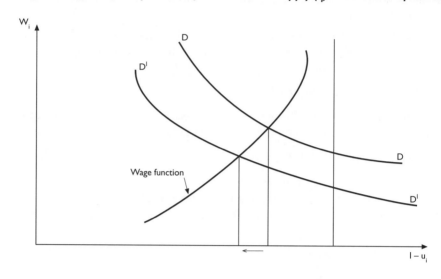

Note: For definitions see text.

wages outweighs the upwards force on unskilled wages ($\phi_2 - \phi_1 > 0$). The third term shows the effect of technical progress raising the relative demand for skilled labour. Since $l_2/\alpha_2 > 1$ and $l_1/\alpha_1 < 1$, a rise in the demand for skilled labour (α_1) *raises* overall unemployment, by raising the demand for labour where the wage pressure responds sharply to extra demand and reducing demand where wages are unresponsive to demand.

Empirical work

Empirical work using this kind of approach is still at a preliminary stage. However Nickell and Bell (1995*a* and *b*) give results using a similar model, with a more general CES production function. They tentatively estimated that on average one fifth of the rise in unemployment from the late 1970s to the late 1980s in Germany, Holland, Spain, the United Kingdom and Canada was due to structural shifts of demand relative to supply. Nickell (1995*b*) gives similar results.

EMPLOYMENT PROTECTION

It is widely believed that labour market flexibility is good for the macroeconomy and that employment protection legislation is an impediment to such flexibility. So it is argued that freedom of action for employers to dismiss workers on economic grounds is necessary for a smoothly functioning economy, though it is of course desirable to protect employees from arbitrary, unfair or discriminating dismissals. However, it may be tricky in practice to protect employees from arbitrary dismissal while simultaneously allowing freedom of action for employers to dismiss on economic grounds. Thus it may be felt necessary by benevolent legislators to circumscribe this freedom of action.[9] The macroeconomic consequences of this are, however, of major importance – both on the process of short-run adjustment and on the long-run equilibrium level of unemployment.

Theoretical background

Employment protection has a potential impact at a number of different points in the operation of the labour market. It obviously impedes employment adjustment by reducing both flows from employment, because of the legal hurdles, and flows into employment by making employers more cautious about hiring. It may also influence wage determination, for example by raising the power of insiders or by lengthening unemployment duration. Finally, because of the excessive caution of employers, it may impede the absorption of new entrants into the labour market thereby reducing participation rates and raising relative youth unemployment rates.

Consider the following model, where we ignore nominal inertia (wage/price stickiness), labour force growth and trend productivity effects. Wage setting is given by

$$\log W = -\gamma_I u - \gamma_{II} \Delta u + z_w$$ (7)

where z_w are wage pressure shocks. The demand for labour is given by

$$n = \lambda n_{-1} - (1-\lambda)\beta_I \log W + (1-\lambda) z_n$$ (8)

n = log employment, z_n = labour demand shifts (e.g., productivity shocks) and β_1 is the *long-run* labour demand elasticity. If we suppose the labour force to be fixed and normalised to unity, (8) can be written as

$$u = \lambda u_{-1} + (1-\lambda)\beta_I \log W - (1-\lambda) z_n.$$ (9)

Then, eliminating real wages from (7) and (9), we obtain

$$u = \alpha_{II} u_{-1} + (1-\alpha_{II}) u^*$$ (10)

where u^* is the equilibrium unemployment rate, given by

$$u^* = \frac{\beta_I z_w - z_n}{1 + \beta_I \gamma_I},$$ (11)

and the speed of adjustment, $1\text{-}\alpha_{11}$, is given by

$$1-\alpha_{11} = \frac{\beta_1\gamma_1 + 1}{\beta_1\gamma_1 + \beta_1\gamma_{11} + (1-\lambda)^{-1}}. \tag{12}$$

From this analysis, we see that there are two important questions. First, how might employment protection influence the *speed of adjustment*, $1\text{-}\alpha_{11}$? Second, how might employment protection affect the *equilibrium unemployment rate*, u^*? The first of these is straightforward. We would expect employment protection to raise employment adjustment costs and this would increase λ. Furthermore, employment protection may tend to increase long-term unemployment by reducing the rate of flow from unemployment to employment, as employers become more cautious about hiring. This will typically generate hysteresis effects in wage determination and thereby raise γ_{11}. Increases in both λ and γ_{11} will tend to reduce the overall speed of adjustment, $1\text{-}\alpha_{11}$.

Turning to the second question, namely the impact on equilibrium unemployment, it is important to recognise that, just because employment protection may tend to lengthen the duration of unemployment spells, this does not mean that it will necessarily raise equilibrium unemployment, u^*. For offsetting the duration effect is the reduction in flows. The flow into unemployment is obviously reduced by regulations designed to restrict dismissals. Since the unemployment rate is the product of the inflow rate and the mean duration, the overall effect of employment protection on u^* is indeterminate.

Looking at the formula for u^* in (11), there are a number of possibilities. First, employment protection may influence wage pressure, z_w, directly, for example, by raising the power of insiders. Second, employment protection can raise the impact of unemployment on wages, γ_1, by making the threat of unemployment more unpleasant (longer duration, harder to find alternative employment). On the other hand, of course, since employees are protected against dismissal to some extent, the threat of unemployment is less germane and this will *reduce* γ_1. So the overall effect on u^* is ambiguous.

Finally, we have not modelled participation in this exercise but we should consider the implications of employment protection for employment rates as well as unemployment rates when we come to our empirical investigation.

Evidence on unemployment dynamics

Our purpose in this section is to explore the evidence on the relationship between employment protection, employment adjustment and both the dynamics of labour demand (λ) and the extent of hysteresis in wage determination (γ_{11}).[10]

We first investigate the relationship between some empirical measures of λ, a measure of the rate of turnover of employees within companies (the percentage of employees with job tenures less than two years, PL2) and the OECD composite ranking of the tightness of employment protection (EP). The data are reported in Table 4. The first point to note is the very strong correlation between EP and PL2, the correlation coefficient between the two variables being 0.9. So the variation in the rate of turnover (as captured by the proportion of employees with less than two years tenure) is explained almost entirely by the strictness of the employment protection laws. The relationship between PL2 and our various measures of λ is set out in Table 5. In two out of the three cases, we see that PL2 is significantly related to the aggregate measure of labour demand sluggishness (λ). Overall, therefore, there is some evidence in favour of the hypothesis that the speed of adjustment in labour demand is negatively related to the strictness of employment protection legislation.

Turning next to wage determination, we are concerned here with the relationship between the degrees of hysteresis (γ_{11}) and employment protection, operating via long-term unemployment. The impact of long-term unemployment on the extent of hysteresis is confirmed explicitly in Layard et al. (1991), Chapter 9, Table 9 and implicitly in OECD (1993, Chapter 3).[11] So we can simply focus on the impact of employment protection on long-term unemployment, in particular on the proportion of the unemployed who have a duration of more than one year. As well as employment protection, we should also expect the long-term proportion to be influenced by the duration of benefit availability (BD) and by expenditure on active labour market policies (ALMP), many of which are designed to prevent the build-up of long-term unemployment. In Table 4 we provide two measures of long-term unemployment. The first is simply the 1985-93 average proportion of unemployed with durations exceeding one year. The second attempts to standardise this proportion, when possible, by measuring it for each country when unemployment lies between 5 and 7 per cent. The idea here is to focus on the extent of long-term unemployment at *given levels of aggregate unemployment.* Because the long-term proportion tends to be an increasing function of the overall unemployment rate in the long-run, anything which explains unemployment in general will tend to be correlated with the long-term proportion in a cross-section. The standardised measure will eliminate this problem.

The relevant regressions explaining the two measures of the long-term proportion are:

$$\text{LTU (standardised)} = 21.5 + 0.24BD - 0.51ALMP87 + 0.55EP + 13.8IT$$

$$(2.7) \qquad\qquad (3.2) \qquad\qquad (1.5) \qquad (2.8)$$

$$N = 19, R^2 = 0.55$$

Table 4. **Further data used for analysing employment protection**

	λ(LNJ)	λ(NS)	λ(BLN)	Percentage of employees with tenure <2 years (PL2)	LTU 85-93	LTU (standardised)	γ_1	Employment rate 1990	Employment protection
Belgium	0.64	0.92	0.76	18	67	35.9	4.06	55.0	17
Denmark	0.48	..	0.26	27	29.4	36.2	1.74	75.7	5
France	0.74	0.90	0.72	22.2	40.8	30.3	4.35	57.9	14
West Germany	0.86	0.86	0.36	21	44.1	21.2	1.01	62.9	15
Ireland	0.85	0.86	0.71	22	54.6	31.8	1.82	50.2	12
Italy	0.81	0.74	0.65	13	66.2	35.8	12.94	52.6	20
Netherlands	0.85	0.91	0.90	26.9	50.4	27.1	2.28	59.2	9
Portugal								67.2	18
Spain	0.66	..	..	13.6	55.4	27.5	1.21	47.4	19
United Kingdom	0.70	0.88	0.37	31	40.9	24.5	0.98	70.4	7
Australia	0.35	0.49	0.43	36.8	29.3	21.1	0.73	68.6	4
New Zealand	0.84	..	..	..	..	14.7	3.23	66.1	2
Canada	0.92	0.91	0.17	33.7	8.8	3.5	2.38	70.5	3
United States	0.38	0.10	0	39.7	8.2	4.2	0.94	71.6	1
Japan	0.85	0.83	0.65	20	15.1	18.8	14.50	71.7	8
Austria	0.85	0.84	0.56	..	..	13.3	3.11	65.0	16
Finland	0.45	0.91	0.32	26.3	17.4	12.0	1.55	73.5	10
Norway	0.88	0	0.07	17	14.5	10.8	10.59	73.6	11
Sweden	0.60	0.78	0.16	..	7.9	6.8	12.16	81.7	13
Switzerland	0.81	0.83	0.12	29.3	18.9	17.0	7.33	79.5	6

Notes:

λ = coefficient on lagged dependent variable in an employment equation. LNJ = Layard, Nickell and Jackman (1991); Ch. 9, Table A1, p. 450. NS = Newell and Symons (1985). BLN = Bean, Layard and Nickell (1986) both as reported in Alogoskoufis and Manning (1988); Table 6 and in Layard, Nickell and Jackman (1991); Ch. 9, Table A3, pp. 454-466.

PL2 = percentage of manufacturing employees with tenure less than 2 years. It is based on Metcalf (1986). Table 4, and on OECD (1993). Table 4.1. Where information for a given country appears in both places, the average is reported. The figure for Spain is derived as follows: In OECD (1993). Table 4.1, it is reported that 31.6 per cent of employees had tenure of less than 2 years. But much of this was a consequence of the introduction of fixed term employment contracts in the mid 1980s. Since our sample period is mostly prior to this date, we must try and remove the impact of these fixed term workers. In 1990, 23.8 per cent of employees held fixed term (≤3 year) contracts so, if we suppose that three quarters of these have a job tenure under 2 years, removing these leaves 13.6 per cent as reported in the table.

EP = a measure whereby countries are ranked by the strictness of their employment protection legislation (*i.e.* 1 = least strict etc.). These data are taken from OECD (1994). Table 6.7, col 5.

LTU85-93 = percentage of unemployed with a duration of unemployment of more than 1 year using survey-based data and averaged over 1985 to 93. (*OECD Employment Outlook* various issues, statistical annex.)

LTU (standardised) = percentage of unemployed with a duration of unemployment of more than 1 year. Where possible, this is measured for each country when the aggregate unemployment rate is between 5 and 7 per cent (OECD. *Employment Outlook*, various issues. The data refer to various dates in the 1980s.)

Employment rate = employment as a proportion of the population of working age. OECD *Jobs Study. Evidence and Explanations*, Table 6.8.

Table 5. **Slope coefficients in a regression of λ on PL2**

Dependent variable	λ(LNJ)	λ(NS)	λ(BLN)
PL2	−0.011 (2.1)	−0.0081 (0.6)	−0.010 (2.4)
N	16.00	14.00	15.00
R^2	0.23	0.04	0.23

$$\text{LTU 85-93} = 37.4 + 0.55\text{BD} - 0.33\text{ALMP91} + 1.77\text{EP} + 30.6\text{IT}$$

$$(3.4) \qquad (3.9) \qquad\qquad (3.3) \qquad (3.6)$$

$$N = 17, R^2 = 0.82$$

(IT is a dummy for Italy, which is included because although Italy has only a short benefit duration, the level of benefit is negligible, so its duration is irrelevant.) The overall picture is that there is some evidence that stricter employment protection legislation raises long-term unemployment and thus enhances hysteresis in wage-setting. When added to the results on labour demand, we feel that we have some fairly strong and coherent evidence that the strictness of employment protection legislation does influence labour market dynamics by raising unemployment persistence. Whether or not it influences the equilibrium level of unemployment is the issue we consider next.

Evidence on equilibrium unemployment

As we noted earlier, employment protection can influence equilibrium unemployment by directly influencing wage pressure and/or by affecting the impact of unemployment on wages (γ_1). This latter parameter is crucial in translating wage pressure into unemployment (see equation 11).

We begin by looking at the effect of employment protection on γ_1 and then move onto consider its overall impact on average unemployment. As we argue in Layard et al. (1991), there are a number of other possible factors which can influence γ_1. These include the structure of the benefit system (replacement rates and benefit duration), and the extent of union and employer co-ordination in wage bargaining. In Table 4, we present estimates of γ_1 from Layard et al. (Chapter 9, Table 7). The relevant regression to explain γ_1 is

$$\gamma_1 = 11.9 - 0.078\text{RR} - 2.12\text{BD} + 1.32(\text{UNCD} + \text{EMCD}) + 0.23\text{EP}$$

$$(0.9) \qquad (4.8) \qquad (2.3) \qquad\qquad\qquad (1.7)$$

$$N = 19, R^2 = 0.71$$

This indicates that if employment protection legislation is very strict, this tends to be associated with high values of γ_1. Of course, EP is not significant at conventional levels but it is most unlikely that there is, in reality, a strong effect in the opposite direction. So, from this channel the data indicate, if anything, employment protection reduces unemployment. But, since we know that employment protection can also increase wage pressure, we must also investigate its total impact on unemployment.

This was done in Table 3. As this showed, there is some weak evidence that employment protection tends overall to increase employment. But the t-statistics are never very significant. We ran a large number of further variations using alternative measures of union density and union coverage and also different measures of employment protection. In some eighteen regressions, we were able to obtain only two significant negative coefficients on EP. So there is no strong evidence that employment protection affects equilibrium unemployment. This is, of course, consistent with the fact that while we have good reason to expect employment protection legislation to reduce flows both into and out of unemployment, we have no strong reasons for believing either effect to dominate.

Conclusions

We would expect employment protection legislation to slow down the speed with which the labour market adjusts to shocks but to have only a minor impact on the long-run equilibrium. It may however affect the position of those entering or re-entering the labour market because of the effective restrictions on hiring. In practice, there is considerable evidence that employment protection reduces adjustment speeds in the labour market. But it is hard to find any significant effects on equilibrium unemployment rates.

TAXES ON EMPLOYMENT

Lowering payroll taxes is a perennial suggestion by those concerned to reduce unemployment. Thus the *OECD Jobs Study* (1994) recommends that we should "Reduce non-wage labour costs, especially in Europe, by reducing taxes on labour..." (p. 46). The European Commission's White Paper on Employment proposes a reduction in payroll taxes in conjunction with an increase in taxes on energy. Another straightforward policy would be to lower payroll taxes and make up the shortfall by raising consumption taxes. Phelps (1994) argues that "such a substitution of tax instruments would achieve a major gain in employment and some gain in the general level of real wage rates as well" (p. 28). Presumably, such a switch would work equally as well in a non-European country, such as the United States, where the sum of payroll and income taxes is substantial.

The general argument for this switch goes as follows.[12] Payroll taxes apply only to labour income; consumption taxes apply to all income (which is spent). So a switch from the former to the latter raises the reward for working relative to not working and thereby reduces unemployment. More formally, we may write total real income in work net of taxes, Y, as

$$Y = \frac{W(1-t_1)(1-t_2)}{P(1+t_3)} + \frac{Y_n(1-t_2)}{P(1+t_3)}$$

where W = labour costs, t_1 = payroll tax rate, t_2 = income tax rate, P = output price at factor cost, t_3 = consumption tax rate, Y_n = non-labour income. This may be rewritten as

$$Y = \frac{\upsilon W}{P}\left(1 + \frac{y_n}{(1-t_1)}\right)$$

where $\upsilon = (1-t_1)(1-t_2)/(1 + t_3) - (1-t_1-t_2-t_3)$, the tax wedge, $y_n = Y_n/W$, the ratio of non-labour income to labour costs. Consider now the real income when unemployed, Y^u. This may be written as

$$Y^u = \frac{B(1-t_2)}{P(1+t_3)} + \frac{Y_n(1-t_2)}{P(1+t_3)}$$

$$= \frac{\upsilon W}{P}\left(b + \frac{y_n}{1-t_1}\right)$$

where $b = B/W(1-t_1)$ = unemployment benefit/wage ratio. The definition of Y^u assumes that benefits are subject to income tax.

In most theories of wage determination, the wage cost which is set depends on Y/Y^u which is increasing in b, y_n and t_1. Increases in b, y_n and t_1 will, therefore, automatically raise equilibrium unemployment. So a reduction in t_1 and an equal increase in t_3 will leave the tax wedge, v, unchanged but will lower equilibrium unemployment so long as y_n is not zero.[13] How big is this effect? The crucial factor is the extent of non-labour income which is not subject to payroll tax. It is arguable that, for the typical person at risk of unemployment, this non-labour income is extremely small. For example, in 1987/88, only 7 per cent of unemployment entrants in Britain had savings of more than £3K, a sum which would produce an annual interest income of around 10 per cent of unemployment benefit.[14] So it may be that this tax switching effect is simply too small to have any noticeable effect.

A more fundamental question is whether any of the taxes (payroll, income or consumption) have an impact on labour costs in the long-run, or whether they are all eventually shifted onto labour. An obvious first approach to this issue is to see whether countries with high taxes have higher labour costs than those with low taxes. We must obviously correct for productivity which suggests that we correlate

$$\frac{W}{P} \Big/ \frac{Y}{N}$$

with tax rates across countries (W = labour costs, P = GDP deflator, Y = GDP, N = employment). But this procedure is open to objection. Real labour costs normalised on productivity is precisely equivalent to WN/PY, the share of labour. In a Cobb-Douglas world, for example, an increase in taxes might lead to a rise in W/P and a fall in N, with the share of labour unchanged. The proposed correlation will then understate the true impact of taxes because of the fall in N when labour costs rise. This suggests that we normalise real labour costs on Y/L where L is the labour force.

Taking average values over the period 1980-90 for thirteen OECD countries[15] we obtain:

$$WL/PY = 7.06 + 0.017t_1 + 0.033t_2 - 0.12t_3$$

$$(0.6) \qquad (0.5) \qquad (0.9)$$

($R^2 = 0.13$, N = 13, t ratios in brackets)

where t_1 is the payroll tax rate, t_2 is the income tax rate, t_3 is the consumption tax rate. Basically there is no relationship between tax rates and labour costs, indicating complete shifting onto labour. A similar result due to James Symons and Donald Robertson and based on changes is reported in OECD (1990), Annex 6A. Using changes between 1974 and 1986 across 16 OECD countries,[16] they obtain

$$\Delta \log W/P = -0.05 + 0.09\Delta t_1 + 0.33\Delta t_2 + 0.68\Delta t_3 + 0.97\Delta \log PROD$$

$$(0.3) \qquad (0.6) \qquad (1.1) \qquad (5.3)$$

($R^2 = 0.80$, N = 16, t ratios in brackets; PROD is labour productivity)

Here again we see no significant effects of tax changes on real labour costs although the numbers suggest that consumption taxes have the biggest impact.

While these cross-section regressions are useful for looking at long-run tax shifting, only time-series analysis can shed light on the dynamics. First we report some further results in the same Annex due to Symons and Robertson, which are the average coefficients and t ratios emerging from individual time-series regressions for 16 OECD countries. Thus we have:

$$\log (W/P)_t = const. + 0.84\log (W/P)_{t-1} + 0.12\log (K/L)_t + 0.46\Delta(t_1 + t_2 + t_3) + 0.07t_1 - 0.07t_2 + 0.26t_3$$

$$(9.6) \qquad\qquad (1.4) \qquad\qquad (2.3) \qquad\qquad (0.3) \quad (0.1) \quad (0.2)$$

(average t ratios in brackets)

These results suggest there is no systematic long-run impact of taxes on labour costs but that the short-run effects are substantial. A one percentage point increase in the tax wedge (from whatever source) leads to a short-run increase in labour costs of around $1/2$ per cent which takes a long time to fade away. So even after four years, labour costs are still $1/4$ per cent higher. Such effects will lead to significant and persistent temporary increases in unemployment, particularly in the light of the fact that tax wedges have risen by 10 to 20 percentage points in the last 30 years in most OECD countries. In the long-run, however, these unemployment effects will disappear.

These significant and long-lasting temporary tax effects imply that, when looking at individual country data, it is very difficult to discriminate between the short and long-run impacts of the individual taxes. There is simply not enough information. Consequently, the impression given by the collection of individual country time series studies of wage determination is that the estimated tax effects are all over the place.

It is not worth repeating the summaries in Layard *et al.* (1991), p. 210 and OECD (1994), p. 247 but we may consider one recent example, namely the work of Tyrväinen reported in OECD (1994).[17] This work focuses on the long-run effects of taxes by using the Johansen method to estimate long-run cointegrating relationships between labour costs, taxes and other relevant variables. The long-run tax effects he obtains are given in Table 6. The first point that stands out is how big the tax effects are. Whereas our previous evidence indicated zero long-run tax effects, here we have a substantial long-run impact of taxes. Second, in all bar two of the countries, the tax effects are uniform across all taxes. Indeed, in no country is there any advantage in switching from payroll taxes to consumption taxes.[18]

We have investigated these matters further in the context of our pooled regression equation of Table 3. The payroll tax rate, as an additional explanatory variable turns out to be insignificant (with a t-statistic of 0.4) though the total tax burden as percentage of GDP comes in with a small significant positive coefficient (though no effect on long-term unemployment). These results require further investigation.

Table 6.   **Labour cost responses to changes in tax rates**

	Semi-elasticity of labour costs with respect to:		
	Employers' payroll taxes (t_1)	Income taxes and employees' social security contributions (t_2)	Value-added and excise taxes (t_3)
Australia	0.5	0.5	0.5
Canada	0.8	0.8	0.8
Finland	0.5	0.5	0.5
France	0.4	0.4	0.4
Germany	1.0	1.0	1.0
Italy	0.4	0.4	0.4
Japan	0.5	0.5	0.5
Sweden	0.0	0.0	1.0
United Kingdom	0.25	0.25	0.25
United States	0.0	1.0	0.0

Source: T. Tyrväinen, "Real Wage Resistance and Unemployment: Multivariate Analysis of Cointegrating Relations in 10 OECD Economies", *The OECD Jobs Study: Working Paper Series.* Shows d log(W/P)/dt_i.

On balance, we may perhaps conclude that taxes may have an adverse effect on unemployment in the long run, but any such effect is smallish, and that it relates to the burden of taxation in total and not to payroll taxes in particular.[19]

WORK-SHARING AND EARLY RETIREMENT

Two final much-canvassed solutions to unemployment are reduced hours of work and early retirement. Advocates of these measures often seem to believe that there is some exogenous limit to the amount of work to be done. But history shows that, for a given institutional structure, the amount of work tends to adjust in line with the available supply of labour – leaving the equilibrium rate of unemployment unchanged. We can begin with some theoretical remarks, before supporting them with evidence.

Theoretical issues

We shall first examine the underlying theory in a long-term context, using for illustration a simple efficiency wage model. Efficiency per worker hour is e, which depends on hourly wages (W_i) relative to the expected wage ($\hat{W}$) and on the unemployment rate: $e_i = e(W_i/\hat{W}, u)$. Output is given by $f(eHN)$ where H is hours per worker, which can be varied exogenously. Then the profits of the representative firm are

$$\pi_i = f(e_i HN_i) - \frac{W_i}{e_i} e_i HN_i \qquad (f' > 0, f'' < 0)$$

The problem is recursive and the firm can first choose W_i to minimise W_i/e_i. The optimum wage is then given by

$$e_l\left(\frac{W_i}{\hat{W}}, u\right) = e\left(\frac{W_i}{\hat{W}}, u\right)$$

Hence in general equilibrium (with $W_i = \hat{W}$) unemployment is determined by

$$e_l(1, u) = e(1, u)$$

This holds irrespective of hours.

This result arises because the change in hours affects both those making the wage comparison and the reference group with which the comparison is being made. In the long run both groups must be paid the same. However in the short run things could be different, especially if people are comparing their wage with what they think they "ought to" be paid – as in many models of real wage resistance. The problem here is that people's ideas of what they should be paid adjust only gradually to the reality of what they are paid. Thus

$$\Delta \log \hat{W} = \gamma(\log W_{-1} - \log \hat{W}_{-1})$$

Suppose there is now a downwards productivity shock. Sluggish adjustment of the reference wage will for a time prevent actual wages falling as much as is needed to preserve employment. In this case reduced hours can be an appropriate adjustment to temporary shocks. Indeed in general there can be no objection to allowing hours to act as shock-absorbers, as in Japan. But this is quite different from saying that lower hours will secure permanently higher employment. They will not, and they will also reduce the national output.

Similar arguments apply to the use of early retirement. Since labour market equilibrium requires a given unemployment rate, reductions in labour supply will simply reduce equilibrium employment. Employment will of course take a while to adjust down, and, until it does, there will be extra inflationary pressure in the economy – which eventually leads to the necessary fall in real aggregate demand (assuming nominal demand follows a steady path). However again a negative productivity shock together with real wage resistance will lead to less unemployment if the labour force is temporarily reduced.

Empirical analysis

It is fairly simple to check on these basic lines of reasoning. We ran the following wage equation for each of our usual 19 OECD countries for the years 1952 to 1990:

$$\dot{w} = a_1 \dot{w}_{-1} + (1 - a_1)\, \dot{p}_{-1} + a_2 (w - p)_{1} + a_3 \log L + a_4 \log N + a_5 \log H + a_6 t + \text{const.}$$

where w is log hourly earnings in manufacturing, p is log consumption deflator, L is labour force, N employment, H is average weekly hours in manufacturing and t is time. We then computed the average value of each coefficient (averaged across all countries) and its average t-statistic.

If our reasoning has been correct we would expect:

– log H to have no significant effect; and

– a_3 to be insignificantly different from $(-a_4)$, indicating that it is the unemployment rate which affects wage pressure and the size of the labour force exerts no independent influence.

Both expectations were born out. The equation looked as follows, with average coefficients and average t-statistics:

w = 0.37w$_{-1}$+0.63p$_{-1}$−0.12(w-p)$_{-1}$−2.10 log L+1.82 log N−0.16 log H+0.008t+const.

   (1.8)   (0.7)   (2.3)   (2.8)   (0.1)   (1.4)

Hours have no significant effect and a cut in the labour force raises wage pressure in a way that can only be offset by an equivalent cut in jobs.

We again examine these effects also in the context of our pooled cross-section regression of Table 3. Average hours worked, as additional explanatory variable, had a small but statistically insignificant (t = 1.1) negative effect on unemployment. A more rapid growth of the labour force was also associated with significantly (t = 2.4) lower unemployment, but this result is not very plausible, and may reflect largely the rapid growth of the labour force in the United States.

CONCLUSIONS

We have found clear evidence that unemployment is strongly affected by how unemployed people are treated and by how wages are determined. There are also indications that problems of skill mismatch have exacerbated European unemployment. As regards employment protection, there is no clear evidence of whether it decreases the outflow rate from unemployment by more or less than it decreases the inflow rate. And there appears to be no long-term effect on unemployment rates from employment taxes or from work-sharing/early retirement.

Thus it is unhelpful to focus the discussion of unemployment on the concept of flexibility. Clearly lower benefits and less employment protection are examples of more flexibility. But active labour market policy, co-ordinated wage bargaining, and skill training are not exactly forms of flexibility.

It seems better to focus on the proper role of government in affecting unemployment. Clearly lower benefits of shorter duration would reduce unemployment, but these policies should be accompanied by more (not less) active labour market policy. Similarly governments would be ill-advised to encourage the dismantling of bargaining structures. And they ought certainly to ensure that most youngsters enter adult life with a basic level of competence.

Indeed if Europe's social chapter is to contribute to lower unemployment in Europe it needs to impose two further obligations on governments: *a)* to prevent entry to long-term unemployment (by replacing long-term benefits by active labour market policy), and *b)* to prevent young people ceasing their education (full-time or part-time) until they have acquired basic literacy, numeracy and vocational competence.

NOTES

1. We are extremely grateful to Tim Hughes and Jan Eeckhout for help with Sections 1 and 7, to Marco Manacorda and Barbara Petrongolo for allowing us to draw on their work in Section 4, to W. Röger for helpful comments, and to Philomena McNicholas for typing the paper presented to the Conference.

2. We also used the less conventional measure of "the change in inflation *relative* to its initial level" – to allow for the extra difficulty of reducing inflation when it is low. This was only marginally more significant than the conventional measure and barely affected the other coefficients. We also tried including the trade deficit since inflation can always be reduced by a real exchange rate appreciation; but it was insignificant and wrongly signed.

3. We are indebted to our discussant, W. Röger, for emphasising this point.

4. The other main influence was co-ordinated wage-bargaining. We reject the view that high employment was based on money illusion and repeated devaluation.

5. Because of cyclical effects on the scale of ALMP it is difficult to study the effect of ALMP on wage pressure (and thus unemployment) from time series data, as has often been tried (Calmfors and Nymoen, 1990; Calmfors and Forslund, 1991). The best evidence must come from cross-sectional comparisons such as our international comparisons in Table 3 or (when available) more microeconomic comparisons of the effects of institutional differences.

6. For a full discussion of the degree of co-ordination in 12 countries see Soskice (1990).

7. This draws heavily on the work of our colleagues M. Manacorda and B. Petrongolo (1995).

8. Since $\ln W_i = \log \alpha_i + \log \left(\dfrac{Y\ L\ L_i}{L\ L_i\ N_i} \right)$

9. There is also an important productivity argument. It is well known that a participatory environment is good for company productivity (see Nickell, 1995a, Chapter 5) and that, as part of this environment, some degree of job security is required. If the remainder of the economy is governed by very loose employment protection laws, any employer who wishes to introduce some degree of job security for the above reasons may be so beset by adverse selection problems that he is unable to operate a participatory system. This mechanism could easily operate to the detriment of national productivity growth.

10. When analysing labour demand dynamics on the basis of aggregate data, it is necessary to face up to some criticisms of this activity set out by Kramaz (1991), Caballero (1992) and Hamermesh (1992). Thus Hamermesh argues that "one cannot use aggregate dynamics to examine or compare the structures or sizes of adjustment costs" (p. 8). Since we intend to do just this, we must examine the arguments closely. Hamermesh looks at three types of adjustment cost structures, namely fixed costs, linear costs and asymmetric quadratic costs. In each case he concludes that, *in aggregate*, the adjustment speed is related both to micro adjustments costs *and* to the cross-section variance of sectoral shocks. When looking across countries there is, therefore, the danger that any correlation between adjustment speeds and adjustment costs is corrupted by our inability to control for the variance of sectoral shocks. It is more or less impossible to obtain comparable measures of the variance of sectoral shocks because of the difficulty of obtaining consistent sectoral breakdowns across a large number of countries. How-ever, this corruption will only be serious if the cross-section variance of shocks is strongly correlated with adjustment costs across countries. While we have no evidence on this, there seem to be no strong *a priori* arguments in favour of such a correlation, in which case the omission of this variable is not a problem. Finally, it is worth remarking that estimated labour market dynamics look very similar at the aggregate and at the firm level. For example, the dynamics of a United Kingdom aggregate annual employment equation have the form $n_t = 1.06n_{t-1} - 0.36n_{t-2} +$ etc., whereas a similar annual equation based on United Kingdom company data has dynamics $n_t = 0.83n_{t-1} - 0.14n_{t-2} +$ etc., (see Layard et al. 1991, Chapter 9, Table 15, and Nickell and Wadhwani, 1991, Table III). Both exhibit a considerable degree of persistence, with shocks dying away at a very similar rate.

11. The results in OECD (1993), Table 3.5 indicate a strong positive relationship between wages and long-term unemployment at given unemployment rates. Since long-term unemployment is negatively related to unemployment changes in the short-run, this asserts a positive relationship between long-term unemployment and hysteresis effects (negative effects of unemployment changes on wages).

12. This is the non-labour income argument. Hoon and Phelps (1995) also provide a real interest rate argument, which we do not consider here.

13. The effect will be enhanced if B is exogenous, rather than B/W(1-t1). Typically, how-ever, most countries (although not Britain) set the replacement ratio rather than the level of benefit.

14. See Layard et al. (1991), Table A6.

15. These are Australia, Belgium, Canada, Denmark, France, Germany, Italy, Japan, Netherlands, Spain, Sweden, United Kingdom, United States.

16. These are those recorded in footnote 15 plus Austria, Finland, Ireland, Norway and Switzerland minus Denmark and Spain.

17. See OECD (1994), p. 246.

18. So long as the tax base for these is the same. If, of course, it happens that the consumption tax base is larger, then a lower consumption tax rate would raise the same revenue and have a lesser impact on labour costs.

19. There is a separate question about the effect of changing the progressivity of the employment tax. If skill formation responds very little to relative wages, there is a strong case for a fiscally neutral shift towards greater progressivity, raising the demand for unskilled labour and reducing it for skilled (Layard, Nickell and Jackman, Sections 6.5 and 10.3).

BIBLIOGRAPHY

Alogoskoufis, G. and Manning, A. (1988), "On the Persistence of Unemployment", *Economic Policy*, No. 7: 427-69.

Atkinson, A.B. and Micklewright, J. (1991), "Unemployment Compensation and Labour Market Transitions: A Critical Review", *Journal of Economic Literature*, 29 (4): 1679-1727.

Bean, C.R., Layard, R. and Nickell, S.J. (1986), "The Rise in Unemployment: A Multi-Country Study", *Economica*, 53: S1-S22.

Budd, A., Levine, P. and Smith, P. (1988), "Unemployment, Vacancies and the Long-Term Unemployed", *Economic Journal*, 28: 1071-1091.

Caballero, R.J. (1992), "A Fallacy of Composition", *American Economic Review*, 82: 1279-92

Calmfors, L. and Driffil, J. (1988), "Centralisation of Wage Bargaining and Macroeconomic Performance", *Economic Policy*.

Calmfors, L. and Forslund, A. (1991), "Real Wage Adjustment and Labour Market Policies: The Swedish Experience", *Economic Journal*, 101.

Calmfors, L. and Nymoen, R. (1990), "Real Wage Adjustment and Employment Policies in the Nordic Countries", *Economic Policy*, 11.

Carling, K., Edin, P.A., Harkman, A. and Helmlund, B. (1995), "Unemployment Duration, Unemployment Benefits and Labour Market Programmes in Sweden", *Journal of Public Economics*.

Fahrer, J. and Pease, A. (1993), "The Unemployment/Vacancy Relationship in Australia", Reserve Bank of Australia Economic Research Department, Research Discussion Paper 9305.

Fay, R. (1995), "Enhancing the Effectiveness of Active Labour Market Policies, the Role of – and Evidence from – Programme Evaluations in OECD Countries", OECD, mimeo.

Hamermesh, D.S. (1992), "Spatial and Temporal Aggregation in the Dynamics of Labour Demand", *NBER Working Paper* No. 4055, Cambridge, Mass.

Hoon, H.T. and Phelps, E.S. (1995), "Taxes and Subsidies in a Labor-Turnover Model of the Natural Rate", Columbia University, mimeo.

Jackman, R. and Layard, R. (1991), "Does Long-Term Unemployment Reduce a Person's Change of a Job?, A Time-Series Test", *Economica*, 58: 93-106.

Katz, L.F. and Meyer, B.D. "The Impact of the Potential Duration of Unemployment Benefits on the Duration of Unemployment", *Journal of Public Economics*, 41(1): 45-72.

Kramarz, F. (1991), "Adjustment Costs and Adjustment 'Speed'", INSEE, Paris, mimeo.

Layard, R. (1995), "The Road back to Full Employment", Rudolf Meidner Lecture, Centre for Economic Performance, London School of Economics, mimeo.

Layard, R., Nickell, S.J. and Jackman, R. (1991), *Unemployment: Macroeconomic Performance and the Labour Market*, Oxford University Press, Oxford.

Manacorda, M. and Petrongolo, B. (1995), "The Race between the Supply and Demand of Skills: Some Evidence from OECD Countries", Centre for Economic Performance, London School of Economics, mimeo.

Metcalf, D. (1986), "Labour Market Flexibility and Jobs: A Survey of Evidence from OECD Countries with Special Reference to Great Britain and Europe", Centre for Labour Economics, WP No.870, London School of Economics.

Narendranathan, W., Nickell, S. and Stern, J. (1985), "Unemployment Benefits Revisited", *The Economic Journal*, 95: 307-329.

Newell, A. and Symons, J.S.V. (1985), "Wages and Unemployment in OECD Countries", Centre for Labour Economics, DP No. 219, London School of Economics.

Nickell, S.J. (1995a), *The Performance of Companies*, Oxford: Blackwells.

Nickell, S.J. (1995b), "The Distribution of Wages and Unemployment across Skill Groups", Oxford, Institute of Statistics, mimeo.

Nickell, S.J. and Bell, B. (1995a), "The Collapse in Demand for the Unskilled and Unemployment across the OECD", *Oxford Review of Economic Policy*, 1: 40-62.

Nickell, S.J. and Bell, B. (1995b), "Changes in the Distribution of Wages and Unemployment in OECD Countries", Oxford, Institute of Statistics, mimeo.

Nickell, S.J. and Wadhwani, S. (1991), "Employment Determination in British Industry: Investigations Using Micro-Data", *Review of Economic Studies*, 58: 955-69.

OECD (1990), *Employment Outlook*, Paris.

OECD (1993), *Employment Outlook*, Paris.

OECD (1994), *The OECD Jobs Study*, Paris.

Phelps, E.S. (1994), "A Program of Low Wage Employment Tax Credits", Russell Sage Foundation Working Paper 55, New York.

Schwanse, P. (1995), "The Effectiveness of Active Labour Market Policies: Some Lessons from the Experience of OECD Countries", paper presented to OECD technical workshop, Vienna, November 1995.

Soskice, D. (1990), "Wage Determination: the Changing Role of Institutions in Advanced Industrialized Countries", *Oxford Review of Economic Policy*, Vol. 6, No. 4.

COMMENTS

by

W. RÖGER

The paper by Jackman, Layard and Nickell (JLN) covers a wide range of possible structural determinants of OECD unemployment. The authors provide a comprehensive analysis of their results, also in the light of recent studies in this area. Given the nearly exhaustive list of factors affecting unemployment dealt with in this paper, my comments must necessarily be very selective. Instead of saying a few words on everything I will rather concentrate on those topics which in my view are likely to be the most controversial but also of the most direct relevance to policy makers. These are first the estimated effects of active labour market policy and unemployment benefits on the level of unemployment and second the assessment of the role a reduction of payroll taxes could play to alleviate the unemployment problem.

ACTIVE LABOUR MARKET PROGRAMMES AND BENEFITS

Before going into the details, let me first start with some methodological remarks on the cross section regressions presented in the first chapter of the paper. This will serve as an introduction to some of my comments on the role of active labour market policies and replacement ratios. The authors present regression results obtained from a cross section of 20 OECD countries, using time averages of 5 years, namely over the periods 1983-88 and 1989-94. My major methodological concern is whether these periods are sufficiently long to allow an interpretation of the regression results as reflecting long-term relationships with causality running from the structural determinants to unemployment and not the other way round. To make this point more precise, consider the following dynamic reduced form equation for unemployment in country i

$$LU_{it} = a_{oi} + a_1 X_{it} + bLU_{it-1} + e_{it} \qquad (1)$$

where LU_{it} is the unemployment rate in country i and year t, X_{it} is a vector of structural determinants, including, for example, benefits and ALMP. The coefficient a_{oi} is a country specific constant and e_{it} is a stochastic error term. This equation can be rewritten as

$$LU_{it} = a_{oi}/(1 - b) + a_1/(1 - b)X_{it} - 1/(1 - b)\Delta LU_{it} + 1/(1 - b)e_{it}. \tag{2}$$

If we define the time average of a variable Y_{it} as $Y_i^* = \Sigma Y_{it}$, then we can rewrite this equation for country i in terms of averages

$$LU_i^* = a_{oi}/(1 - b) + a_1/(1 - b)X_i^* - 1/(1 - b)\Delta LU_i^* + 1/(1 - b)e_i^*. \tag{3}$$

This formulation is intended to show two possible problems associated with the JLN regressions. They present results in which the last two terms of (3) are neglected. In my view this may be perfectly valid if the time interval over which the time averaging is performed is sufficiently long such that e_i^* and ΔLU_i^* approach their expected value of zero (provided this exists for the latter term). Given the persistence of the unemployment rate in most OECD countries these conditions in the data are most likely not fulfilled over periods of five years and the effects of cyclical shocks and dynamics should therefore be accounted for in those regressions.

Ignoring the last two terms has two consequences. First, since there may be important interactions between X_i^* and ΔLu_i^*, the estimated coefficients could be biased. A term like LU_i^* could to some extent also capture effects ignored in the current regressions and thus treating it properly could give us a further indication on the comprehensiveness of the considered determinants. To remedy this problem one could rewrite the regression in the following form

$$\Delta LU_i^* = \beta\alpha X_i^* - \beta LU_{io} + e_i^* \text{ with } \alpha = a/(1 - b) \tag{4}$$

where LU_{io} denotes the unemployment rate at the beginning of the period over which the averaging is performed. The parameter β measures the speed of adjustment and the vector α gives the long run effect of elements in X_i on LU_i. This formulation is of course well known from the literature on convergence regressions. It also has the advantage that there is no correlation between e_i^* and lagged unemployment which is used as a regressor. Though I don't have any priors on the direction of bias inflicted by the JLN procedure of neglecting the adjustment dynamics, I do, however, know from various cross section studies that results obtained by controlling for the dynamics can make a substantial difference.

The presence of a non zero e_i^* points in another direction, namely to a possible simultaneity problem. Notice, both terms appear in the regressions as active labour market spending (ALM) or benefits (BEN) per unemployed person (LU), i.e. LU also appears on the right hand side of the regression. Now, if governments have a tendency to lower unemployment benefits per person when the unemployment rate is high because of expenditure constraints or as a measure to fight unemployment then there is a downward bias in these estimates. Similarly, if authorities dispose of a relatively fixed absolute amount for active labour market spending, for example, then we would observe a tendency for countries with temporarily high unemployment rates to have low ALMP 's and vice versa. In the unemployment regressions this would show up as a negative sign of ALMP in these regressions, even if in fact active labour market policy would not contribute at all towards a reduction in the unemployment rate. In the revised version of the paper, the authors have taken this simultaneity problem into account by resorting to instrumental variable methods. And indeed, as should be expected, the effect of ALMP on long-term unemployment is now more than halved (the coefficient is reduced in absolute value from .07 to .03). This estimate does, however, so far not take into account the "cross sectional endogeneity". Because these programmes are expensive it is unlikely that countries with high unemployment rates can afford to be very generous. This could again easily be picked up by the regression as a strong negative effect of ALMP for the unemployment rate. An indication that this could be present in the current regression results is the fact that the ALMP coefficient is not robust with respect to the exclusion of Sweden which renders the ALMP coefficient insignificant. The authors interpret this as an indication that only Swedish style labour market policies are effective. While they may be right on analytical grounds, it nevertheless appears to be a very novel conclusion one draws from regression results where outliers are important.

Finally, if we accept the estimate as it stands, what does it imply for the effectiveness of ALMPs on a macroeconomic level. Take for example the case of the European Union with an average unemployment rate of roughly 10 per cent. According to the estimates a reduction in the unemployment rate by 1 per cent could be achieved by an increase of ALMP by tripling its current rate of roughly 10 per cent. If this is financed by an increase in labour income taxes or social security contributions the net labour market effect of these programmes will depend heavily on who is finally bearing the increased labour tax. The authors seem to believe that employees would eventually bear the heavier tax burden by accepting a decline in their net wage income by more than 4 per cent. However, if that is the case one can pose the question whether larger reductions in unemployment could not be realised if workers and firms agreed to lower wages by 4 per cent in the first place. With a wage elasticity of labour demand between .5 and 1 this seems to be a more effective (though admittedly unrealistic) option. In any case all this boils down to the following: a reduction in the unemployment rate by 1 per cent will eventually require a substantial reduction of net wages. Active labour market programmes do therefore not seem to offer an easy way out of the trade off between wages and unemployment, at the given high level of the unemployment rate. This of course also suggests that active labour market programme s should only be applied to very well targeted groups of the unemployed in order to avoid unnecessary costs.

TAXATION AND EMPLOYMENT

Let me now turn to the section on taxation and employment which is also of considerable policy relevance. Here the authors reach the very strong conclusion that wages will not be affected by labour taxes in the long run. In other words, pay roll taxes are in the long run completely shifted on to labour. I agree completely with this result, however, my interpretation of this finding is most likely entirely opposite to the conclusions the authors would draw from it. The interpretation in the paper seems to be that because wages are not affected by tax rates in the long run, employment or unemployment will also not be affected in the long run. In my view, this conclusion cannot be drawn from this result. For example, a standard neo-classical growth model augmented by a wage rule to close the labour market would arrive at this result, namely that wage costs are independent from the level of labour taxation in the long run, irrespective of any particular tax shifting hypothesis imbedded in wage behaviour. The only requirement for this result is that the increase in the tax rate for labour does not lead to a change in the capital costs for firms in the long run. This could only happen if corporate income taxes or the real interest rate would change as a result of the change in labour income taxes. The first option is excluded by definition and the second possibility is not a possible outcome for most countries, since their influence on the real long-term interest rate in a world of capital mobility is negligible. But even in a closed economy setting the interest rate (at least in the neo-classical model) is primarily determined by the rate of time preference of households and governments. To clarify this argument we only have to look at the marginal productivity conditions. Given any constant returns to scale production function, the capital labour ratio k is determined by capital costs only

$$f'(k) = (r + d) \qquad (5)$$

where r is the real rate of interest and d is the depreciation rate and we neglect corporate taxes in the expression for capital costs. Of course this has the strong implication that in the long run wages will essentially be determined by technological conditions and the capital labour ratio and therefore eventually by capital costs. This can clearly be seen by looking at the marginal productivity condition for labour

$$[f(k) - f'(k)k] = w. \qquad (6)$$

Now consider any wage rule linking (gross) wage claims of workers to major determinants like for example labour income tax rates (t), the replacement ratio (ben), productivity (Y/N) and/or the unemployment rate (LU)

$$w = w(t, ben, Y/N, LU). \qquad (7)$$

Given the marginal productivity conditions (5) and (6) and the fact that r is not controllable by a change in labour taxes it seems obvious that real gross wage rates are not influenced by the level of payroll tax rates. What is therefore likely to happen in this world, if government decides to increase labour taxes? Unless the elasticity of wages with respect to changes in the unemployment rate is infinite, real wages will generally increase together with the rate of unemployment. This will be associated with an increase in labour productivity. Of course in order to meet the optimality condition for capital the optimal response of firms is to reduce the capital stock along with the reduction in employment, *i.e.* invest less. This process will continue until the Phillips curve mechanism sets in strong enough to reduce gross wages to the level prior to the tax increase.

Notice especially, this adjustment story for wages seems to be entirely consistent with the other result in the paper concerning strong and long lasting temporary effects of tax reforms on wages. My guess is, that any alternative interpretation of the adjustment story – which would not be associated with the result that higher labour tax rates will eventually lead to higher unemployment (or lower levels of employment) – can only be based on wage rules that link real wage claims to the change in the tax rate, but not its level. I am not aware of any such theoretical hypothesis. Indeed, from the wage rule, as written above, an alternative adjustment possibility, with wages unaffected by tax rates, seems to be that the economy moves to a new equilibrium with lower labour productivity. But not only is this extremely unlikely given the wage pressure imposed by the tax increase, it would not avoid the unemployment problem in the long run. The efficiency conditions for employment would certainly be violated if wages return to the baseline level but productivity stays below base. Thus employment must fall.

The authors are aware of the difficulties of testing for long-run tax effects in wage equations and they avoid including a direct measure for labour productivity in the regression. When I translate this into my framework, then instead of my equation (6) they decompose employment into labour force and the unemployment rate and they estimate an equation of the following form

$$w = w(K/L,LU(tax)) = a_1\log(K/L) + a_2LU(tax) \tag{6'}$$

where L is the labour force. The argument implied by this regression is the following. If taxes have a long run effect on unemployment this should show up as a positive coefficient of the unemployment term or alternatively as a positive coefficient of those factors which influence the unemployment rate, such as taxes for example. While this goes a step beyond other results shown in the paper where only labour productivity is used in the regression, this strategy seems nevertheless problematic, at least for the following reasons. First it should be seen that equation (6') looks suspiciously close to a standard wage equation, when an equality constraint on the two coefficients a_1 and a_2 is not imposed, as would be implied by the marginal productivity condition (6).* But this means that LU could appear with a negative instead of a positive sign as implicitly required by the authors. I therefore have the strong suspicion that the authors regression is picking up a mixture of both a wage and a labour demand equation, resulting in coefficients for the tax terms which are biased towards zero. Notice also, by using capital instead of GDP,

---

* Of course it is difficult to impose such a constraint since it would require knowledge on how taxes affect unemployment in the first place.

one also allows for large tfp shocks in the marginal productivity condition which makes it even more likely that OLS is picking up a wage equation instead of the required inverted labour demand schedule.

To summarise the argument, I would conclude that an increase in labour taxes and any attempt of workers to shift these taxes forward onto firms will most likely be accompanied by declining rates of investment until a new equilibrium, consistent with the long run real interest rate, is re-established. As long as the authors have no convincing story why investment should accelerate again towards the end of the transition process, the decline in the capital stock will most likely be permanent and be accompanied by a lower level of employment. Some recent indirect evidence supporting this view comes from a study by Mendoza *et al.* (1995). These authors present results from panel regressions of 5 year averages for 18 OECD countries over the period 1965-91 exhibiting a significant negative impact of both the corporate tax rate and labour income tax rate on the investment rate. Furthermore this result seems to be remarkably robust with respect to the estimation method and the choice of additional explanatory variables. In the current context, this result indicates that there does indeed seem to exist a link between labour taxes and investment activities of firms as emphasised in the argument above.

Let me finally stress, though I have concentrated my comments on only a small number of policy aspects, this does, of course, not mean that all the other aspects dealt with in the paper are unimportant. In view of the world wide increase in the supply of unskilled labour and the increased ability of firms to shift production plants abroad, the work on the impact of skill imbalances and relative wages, briefly cited and outlined in the paper seems highly relevant to me. I look forward to forthcoming work by the authors.

BIBLIOGRAPHY

Mendoza, E. G., Milesi-Ferretti, G. M. and Asea, P. (1995), "Do Taxes Matter for Long-Run Growth? Harberger's Superneutrality Conjecture", *International Finance Discussion Papers* No. 511.

GENERAL DISCUSSION

The discussion focused on four main issues:

- labour market performance and the systems of wage determination;
- the respective roles and design of "active" and "passive" labour market support measures in improving labour market outcomes;
- the influence of taxes and tax structures on employment/unemployment;
- the impact of employment protection on unemployment, its components by duration and labour force participation.

Several participants challenged the empirical results of the Jackman/Layard/Nickell paper, according to which a higher degree of co-ordination of wage bargaining on the employers' and the union side must be viewed positively from the viewpoint of unemployment. It was argued that countries' positions with respect to the strength and structure of their unions and employers' associations, and their influence on actual wage developments, differ much and that with labour becoming increasingly heterogeneous, the arguments for centralised and co-ordinated bargaining become in any case less powerful. In response to these observations it was pointed out that the importance of co-ordination lies in the fact that it serves to reduce social conflicts and tensions. People with a strong common interest to create favourable conditions for output and employment are thereby bound to listen and to talk to each other. In this way social consensus will be promoted with beneficial influences on wage behaviour.

There was a lively debate on how to establish an optimal mix between "active" and "passive" labour market measures. Financing training and retraining tends to be more costly than passive income support but could be justified from an economic point of view if the employment prospects of the persons involved are clearly improved and the risk of major displacement effects relatively small. It was pointed out, however, that there is no guarantee for these conditions to be met. What needs to be avoided is that "unsuccessful" participants in active labour market programmes would automatically get renewed eligibility for unemployment benefits. The answer of how to deal with the relationship between active and passive labour market measures greatly depends, therefore, on both the design of income-

and activity-support programmes, and the way they are administered. One participant suggested in this context that the funding of unemployment insurance systems should seek to reduce the subsidy elements by greater use of experience rating.

On taxes and tax structures there was a majority view among participants that changes in the level and structure of taxation on different sources of incomes and factors of production are more important to labour market outcomes than was suggested by the Jackman/Layard/Nickell paper. However, the effects of tax rate changes will be mainly felt in the short- to medium-run as due to tax shifting the long-run equilibrium rate of unemployment may not be affected in any significant way. The point was also made that if payroll taxes are used to finance spending on active labour market programmes, the efficiency costs should be compared with the positive employment effects that may occur due to these programmes.

Finally, some participants wondered whether the relationship between unemployment protection legislation and unemployment was as weak or ambiguous as indicated by the model results shown in the Jackman/Layard/Nickell paper. While employment protections clearly slows the speed of adjustment of employment to changes of demand and output, it may also permanently affect the demand for labour as employers become more cautious about hiring. A crucial question was to what extent the lower demand for labour would be accompanied by a parallel reduction of labour force participation as suggested by the authors of the paper. Although it was claimed that the institutional cross-section results were reasonably robust, it was agreed that it would be useful to do more work in this area and in particular to look further into individual case studies.

THE MACROECONOMIC EFFECTS
OF FINANCIAL SECTOR REFORMS:
AN OVERVIEW OF INDUSTRIAL COUNTRIES

by

Palle S. Andersen[1] and William R. White
Bank for International Settlements

"The [US financial] system is correctly described as a well-kept and orderly zoo. Different species, such as banks, securities dealers, insurance companies, and so on, were neatly housed and fed in separate cages segregated by function and geographical scope. The bars between the cages prevented the various species from preying on one another. ... The relations between the animals and the visitors, between the financial institutions and their clientele, were sober and sedate. The deregulation of the 1970s and 1980s destroyed this idyllic arrangement. The destruction was done piecemeal, with little appreciation for the rationale of the existing arrangement, and with no particular plan or vision for the outcome. ... This is not to suggest that the old zoo could have been preserved in a changing world. Rather, I want to underline that, be it the US financial system or the Soviet economy that is to be renovated, the mere abolition of constraints will not automatically give birth to desirable new structures." Wojnilower (1991), p. 209-210.

INTRODUCTION

Given the numerous conferences and studies, including several here at the OECD,[2] that have addressed the issue of financial sector reform in recent years, it is not easy to say something that has not already been said. What we attempt in this paper is to provide an extensive, but by no means comprehensive, review of the principal issues and consequences. Where possible, we emphasise work carried out at the BIS and we focus on those aspects of financial reform that are of particular relevance to central banks. In doing so we define financial reform "broadly" to include deregulation as well as financial innovation. Conversely, we take a "narrow" view of the macroeconomic effects of financial reforms by attempting to abstract from the other policies and circumstances which will condition those effects in the real world. This is clearly a deficiency since initial macroeconomic imbalances, contemporaneous macro policies and the stage of other structural reforms in the economy (in particular those affecting the rigidity of labour markets) can all significantly affect the outcome of financial reforms.

There are numerous examples from both industrial and developing countries which show that introducing financial reforms in conditions of macroeconomic imbalances can cause serious problems. We only need to think of the Latin American "Southern Cone" countries, which in the 1970s deregulated their financial sectors when inflation was high and their governments were running very large budget deficits. In the Nordic countries, a major reason for the speculative bubble of the mid-1980s and the subsequent banking crisis was that the level of spending was already excessive when the financial sector was deregulated. An additional problem in both cases was that adherence to a fixed exchange rate regime seriously constrained the central banks in counteracting rapid credit growth; nor was fiscal policy tightened sufficiently.[3]

The sequence of the reform process can also affect the outcome. For instance, liberalising the financial sector while maintaining high marginal tax rates and full deductibility of interest payments creates a strong incentive to incur debt. In several countries, such an unfortunate combination of circumstances provided an additional "boost" to the asset price cycle in the 1980s. The sequencing of "real-side" and financial reforms is also important. Recent work by the OECD Secretariat on product market reform concluded that the benefits of such reforms would only be fully realised when labour markets were also reformed, a difficult process that might take years.[4] The same conclusion might apply even more strongly in the case of financial market reforms, which in many countries are much further advanced than even the reform of product markets. In sum, there is no guarantee in real-world circumstances that financial sector reform will not move a country from a "second best" to a "third best" equilibrium rather than closer to a "Pareto optimum".

The paper has five sections. The first summarises the salient features of financial sector reforms, including both domestic and international aspects. In the second section we look at financial reform and long-term growth, focusing on three channels through which growth might be affected. In the third section there is a discussion of the effects of financial reform on the short-term (cyclical) behaviour of the economy, including changes in the capacity of the economy to stabilise itself in the face of shocks. In this section, we also evaluate the impact of financial deregulation on the conduct of monetary policy, including the implications of resulting changes in the transmission mechanism. In the fourth section we attempt to disentangle the permanent and transitory effects of financial reforms and focus on some transitional problems. In the fifth section the principal policy conclusions of the paper are summarised.

SOME SALIENT FEATURES OF FINANCIAL REFORMS

On the basis of historical developments, three phases of financial reform can be distinguished. The first phase has generally involved the deregulation of domestic financial markets, with interest rates and market mechanisms generally replacing quantitative restrictions as the principal means for effecting monetary policy. This increased reliance on market-based mechanisms is likely to have raised equilibrium levels of real interest rates and to have affected the size of the interest rate adjustments required to maintain economic stability (Bennett, 1990 and Wojnilower, 1985). A second phase was generally characterised by financial innovation taking over as the "driving force" behind financial developments, with further deregulation being prompted in turn. The third and final stage has been marked by the growing international integration of financial markets, as more and more countries have removed exchange controls and other impediments to international capital flows.

This last phase of the financial reform process might be thought unremarkable, marking only a return to the conditions which prevailed at the beginning of this century. Yet, the recent changes have been of such a magnitude as to command the interest of academics, policy-makers and the general public. There has been an explosive growth of cross-border flows, increasingly involving private flows to and among emerging economies. Along with this has come greater international competition, not only among financial institutions but also between institutions and markets, and profits have already started to come under pressure (Borio, 1995 and *The Economist*, 1995). Finally, there has also been growing convergence in both the means and second moments of price changes (*i.e.* the unconditional variance of price or yield changes) on internationally traded financial assets (Morton, 1996).

Notwithstanding the significant "globalisation" of financial markets seen to date, there are also indications that this phase of the reform process is far from complete. So far, international competition and integration have been largely confined to wholesale markets. Moreover, cross-country correlations between domestic investment and national saving remain high and significant (Feldstein, 1995 and Goldstein and Mussa, 1993), indicating that long-term capital flows still suffer from a "home-country bias". Finally, there are marked differences in the degree of international diversification of investment portfolios managed in different countries. This implies considerable potential for a further increase in cross-border flows.

A final point worth emphasising is that, despite globalisation, financial structures continue to differ between countries. Until a few years ago it was generally assumed that, given the global nature of financial reforms, financial structures and the transmission mechanism of monetary policy would converge rapidly. This process may well be under way, yet the 1992 turbulence in the ERM clearly pointed to remaining and significant differences across countries in the transmission mechanism of monetary policy. Moreover, such differences have been clearly identified econometrically in a number of studies recently carried out at the BIS (BIS, 1995b). On the basis of simulations of structural macroeconomic models used by individual central banks, it generally appears that changes in monetary policy are transmitted more quickly to real GDP and inflation in the Anglo-Saxon countries and Japan than in the continental European countries.

A number of other findings of these BIS studies point to differences in financial structure as being responsible for these econometric results.[5] Most importantly, significant differences between the financial structures of the two country groups defined above can be easily identified. In the Anglo-Saxon countries, Japan and Sweden, wealth effects arising from changes in interest rates are particularly important because the share of housing and equity in household assets is relatively high and collateral values play a major role in the availability of credit. These countries are also characterised by relatively large cash-flow effects in response to changes in monetary conditions because a large proportion of debt is at adjustable interest rates, and because loan rates adjust relatively quickly to policy rates. Moreover, while capital gearing has tended to rise, the corporate control mechanism in most of these countries is still characterised by an "arm's length" relationship between users and suppliers of external funds and by a high share of securities in total credit. The second group of economies, including most of the continental European countries, are characterised by rather low wealth and credit availability effects. Moreover, while debt ratios tend to be much higher than in the first group of countries, most of the debt is at fixed rates or at rates linked to long-term bond rates.

FINANCIAL REFORMS AND LONG-RUN GROWTH

Three potential effects of financial reform on growth can be distinguished using a simple endogenous growth model based on work by Pagano (1993). Steady state growth (g) can be written as:[6]

$$g = A \phi s - \delta$$

where δ is the rate of depreciation, s the national saving rate, A the marginal productivity of capital and ϕ the proportion of saving which is channelled into investment. While a rise in δ will reduce growth (see below), financial market reforms enhance long-term growth if they: increase the aggregate saving rate(s); improve the allocation of saving and thus the marginal productivity of capital (A); or raise the proportion of saving channelled into investment (ϕ) by improving the efficiency of the intermediation process and the competitiveness of the financial sector.[7] Consider the effects of financial reform on each of these terms in turn.

Saving and growth[8]

A higher saving rate arising from financial reforms was the main source of higher growth projected by the models of McKinnon (1973) and Shaw (1973). In practice, actual developments seem to have differed markedly from those assumed. There is clear evidence from a number of industrial countries that financial deregulation has instead tended to lower household saving by lessening liquidity constraints. Consider, for example, the consumption functions estimated by Blundell-Wignall and Browne (1991), which show a significant decline in the coefficient on current disposable income in periods following deregulation.[9] The existence of such an effect in France and the United Kingdom seems to be supported by the movements in personal saving rates recorded in Figure 1. Such effects are even more clearly evident in the figures for some of the Nordic countries, where personal saving rates actually turned negative as households doubled the ratio of debt to net disposable income in the course of the 1980s (see Drees and Pazarbasioglu, 1995, for further evidence).

While it seems that most of this decline was only transitory (see below),[10] there is also some econometric evidence that household saving has fallen permanently (Bayoumi, 1993 and Jappelli and Pagano, 1994). Moreover, to further support the hypothesis of permanent effects, Figure 1 indicates that there is a marked contrast between saving rates in countries which undertook extensive deregulation in the early 1980s (largely Anglo-Saxon countries) and countries where deregulation is of a more recent date and has proceeded more slowly or had already occurred in the 1950s and 1960s. Counter-evidence to the view that the effect is only transitory might be seen in the Scandinavian countries, where earlier saving rates have been restored. However, because of the deep recession in the post-reform period, it cannot be excluded that saving rates have "overshot" as households have been forced to repay part of their debt and that Scandinavian saving rates will eventually revert closer to Anglo-Saxon norms.

Based solely on the above evidence one would be tempted to conclude that, as far as the saving channel is concerned, financial sector reforms reduce long-run growth and general welfare. However, before drawing this conclusion, three observations should be made. First, it depends on the growth model assumed. In a neoclassical model only the *level* of income will be affected, not the rate of growth. Conversely, in an endogenous growth model, it is the *growth rate* which is adversely affected (Jappelli and Pagano, 1994). Secondly, even if the growth effect is adverse, it is possible (though not likely) that consumer welfare is enhanced, as the gains from the removal of liquidity constraints outweigh the loss of lifetime income.

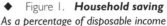

◆ Figure 1. **Household saving**
As a percentage of disposable income

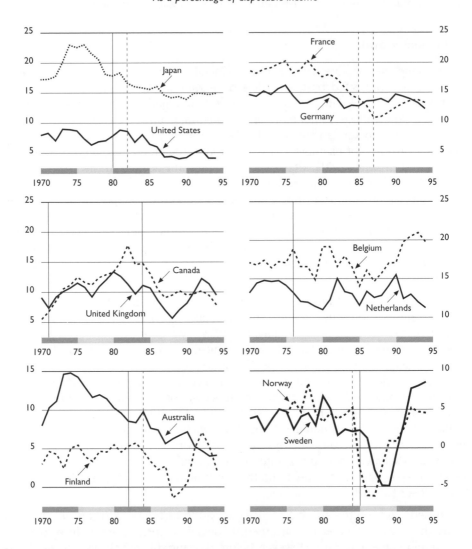

Note: The vertical lines indicate the initial year of major financial reform: for the United States the phasing-out of Regulation Q; for Japan, the New Bank Law and Securities and Exchange Law; for France, the introduction of a new credit control system, with controls abolished in 1987; for the United Kingdom, the abolition of the Competition and Credit Control Policy (1971) and the deregulation of building society interest rates (1984); for the Netherlands, the liberalisation of mortgage lending; for Australia, the removal of interest rate ceilings and credit directives; for Finland, the first phase of deregulation of interest rates; for Sweden, the removal of a ceiling on lending rates; and for Norway, the abolition of supplementary reserve requirements and interest rate regulations.

Source: National data.

A third reason for questioning the conclusion that financial reform reduces saving and long-run growth is that it rests on the crucial assumption that the model used above is correct. This need not be so. Indeed, there seems to be as much evidence to support the proposition that growth drives saving as there is to support the proposition that saving drives growth. Consider, for example, the experience of the Asian countries, where saving rates only started to rise *after* the increase in economic growth. Moreover, using aggregate time series and cross-country data, as well as household surveys, Carroll and Weil (1994) have found significant evidence that the direction of causality is from growth to saving.[11] These results would imply that financial reforms, if they affected growth positively through other channels, could then have a secondary positive effect (a virtuous circle) through the increased saving which growth encourages.

Resource allocation and growth

There are many well-known theoretical arguments in favour of deregulation of the domestic financial system. For example, deregulated financial institutions can improve the allocation of savings and growth, given their "potential" ability to screen proposed investment projects, to assess the collateral of various borrowers, to monitor the performance of projects for which funds have been lent, to aggregate idiosyncratic risks and to reduce individual agents' need to hold liquidity balances. In principle, the removal of exchange controls and the marked rise in cross-border capital flows, notably foreign direct investment, should also contribute to better global allocation of capital and provide opportunities for diversification allowing investors higher returns as well as a reduction of risks.[12]

Some of these theoretical arguments have been supported empirically. Studies, mostly based on Asian countries, have found that the marginal productivity of capital (measured by the growth of GDP divided by the investment/GDP ratio) is a positive function of financial deregulation. Moreover, in cross-country growth regressions (King and Levine, 1993), growth is shown to be positively related to variables measuring financial developments and financial depth.

In contrast, Englander and Gurney (1994) show that the King-Levine results do not hold for industrial countries. There is also a risk that financial reform will make resource allocation worse rather than better if deregulated financial institutions do not have the "potential" ability required to make sound investments (previous state ownership, etc.). As discussed further below, financial reforms in several industrial countries have contributed to excessive investment in real property markets and asset market "bubbles". While such bubbles are unlikely to be a permanent consequence of financial reforms, the adverse *effects* of the bubbles experienced in the 1980s seem to be, if not permanent, at least of a very long duration given the long-lived nature of the physical investments and resulting problems of financial fragility.

A related possibility is that financial reforms may generate a perception of greater uncertainty and financial fragility, and thus may induce a shift from long to short-term investment (*i.e.* a rise in δ without a corresponding rise in gross saving in the equation shown above). It is incontestable that in recent years, characterised by significant financial reforms, there has been a clear shift towards investment with a shorter duration. However, much of this can be explained by technological changes and falling capital goods prices (notably computers). Nor is it clear that financial markets have become more uncertain and volatile, as much depends on how volatility is measured. Indeed, as is discussed further below, the evidence seems to suggest less financial volatility over the last decade or so rather than more.

The intermediation process

Financial reforms have generated numerous changes in the structure of the intermediation process. Among the factors likely to have raised ϕ and to have benefited long-run growth would be the reduction in reserve requirements imposed on financial intermediaries[13] as well as the increase in competition and the accompanying narrowing of interest margins. Moreover, the cost of financial transactions has declined dramatically, mainly as a result of technical innovation, but also because financial reforms have provided financial intermediaries with an incentive to adopt the most cost-efficient methods to remain competitive. We have also witnessed a vast expansion in the range of financial instruments available to borrowers and lenders, and a decline in agents' demand for liquidity as insurance against failure. Finally, in many developing countries financial saving has tended to rise in the wake of financial reforms (*i.e.* a higher ϕ in the above equation) even when aggregate saving declined.

There are also developments indicating that the increase in ϕ arising from all these changes may be only modest. First, financial reforms combined with technical progress have generated a marked expansion of employment and investment in the financial sector, but in virtually all countries the measured growth of financial sector output has not kept pace with the use of resources. This implies that measured productivity growth has been negative.[14] Secondly, real interest rates have risen since the regulated 1960s. This is partly because of higher equilibrium rates as quantitative restrictions were dismantled and the return to capital has increased, but it is mostly due to a fall in government[15] and household saving. Even accounting for these factors, there is a positive residual which Orr et *al.* (1995) ascribe to financial innovations and reforms. Thirdly, it is worth noting that a high proportion of investment is still financed by enterprises' own saving, suggesting that financial reforms have not yet eliminated the problem of asymmetric information and the premium on external relative to internal funds. Fourthly, while financial deregulation has led to a large number of mergers and acquisitions in the banking sector, it remains an unsettled issue whether these have improved efficiency and created positive economies-of-scale effects.[16] Finally, some of the increase in ϕ arising from the dismantling of previous regulations has been offset by the marked rise in financial institutions' provisions for "bad" loans and in the costs of supervision. Part of this rise may be only temporary, reflecting the costs of getting used to operating in a liberalised environment, but the costs of supervision and of providing a public safety net are likely to increase further in future years.

A special feature of financial innovation and the intermediation process has been the declining role of banks, as they have lost their cost advantages on the liability side of their balance sheets as well as their income advantages on the asset side. This development has been most noticeable in the United States, whereas in countries with universal banking systems there has been relatively little change to date. It is also the case that, in all countries, banks remain the principal source of funds for most small and medium-sized firms. Although more sophisticated financial arrangements have not eliminated the need for screening, evaluation and monitoring which is met by banks, their general loss of market share is likely to continue, with potential implications for the effectiveness of monetary policy. This is discussed in the concluding section of the paper.

Concluding remarks on financial reforms and growth

Most of the empirical studies reviewed above have dealt with only one aspect of financial reform and have included only one financial measure in their empirical estimates. As the above analysis makes clear, financial reforms could affect growth in a number of ways simultaneously. This problem has been addressed in a recent empirical study by Johnston and Pazarbasioglu (1995) which builds on the model proposed by Pagano and uses panel data for forty industrial and developing countries. Their empirical analysis takes more explicit account of the different dimensions of financial reforms by simultaneously including variables which attempt to capture financial saving and allocational effects (real interest rates) as well as effects arising from higher volume (ratio of private credit to GDP) and more effective financial intermediation (interest rate spreads). Moreover, they allow for sufficiently long adjustment periods by distinguishing between developments before, during and after financial reforms, and they provide separate estimates for countries that suffered a resulting financial crisis and those that did not.[17] This last distinction leads on to some powerful policy implications.

Their main results are shown in Table I and can be summarised as follows. For non-crisis countries GDP growth rises significantly between the pre-reform and post-reform periods and the change in real interest rates from negative to positive has supported the increase. The rise in the volume of intermediation has also stimulated growth, notably in the post-reform period, whereas the modest

Table 1. **Financial sector reforms and growth**[1]

Variables	Non-crisis countries			Crisis countries		
	Pre-reform	Reform	Post-reform	Pre-reform	Reform	Post-reform
GDP	2.6	4.2	4.4	4.2	3.5	2.2
RI	−5.8	1.4	2.5	−3.2	−6.6	6.1
	(0.01)	(0.04)*	(0.07)*	(0.03)	(0.10)*	(−0.04)*
CRED	0.32	0.42	0.53	0.34	0.48	0.43
	(−1.2)	(0.2)*	(6.0)*	(−3.4)	(−7.0)*	(−3.6)*
RMDEP	0.35	0.30	0.26	0.37	0.27	0.39
	(−0.9)	(−0.2)	(−2.2)	(−3.4)	(−8.1)	(−0.5)
SPREAD	4.1	4.6	4.1	5.9	8.3	11.1
	(−0.4)	(−0.02)	(−0.5)	(−1.9)	(−0.5)	(−1.5)

Notes: GDP = rate of growth of real GDP, five-year averages.
RI = deposit rates less annual rate of inflation.
CRED = ratio of private sector credit to GDP.
RMDEP = ratio of reserve money to total deposits.
SPREAD = difference between lending and deposit rates.
1.   GDP is the dependent variable and RI, CRED and RMDEP or SPREAD are included as independent variables together with other variables from a Barro growth equation. Unbracketed figures show averages for the three sub-periods and bracketed figures estimated coefficients, with * denoting whether they are found to be significant.
Source: R.B. Johnston and C. Pazarbasioglu, 1995.

improvement in the efficiency of the intermediation process has had no significant impact. In contrast, for the countries that experienced financial crises, the average growth rate was halved between the pre-reform and the post-reform periods. Although this is not entirely due to financial reforms, it is worth noting that developments in real interest rates reduced growth both in the reform period (when they were negative) and during the post-reform period (when they turned sharply positive). Moreover, the marked rise in credit growth during the reform period appears to have been misallocated and in the post-reform period the large widening of the spread as well as the more cautious lending behaviour (as measured by the rise in RMDEP) had a negative, though not significant, effect on growth.

On balance, these results suggest that the long-run effects of financial reforms are likely to be positive, in particular, if crisis can be avoided during the process. However, so far, few countries have been able to fully realise these benefits because, in the immediate post-liberalisation phase, the positive effects have been to a large extent offset or superseded by distortions in other areas and sectors and/ or by transitory problems. In particular, when financial reforms lead to excesses in the form of negative real interest rates and too rapid credit growth, there is a risk of resource misallocation with real economic consequences that may extend well into the post-reform period.

FINANCIAL REFORMS, SHOCKS AND CYCLICAL FLUCTUATION

Has the real economy become more exposed to financial shocks?

As financial markets have become increasingly liberalised and more subject to international influences and to the use of new instruments, fears have grown that financial markets themselves have become a new source of instability for the real economy. One set of concerns is that financial reforms have led to increased volatility in asset prices, misalignments and contagion effects, all with potentially adverse effects for macroeconomic performance *over time*. A second set of concerns has to do with the threat of systemic risk; that is, the possibility that a failure somewhere in the financial system (at the level of an institution, a market or in the underlying payments system) could *suddenly* have sharp reverberations in other markets of such a magnitude as to have significant macroeconomic implications. The nature and validity of these concerns warrant consideration.

There is a general perception that financial market volatility has permanently increased as a result of deregulation and financial innovation, notably the growing use of derivative instruments. This perception is invalid insofar as volatility is measured by the second moments of changes in financial asset prices. Such statistics generally have shown no trend over the last twenty years, and in many cases actually seem to indicate a trend to less volatility (see, in particular, Anderson and Breedon, 1996 and Morton, 1996). Moreover, there is now a large body of literature (Cohen, 1996) indicating that the introduction of a derivative market in most cases seems to reduce the volatility of the spot price rather than increase it.[18] Finally, it bears noting that there is virtually no evidence in the literature that short-term financial volatility reduces economic welfare.[19]

A counter-argument to the above conclusion is that standard deviations, being averages, do not adequately reflect the occasional large price movements which might have potential systemic implications. Indeed, the very assumption of normality, which underlies such measures, must be questioned in light of the body of evidence, indicating that distributions describing changes in financial asset prices typically have "fat tails".[20] While there has been increasing interest, both in the academic literature and in the market-place, in using financial market data to calculate the full distribution of expected price changes, we know of no attempts to date to determine whether the likelihood of "large" price movements is now greater than in the more regulated past. However, simple observation of such events as the 1987 stock-market crash, the collapse of bond prices in the spring of 1994 and the sharp rise and fall in the value of the yen in the middle of 1995 would seem consistent with such a proposition.[21]

Contagion effects refer to the possibility that asset price movements may now be more easily transmitted from market to market and country to country. It is clear that correlations between the international prices of similar assets (especially bonds) have risen sharply in recent years (Morton, 1996), though it is not so clear that correlations between prices in different national markets have risen as well (Goldstein and Mussa, 1993). Such international transmissions are not necessarily adverse to economic activity as they might dilute the impact of shocks and be thought to play a stabilising role. On the other hand, the effects may be thought less benign. Sutton (1996) documents that "excessive" (relative to risk-neutral expectations) rate movements in the US bond markets now tend to be reflected in similar "excessive" movements in other bond markets. The immediate after-effects of the Mexican crisis, which were felt elsewhere in Latin America and to some degree in Asia, provide a further illustration of such risks. Finally, a striking example of international contagion effects with systemic potential was the fall in London real property prices in 1990. This decline was catalysed by the collapse of several Swedish financial companies with speculative positions in that market. The subsequent slump in the London real property market led to the bankruptcy of the Canada-based Olympia & York building corporation, which in turn weakened the financial balances of several international banks (some of them with a AAA rating) throughout the world.[22]

It is still more difficult to test whether the financial market reforms of recent years have increased the frequency and magnitude of "misalignments" in the prices of financial assets. Whereas a particular measure of volatility can be objectively calculated and priced by the market, identification of a speculative bubble demands an estimate of the level of asset prices consistent with macroeconomic fundamentals. In general, reliable equations of such a nature are not available. While it is tempting to refer to the behaviour of the dollar in the early 1980s, and the behaviour of asset prices in Japan and a number of other countries more recently, as indicating a new bias towards "bubble-like" behaviour, counter-arguments can be made. First, speculative bubbles have a very long history which substantially predates recent incidents. Moreover, to the extent that recent financial reforms can be linked to subsequent bubble-like behaviour, for example in property and equity markets, it seems more likely that this was a transitional problem rather than something likely to be a permanent feature of such markets. We return to this issue in some detail below.

The second set of concerns arising from recent changes in financial markets has to do with systemic risk. As one of us said in an earlier paper (White, 1991):

"... there are also new and more serious risks to manage in global financial markets where competition is more fierce, where profit margins are less comfortable, and where markets are increasingly interrelated in new ways that are not fully understood."

Indeed, it could be contended that systemic concerns would seem even more justified today than five years ago given recent changes in the weights attached to the various kinds of risk (market risks, counterparty risks and liquidity risks) confronting market participants. Today, with the explosive rise in gross cross-border flows, a much greater weight must be attached to counterparty risk and the associated possibility, given that receipts and payments are generally not synchronous, that one major default could generate chain reactions which would threaten the stability of the global financial system. Such possibilities have been extensively considered in a number of fora.[23] Moreover, a variety of policy measures[24] have been introduced to minimise the risk of systemic failures. On the one hand, the fact that policies have actually been adapted in this way suggests that there is a real problem to address. On the other hand, the fact that the industrial countries have in recent years been subjected to some very large financial shocks, and there have been no systemic repercussions, must be judged comforting. It is of course impossible to say whether this welcome outturn was due to the preventive policies just referred to, or implies that there was nothing to worry about in the first place.

Has the real economy become more resilient to shocks?

There is little doubt that, in some respects at least, financial reforms have reduced the sensitivity of the real economy to both real and financial shocks. With the removal of credit controls, economic agents have greater access to borrowing and are less reliant on current income and cash flows. Moreover, the development of various derivative markets has not only made it easier for market participants to achieve the combination of risk, return and liquidity which they desire but has also permitted hedging against movements in market prices. [25] As a result, the multiplier and accelerator implications of shocks for real variables may be smaller than previously (BIS: ECSC, 1994b). Finally, recent developments in financial markets imply that risks of all sorts are increasingly being transferred to those willing and (hopefully) able to bear them. This might also be presumed to increase the capacity of the economy to shrug off shocks of various sorts.

At the same time, it is possible to cite counter-arguments to some of these points. The fact that economic agents have been given greater access to credit has permitted the marked increase in debt and debt ratios observed over the last decade. In turn, increases in debt ratios have made households, enterprises and even governments considerably more vulnerable to shocks than before. It is surely significant that there are a number of industrial countries today whose debt position is such that they would no longer contemplate discretionary fiscal action to offset an economic downturn; indeed, in recent years even the traditional use of automatic stabilisers has in some countries been questioned. Similarly, while the concentration of risk-taking in fewer, better hands is likely to imply a lower probability of defaults with attendant positive effects on confidence and spending propensities, the knock-on effects could be significantly greater should such a default in fact occur.

When confronted with demand-side or supply-side shocks affecting output gaps, unemployment and inflation, the economy has its own "automatic stabilisers". Subject to the monetary authority pursuing some nominal target, interest rates and the exchange rate should normally move in such a way as to cushion the real-side shock while at the same time avoiding a longer-run inflationary bias. This leads one directly to the question of whether financial reforms have altered the transmission mechanism of monetary policy, and if so, whether they have tended to make the conduct of monetary policy less or more difficult.

Implications for the conduct of monetary policy

Recent changes in financial markets have affected the conduct of monetary policy in three important ways. First, they have altered the transmission mechanism of monetary policy. Secondly, they have made monetary indicators less reliable as guides for the conduct of monetary policy. And finally, to the extent that they have contributed to greater financial market volatility and misalignments of asset prices, they have complicated the short-run implementation of monetary policy.

Before turning in detail to the ways in which financial market reforms may be expected to have affected the *transmission mechanism*, it may be useful to refer to some empirical evidence. Turning first to the US economy, the evidence is somewhat conflicting. On the one hand, four important studies (Friedman, 1989, Bosworth, 1989, Kahn, 1989 and Mauskopf, 1990) all come to the conclusion that a one percentage point change in the interest rate set by the Federal Reserve has more or less the same effect on GDP as it did fifteen years ago. This can be seen both from reduced form equations, relating GDP directly to monetary instruments, and from simulations based on large scale macroeconomic models.

However, within these unchanged aggregate effects, the same studies also identify a number of offsetting influences.[26] In particular, the effects of a faster and somewhat larger transmission of interest rate changes to other financial variables in recent years (for instance yield curves, financial asset prices and exchange rates) tend to be "cancelled out" by a smaller and slower reaction of various demand components (residential investment, private consumption, business fixed investment, inventories and net exports) to variations in financial variables. Moreover, when changes in the interest sensitivity of individual demand components are found to be significant, they more or less offset each other, leaving the aggregate response of real GDP relatively unchanged.

A more recent study by Mosser (1992) provides stronger evidence that the transmission mechanism of US monetary policy has changed. She uses an approach that differs from those reported above in two important respects. First, it applies dynamic simulations, allowing for feedback effects. Secondly, instead of attempting to identify parameter changes within the same model, her intertemporal comparisons are based on four different macroeconomic models, each specified appropriately for the conditions of 1975 and 1990 respectively. On this basis, and using changes in non-borrowed reserves instead of interest rates as the policy instrument, Mosser concludes that for the United States GDP and inflation multipliers are about twice as large in the later vintage models.[27]

Turning to other countries, Kasman and Rodrigues (1991) find that in *Japan* long-term interest rates have become significantly more sensitive to changes in the interbank rate (the principal operating instrument of the Bank of Japan) since the abolition of credit and interest rate controls, and that the Bank's ability to influence broad monetary aggregates appears to have declined.[28] White (1991) reports that the response of spending to interest rate changes in *Canada* does not seem to have changed greatly in recent years. However, he too makes reference to the possibility of a number of offsetting influences being at work, and notes that financial deregulation took place in Canada much earlier than in most other countries. In contrast, in the *United Kingdom*, the sensitivity of aggregate spending to interest rates appears to have increased, largely owing to the fact that a larger proportion of households is now affected by changes in mortgage rates (Bank of England, 1990). Indeed, as a result of this development, higher mortgage rates seem to affect not only residential construction but, through cash-flow effects, expenditure on non-durable consumption.

Recognising the enormous variety of experiences across countries, let us now look more systematically at the offsetting ways in which changes in the financial sector may have affected the transmission mechanism. The removal of credit and interest rate controls in many countries has had particularly important effects. The previous process through which higher interest rates led to disintermediation and credit rationing has been weakened, leading to a marked reduction in the measured interest rate sensitivity of the demand components most affected by the earlier controls (notably residential construction, see Gunther, 1994). In itself, such a change would seem to imply that cyclical stabilisation may require rather larger interest rate movements than hitherto (Wojnilower, 1985 and 1991). A similar conclusion would be suggested by the fact that agency costs also seem to vary more procyclically than they did before, perhaps reflecting the fact that capital adequacy requirements for supervisory purposes are themselves affected by the prices of financial and real assets. In addition, the transmission of monetary policy changes to the real economy has become subject to longer lags and shifts in the sensitivity of various demand components.[29] Moreover, rapid growth in the use of financial derivatives seems likely to have lengthened the lags even further.

In contrast, asymmetry effects linking interest rate changes to consumption and business investment may now be greater than they were previously, implying the need for smaller interest rate movements. The distributional (rather than the substitution) effects of higher interest rates generally tend to reduce household spending[30] because creditors are typically older households with low spending propensity while debtors tend to be young housebuyers with high spending propensity (King, 1994). In addition, creditors are not compelled to spend higher interest income in the same way that cash-constrained debtors may be forced to cut consumption to meet higher debt servicing requirements. Indeed, if interest income accrues largely to pension funds, the creditor may not even realise that his or her wealth has increased. Evidently, this asymmetry effect will grow more pronounced as debt (and asset) levels of different households grow relative to levels of real disposable income.[31] A similar phenomenon may exist in the business sector. Bernanke and Campbell (1988) and Bernanke, Campbell and Whited (1990) have found that, while a majority of indebted firms in the United States would not be seriously affected by a monetary tightening, the distribution of debt is skewed to the left. Moreover, there is a not insignificant proportion of firms so heavily indebted that they could face bankruptcy. In the same vein, Smith and Sterne (1994) found for the United Kingdom that the most highly indebted firms suffered the steepest profit declines during the 1990-92 recession.

For many countries, another important effect of financial reforms is that a larger part of monetary policy changes is now transmitted via exchange rate changes rather than via changes in domestic interest rates. All other things being equal, in particular unchanged expectations about the future value of the exchange rate, a rise in interest rates will initially lead to a real appreciation and downward pressures on price inflation.[32] Given this new channel of transmission, the implication is again that the size of interest rate changes required for purposes of cyclical stabilisation will be less than before. The fact that prices are directly affected by exchange rate changes might also seem to imply that the real output costs of disinflation would be less.[33] However, it must be remembered that the direct effect on prices of a monetary-induced exchange rate appreciation must be given back when monetary policy is eased once again. Broadly stated, the existence of an exchange rate channel does more to affect the incidence of monetary policy than its ultimate costs and benefits.

A second important implication of financial reform and financial innovation[34] is that traditional monetary aggregates have become less useful as *intermediate targets*. This reflects two changes (Filosa, 1995). Most importantly, money demand functions became increasingly unstable so that the link between the intermediate target and the ultimate target was broken. This break can be clearly seen from the marked drop in the correlation between intermediate targets and nominal income in many countries and from numerous VAR studies looking for the predictive power of various intermediate targets (Friedman and Kuttner, 1992).[35] The break can also be seen from money demand specifications with time-varying parameters or from specifications with variables, such as term structures, exchange rates and asset prices (Borio et *al.*, 1994 and Filosa, 1995), which are not included in traditional money demand equations. Consequently, several central banks, while still monitoring changes in monetary aggregates, have lowered their priority from targets (essentially the sole indicator of whether interest rates should change) to indicators (but only one among many).

A further development which reduced the usefulness of monetary aggregates as targets of monetary policy was stronger competition between banks and non-banks. With new non-bank financial institutions offering highly competitive deposit instruments, the interest rate sensitivity of narrow money aggregates increased significantly. One consequence was that the predictability of the link between monetary instruments and narrow money was weakened. Another consequence of a greater interest rate elasticity was that the interest rate changes required to keep the rate of growth of the money supply under control became too small to adequately respond to cyclical pressures. In response to these developments, a few central banks chose to maintain the intermediate targets by extending the definition of "money", but most opted to reduce the emphasis on monetary aggregates as described above.

A third effect of recent financial developments has been to *complicate the implementation* of domestic monetary policy. A greater reliance on market-driven processes may or may not imply more financial market volatility and misalignments, but it certainly does imply that monetary authorities must treat the market's perceptions and concerns more seriously than before. This has led in recent years to a growing transparency on the part of many central banks, with respect both to their ultimate objectives and to their reasons for changing the setting of operating instruments and with the purpose of minimising the probability of the central bank itself becoming a source of instability.

FINANCIAL REFORM: PERMANENT EFFECTS AND TRANSITIONAL PROBLEMS

The heading of this section no doubt promises more than it can deliver. Given that our experience with financial reforms is relatively recent, our ability to distinguish between permanent and temporary phenomena is very limited. Moreover, it is undoubtedly wrong to characterise financial sector reforms as moving from one equilibrium to another. Rather, given the relatively broad definition of financial reform used in this paper, we should think of reform as a continuous process. Finally, while certain *events* related to financial reform may be only transitory, their macroeconomic *effects* may nevertheless be persistent and long-lasting.[36] Consequently, the distinctions drawn between permanent and temporary phenomena in this section must be viewed sceptically.

The discussion earlier in this paper indicates that the following changes and effects of financial reform will eventually prove to be more or less permanent: lower household saving rates; higher real interest rates; a larger role in the transmission mechanism of monetary policy for balance-sheet variables and the exchange rate; an associated need for monetary authorities to rely on a broader set of indicators or information variables than previously; and a better allocation of resources both within and between countries. Without repeating arguments made above, most of these effects can be judged as being welfare-enhancing, or at least not likely to reduce welfare. Since permanent benefits would generally seem to dominate temporary costs, this leads to the conclusion that financial reforms have generally been desirable.

To draw this conclusion is not to deny that financial reforms can have significant transitional effects whose costs may be heavy and persistent. Perhaps most important, considering the experience of both developed and developing economies, has been a sharp increase in credit growth after the introduction of financial reforms. In part, this may have been an adjustment to a permanently higher debt/income ratio in response to new market forces. However, in many countries, this expansion of credit seemed to be associated with a greater appetite for risk on the part of lenders and inadequate credit-screening procedures on the part of banks in particular. The fact that, in a number of countries, heightened competition between lenders took the form of "competing for size" further contributed to the rapid growth of credit.[37]

One associated effect of this sharp expansion in credit availability has been noted earlier: a "downward overshooting" of household saving rates in the 1980s, particularly in France, the United Kingdom and the Scandinavian countries. This may have contributed to the pick-up in inflationary pressures (for currently produced goods and services) in the latter part of the 1980s. In the same vein, the availability of credit to finance governments, particularly funds imported from overseas, may have an expansion of government spending which may have contributed to the same outcome. The fact that generalised inflationary pressures were not even more severe may owe something to the structural changes related to new technology that were taking place at the same time, as well as the influence of stronger international competition in product markets.[38]

What seems clearer is that a strong relationship developed between credit growth and the rate of increase of real asset prices in the 1980s. As can be seen from Figure 2, asset price cycles are not unique to the 1980s, but there has undoubtedly been an unusually strong correlation between asset prices and credit during the last fifteen years (Table 2) in many countries. This reflected not only the sharp rise during the 1980s, but also the marked declines during 1990-94, which have not yet bottomed out.[39]

Recalling that the 1980s was a period of very high real interest rates, the fact that asset booms occurred simultaneously in so many countries raises questions about the underlying causes.[40] While the evidence from Table 2 and Figure 2 is

◆   Figure 2. **Real aggregate asset prices and credit**

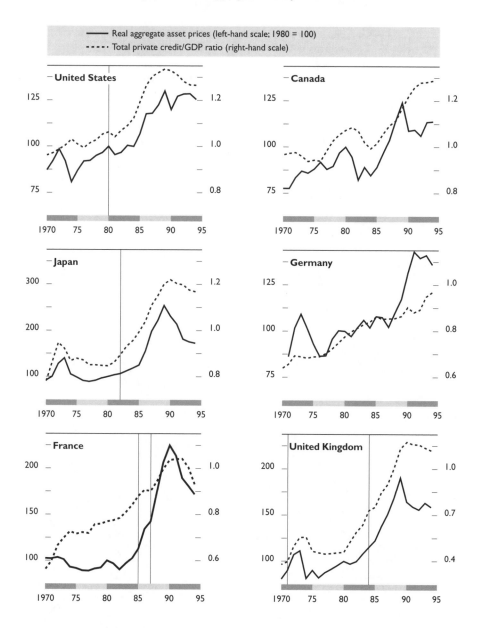

Note: The vertical lines indicate the initial year of major financial reform; for details, see note to Graph 1.
Source: See Table 2.

◆ Figure 2 (cont.). **Real aggregate asset prices and credit**

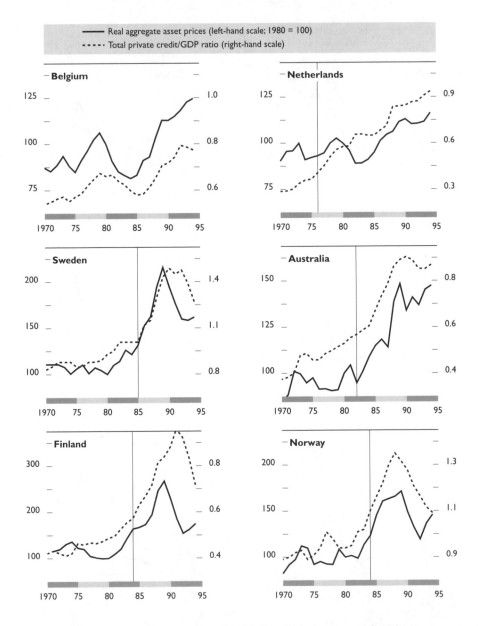

Real aggregate asset prices (left-hand scale; 1980 = 100)
Total private credit/GDP ratio (right-hand scale)

Note: The vertical lines indicate the initial year of major financial reform; for details, see note to Graph 1.
Source: See Table 2.

Table 2. **Bilateral correlation coefficients between asset prices and credit**

	1970-79	1980-94
United States	0.00	0.93
Japan	0.75	0.90
Germany	0.00	0.82
France	−0.74	0.96
United Kingdom	0.34	0.93
Canada	0.28	0.72
Australia	−0.14	0.94
Belgium	0.94	0.92
Finland	−0.72	0.65
Netherlands	0.54	0.85
Norway	−0.00	0.89
Sweden	−0.49	0.85

Note: For a definition of the variables, see Figure 2.
Source: Bank of International Settlements; R.B. Johnston and C. Pazarbasioglu, 1995.

suggestive, the thorough analysis undertaken in Borio *et al.* (1994) clearly points to a dominating role of both domestic and international aspects of financial reforms, operating via a credit channel:

"To a large extent, the major expansion of credit during the past decade reflected a relaxation of credit constraints in the financial industry in the wake of both market-driven and policy-determined structural developments. Their end-result was greatly to increase competitive pressures in the industry and to broaden the range of borrowing opportunities. In the process, they also heightened the impact of pre-existing tax provisions which encouraged indebtedness and which had been less powerful during the period when credit rationing was prevalent. The resulting environment provided fertile ground for a self-reinforcing spiral of credit and asset prices, with faster credit expansion raising asset prices and higher asset prices in turn relaxing credit constraints further. The likelihood of such a process is especially high in the transition period, as agents adjust to the newly-found freedom and a lack of familiarity with the new financial conditions leads to errors of judgement on the part of both lenders and borrowers. ... From a broader perspective, the heightening of competitive pressures has influenced asset prices not only within the narrow confines of domestic markets, but also through the linkages between them. The growth of cross-border capital flows has played a role." (Borio *et al.*, 1994, p. 28-32).

It would clearly be inappropriate to put all the blame for the credit expansion and asset price bubble of the 1980s on financial reform.[41] In the same vein, it would also be inappropriate to say that the financial fragility and crises of the 1990s had a similar, simple cause. Other factors such as recessions, inadequate risk management and prudential procedures, exchange rate changes, tax-induced incentives to take on too much debt, undercapitalisation and structural weaknesses due to the previous regulations also played a role. Yet, there can be little doubt that the credit bubble contributed to the general weakness of financial systems in the 1990s and that in many countries the effects of that weakness continue to be felt, particularly by small and medium-sized businesses. Nor can there be any doubt that the competitive pressures unleashed by financial reform will intensify in the 1990s, implying ongoing challenges for those banking systems which have not yet fully recovered from earlier excesses. In such cases, the "temporary" costs of financial reform may be felt for a particularly long time.[42]

SOME POLICY CONCLUSIONS

Looking back at the experience with financial reforms in industrial countries over the last ten to fifteen years, a few lessons can be learned with respect to the way in which reforms should be carried out, the conduct of monetary policy and the implications for prudential supervision. Needless to say, at this stage of our understanding all conclusions must be treated as highly tentative.

Liberalising the financial sector ahead of other sectors, particularly labour markets, may mean that the full benefits of reform will be hard to realise. Given such a sequencing, shocks requiring real wage adjustments are likely to be diverted to financial markets, with an attendant risk of increased volatility and misalignments. If imperfections elsewhere in the economy distort financial decisions by creating incentives to take on too much debt, or incur too high risks, the probability of credit bubbles will be heightened. As to the pace of financial reform, most countries that chose to deregulate within a very short period seemed to run into problems, because both the banks and the monetary and supervisory authorities needed time to adapt. Conversely, partial deregulation has the potential to channel excess demand into the liberalised sector, further increasing the likelihood of bubbles.

As for lessons concerning macroeconomic policy, it is important that financial reforms should not be introduced in a period of excess demand. While in some cases it may be imperative to do so, the associated risks should be clearly recognised. Markets' tolerance of "bad" or unsustainable policies has declined in step with their growing influence. Countries with high public debt/GDP ratios have to pay a risk premium on government bonds and the 1992-93 European exchange rate crisis can be seen as the markets' reaction to a perceived inconsistency between the interest rates needed to maintain stable exchange rates and those required to reduce unemployment. The Mexican crisis last year and the way in which it affected other emerging market economies is widely interpreted as a reaction to an inconsistency between a growing external imbalance and a fixed exchange rate. It also shows that market judgements may be restrained and indeed even inadequate for a time, but when imposed these judgements may be severe (BIS, 1995a).

The need to tighten fiscal policy during periods of financial reform should also be recognised. With the removal of liquidity constraints, private sector saving is bound to decline, at least temporarily. This implies that, with an unchanged government budget balance, the overall saving-investment balance will deteriorate, as well might the current account. Moreover, because financial reform typically leads to higher real interest rates, it also tends to worsen the budget balance because of higher interest payments on the public debt. This makes it still more imperative to cut non-interest expenditures or raise taxes in the context of financial reforms. The need for fiscal tightening tends to be even greater in countries with a fixed exchange rate because the burden of adjustment to financial reform falls entirely on fiscal policy, which might not be sufficiently flexible.

Financial reforms can lead to temporarily higher credit growth and can contribute to generalised inflationary pressures. Recognising this possibility, and bearing in mind some of the insights of the recent literature on "credit channels", perhaps more attention should be paid to credit aggregates than in the recent past. This conclusion also applies in periods of weak demand if one accepts the possibility of credit rationing, especially to the small and medium-sized customers of banks. However, if faster credit growth arising from financial reform primarily affects the price of financial assets, the monetary authorities are confronted with a dilemma. Raising real interest rates to restrain asset price increases could impose excessive costs on the real economy.[43] There is no consensus at this point as to how this problem should be handled.

Because financial reforms can lead to a temporary rise in credit growth, it is also important that the monetary authorities be free to react if they want to. Virtually all countries with fixed exchange rate regimes found it difficult to control credit growth during the reform period, and most eventually had to devalue their currencies because of their weakened competitive position. However, excessive credit growth cycles were not unique to countries with fixed exchange rate regimes, clearly suggesting that a flexible exchange rate regime is no panacea.[44]

The fact that banks responded to financial reforms by expanding their traditional lending activities into more risky areas (commercial real estate, corporate takeovers, etc.) and by pursuing new off-balance-sheet activities (notably derivatives) has raised important prudential and regulatory issues (Edwards and Mishkin, 1995). To reduce the risk of bank failures and financial fragility, it could be argued that efforts should be made to strengthen the competitive position of banks in the intermediation process. In some countries this may require that remaining regulations which "overly" restrict banks be removed. At the same time, it might also be argued that the events of the late 1980s could only have been prevented through stronger prudential regulation. Ultimately, this line of thought leads back to the issue of "narrow banking" (see Nakajima and Taguchi, 1995, in particular their "Regime II").

Finally, if some lessons have been learned about preventing crises arising from financial deregulation, there are also lessons about dealing with crises when they do arise. Unsound financial institutions should be closed, restructured or merged as quickly as possible since delays can be very costly. It is also important that such problems be solved without distorting competition in the financial sector; that is to say, the end-result should be a clear reduction in the amount of capital directed to the banking industry. Apart from these general points, past experience does not help us to clearly identify a "least-cost" solution. Each of the Nordic countries dealt with its financial sector problem in its own way, while the United States took yet another approach in dealing with unsound saving and loan institutions. To note that the US approach was successful in large part because of rising asset prices at the time only reminds us that all restructuring solutions must be circumstance, time and country-specific.

Annex

THE "CREDIT CHANNEL" VIEW

As a slight extension to the discussion of changes in the transmission mechanism of monetary policy, this annex briefly considers the "money vs. credit channel" debate, which has been especially intensive in North America. Since the "rediscovery" of and interest in the credit channel has, to some extent, coincided with financial reforms and asset price volatility, it is tempting to conclude that the credit channel has permanently gained in importance as a result of financial reforms. However, as noted by one of the leading proponents (Bernanke, 1992), the credit channel can be traced back to Fisher (1933). Although modern versions tend to split the credit channel into a bank lending and a balance sheet (or financial accelerator) channel, is not a new phenomenon related to financial reforms. In fact, if anything, financial reforms are likely to have reduced the importance of this transmission channel as a result of securitisation, better channels of information via derivative markets and the development of alternative sources of credit, including foreign credits.[45] Moreover, while there is a growing number of studies providing impressive and convincing evidence of the banking lending component of the credit channel (Akhtar, 1994 and Kashyap and Stein, 1993), there is an almost equally large number which fails to find any significant evidence, including two authors (Oliner and Rudebusch, 1995) who have actually "switched side" in the course of the debate. Attempts to identify credit channels in the monetary transmission process in Canada have also produced mixed results (Bank of Canada, 1994) and the same applies to countries for which one might presume a major role for bank loans because they account for a large proportion of total credit and security markets are less developed than in North America.[46]

Nonetheless, the balance sheet component of the credit channel view, with its emphasis on "financial accelerator effects" (Hubbard, 1994) stemming from asymmetric information problems, provides a particularly useful framework for understanding the effects of changes in asset prices and financial reform, including the consequences for the transmission process:

- the enhanced role of balance-sheet considerations in the credit creation process. As noted in the text, debt/income ratios are likely to be permanently higher for households as well as enterprises, which affects their desire and capacity to borrow. In addition, new capital requirements combined with fluctuations in asset prices have increased the role of financial institutions' own balance sheets in their lending decisions;

– a better understanding of the distributional *and sectoral* effects of changes in monetary policy as different agents have different sensitivities to such changes, depending on whether they rely on banks or have access to other sources of credit. Agents in the former group are particularly vulnerable to changes in banks' credit policies whereas those in the latter group may have become less sensitive to policy changes owing to the development of new markets and instruments;[47]

– the importance of institutional changes, including the rise of "non-bank" banks, securitisation, the "junk bond" market, etc.;

– a broader and better understanding of how interest rate changes affect various demand components, especially in the light of the low and uncertain interest rate elasticities found in empirical studies; and

– a better appreciation of the lags with which monetary policy changes affect real demand.

Many of these effects are discussed in the extensive survey of the sources of the 1990-92 slowdown in US credit growth (Akhtar, 1994) as well as in numerous other recent studies. However, rather than reviewing this large and rapidly growing literature, we conclude by referring to the discussion of the asset price cycle of the 1980s. In many ways this episode provides a good illustration of how credit growth and movements in asset prices interact with changes in the stance of monetary policy, partly by strengthening the impact of expansionary policies, but also, perhaps even more importantly, by delaying and subsequently reinforcing the effects of tighter policies.

NOTES

1. The views expressed in this paper are those of its authors and not necessarily the views of the BIS.

2. See in particular Edey and Hviding (1995) *Economic Studies No. 25*, 1995/II.

3. For instance, in countries with a fixed exchange rate regime, fiscal policy becomes the main instrument in helping the economy to adjust to reform of the domestic financial sector because the hands of the monetary authorities are "tied" by the exchange rate target. Consequently, if financial reform leads to excessive credit growth, the principal instrument for counteracting this is to strengthen the budget balance.

4. New Zealand is probably the only OECD country which has deregulated all its major markets, and even there the benefits have been difficult to realise because the labour market was the last in the sequence. New Zealand is also unique in that, forced by a crisis in the exchange market, the authorities abolished all financial market controls and regulations before taking steps to correct severe macroeconomic imbalances; and this "reverse sequence" may have been a principal cause of the slow recovery.

5. When the transmission mechanism was estimated from models which impose the same structure on all countries (structural VAR models or the Multi-Country Model maintained by the Federal Reserve Board), the effects of a standardised change in monetary policy were broadly similar in the United States, Canada and Germany, but somewhat smaller in the United Kingdom, France and Italy.

6. Pagano assumes an economy which produces only one good with a linear production function between output (Y) and the capital stock (K):
(i) $Y(t) = A\,K(t)$
There is no population growth and the capital stock depreciates at a rate of δ per period so that gross investment is:
(ii) $I(t) = K(t + 1) - (1 - \delta)K(t)$
If the economy is closed, gross investment has to equal gross saving (S), but a proportion of saving $(1-\phi)$ may be "lost" in the intermediation process:
(iii) $I(t) = \phi\,S(t)$
Defining the rate of output growth as $[Y(t)/Y(t - 1)] - 1$ and dropping the time indices (i)-(iii) can be combined to yield the equation in the text.

7. Bisignano (1991) uses the following categorisation in discussing the potential growth effects: *allocative efficiency* (which coincides with raising A; *operational efficiency* (which

overlaps with increasing φ; and *dynamic efficiency* (which may interact with all the potential effects).

8. There is a rather long literature on the optimal saving rate under "golden rule" conditions, which we shall largely ignore. Most empirical tests seem to suggest that in virtually all industrial countries actual saving rates are well below optimal rates, whereas one might doubt whether this is also the case in some of the Asian countries (Singapore, for instance), where national saving rates are close to 50% of GDP and a large part is accounted for by obligatory pension fund contributions.

9. Germany and Canada, which liberalised financial markets at a much earlier date, are exceptions to this result, as for both countries the coefficient increases in the 1980s. In the case of Canada this increase seems to coincide with the severe recession and the period of unusually high interest rates in the early 1980s; see Wirjanto (1994).

10. In estimating consumption functions for Sweden, Berg and Bergstrom (1995) find that real household debt has a positive effect on consumption and that higher debt contributed significantly to the fall in household saving in the 1980s. The influence, however, is only transitory, in contrast to net financial and housing wealth, which both have a permanent effect.

11. There are, however, also studies showing more ambiguous effects. For instance, Masson *et al.* (1995), looking at the determinants of private saving in both industrialised and developing countries, find that real income growth is a causal factor only for high-income developing countries and that for all countries the saving rate tends to decline with the level of per capita income. In addition, Paxson (1995) concludes that while growth has a causal and positive effect on saving, it explains only a fraction of the correlation observed in cross-country data.

12. It should, of course, be kept in mind that a good part of the rise in international capital flows has been of a short-term and rather speculative nature and, in several instances, has made it more difficult for central banks in the recipient countries to maintain stable policies. However, neither time nor space permits further discussion of this issue.

13. Haslag (1995) estimates a model that merges the literature on financial intermediaries and growth with that on inflation and growth. Using reserve requirements as a proxy for a tax on intermediation and cross-section data for both industrialised and developing countries, he finds that both high reserve requirements and high inflation tend to reduce growth. However, neither coefficient is statistically significant and his model also excludes other variables with a potential effect on growth.

14. If productivity levels in the financial sectors are higher than on average in the economy, a shift of resources into this sector could nevertheless raise average productivity. It should be noted, however, that the national accounts measures of output and prices in this sector are subject to serious problems; see Gordon (1995) and Lowe (1995) for a more detailed discussion of this issue. One inconsistency noted by Lowe is that in Australia, a sharp rise in financial sector relative wages has been accompanied by falling real product wages, suggesting that price changes are overstated and output and productivity growth understated.

15. It is not unlikely that the rise in φ has made it easier for governments to finance deficits and that, indirectly, this has contributed to the misallocation of resources and the rise in real interest rates. For further discussion of the causes of higher real interest rates and the influence of government dissaving, see King (1995) and Orr et al. (1995).

16. A recent study by Elyasiani and Mehdian (1995), which compares the performance of large and small US banks before and after financial deregulation, finds that the former improved their efficiency relative to the best-practice frontier, while the performance of small banks remained largely unchanged. However, in contrast to the large banks, which recorded a negative rate of technological progress, the small banks achieved a positive rate, thanks to the technological advance of a few high-performing banks.

17. Nonetheless, while this part of the analysis is a good illustration of what can go wrong, the results may not be very robust as there is a clear risk of a pre-selection bias.

18. Generally, this is attributed to the lower costs of derivative transactions and a more efficient process of price discovery.

19. See, for example, Côté (1994). Admittedly, this survey draws primarily on Canadian and US data.

20. Moreover, there is a general consensus that asset prices (except for exchange rates) behave asymmetrically in that downward price movements tend to be larger than increases. The same phenomenon has been observed with respect to changes in real output, but little is known about the sources of these asymmetries.

21. In discussing these events, Davis (1995a) attributes a major role to institutional investors, stressing the growing internationalisation of their portfolios as well as a tendency towards herding due to various means of resolving principal-agent problems in fund management.

22. As further discussed in Mishkin (1994) and White (1995), this development has policy implications. Since a financial crisis, if it were to occur, is now more likely to be a global phenomenon, there is a clear need for closer cooperation between central banks and banking regulators of different countries, including standardisation of regulatory requirements and clarification of legal and jurisdictional issues concerning the bankruptcy of multinational firms.

23. The most well-known would include the Basle Committee on Banking Supervision, the Euro-currency Standing Committee and the Committee on Payment and Settlement Systems (all reporting to the G-10 Governors meeting at the BIS) and the Institute of International Finance.

24. See, for example, BIS (ECSC, 1994b and 1994c), BIS (ECSC, 1994a), BIS (ECSC, 1995c) and other recent publications of the various committees referred to in the above footnote.

25. There may, however, be a "matching problem" in that very few hedging instruments are well suited for those demand components that are most cyclically sensitive (residential construction, purchases of consumer durables and inventories).

26. See Friedman (1989), p. 98: "Taken together the specific changes reported in this paper probably leave the Federal Reserve System neither more nor less able to influence real

economic activity than it used to be. But they also mean that monetary policy works in different ways, which present different opportunities as well as different risks".

27. On the other hand, using a structural VAR model, de Kock and DeLeire (1994) find that output effects of monetary policy changes in the United States have fallen to only one-third of the pre-deregulation impact. However, because they regard their results as suggestive rather than definitive, we have treated them as "an outlier".

28. Detailed accounts of financial deregulation in Japan can be found in Nakajima and Taguchi (1995) and Horiuchi (1995).

29. For instance, the sensitivity of net exports to changes in interest rates has increased in countries with flexible exchange rates while the sensitivity of domestic demand components (for instance residential investment) has declined. In the long run, the two changes may be offsetting, but because net exports react so slowly to changes in the exchange rate while domestic demand reacts more quickly to interest rate changes, the average lag tends to lengthen.

30. This appears to hold even when allowing for the fact that a growing proportion of households' net financial wealth is held in interest-earning assets with flexible rates (see Cantor, 1989). As far as government debt is concerned, there may be two offsetting factors to the net income gain for the household sector. First, if the government respects its intertemporal budget constraint, it will have to reduce non-interest spending or raise taxes. Secondly, if the government allows the current deficit to rise, empirical evidence suggests that about one-half of the rise will be met by higher private saving.

31. This is particularly the case when, as in Australia and the United Kingdom, a very high proportion of debt is at variable interest rates. At the same time, the net effect on aggregate spending of a change from fixed to variable rates is uncertain. On the one hand, current spending will be more strongly affected because of larger fluctuations in cash flows; on the other, spending on consumer durables and fixed investment may become less sensitive to changes in interest rates, as the "locking-in" effect is reduced.

32. Simulations on the model maintained at the Bank of England show that the price-dampening effect of a rise in interest rates doubles with a move from a fixed to a floating exchange rate regime.

33. That is, the "sacrifice ratio" could improve, depending on the pass-through of exchange rate changes into domestic inflation and the time horizon over which the sacrifice ratio is estimated.

34. The initial phase of financial deregulation and the shift from direct to indirect instruments of control went relatively smoothly because the markets for the indirect instruments were already in place. The situation is somewhat different in developing countries which, forced by international competition and global integration, have moved from direct to indirect instruments of control but often lack well-developed markets for these new instruments (see Alexander et al., 1995). This has in many cases made it difficult to sterilise the effects of capital inflows.

35. Poole (1994) points out that the correlation between the growth of the money aggregate and the rate of inflation generally declines in conditions of low inflation and low

nominal interest rates because the "penalty" for holding money is low. Consequently, a money supply shock tends to be absorbed in larger money holdings rather than in higher inflation. He also claims, using a simple reduced-form relationship, that the general success of monetary policy in achieving the ultimate target implies that the covariance between monetary instruments or intermediate targets and the ultimate target approaches zero:

$$Y = a + bX + cM$$

where Y = the ultimate target, X = exogenous disturbances and M = the monetary instrument or target. An optimal monetary policy would imply:

$$M^* = (Y^* - a - bX)/c$$

and if the central bank always manages to offset changes in X and keep M close to M* the covariance between M and Y would approach zero. If this were true, it would, indeed, be highly favourable to central bank policies but, unfortunately, it does not hold (Friedman, 1994) because the *partial* correlation between Y and M has virtually disappeared so that the parameter c can no longer be identified. Although something of a detour there are important lessons to be drawn from this exchange. Using Poole's argument, "good" monetary instruments or intermediate targets cannot be found from bi-variate relations. On the other hand, and this is what makes empirical work in this area so difficult, success in identifying such an instrument requires a very precise estimate of the parameter b; in other words, a complete model with a well-specified transmission process. This is not a new point, having been made in White (1979).

36. To illustrate, we do not see asset price cycles of the magnitude experienced in the 1980s as a permanent feature, but their effects on investment and capital stocks via weakened balance sheets of banks and non-financial enterprises could be with us to the end of this decade.

37. See also Nakajima and Taguchi (1995), who, after reviewing the asset price cycle of the late 1980s and the subsequent bank problems, conclude that: *"While the non-monetary factors and macroeconomic policy settings contributed to the hike in asset prices, the main reason was obviously the aggressive lending behaviour of banks"* (p. 61) and *"the main reason for the bank problem was their mismanagement in responding to intensified competition"* (p. 60).

38. See Schinasi and Hargraves (1993).

39. The high positive correlations are likely to reflect a dual causal relationship as an exogenous rise in real asset prices makes banks more willing to expand lending, which in turn provides a further boost to asset prices (see Higgins and Osler, 1995). However, as shown by Borio et al. (1994) and BIS (1993), the positive influence of credit on real asset prices remains even after allowance is made for other determinants of real asset prices. New Zealand, which abolished virtually all financial regulations in the course of just nine months in 1984-85, experienced a similar credit-induced boost to real property and equity prices. Between 1984 and 1987 the ratio of private sector credit to GDP rose from less than 20% to almost 30% and over the same period equity prices increased by 135% and real property prices by 40-55%, while consumer prices recorded a cumulative rise of over 35%. In the case of Japan, Ito and Iwaisako (1995) find that the initial rise in land and equity prices can largely be attributed to strong credit growth, while the continued rise during the late 1980s is difficult to explain by "fundamentals".

40. Saarenheimo (1995) provides an instructive illustration of how bank lending in Finland "overreacted" to the removal of earlier controls. Moreover, according to his estimate the loan supply "bubble" not only led to a boom in asset prices but also generated a rise in private investment of almost 25%, followed by an equally large decline and a prolonged slump when the bubble burst. In a related paper, Takala and Viren (1995) find that the bankruptcy rate, which more than doubled during Finland's recent recession, is positively related to indebtedness and real interest rates, while a rise in the bankruptcy rate tends (with a one-year lag) to reduce bank credit and real output growth. Though the results are still preliminary, it thus appears that bankruptcies may play a role in the transmission of financial market developments to real economic activity and that the exceptional rise in debt following financial reform was a major cause of the subsequent recession.

41. It should be stressed that asset market bubbles and excessive debt creation have not been confined to countries with liberalised financial systems. In South Korea and Taiwan excess demand pressures combined with tight controls on capital outflows and most domestic financial markets can lead to strong pressures in those markets (mainly equity and real property markets), which are largely free of regulations. In Canada, which liberalised financial markets as early as the 1960s and 1970s and which in Table 2 shows a comparatively low correlation between credit growth and asset price increases, attempts by households and enterprises to cut back their debt, nonetheless, significantly reduced credit demand and overall growth during the 1991-92 recession (see Fillion, 1994). Moreover, as is shown in Montplaisir (1995), including debt service payments and household debt in a reduced-form IS equation improves its predictive power.

42. On this point see also Davis (1995b) and Nakajima and Taguchi (1995). Davis argues that the appropriate macroeconomic response to financial fragility is not straightforward. He further takes the view that there are sufficient secular factors (inter alia increased financial competition) to expect greater financial fragility to be a permanent feature of liberalised financial markets. Nakajima and Taguchi recognise that the increased competition is likely to be a permanent feature and that deregulation tends to encourage banks to take excessive risks if moral hazard incentives are allowed to remain. They, therefore, believe that coupling deregulation with the removal of these incentives is a necessary condition for reducing the risk of financial instability.

43. It is also uncertain how much interest rates should have been raised in the late 1980s; see Macfarlane (1991), p. 187: "We will never know how high interest rates may have had to go, and how long they may have had to be held there, to achieve a low growth rate for credit during this period. Real interest rates of 10% or so and nominal interest rates to borrowers of over 20% did not do the job".

44. While the credit-asset price cycle was most pronounced in the Nordic countries, banking problems related to real estate lending also occurred in the United States, Japan, the United Kingdom and Australia, all of which have flexible exchange rates. Even in Switzerland, 84 ailing banks were merged or taken over during 1990-94, in most cases because of poor management and excessive risk-taking on real estate lending.

45. See Duca and Garrett (1995), who find that the effect of changes in monetary policy are partly transmitted via changes in banks' willingness to grant loans to the household sector, but also that this effect has declined since the abolition of deposit rate regulation. Mosser (1992) comes to the same conclusion by comparing the financial structure of older and more recent vintages of US macroeconometric models.

46. According to results reported in BIS (1995b) this holds for Japan but not for Germany, where banks seem to have the incentive and the balance-sheet strength to, at least temporarily, insulate borrowers from more restrictive policies.

47. Because of banks' aggregate balance-sheet constraint, it is not surprising that studies based on disaggregated data are better able to identify separate credit channel effects than analyses using aggregate data. For the United States such studies tend to show that small to medium-sized enterprises are much more affected by policy changes than larger enterprises, because, unlike the latter, they mainly rely on bank credit and have little access to alternative sources of credit. For European countries, on the other hand, disaggregated studies point to somewhat different sectoral patterns. For Italy, where the removal of credit ceilings led to a shift in banks' asset composition in favour of credits, Angeloni *et al.* (1995) find clear evidence that the widening of loan spreads (their principal indicator) is most pronounced for large banks and firms, since smaller banks often operate in isolated regions with few banks and maintain closer relations with their customers, which tend to be small to medium-sized companies. For the United Kingdom, Dale and Haldane (1995) identify a credit channel effect for the personal sector, whereas for the enterprise sector the effects of a monetary tightening seem to be mainly transmitted via changes in deposit holdings. At the same time, the enterprise sector is much more affected by a given change in monetary policy than the personal sector because the latter is shielded by "sticky" loan rates.

BIBLIOGRAPHY

Bank of Canada (1994): "Credit, interest rate spreads and the monetary policy transmission mechanism". Proceedings of a conference held at the Bank of Canada.

Bank of England (1990): "The interest rate transmission mechanism in the United Kingdom and overseas". Bank of England, *Quarterly Bulletin*, May, pp. 198-214.

BIS (1993): Bank for International Settlements, 63rd Annual Report.

BIS (1994): Bank for International Settlements, 64th Annual Report.

BIS (1995*a*): Bank for International Settlements, 65th Annual Report.

BIS (1995*b*): "Financial structure and the monetary policy transmission mechanism". CB 394.

BIS (Euro-currency Standing Committee, 1994*a*): A discussion paper on "Public disclosure of market and credit risks by financial intermediaries" (*Fisher Report*). September.

BIS (Euro-currency Standing Committee, 1994*b*): "Macroeconomic and monetary policy issues raised by the growth of derivatives markets" (*Hannoun Report*). November.

BIS (Euro-currency Standing Committee, 1994*c*): Compendium of annexes to the report on "Macroeconomic and monetary policy issues raised by the growth of derivatives markets" (*Hannoun Report*). November.

BIS (Euro-currency Standing Committee, 1995*c*): "Issues of measurement related to market size and macroprudential risks in derivatives markets" (*Brockmeijer Report*). February.

Akhtar, M.A. (1994): "Causes and consequences of the 1989-92 credit slowdown: overview and perspective". Federal Reserve Bank of New York, *Quarterly Review*, Winter, 18(4), pp. 1-23.

Alexander, W.E., T.J.T. Balino and C. Enoch (1995): "The adoption of indirect instruments of monetary policy". *IMF, Occasional Paper*, No. 126.

Anderson, N. and F. Breedon (1996): "UK asset price volatility over the last 50 years, in BIS, CB 395", *Financial market volatility: measurement, causes and consequences*. Forthcoming.

Angeloni, I., L Buttiglione, G. Ferri and E. Gaiotti (1995): "The credit channel of monetary policy across heterogeneous banks: the case of Italy". Banca d'Italia, *Temi di Discussione*, No. 256.

Bayoumi, T. (1993): "Financial deregulation and household saving". *The Economic Journal*, 103(421), pp. 1432-43.

Bennett, P. (1990): "The influence of financial changes on interest rates and monetary policy: a review of recent evidence". Federal Reserve Bank of New York, *Quarterly Review*, 15(2), Summer, pp. 8-30.

Berg, L. and R. Bergstrom (1995): "Housing and financial wealth, financial deregulation and consumption – the Swedish case". *Scandinavian Journal of Economics*, 97(39), pp. 421-39.

Bernanke, B.S. (1992): "Credit in the macroeconomy". Federal Reserve Bank of New York, *Quarterly Review*, 18(1), Spring, pp. 50-70.

Bernanke, B.S. and J. Campbell (1988): "Is there a corporate debt crisis?" *Brookings Papers on Economic Activity*, Vol. I, pp. 83-141.

Bernanke, B.S., J. Campbell and T.M. Whited (1990): "US corporate leverage developments in 1987 and 1988". *Brookings Papers on Economic Activity*, Vol. I, pp. 255-78.

Bisignano, J. (1991): "European financial deregulation: the pressures for change and the costs of achievement", in I. Macfarlane (ed.), *The deregulation of financial intermediaries*. Proceedings of a conference, Reserve Bank of Australia, pp. 246-90.

Blundell-Wignall, A. and Brown, F. (1991): "Monetary Policy in Liberalised Markets", *OECD Economic Studies*, No. 15, Autumn.

Borio, C., N. Kennedy and S.D. Prowse (1994): "Exploring aggregate asset price fluctuations across countries". *BIS Economic Papers*, No. 40.

Borio, C (1995): "The changing shape of the banking industry". Paper presented at the All Governors Meeting, *BIS*,December.

Bosworth, B. (1989): "Institutional change and the efficacy of monetary policy". *Brookings Papers on Economic Activity*, Vol. I, pp. 77-110.

Cantor, R. (1989): "Interest rates, household cash flow and consumer expenditures". Federal Reserve Bank of New York, *Quarterly Review*, 14(2), Summer, pp. 59-67.

Carroll, C.D. and D. Weil (1994): "Saving and growth: a reinterpretation". *Carnegie-Rochester Conference on Public Policy*, Vol. 40, pp. 133-92.

Cohen, B.H. (1996): "Derivatives and asset price volatility: a test using variance ratios", in BIS, CB 395, *Financial market volatility: measurement, causes and consequences*. Forthcoming.

Côté, A. (1994): "Exchange rate volatility and trade: a survey". Bank of Canada, *Working Paper* 94-5.

Dale, S. and A.G. Haldane (1995): "Interest rates and the channels of monetary transmission: some sectoral estimates". *European Economic Review*, 39(9), pp. 611-26.

Davis, E.P. (1995a): "Institutional investors, unstable financial markets and monetary policy". LSE Financial Markets Group, *Special Papers*, No. 75.

Davis, E.P. (1995b): "Financial fragility in the early 1990s - what can be learnt from international experience?" LSE Financial Markets Group, *Special Papers*, No. 76.

de Kock, G. and T. DeLeire (1994): "The role of the exchange rate in the monetary transmission mechanism: a time-series analysis". Federal Reserve Bank of New York, *Research Paper*, No. 9412.

Drees, B. and C. Pazarbasioglu (1995): "The Nordic banking crisis: pitfalls in financial liberalization". *IMF Working Paper,*No. 95/61.

Duca, J.V. (1995): "The interest rate sensitivity of GDP and accurate Reg. Q measures". Federal Reserve Bank of Dallas, Research Department *Working Paper,* No. 95-13.

Duca, J.V. and B. Garrett (1995): "Credit availability, bank consumer lending and consumer durables". Federal Reserve Bank of Dallas, *Working Paper,* No. 95-14.

Economist, The (1995): "The wanderlust in Germany". December 2nd, 337(7943), pp. 83-84.

Edey, M. and K. Hviding (1995): "An assessment of financial reform in OECD countries". *OECD Working Papers,* No. 41.

Edwards, F.R. (1993): "Financial markets in transition – or the decline of commercial banking", in *Changing capital markets.* A symposium sponsored by the Federal Reserve Bank of Kansas City, pp. 5-63.

Edwards, F.R. and F.S. Mishkin (1995): "The decline of traditional banking: implications for financial stability and regulatory policy". Federal Reserve Bank of New York, *Economic Policy Review,* July, pp. 27-45.

Elyasiani, E. and S. Mehdian (1995): "The comparative efficiency performance of small and large US commercial banks in the pre-and post-deregulation eras". *Applied Economics,* 27, pp. 1069-79.

Englander, A.S. and A. Gurney (1994): "Medium-term determination of OECD productivity". *OECD Economic Studies,* No. 22, pp. 49-109.

Feldstein, M. (1995): "Global capital flows: too little not too much". *The Economist,* June 24th, 335(7920), pp. 90-91.

Fillion, J-F. (1994) "L'endettement du secteur privé au Canada: un examen macroéconomique". Bank of Canada, *Working Paper,* No. 94-7.

Filosa, R. (1995): "Money demand stability and currency substitution in six European countries". *BIS Working Paper,* No. 30.

Friedman, B. (1989): "Changing effects of monetary policy on real economic activity", in *Monetary policy issues in the 1990s.* A symposium sponsored by the Federal Reserve Bank of Kansas City, pp. 55-111.

Friedman, B. (1994): "Discussion", in J.C. Fuhrer (ed.), *Goals, guidelines, and constraints facing monetary policy makers.* Federal Reserve Bank of Boston, conference proceedings, pp. 122-29.

Friedman, B. and K.N. Kuttner (1992): "Money, income, prices, and interest rates". *American Economic Review,* Vol. 82(3), pp. 472-92.

Goldstein, M. and M. Mussa (1993): "The integration of world capital markets", in *Changing capital markets.* A symposium sponsored by the Federal Reserve Bank of Kansas City, pp. 245-315.

Gordon, R. (1995): "Problems in the measurement and performance of service-sector productivity in the United States", in P.S. Andersen, J. Dwyer and D. Gruen (eds.), *Productivity and growth.* Proceedings of a conference, *Reserve Bank of Australia,* pp. 139-66.

Gunther, J.W. (1994): "Changing channels of monetary transmission: evidence from the home mortgage market". Federal Reserve Bank of Dallas, Financial Industry Studies, *Working Paper*, Nos. 4-94.

Haslag, J.H. (1995): "Monetary policy, banking and growth". Federal Reserve Bank of Dallas, Research Department, *Working Paper*, No. 95-15.

Higgins, M. and C. Osler (1995): "Asset market hangovers and growth in the industrial world". *Memo*, Federal Reserve Bank of New York.

Horiuchi, A. (1995): "Financial sector reforms in postwar Japan: an overview". University of Tokyo, *Discussion Papers*, No. 95-F-34.

Hubbard, G.R. (1994): "Is there a 'credit channel' for monetary policy?" *NBER Working Paper*, No. 4977.

Ito, T. and T. Iwaisako (1995): "Explaining asset bubbles in Japan", *NBER Working Paper*, No. 5358.

Jappelli, T. and M. Pagano (1994): "Saving, growth and liquidity constraints". *Quarterly Journal of Economics*, 109(1), pp. 83-109.

Johnston, R.B. and C. Pazarbasioglu (1995): "Linkages between financial variables, financial sector reform and economic growth and efficiency". *IMF Working Paper*, No. 95/103.

Kahn, G.A. (1989): "The changing interest rate sensitivity of the US economy". Federal Reserve Bank of Kansas City, *Economic Review*, 74, November, pp. 13-34.

Kashyap, A.N. and J.C. Stein (1993): "Monetary policy and bank lending". *NBER Working Paper*, No. 4317.

Kasman, B. and A.P. Rodrigues (1991): "Financial liberalization and monetary control in Japan". Federal Reserve Bank of New York, *Quarterly Review*, 16(3), Autumn, pp. 28-46.

King, M. (1994): "Debt deflation: theory and evidence". *European Economic Review*, 38(3/4), pp. 419-45.

King, M. (1995): Report to G10 industrial countries on *Saving, investment and real interest rates*.

King, R.G. and R. Levine (1993): "Finance, entrepreneurship and growth: theory and evidence". *Journal of Monetary Economics*, 32(3), pp. 513-42.

Lowe, P. (1995): "Labour-productivity growth and relative wages: 1978-94", in P.S. Andersen, J. Dwyer and D. Gruen (eds.), *Productivity and growth*. Proceedings of a conference, Reserve Bank of Australia, pp. 93-134.

Macfarlane, I. (1991): "The lessons for monetary policy", in I. Macfarlane (ed.), *The deregulation of financial intermediaries*. Proceedings of a conference, Reserve Bank of Australia, pp. 175-200.

Masson, P.R., T. Bayoumi and H. Samiei (1995): "International evidence on the determinants of private saving". *IMF Working Paper*, No. 95/51.

Mauskopf, E. (1990): "The transmission channels of monetary policy: how have they changed?" *Federal Reserve Bulletin*, 76(12), December, pp. 985-1008.

McKinnon, R.I. (1973): *Money and capital in economic development*, Washington: Brookings Institution.

Mishkin, F.S. (1994): "Preventing financial crisis: an international perspective". *NBER Working Paper*, No. 4636.

Montplaisir, M-C. (1995): "Effets des variables financières dans la courbe IS". Bank of Canada, *Internal Note*, No. 95-141.

Morton, J.E. (1996): "Trends in financial market volatility in the G7 countries", in BIS, CB 395, *Financial market volatility: measurement, causes and consequences.* Forthcoming.

Mosser, P.C. (1992): "Changes in monetary policy effectiveness: evidence from large macroeconometric models". Federal Reserve Bank of New York, *Quarterly Review*, 17(1), Spring, pp. 36-51.

Nakajima, Z. and H. Taguchi (1995): "Toward a more stable financial framework: long-term alternatives – an overview of recent bank disruption worldwide", in K. Sawamoto, Z. Nakajima and H. Taguchi (eds.), *Financial stability in a changing environment.* Basingstoke: Macmillan, pp. 41-98.

Oliner, S.D. and G.D. Rudebusch (1995): "Is there a bank lending channel for monetary policy?" Federal Reserve Bank of San Francisco, *Economic Review*, No. 2, pp. 3-20.

Orr, A., M. Edey and M. Kennedy (1995): "The determinants of real long-term interest rates". *OECD Working Papers*, No. 42.

Pagano, M. (1993): "Financial markets and growth: an overview". *European Economic Review*, 37(2-3), pp. 613-22.

Paxson, C. (1995): "Saving and growth: evidence". *NBER Working Paper*, No. 5301.

Poole, W. (1994): "Monetary aggregates targeting in a low-inflation economy", in J.C. Fuhrer (ed.) , *op. cit.,* pp. 87-122.

Saarenheimo, T. (1995): "Credit crunch caused investment slump". Bank of Finland, *Discussion Papers*, Nos. 6/95.

Schinasi, G.J. and M. Hargraves (1993): "Boom and bust in asset markets in the 1980s: causes and consequences". *IMF Staff Studies*, pp. 1-27.

Shaw, E.S. (1973): "Financial deepening in economic development". New York [etc.]: *Oxford University Press.*

Smith, J. and G. Sterne (1994): "Personal and corporate sector debt". Bank of England *Quarterly Bulletin,* 34(2), May, pp. 144-56.

Sutton, G. (1996): "Is there excess comovement of bond yields between countries?", in BIS, CB 395, *Financial market volatility: measurement, causes and consequences.* Forthcoming.

Takala, K. and M. Viren, (1995): "Bankruptcies, indebtedness and the credit crunch". Bank of Finland, *Discussion Papers,* Nos. 28/95.

White, W.R. (1979): "Alternative monetary targets and control instruments in Canada: criteria for choice". *The Canadian Journal of Economics,* 12(4), November, pp. 590-604.

White, W.R. (1991): "Some implications of international financial integration for Canadian public policy". Bank of Canada, *Technical Report*, No. 57.

White W.R. (1995): "International financial integration: some implications for central banks". Bank of Korea, *5th Central Banking Seminar,* November.

Wirjanto, T.S. (1994): "Aggregate consumption behaviour and liquidity constraints: the Canadian evidence", *Canadian Journal of Economics,* 28(4*b*), pp. 1135-52.

Wojnilower, A. (1985): "Private credit demand, supply, and crunches – how different are the 1980s?" *American Economic Review,* 75(2), May, pp. 351-56.

Wojnilower, A. (1991): "Some principles of financial deregulation: lessons from the United States", in I. Macfarlane (ed.), *The deregulation of financial intermediaries.* Proceedings of a conference, Reserve Bank of Australia, pp. 203-216.

COMMENTS

by

A. WINTERS

I learned a lot from reading the Andersen and White paper and my making a public comment on it is like the blind leading the sighted. As an economist who has spent most of his career on the real economy, I can merely hope that I might identify some of the insights in the paper that are so obvious to experts in the financial sector that they have not been fully articulated.

The most fundamental suggestion of the paper is, I think, that financial deregulation is leading to a decline in household savings, and that at least part of this decline is permanent rather than transitory. It is not at all difficult to understand how deregulation could have a transitory effect on savings rates. For example, households may wish to rebalance their portfolios of assets, using their greater borrowing ability to finance the purchase of real assets, and it is also possible that they would want to reassess their ratios of income to assets. The suggestion that the change in the savings rate is permanent, however, I find somewhat more difficult to credit. In any model with infinitely lived agents, or with a strong bequest motive, it seems to me that agents will rebalance their portfolios and that flows of savings and dissavings will then return to their previous rates. Thus I suspect that it is only in an overlapping generation model that there is any likelihood of finding a permanent savings effect.

A simple overlapping generations model has some people saving and others dissaving at the same time. Recorded household savings is the sum of these two parts. It is easily comprehensible that if borrowing is restricted individuals might try to accumulate more financial assets early in their lives, for, say, precautionary reasons, or might, as in Jappelli and Pagano, be unable to borrow as much as they would wish in their early lives. In each of these cases, a financial deregulation will allow the young to reduce their net savings and thus appear to reduce the savings rate overall. In steady state, however, it seems to me that the latter conclusion does not follow, for once the "deregulated generation" with lower savings has become old their dissavings (bounded by zero assets) will be correspondingly lower.

So how do Jappelli and Pagano get savings rates to fall? First, they assume that the economy is growing so that the generation which is dissaving is smaller and/or poorer than the generation that is saving. Imagine that before deregulation stocks of assets were growing because the young saved more than the old dissaved; then after deregulation, which reduces the level of savings, this effect will be less marked. That is, the savings rate will have fallen. This story is very elegant, and Jappelli and Pagano's empirical results look rather convincing, but it seems unlikely to me that such effects as these would show up in the first ten years' data following a deregulation. Moreover, this effect depends on the margin of a margin (it refers to changes in the allocation across uses of the increment in income), so it seems quite likely to be dominated by other phenomena in the real data. Thus, I suspect, that it is only in the very long run, if at all, that we will be able to determine from time-series data whether deregulation has reduced savings rates.

An implication of Andersen and White's paper is that a decline in the savings rate is costly. One route through which this might occur is also due to Jappelli and Pagano Even if net savings is zero, a financial regulation that caused the young to save more and the old to dissave more, would still be associated with a higher average stock of assets. If this stock of assets is equated with the capital stock of the economy, and if one has an endogenous growth model which relates the growth rate to the capital stock, then financial regulation is good for growth, or conversely, financial deregulation is bad for growth. I should have found it useful if the authors could have identified the market failure (such as this growth externality) which they felt was responsible for declining welfare resulting from the removal of barriers to choice. One of the lessons which I think international trade economists have learned over the years is that it is always useful to identify precisely which market failure is distorting the link from choice to welfare. This intellectual discipline is necessary (a) to be quite sure there really is a failure, (b) because not all failures have the same effects and (c) because one can only devise efficient corrective policy by identifying the precise point of breakdown.

Finally on savings, we should note that households are not the only source of savings. In general, it is total savings that matters. If financial regulation allowed governments to alter their savings behaviour – for example, to borrow more easily at least before there was any question about their liquidity or solvency – these effects could easily outweigh the effects on household savings.

Another point on which I should press the authors is their statement that financial institutions may not (yet) have the ability to make sound investments. This is clearly possible, but it does not change my mind about the policy implications of deregulation. First, won't the financial institutions learn to invest better? We could think of the whole process of transition in Eastern Europe as being one whereby firms, governments and institutions learn to manage the market economy better, even though in the short term learning is costly with errors of judgement contributing to declining output. Similarly with financial deregulation in OECD; if in the long run it permits us to make better use of financial instruments, the investment of making a few mistakes while we learn is very likely to be worthwhile. Moreover, what is the alternative? Governments do not have a record of unmitigated success in investment. Since this conference is at the OECD, perhaps I should merely note David Henderson's work on the costs of Concorde and Advanced Gas Cooled reactors, (Henderson, 1977).

Andersen and White comment that financial deregulation has led to increased perceptions of uncertainty. That seems true, but again as we have learned in the literature on resource allocation, not all perceptions of uncertainty are harmful. Indeed, if the world is uncertain, resource allocation is improved by our all understanding that and reacting accordingly. Thus, for example, I do not think that one would argue that the very stable internal prices for agricultural produce in the EU are socially welfare enhancing. They are very nice for farmers, but they almost certainly encourage too much activity in agriculture. Put another way, one needs to consider risk overall, and squeezing it out of the financial markets does not mean that it disappears altogether. Indeed, since financial markets are sometimes characterised as being primarily markets for risk, it might seem that they are exactly the right place to have risk concentrated.

The Mexican crisis was scary, but whether it is evidence of fragility or robustness in markets, I am less sure. There is no doubt that a lot of people made a lot of mistakes and that, with relatively liberal financial markets, when these came home to roost they came home with a vengeance. On the other hand, the contagion effect was not particularly large nor long-lived. Moreover, Mexico taught us a very important lesson: that we have to consider each investment on its merits, and that those merits reside very firmly in economic fundamentals. If, as a result of the Mexican crisis, investors have learned to be more careful and to seek better information, it seems to me that the scare has been worthwhile. Also, on the question of contagion, the authors mentioned the way in which the London property crash filtered through the international financial system. They imply that this was unfortunate and dangerous. I really do not know, but again I would ask "what was the alternative?" Should we have continued to invest real resources in excess office space?

The policy lessons which I draw from all this are not that we should put sand in the wheels, and thus hinder good investment as well as bad investment. Still less should we look to government and central banks to make all our investment decisions. Rather they are that errors are costly and that information and responsible entrepreneurship are now even more important than previously. The case for prudential supervision is perhaps stronger than ever, and given that markets are international it is clear that supervision should be managed with a similar scope. It also seems necessary that we have provision for co-ordinated rescues, for when one is trying to do something as complicated as global investment, errors are bound to occur. As the corollary of recognising that errors are inevitable, I would urge that we make it very clear, and if possible tie our hands to ensure such an outcome, that the costs of carelessness or excessive risk-taking will fall directly on the individuals who are responsible. That is, while one might rescue small depositors in the event of a crash, very large depositors who have the means to obtain necessary information, shareholders, and most importantly, managers, will suffer severe consequences if they mess up. It seems to me that only by fixing private costs firmly where decisions are taken can we expect the invisible hand to ensure that private decisions generate social benefit.

GENERAL DISCUSSION

The discussion focused on five main issues:

– the relationship between financial deregulation and saving;

– the effect of financial deregulation on the conduct and transmission mechanism of monetary policy;

– the need for strengthening supervision;

– the extent of completeness and open-endedness of the financial market reform process;

– transitions problems and expected benefits of financial deregulation and innovation.

There was general agreement that financial deregulation tends to lower national saving in the short-to-medium-run but that it is too early to say what is going to happen in the longer-run. After deregulation private households have had easier access to credit and governments have found it easier to finance large budget deficits for much longer than they otherwise would have done. As to private saving behaviour it was observed, however, that there have been many other factors effecting saving and the portfolios of assets and that one may get different results if the national income accounting concept of saving were augmented by capital gains and losses.

There was also agreement that the conduct of monetary policy has become more difficult after deregulation and that the transmission mechanisms to the real economy has become weaker and slower to "bite". For the United States two factors were mentioned in particular for the lengthening of the lag; the easing of credit restraints on housing and that much more of the channel of monetary policy works through exchange rates whose influence on net exports are slow to come through. As far as international transmission processes are concerned it was pointed out that globalisation of financial markets leads to undesirable spill-over effects between national economies if cyclical positions are different. A case in point was the US-triggered rise in bond rates in 1994 which was definitely not what Europe needed.

Many participants acknowledged that in deregulated markets there was a need for greater supervision to contain the enhanced risk of default. It was noted in this context, however, that regulation and supervision are not always easily distinguishable and that over-regulation, for instance by setting too rigid adequacy rules, should be avoided. The question was raised whether supervisors can really "be ahead" of evaluations of financial markets. Another control-related issue was raised with respect to possible consequences of financial reform on corporate governance.

In response to these latter two queries it was argued that the ability to operate in a deregulated world would increase over time. It is a learning-by-doing process. Banks are unlikely to go again on a very risky expedition into the real property markets but that does not mean that future "bubbles" in financial markets can be avoided. On corporate governance it was argued that one control system is not necessarily better than others. Different systems may continue to co-exist in different countries. Serious real problems would only arise in a period of transition, when former control mechanisms disappear and nothing has been done to replace them.

In debating the question of costs and benefits of the financial reform process it was noted that the process is not only policy-determined but, in large measure, also driven by technological and socio-economic changes. Whatever its merits the process is not reversible and never complete. Given the ever-changing external environment there is a continuous need for adjustment. In general, costs are mostly transitory as they arise during the adjustment period. By contrast, benefits are permanent but take longer to occur and are more difficult to measure. On theoretical reasoning, deregulation of financial markets should provide for a better match between savings and investment opportunities while at the same time increasing consumers' choice and welfare.

TRADE LIBERALISATION AND ECONOMIC PERFORMANCE

by

Jan Haaland and Victor Norman
Centre for International Trade and Shipping
Norwegian School of Economics and Agder University College

INTRODUCTION

The combined effects of the single European market, the Europe agreements between the European Union (EU) and Eastern Europe, North American Free Trade Agreement (NAFTA), and the Uruguay round agreements could well be the most comprehensive liberalisation of world trade since the 1840s. At the same time, these measures to liberalise trade differ fundamentally from previous ones, in that freer trade now has followed, and to a great extent been induced by, domestic deregulation; and the stated objective of trade liberalisation has been better domestic performance rather than traditional gains from trade.

The purpose of this paper is to look at some of the links between trade policy and economic performance, and to assess their quantitative importance.

In traditional trade theory, trade occurs between undistorted national economies. The only effect of freer trade is to reduce international price wedges. By so doing, comparative advantages will be exploited more fully, thus raising real incomes. At initially low-to-intermediate levels of trade barriers, however, the income effects (like other Harberger triangles) will be small. Beyond comparative-advantage effects, freer trade will not affect economic performance.

Quantitatively important links between trade and performance must therefore have to do with domestic distortions in the trading countries. Of these, the most interesting have to do with scale economies and imperfectly competitive product markets, trade unions and other labour market imperfections, and with external economies and co-ordination failures.

The most obvious link, and the one studied in greatest detail, is the link between trade and performance in the presence of scale economies and imperfect competition. If domestic markets are too small to allow a large number of firms of technically efficient scale, international trade could give gains both through larger (and thus more efficient) firms, and through greater competition.

There could be further gains. Firms with market power have incentives to segment markets in order to price discriminate. Segmentation along national lines is a natural consequence, at least as long as formal trade barriers are in place. If so, reduction or elimination of trade barriers could facilitate market integration (in the strict sense of the term), which could be beneficial by itself.

The second possible link is through the labour market. To the extent that market power or asymmetric information produce wedges between the marginal productivity of labour and the marginal value of leisure, trade policy could have second-best effects on labour market performance. We could imagine two types of such effects. One would be straightforward second-best quantity effects: by shifting labour-demand curves, trade policy could (for given price wedges in the labour market) affect employment. The other would be price-setting effects. It is sometimes argued, for example, that free trade disciplines trade unions. If so, freer trade could reduce the monopoly wage wedge.

A third link between trade policy and performance is through economic growth. It is commonly asserted that free trade fosters rapid growth. Although the links between trade and growth are considerably more complex than many who subscribe to this view seem to think, there may be some truth to it. In particular, to the extent that trade barriers prevent international diffusion of knowledge, or prevent the formation of industrial agglomerations, there may be an important relationship between trade policy and potential economic growth.

In the following, these links are discussed in somewhat greater detail, and an attempt is made to assess their relative importance, by means of numerical, dynamic, general-equilibrium simulations. The simulations use a model of the world economy which distinguishes five world regions – United States, Japan, European Community (EC) prior to expansion, European Free Trade Association (EFTA), and the rest of the world (treated exogenously). European markets are initially segmented along national lines. The model has 14 traded goods and services, and a non-tradeables sector in each country. Each traded good is produced in industries with product differentiation and imperfect competition. There are three primary factors – capital and two types of labour (skilled and unskilled). The simulations use as a base case a scenario for the year 2005, based on ILO labour force projections and historical savings behaviour, but in which trade policies are as they were in the early 1980s.

The following three sections discuss scale and competition effects, labour-market effects, and growth effects. The model and the reference case used for the simulations are presented in somewhat greater detail in the appendix.

PRODUCT MARKET EFFECTS

The direct effect of trade policy is to change the terms at which foreign goods can enter domestic product markets (and domestic goods can enter foreign markets). All effects on domestic variables must derive from this.

Channels

In a perfectly competitive economy, the channel through which trade policy affects the domestic economy is straightforward: domestic prices of tradeables equal foreign prices plus trade costs, so changes in trade costs map directly into changes in domestic prices, and thus into changes in domestic consumption, production, and employment patterns.

With imperfectly competitive markets, the transmission mechanism is more complex. The obvious complication is that firms and other agents are price-setters, not price-takers; so there is no automatic equalisation of foreign and domestic prices. The more profound complication is that the degree of competition matters as much as the level of tariffs (or other trade costs) *per se*. Both aspects are illustrated in Table 1, which gives simulated effects of liberalisation for a stylised industry. The industry produces differentiated products, with a constant elasticity of substitution between product varieties from different firms. Initially, the industry

Table 1. **Illustration of product market effects of liberalisation**

Model assumptions		
Industry elasticity of demand		1.4
Elasticity of substitution between product varieties		5
Cournot competition		
Initially two domestic and two foreign sellers		
Trade costs initially = 50 per cent of marginal cost		
Effects on home price	*Percentage*	
Trade cost reduction	30	60
Number of foreign sellers		
2	−1.8	−3.8
3	−4.1	−6.3
4	−5.9	−8.1
Effects on total sales		
Trade cost reduction	30	60
Number of foreign sellers		
2	6.3	15.4
3	13.0	25.0
4	18.5	32.6

has two domestic firms competing with each other and with two foreign sellers. All four firms have equal and constant marginal production costs, but the foreign firms face trade restrictions equivalent to a 50 per cent tariff. The table gives the effects on the price charged by the domestic firms and on total domestic sales (from domestic firms and imports), of, respectively, a 30 per cent and 60 per cent cut in the tariff, under varying assumptions regarding the subsequent number of foreign competitors in the market.

Two points should be noted. First, the price charged by domestic firms will typically fall by far less than the trade cost reduction – in the example, a 60 per cent tariff cut is equivalent to a 20 per cent marginal-cost reduction for foreign firms. That is almost fully reflected in import prices: They fall by 17-19 per cent, depending on the number of foreign firms. By contrast, the prices charged by domestic firms fall by only 4-8 per cent. Second, entry by more foreign firms is at least as important as the tariff reduction *per se*: a small tariff reduction, if it induces new foreign entry, could have a greater impact than a large tariff reduction under circumstances which do not encourage entry.

Effects

The counterparts to more complex transmission mechanisms are more varied and quantitatively larger effects. Freer trade, by affecting the degree of competition and the population of firms, could – even at initially low levels of trade barriers – have first-order real income effects through changes in demand, production and the range of product varieties available to consumers.

To illustrate the difference between the effects with perfectly and imperfectly competitive product markets, consider a national market in which there is a fixed number of active firms, some domestic and some foreign (so we ignore effects on the product range or the population of firms; we also ignore possible export-market effects). Changes in trade policy will affect the quantity produced and sold by each firm. For small changes, the real-income (welfare) effect of any such change will be the quantity change times the difference between the consumer price and the marginal cost. The total effect of a change in trade policy will be the sum of the effects associated with each firm, *i.e.* the sum of the output increases multiplied by price-marginal cost margins.

For simplicity, assume that all domestic firms are alike and that the same is true for all foreign firms, and denote by subscript h prices, marginal costs and total sales from domestic firms, and by subscript f the corresponding values for foreign firms. For small changes (and as an approximation for larger changes), the welfare effect of freer trade will then be

$$Gain = (P_h - MC_h)\Delta X_h + (P_f - MC_f)\Delta X_f \qquad (1)$$

Relative to total consumer expenditure on the products in question (Exp), this can be written as

$$\frac{Gain}{Exp} = \frac{P_h - MC_h}{P_h}\left(\frac{P_h X_h}{Exp}\right)\frac{\Delta X_h}{X_h} + \frac{P_f - MC_f}{P_f}\left(\frac{P_f X_f}{Exp}\right)\frac{\Delta X_f}{X_f} \tag{2}$$

where $(P_h X_h / Exp)$ and $(P_f X_f / Exp)$ are the shares of home-market firms and foreign firms in total domestic sales, so the latter is the import share (call it m), and the former is $(1 - m)$.

If the market is perfectly competitive, price will equal marginal cost for the domestic firms, so the first term in (2) vanishes. For imports, price will equal marginal cost plus the tariff or tariff equivalent (T). Thus (2) reduces to

$$\frac{Gain}{Exp} = \frac{T}{P_f} m \frac{\Delta X_f}{X_f} \tag{3}$$

If the market is imperfectly competitive, the price-marginal cost margins will depend on the price elasticities facing individual firms. They reflect two sources of market power. One derives from product differentiation: the more different the products, the greater the market power of each firm in its particular market niche. The other derives from a dominant position in the total market: the larger the share of the total market, the greater the firm's market power. Specifically, if we assume quantity (Cournot) competition between the firms, the mark-up of firm i will be

$$\frac{P_i - MC_i - T_i}{P_i} = (1 - s_i)\frac{1}{\sigma} + s_i\frac{1}{e} \tag{4}$$

where $1/\sigma$ a measure of the degree of product differentiation (equal to zero if the products of different firms are identical), e is the industry-level price elasticity of demand, s_i is the firm's market share, and T_i is the tariff or tariff equivalent facing firm i (zero for domestic firms). Using (4), the gains from freer trade in the imperfectly-competitive case becomes

$$\frac{Gain}{Exp} = \left((1 - s_h)\frac{1}{\sigma} + s_h\frac{1}{e}\right)(1 - m)\frac{\Delta X_h}{X_h} + \left[\left((1 - s_f)\frac{1}{\sigma} + s_f\frac{1}{e}\right) + \frac{T}{P_f}\right]m\frac{\Delta X_f}{X_f} \tag{5}$$

Note that s_h here is the market share of each individual, domestic firms (and correspondingly for s_f); not to be confused with the total shares of domestic and foreign firms in the domestic market.

We can use (3) and (5) to compare the two cases. Suppose, in line with what might be called stylised European facts, that in a typical market imports account for 20 per cent of total sales, each home-market firm has a market share of 20 per cent, and each foreign seller has a market share of 10 per cent. To make things simple, assume that the market price elasticity of demand is unity and that products are not differentiated. To account for the difference in market shares between domestic and foreign firms, we must assume that foreign sellers incur higher costs than domestic ones. Assume that the entire cost difference is due to initial tariffs, which in that case have to be 10 per cent. Assume, finally, that elimination of the tariff raises sales by home-market firms by 5 per cent, and by foreign ones by 15 per cent. With perfect competition (equation (3) above), the gain from free trade would be the tariff rate times the import share times the percentage rise in imports, *i.e.*

10 per cent · 20 per cent · 15 per cent = 0.3 of consumer expenditure

With imperfect competition (equation (5)), the corresponding gain (with e=1 and $1/\sigma = 0$) becomes

- $- (1 - m)s_h$ · % increase home sales
- $+ m(s_f + $ tariff rate) · % increase imports, *i.e.*
- $-$ 80 per cent · 20 per cent · 5 per cent + 20 per cent · (10 per cent + 10 per cent) · 15 per cent
- $- = 1.4$ per cent of consumer expenditure

In other words, the gain is almost four times higher in the imperfectly-competitive case. Had we added product differentiation, the difference would have been even greater: with an elasticity of substitution of 10, the gain would have increased from 1.4 per cent to 2 per cent of expenditure.

Simulated effects

It is clear, then, that the degree of competition in product markets matters a lot to the quantitative effects of freer trade. There are important differences within the OECD area in that respect. In particular, there are strong indications that, prior to the current round of trade liberalisation, American, and to some extent Japanese, markets were substantially more competitive than European ones. The comprehensive survey material gathered in connection with the plans for the single European market (see Emerson, 1988) is one such indication. Another is given by Herfindahl concentration indexes. Table 2 gives the values of the 1985 Herfindahl-indexes for the main industrial sectors in the United States, Japan, and the previous EFTA-countries; all expressed relative to the corresponding average values for the EC countries (prior to EC expansion). As is seen, on the average, US concentration was only one-tenth of the concentration in the EC, while EFTA industrial concentration was five times that of the EC. Japan had slightly higher average concentration than the EC.

These differences are reflected in our simulations of the product market effects of liberalisation.

Table 2. **Herfindahl concentration indexes**

EU = 1 for each industry

NACE	Category	EFTA	United States	Japan
17	Chemical products	3.4	0.0	0.3
19	Metal products	3.2	0.0	1.0
21	Agricultural and industrial machinery	4.8	0.0	2.4
23	Office machinery	12.0	0.3	3.3
25	Electrical goods	0.9	0.1	0.8
28	Transport	3.1	0.1	1.4
36	Food products	0.3	0.1	0.5
42	Textiles, clothing and leather	5.7	0.0	1.3
47	Paper and printing products	9.0	0.0	0.5
48	Timber and other n.e.s.	8.5	0.5	1.0
49	Rubber and plastic products	3.1	0.1	0.5
	Unweighted average	4.9	0.1	1.2

Source: Computed from Haaland and Norman (1992).

Our simulations use a reference scenario for the year 2005 as their base case. In that scenario, trade policies are as they were in the early 1980s; *i.e.* prior to liberalisation. There is, compared to the 1980s, moderate growth in OECD trade with the rest of the world. At the same time, technical progress, labour force growth, and capital accumulation create considerable growth in real incomes and real wages. Details on the reference scenario are given in the appendix.

We compare this reference scenario with a scenario in which world trade is liberalised. Liberalisation is modelled as *a)* integration of European (EC and EFTA) markets, *b)* a 33 per cent reduction in tariffs, non-tariff barriers and other trade costs between OECD countries, and *c)* a doubling of the reference-scenario increase in OECD trade with the rest of the world. Other parameters (technical progress, labour force growth, and capital accumulation) are as in the reference case.

The effects of liberalisation (compared to the reference scenario) on real income (real GDP) and consumer real wages (wages deflated by the true consumer price index) are given in Table 3.

The simulated effects are large, at least compared to traditional Harberger triangles. Non-traded goods account for 60-70 per cent of total production, so a real-income effect of 1 per cent means an increase in tradeables value added of around 3 per cent.

As should be expected from the Herfindahl concentration indexes, the gains from liberalisation are much smaller for the United States, and to some extent for Japan, than for Europe. The differences are not only due to differences in initial

Table 3. **Competition effects of liberalisation**

Percentage change

	Real income	Unskilled real wage	Skilled real wage
EU	0.66	0.70	0.71
EFTA	1.03	1.10	1.36
United States	0.09	0.00	0.11
Japan	0.82	0.75	1.18

concentration, however. They also reflect the specific stimulus to European competition following from the single European market.

Even though the numbers in Table 3 are relatively large, they are somewhat smaller than those obtained in other studies. In the first attempt at numerical assessment of trade liberalisation in the presence of scale economies and imperfect competition, Harris and Cox (1985), found that Canada could gain as much as 8.6 per cent of GDP as a result of free trade with the United States. Gasiorek, Smith and Venables (1992), estimated that the single market alone would raise EC real incomes by 1.35 per cent. In previous studies using roughly the same model as we use in this paper (see e.g. Haaland, 1993), we have estimated gains from European integration alone which are larger than the gains from European integration plus global liberalisation reported in Table 3.

To some extent these differences have to do with modelling format and assumptions regarding pricing rules with imperfect competition. An important reason for the differences, however, is that we compare with a future scenario, whereas previous studies have compared with an initial equilibrium in the 1980s. General economic growth over the 20-year period creates larger domestic markets in all countries. As a result, some of the increased competition that would otherwise have been the result of freer trade, in our simulations materialises even without trade liberalisation.

LABOUR MARKET EFFECTS

The direct link between trade liberalisation and the labour market would be through migration. We have no basis for assessing the possible extent of future labour migration, and we shall therefore ignore it in this paper. Instead, we focus on indirect links, through the product market effects discussed above. The question we ask is how freer trade will affect the demand for labour, and how it might affect wage setting.

Labour demand

The typical low-brow view is that protection saves jobs, and thus that free trade is a threat to employment. While often brushed aside by economists as a populist misconception, the view can be supported by traditional, Heckscher-Ohlin type trade theory. If it is correct that the OECD countries are relatively capital-abundant, global trade liberalisation should lead to exports of capital-intensive goods from the OECD area, and imports of labour-intensive goods to the OECD countries from the rest of the world. If so, at given real wages, freer trade should eliminate more OECD jobs in labour-intensive sectors than the number of capital-intensive jobs created.

Nevertheless, as regards total labour demand in the OECD area, the populist view is likely to be wrong. There are two reasons for this. First, the major effect of the measures actually taken to liberalise trade will probably be more trade *within* the OECD area, rather than between OECD and the rest of the world. Intra-OECD trade expansion will not primarily reflect Heckscher-Ohlin specialisation. Instead, it is likely to reflect market imperfections and demand for product variety; and it will generate higher real incomes. As such, it is likely to be job-creating everywhere. Second, to the extent that there will be increased Heckscher-Ohlin specialisation between the OECD and other countries, the OECD countries are as likely to expand in skill-intensive and R&D-intensive industries as in capital-intensive ones. Even with factor endowments as the driving force, therefore, it is not at all clear what will happen to aggregate labour demand. All told, therefore, there is no basis for a presumption that freer trade means a negative labour-demand shift for the OECD countries. If anything, the opposite hypothesis seems more likely.

When it comes to the composition of labour demand, one could make a better *a priori* case for unambiguous effects. Increased trade between rich and poor countries should lead to a negative shift in the demand for unskilled labour in rich countries, and to a positive shift in the demand for highly skilled labour.

Even that may be wrong, however, once we include income effects and take into account production of non-tradeables. There are clear and positive income effects from increased trade. Some of the increased income will be spent on non-traded goods and services. If non-tradeables use unskilled labour intensively, the number of extra unskilled jobs created there could well outweigh the number of unskilled jobs lost in tradeables production.

In our simulations, we focus on Europe, since unemployment seems to be a more persistent problem there than elsewhere. To find the labour demand effects, we simulate the effects of global liberalisation (specified as before), but keep real consumer wages in the two European regions, for both skilled and unskilled labour, fixed at their base-case levels. We further assume that the supply of labour is sufficient to meet whatever demand materialises; so actual employment equals

Table 4. **Employment effects of liberalisation**

Percentage change

	Unskilled employment	Skilled employment
EU	4.84	4.78
EFTA	16.05	16.51

labour demand. For the United States and Japan we assume unchanged employment and flexible wages.

The results are shown in Table 4. As is seen, trade liberalisation has a positive effect on the demand for both unskilled and skilled labour, and there is not even any substantial difference in the projected demand effects for the two labour types.

In part this surprising result may have to do with our classification of labour types. Unskilled labour in our model is labour with a secondary education only. That is, however, a relatively wide definition, and probably a wider one than most people have in mind when they think of job opportunities for unskilled workers.

Even allowing for this, the result may seem surprising, considering the extent to which job losses in OECD countries are blamed on overseas competition. The result accords well with detailed factor-content studies of the impact of trade on jobs in the United States, however – for a survey, see Freeman (1995). Typically, these studies find that trade with less-developed countries can account for only 10-20 per cent of the fall in demand for unskilled workers. With a general labour-demand stimulus from increased intra-OECD trade and from the real-income effect of trade counteracting the negative effect of trade with non-OECD countries, it is not really surprising, therefore, that we find that global liberalisation will raise demand for both skilled and unskilled workers.

By this we do not mean to say that there is no reason to be concerned about employment or earnings of unskilled workers – only that the problems of unskilled workers have little to do with freer trade.

The more striking feature in Table 4 is the sensitivity of employment to trade policy. For the EC, liberalisation gives a positive shift in the aggre-gate demand curve for both types of labour of almost 5 per cent. For the EFTA countries the corresponding numbers are 16-17 per cent. These numbers are surprisingly high considering the modest effects of freer trade on the constant-employment real wages reported in Table 3. That suggests that labour demand is highly wage-sensitive as well. That turns out to be the case, as is shown in Table 5, which reports the effects, in the liberalisation case, of an exogenous reduction of 0.5 per cent in real wages in Europe. Such a reduction would, according to the model, give an

Table 5. **Effects of 0.5 per cent lower real wages in Europe**

Percentage change

	Real income	Unskilled employment	Skilled employment
EU	3.35	3.69	3.67
EFTA	5.98	6.24	6.27
United States	0.00		
Japan	0.00		

increase in labour demand of 3.5 per cent in the EU and 6.0-6.5 per cent in the EFTA countries. Increased employment would give correspondingly large real income gains.

It is natural to ask why labour demand in the model is so sensitive to both trade policy and wages. The contrast to most macro models is striking. The main reason is probably entry and exit of firms. Most macro models capture (although crudely) imperfect product-market competition in the form of mark-up pricing and product differentiation, but they are typically estimated in a way which does not capture changes in the population of firms. Our model has zero profits and free entry and exit, and as such a supply side which is more flexible and much more sensitive to wages and other factor prices.

Wage setting and employment

The other possible link to the labour market is through wage setting. To the extent that wages are set by monopoly trade unions, or through collective bargaining, we should expect labour demand to affect wages. The effect depends on the particulars of the wage setting system, which obviously varies from country to country. In general terms, however, it may be useful to think of the wage setting process as some trade-off between wages and unemployment, resulting in a wedge between the demand and supply wage. Under such a system, both the level and the wage elasticity of labour demand matters for the equilibrium wage and the resulting level of employment.

As trade liberalisation will make labour demand more wage elastic, it should reduce the wedge between the demand and supply wage. At the same time, as we have seen, freer trade gives a positive labour demand shift. The two effects should unambiguously raise employment, while the net effect on the real wage is unclear.

We do not have data permitting a careful analysis of possible wage and employment effects. As an illustration, however, assume that the labour supply

Table 6. **Illustrative employment and wage effects**

	EU	EFTA
Employment	0.96%	1.16%
Real wage	0.56%	1.06%

elasticity in Europe is 0.2, and that there is an initial wage wedge of 10 per cent, which is reduced to 9 per cent as a result of freer trade. The effects of freer trade, using the labour demand effects discussed above, will then (as shown in Table 6) be an increase in European employment of around 1 per cent, and an increase of real wages of around 0.5 per cent in the EC, and around 1 per cent in the EFTA countries.

INVESTMENT, PRODUCTIVITY AND GEOGRAPHY EFFECTS

The last link we look at is between trade policy and long-term growth.

The most obvious link in that respect is capital accumulation. To the extent that trade policy affects real incomes and the rate of return on investment, it should affect saving and investment. Since our model has endogenous saving, this link is captured in the model, but in the simulations reported above, we have kept the capital stock constant at the base case level.

Table 7 gives the additional effects, compared to the constant-employment liberalisation case, of endogenous capital accumulation – i.e. the steady-state rise in income and wage levels caused by the additional saving with freer trade. As is seen, the effects are very small, and in the case of Japan, negative. The result for Japan reflects a negative Stolper-Samuelson type effect on the rate of return on capital, which reduces saving incentives.

These results strongly suggest that the link between trade and growth – if it exists – relates to other mechanisms than domestic saving and investment as such.

It is natural to start by asking whether, in fact, there is such a link. There are numerous examples – the Scandinavian countries in the latter half of the 19th century, Argentina and Czechoslovakia in the interwar period, Korea and Taiwan during the past 20 years – of a positive correlation between openness and rapid growth. There are, however, as many examples to the contrary: the United States and Germany from 1870 onwards had rapid industrial growth with protected domestic markets, many claim the same to be true of Japan after World War II, and a number of Latin American countries have failed to take off even though they have practised free trade.

Table 7. **Capital accumulation effects of liberalisation**

Percentage change

	Real income	Unskilled real wage	Skilled real wage
EU	0.06	0.05	0.05
EFTA	0.07	0.09	0.06
United States	0.06	0.05	0.06
Japan	–0.14	–0.20	–0.15

In a careful survey of the experience of Korea and Taiwan, Rodrik (1995) may provide the most reasonable resolution of the conflicting correlations. He argues that export orientation by itself does not explain the success of the two countries. Rather, the key to success was active domestic policies – including investment tax incentives – to overcome the investment co-ordination failure typical of countries in the early stages of economic development. At the same time, however, large-scale imports of capital goods embodying state-of-the-art technology was necessary, as was access to export markets which enabled firms to operate on an efficient technical scale.

The attraction of the Rodrik story is that it explains why large countries with domestic access to new technology, such as the United States and Germany, could succeed with protection, while smaller ones, such as the Scandinavian countries, could not. At the same time, it clarifies the links between trade policy and domestic economic policies in a way which may help to explain the Latin American failures.

The story also fits in well both with the "new" growth theory and with the Krugman-Venables theories on trade policy and economic geography (see, e.g., Krugman and Venables, 1995, and Venables, 1996). According to these, externalities or other linkages within or between industries could generate agglomeration effects and endogenous productivity growth as trade barriers are reduced. The literature on trade and geography has identified a number of such agglomeration forces: direct knowledge spillovers between firms, labour-market pooling, labour mobility, intermediate goods to mention some.

To capture such effects fully, one needs much more careful modelling of individual industries than is possible in our modelling format. We have not, therefore, attempted to quantify possible effects. The theory suggests, however, that the effects could be large. Moreover, agglomeration effects could give much less evenly distributed gains – in fact, countries or regions with initially weak industrial clusters could experience de-industrialisation and lower real incomes as a result of freer trade.

CONCLUSIONS

In this paper we have argued that trade liberalisation could have a major impact on domestic economic performance, and through other channels than traditional exploitation of comparative advantages. It is likely that freer trade, through increased domestic competition, could make domestic product markets substantially more efficient. Trade liberalisation could also reduce European unemployment. Despite expectations to the contrary, freer world trade is likely to raise labour demand. It will also make labour demand more wage-elastic, and thereby reduce the wedge between the demand and supply wage to the extent that there is an element of monopoly wage setting. For both reasons, employment is likely to increase. Surprisingly, we find that freer trade could raise employment for unskilled as well as for skilled workers. Finally, trade liberalisation could generate more rapid (intermediate-term) economic growth; but the growth could be unevenly distributed; and we should be prepared for greater geographical concentration of industrial activity.

Our discussion suggests that assessments of trade liberalisation, which so far have tended to concentrate on product-market effects, should focus more on labour-market and economic-geography effects. There is a need for careful estimates of the effects of freer trade on the demands for skilled and unskilled labour, taking into account not only the direct effects of increased trade, but including the indirect effects on labour demand in the non-tradeables sectors of OECD economies. There should also be more empirical work on how international competition affects wage formation. At the same time, the possible effects of trade on the location and geographic concentration of production should be quantified; both because these effects are important by themselves, and because they could have substantial impact on local and national labour markets.

Appendix

MODEL AND REFERENCE CASE

The model we use is a variant of one documented elsewhere (Haaland and Norman, 1992, Haaland, 1993, Baldwin, Forslid and Haaland, 1995), so only a brief sketch will be given.

The model distinguishes four world regions – the EU prior to admission of EFTA countries, the old EFTA, the United States, and Japan. In addition, there are exogenous trade flows with the rest of the world. Initially, EFTA and the EC regions each consist of separate (but, for simplicity, identical) countries and submarkets. The United States and Japan are modelled as fully integrated economies.

Each country produces twelve traded manufactured goods, two traded services, and one non-tradeable from three primary factors, capital and two types of labour (skilled and unskilled). The non-traded good and one of the traded goods are sold in perfectly competitive markets; the remaining products come from imperfectly competitive industries with economies of scale in production. Each of these industries are modelled as Cournot equilibria with firms producing differentiated products. Thus, the model captures the interaction between competition, scale economies and product differentiation.

Final demand in each country is derived from a two-level utility function. At the top level (assumed to be Cobb-Douglas), income is allocated to each of the 15 product groups; at the bottom level (CES), we find demand for the differentiated products from each industry.

Capital and labour markets are perfectly competitive, and factors are not traded between regions. The variant of the model that we use has endogenous capital accumulation, in the sense that the model solves for the optimum steady-state capital stock.

Labour supply is exogenous, and the model solves for the equilibrium (Walrasian) wage rate. It is possible, however, to solve the model for rigid wages and endogenous employment as well; thus permitting us to study some aspects of the interaction between trade and employment.

The model is calibrated to 1985 data (including actual 1985 employment).

As our base case, we have solved the model for an equilibrium in 2005, based on the following assumptions:

- Labour force growth according to ILO projections, which implies moderate growth in the United States, no growth in Japan, and a reduction in the European labour force of 0.2 per cent per year.
- Unchanged educational composition of the labour force.
- Reduction in European unemployment equivalent to the reduction in the European labour force; *i.e.* constant total employment.
- 1.5 per cent annual, exogenous, Hicks-neutral technical progress in all industries.
- Unchanged trade policies (from 1985; *i.e.* prior to liberalisation).
- Modest growth in trade with the rest of the world (OECD imports of labour-intensive manufactures [NACE 19, 28, 42, 49] equivalent to 10 per cent of 1985 consumption; equivalent OECD exports of skill-intensive products [NACE 21, 23, 25]).

The base case gives roughly 2 per cent annual real income growth in all regions. Real incomes and real wages in 2005, relative to the 1985-levels, are:

Base case projections (1985 = 1)

	Real income	Unskilled real wage	Skilled real wage
EU	1.81	1.86	1.84
EFTA	1.84	1.89	1.88
United States	2.10	1.88	1.86
Japan	1.85	1.91	1.89

BIBLIOGRAPHY

Baldwin, R.E., R. Forslid and J.I. Haaland (1995), "Investment creation and investment diversion: simulation analysis of the single market programme", *NBER Working Paper* No. 5364.

Emerson. M. *et al.* (1988), *The Economics of 1992*, Oxford University Press.

Freeman, R.B. (1995), "Are your wages set in Beijing?", *Journal of Economic Perspectives*, Vol. 9, No. 3, pp. 15-32.

Gasiorek, M., A. Smith and A. Venables (1992), "1992: trade and welfare – a general equilibrium model", in L.A. Winters (ed.), *Trade Flows and Trade Policy after 1992*, Cambridge University Press.

Haaland, J.I. and V. Norman (1992), "Global production effects of European integration", in L.A. Winters (ed.), *op. cit.*

Haaland, J.I. (1993), "Welfare effects of 1992: A general equilibrium assessment for EC and EFTA countries", *Empirica*, Vol. 20, pp. 107-127.

Krugman, P.R. and A.J. Venables, 1995, "Globalization and the inequality of nations", *Quarterly Journal of Economics*, Vol. 110, No. 4, pp. 857-880.

Rodrik, D., 1995, "Getting interventions right: how South Korea and Taiwan grew rich", *Economic Policy*, No. 20, pp. 54-107.

Venables, A.J., 1996, "Equilibrium locations of vertically linked industries", *International Economic Review*, forthcoming.

COMMENTS

by

N. Vanston

Economists firmly believe that stronger competition results in higher output and incomes, and that foreign trade is an especially effective means of achieving this. But standard computations of the static real income gains that one could expect in the real world if an economy or a sector moves to the perfect competition ideal with free trade are usually disappointingly meagre, at least for the relatively undistorted economies of OECD countries. Faced with this, economists tend to invoke less well-understood but possibly more powerful mechanisms involving imperfect competition, technology diffusion and increasing returns to scale. The Haaland and Norman paper follows this approach.

To illustrate their point, the authors go through some simple but useful calculations of the impact of trade liberalisation in a stylised world of imperfect competition, showing that the welfare gains are likely to be far higher than if there was perfect competition, on reasonable assumptions concerning elasticities and concentration. The authors hold that Europe (the EU and EFTA) is characterised by weak competition, relative to the US and Japan, as measured by Herfindahl concentration indices. The indices show EFTA with an average index 5 times higher than that of the EU, which is in turn about the same as Japan, but 10 times higher than the United States. Probably the indices for EU and EFTA are calculated as weighted averages for the individual countries. If so, they exaggerate the degree of concentration in Europe, as European manufacturing firms essentially compete in the entire European market (tariff and most non-tariff barriers for manufactured goods were very small within and between both the EU and EFTA by 1980). But it seems reasonable to assume that competition in the European market is less strong than in the United States, and possibly than in Japan in some sectors.

The heart of the paper is a report of simulations, using a CGE model, of trade liberalisation. Notable features of their model include perfect competition in labour and capital markets and free entry and exit of firms. This is a very flexible world with quantities responding rapidly and sensitively to even small changes in relative prices (it differs from current European reality, though, and this probably explains some of the odd results). In the baseline case, there is no trade liberalisation after 1980. Real incomes approximately double everywhere by 2005, and wages for both skilled and unskilled labour increase by roughly the same proportion. In a simulation in which there is full integration of EFTA and EU markets, a 33 per cent reduction in other tariff barriers, and a doubling in the increase of OECD/non-OECD trade, real incomes in Europe and Japan are higher than baseline 2005 levels by about 1 per cent for Europe and Japan, with little change for the United States. Skilled wages rise somewhat more than unskilled.

It is hard to know how to assess the results. The baseline scenario results themselves are a bit puzzling, in that the United States grows at about a 3.8 per cent rate over 20 years, which is significantly faster than most estimates of potential. It is also a little surprising that the baseline growth rates of Europe and Japan are similar, at around 3 per cent. The simulated results from trade liberalisation do not change the baseline results much. An additional one percent of GDP is significant, but hardly exciting. At first sight, it seems that the impact on real incomes of what is described in the first paragraph as "the most comprehensive liberalisation of world trade since the 1840s" is small beer indeed, even when the amplifying effects of imperfect competition and economies of scale are taken into account. Is it too low?

One possible source of underestimation is that potentially faster diffusion of better technology via trade channels is not taken into account. Some recent in-house work in the Secretariat indeed suggests both that productivity differences between similar industries in different countries are surprisingly large, and that they tend to be narrowed via more intense trade. Even quite small rises in underlying rates of technological progress result in substantial boosts to income after 25 years. It could also be argued, following the logic of the paper, that some part of the "baseline" growth of GDP after 1980 is itself due to trade liberalisation in an earlier period. Hence the true impact on 2005 income levels from trade liberalisation is likely to be greater than the figure put forward, but by an unknown margin.

The paper also goes into some detail on labour market impacts, and here some of the results seem to depend critically on the assumption of perfect competition in labour markets. If wages are kept at baseline levels, so that the (actually quite small) increase in income and output is encountering an elastic labour supply, employment levels rise by nearly 5 per cent above baseline for the EU and by over 16 per cent for EFTA! Similarly, if real wages are somehow lowered by 0.5 per cent below baseline, employment is raised by nearly 4 per cent in the EU and by over 6 per cent in EFTA. If employment levels really were so sensitive to real wages, taking into account secondary effects via output, then one suspects that the evolution of employment in Europe would have been more volatile than in practice it has been, and that the behaviour of governments and trade unions would have been different. As the authors note, their atypical findings probably reflect also their assumption of free entry and exit of firms, and hence a very elastic supply side. But if one were to assume, for example, that each time a firm exits, a portion of its labour force either quits the labour force or remains unemployed for a significant time, then the results would probably look very different.

A further unexpected finding, but one that is more plausible, and certainly interesting, is that more intense trade does not lead to a worsening in the relative position of unskilled workers. Partly this is because much of the increased trade is between OECD countries rather than with developing countries. The mechanism is exploitation of economies of scale rather than Heckscher-Ohlin, and there is no *a priori* reason why the demand for unskilled workers should evolve differently from that for skilled workers. Furthermore, rising real incomes lead to higher demand for non-trade services, which are unskilled labour intensive. Again, though, this result probably depends very heavily on the assumption of flexible labour markets: it is contrary to experience in the past 10-20 years, when the same mechanisms were at work as in the simulation.

In summary, although the use of a CGE model is a potentially powerful means of analysing macro-structural issues, and one of the very few with a sound theoretical backing, results from them continue to be very sensitive to assumptions (in this case, the competitiveness of the labour market, and free entry and exit of firms), and there is not enough comparative information yet on their properties for them to be reliable guides for policy-makers. Still, they represent a promising way forward, and one that has not yet been fully explored.

GENERAL DISCUSSION

As the paper and the numerical results of the simulation exercise actually presented to the meeting were of a very preliminary nature and subsequently extended in several areas, the general discussion could not cover the full range of issues addressed in the revised version of the paper.

The discussion focused on the following issues:

– the output and income effects of further trade liberalisation;

– the labour market effects;

– the role of foreign direct investment and its treatment in the model.

Several participants queried the realism of the numerical results. The main disagreement related to the estimated output and employment effects of trade liberalisation and market integration relative to the 1980-2005 baseline scenario. It was argued in this context that the benefits in terms of productivity and real income gains which flow from increased foreign competition may well be bigger than those from greater domestic competition, and that OECD countries collectively would be less self-sufficient than suggested by the model.

As to employment, it was felt that the simulated positive effects were much too big to be taken seriously. It was argued that the supply of labour was clearly not as elastic with respect to real wages as assumed and that competition in the labour market, notably in Europe, is certainly far from being perfect. There was also a question about the impact of further liberalisation on the demand for different categories of labour, notably, unskilled labour. A generally shared view probably was that trade along with the impact of new technology would shift the structure of demand away from low skill types of labour.

On foreign direct investment, it was pointed out that over the past decade it has tended to expand much faster than trade and that at present roughly 50 per cent of world trade is accounted for by inter-firm relationships, or operators of multinationals. Access to foreign markets is no longer exclusively through exports and imports but increasingly so via foreign direct investment. The question was therefore raised whether the model results need to be adjusted in order to take account of these developments.

In response to these various queries and questions it was pointed out that the positive impact of trade liberalisation on growth is not fully captured to the extent that the baseline figures include lagged trade effects from earlier liberalisation. As to the strikingly high elasticity of labour demand with respect to wages it was pointed out that, among other things, this is brought about by the assumed free entry and exit of firms, implying long-term horizontal industry supply curves, which generate large quantity effect in response to lower costs.

Finally, in response to the question on foreign direct investment and how it interacts with trade, it was noted that foreign direct investment is a way of reducing trade costs and it is through this effect, equivalent to that of a cut in official trade barriers, that it can be taken into consideration in the model. In the model the rate of return to capital is equalised across regions as trade is liberalised. For this reason it is not gains from capital flows which are of interest but the induced trade flows and the associated larger gains from integration.

INTERACTION AMONG MACROECONOMIC POLICIES AND STRUCTURAL REFORM

STRUCTURAL REFORMS AND THEIR IMPLICATIONS FOR MACROECONOMIC POLICIES

by
Hans Gersbach and George Sheldon[1]
Alfred-Weber Institut, University of Heidelberg

SUMMARY

This paper synthesises a series of comparative industry studies undertaken by the McKinsey Global Institute and analyses the evolution of unemployment hazard functions across business cycles and changes in unemployment insurance (UI) regulation. We take a European perspective and discuss policies with respect to two objectives: curing unemployment in Europe in the mid-term and facilitating productivity gains in product markets. In particular, we discuss the impact of product market reforms on productivity, the interaction of labour and product market reform in reducing unemployment, and the limited scope for macroeconomic policies to reduce unemployment.

Product market reforms to increase productivity

Further product market reforms and increased globalisation through trade and foreign direct investments promise significant labour productivity gains in manufacturing and service industries, where labour productivity is lagging, via the diffusion of existing knowledge across all countries.

Productivity gains result from the adoption of new ways to produce goods and to deliver services and from the improved organisation of tasks, and less from increased capital intensity or scale. The United States manufacturing sector experienced a substantial reform and recovery in productivity relative to France and Germany in the eighties and early nineties.

Interaction between labour and product market reform to combat unemployment

Product market and labour market reforms appear to be complementary in reducing structural unemployment since both transition rigidities and a lack of labour demand inhibit the reallocation of labour. Product market reforms together with incremental labour market reform can also ease political constraints.

Interaction between structural reforms and macroeconomic policies to combat unemployment

The extension of UI entitlements has a pronounced effect on steady-state unemployment. Extending the length of UI entitlement periods is shown to counteract the unemployment-decreasing effects of cyclical upswings. Hence, shortening UI benefit entitlements would improve the effectiveness of macroeconomic policies. Moreover, it would reduce the share of long-term unemployed.

Although supportive macroeconomic policies can in principle enhance the benefits of structural reforms and could increase their political acceptance, there is little room and potential to use such strategies systematically.

INTRODUCTION

Many countries have embarked, at least partially, on so-called structural reforms in a variety of markets (see OECD, 1994a). In general, structural reforms should bring economies closer to Walrasian-style market economies in which prices and wages are fully flexible, product prices equal marginal costs, etc. Since advocating structural reforms is not supported by theoretically well-founded second best arguments, empirical evidence is needed to assess their implications.

In this paper we derive implications for structural market reforms and their interaction with macroeconomic policy from a series of industry studies and from new evidence based on the cyclical behaviour of the hazard rates of the unemployed. Comparative industry studies are complementary to more standard approaches and regression examinations since they can point to issues which are otherwise not visible. On the other hand, synthesising conclusions from micro studies has to be framed with caution since it is difficult to account for general equilibrium effects. The tentative conclusions, however, can serve as a guideline for policy.

The paper is organised as follows: In the next section we discuss some conceptual issues relating to structural reforms and their implications for macroeconomic policy. Then, we use recent comparative industry studies to assess the productivity-raising effect of market reforms. In the fourth part we provide evidence and underlying arguments for the interaction of product and labour market reform to reduce unemployment. In the final section, we discuss the interaction of these reforms with macroeconomic policy to combat unemployment.

STRUCTURAL REFORMS AND MACROECONOMIC POLICIES

Structural Reforms

Structural reforms in a market are an attempt to eliminate a number of market rigidities (e.g. OECD, 1994a). In this paper we deal with product and labour market reforms. Hence it is helpful to get a more specific understanding of the changes envisioned by structural reforms.

We have to distinguish between rigidities arising from regulatory actions or monopoly power (e.g. minimum wages, insider/outsider phenomena, high and stable mark-ups) and those arising from transaction costs (e.g. menu costs) or information barriers (e.g. efficiency wages). Although this distinction is not always clear cut, e.g., the latter may cause the former, structural reforms can only reduce the first group of rigidities and hence can only be effective if rigidities of this type are responsible for the inefficiencies structural reform should cure. Therefore, we distinguish between structural rigidities, which can be eliminated by reforms, and transaction and informational rigidities which cannot be directly eliminated by policies.

Product market reform can aim to change various structural aspects, such as the decrease of mark-ups, the increase of the flexibility of mark-ups in response to demand shocks, the reduction of X-inefficiency, and the triggering of process and product innovations. Such changes have to be evaluated against the potential benefits of current regulations in curing market failures such as externalities or incomplete information. A particular concern is that some regulations, while rationalised by political economic considerations, may not be easily justified on a cost-benefit basis. In particular, the costs of regulation in terms of productivity losses and narrower product variety could be quite large. In this case, structural reform in product markets can be viewed as a vehicle to reduce these costs.

For structural rigidities in the labour market, a further distinction has to be made between structural rigidities related to a one-sector, one-firm view, such as nominal or real wage rigidity and structural rigidities related entirely to the fact that different types of labour and different types of firms and industries exist. The latter can be termed transition rigidities and refer in many cases to relative wage rigidities.[2] A typical example of transition rigidities is the disincentive faced by low-skilled people in relatively high-paying industries to accept lower-paying jobs in other industries if they become unemployed since income support measures, e.g. unemployment benefits, are tied as a rule to the wage last received.

Interaction of macroeconomic policies and structural reforms

Structural reforms and macroeconomic policies can interact in several ways. First, structural reforms can alter the effectiveness of macroeconomic policies if the effectiveness depends on structural rigidities that reforms are intended to eliminate.[3] Second, reforms can change the mix of monetary and fiscal policy by affecting money demand and the size and composition of public sector finance (e.g. subsidies, unemployment benefits etc.). Third, macroeconomic policies could affect the level of structural unemployment and, by extension, the effectiveness of structural reforms if policies had an effect on cyclical unemployment and if unemployment exhibited hysteresis or persistence. Fourth, from a political-economic perspective, macroeconomic policies could be used to enhance the chances of structural reforms being implemented.

Objectives of policies and framework

Policy can only be designed appropriately if clear objectives are stated. We view two objectives as indispensable for structural reforms and macroeconomic policies. Curing the unemployment problem in Europe in the mid-term and facilitating productivity gains in product markets. We do not view these aims as being conflicting per se. Clearly, this is a European perspective and even in Europe these are not the only issues, in particular, since the development of the European Union poses additional challenges and constraints for macroeconomic policies. In this paper, we assess structural reforms and macroeconomic policy with respect to these two objectives and do not consider other objectives and related polices, such as the convergence towards a monetary union in Europe or maintaining a socially accepted income distribution and social cohesion.

We use empirical studies to examine the effectiveness of policies. Naturally, this also calls for a coherent theoretical framework. A natural candidate would be the standard labour-market model consisting of a wage-setting schedule, an individual labour supply schedule, and a price-setting (labour demand) schedule. Although this framework can be used directionally, it has the drawback that transition rigidities in the labour market and structural differences in product markets cannot be easily integrated. Therefore we take the standard labour market model as a starting base, complementing it with a multi-sector general equilibrium view that contains structural rigidities in specific parts of the labour and product market.

PRODUCT MARKETS

Productivity differences in services and manufacturing

In the first part we show the potential of market reforms in fostering productivity gains in specific industries. In order to assess the potential gains, we first review differences in industry productivity level in the manufacturing and services across countries. We do not, however, survey the large list of individual regulatory items in each market. These can be found in detail elsewhere (e.g. Baily, 1993, OECD, 1994a, OECD, 1995).

Productivity comparisons in manufacturing were estimated using a industry purchasing power parities (see Baily and Gersbach, 1995, van Ark and Pilat, 1993). Productivity in the service industries was measured using a variety of approaches, in particular physical productivity measures and the use of expenditure purchasing power parities (see Baily 1993).

In manufacturing, productivity comparisons for a sample of nine industries are available. The industries account for between 15 and 20 per cent of employment and between 17 and 22 per cent of value added in the manufacturing sector in three countries studied: the United States, Germany, and Japan. Table 1 provides a summary comparison of productivity in all nine industries, with value added per hour worked set at 100 for the United States. It is interesting to note the strikingly wide variation in relative productivity across these three countries, even in such heavily traded sectors as automobiles.[4]

An additional look at the overall development of productivity in manufacturing gives us a much broader view. We turn to Table 2, which presents relative productivity levels for selected years from 1970 -93. The table points to the strong recovery of United States manufacturing from the slowdown in productivity during the 1970s. For manufacturing as a whole, the United States has maintained its position as a leader in terms of labour productivity. The performance of European countries has been diverse. Germany lost some of its edge in several manufacturing industries in

Table 1. **Labour productivity of case studies in 1990**

Value added at industry PPP per hour worked (US = 100)

Industries	Relative productivity		
	Germany	Japan	United States
Auto cars	66	116	100
Auto parts	76	124	100
Metalworking	101	119	100
Steel	100	145	100
Computer	89	95	100
Consumer electrical	62	115	100
Detergents	88	94	100
Beer	44	69	100
Food	76	33	100

Source: Baily and Gersbach (1995) taken from McKinsey (1994).

Table 2. **Labour productivity of manufacturing, selected years 1970-93**

Value added at industry PPP per hour worked (US = 100)

Country pair	1970	1975	1980	1985	1990	1993
France-United States	73	79	90	90	91	88
Germany-United States	76	84	92	88	83	80
Japan-United States	43	52	64	68	76	74
United Kingdom-United States	51	53	52	58	66	70

Source: Van Ark (1995), Gersbach and Van Ark (1994). Updated from 1990 using information from the US Bureau of Labor Statistics.

which they were leaders by 1980 (*e.g.*, machinery). France and especially the United Kingdom benefited from a faster rise in productivity, although France did not catch up fully with the United States.

In services, aggregate productivity comparisons are more difficult than in manufacturing since output is difficult to measure in the service sector and sectoral PPPs are not available. There are some important attempts to measure service sector productivity from the expenditure side of national accounts (*e.g.* Jorgensen and Kuroda, 1992, Dollar and Wolff, 1993). However, these cannot be used for detailed inter-industry productivity comparisons, due to the underlying methodology of the expenditure approach as well as to the inherent problems in measuring service sector outputs.[5]

Recent comparative studies examine a sample of five service industries: airlines, retail banking, general merchandise retailing, restaurants, and telecommunications, which comprise roughly 21 per cent of the market service sector. The following methods were chosen to measure labour productivity. In three case studies (airline, retail banking, telecommunication) a weighted average of physical productivities on the functional level was used. In this approach it is assumed that an industry consists of separate functional activities each of which produces a relatively homogeneous output. However, since no meaningful revenue shares are available for the separate activities, the preferable Divisia output index cannot be constructed and one has to use the employment shares as weights. In retailing and restaurants corresponding expenditure PPPs were used. Since these industries provide a broad range of goods, a broad PPP is needed.

Although measurement and interpretation issues (see *e.g.* Gordon, 1993) remain in such detailed approaches, the results appear to be directionally robust. Table 3 summarises the labour productivity results for the five service sector case studies.[6] The cases show that the United States exhibits higher productivity in most sectors; the only exception being the restaurant industry.

Table 3. **Labour productivity of case studies in services**

(United States = 100)

Industries	Relative productivity				
	Germany	France	United Kingdom	Japan	United States
Airlines	72[1]	72[1]	72[1]		100
Telecommunications[2]	50	55	51	74	100
Retail banking	68		64		100
General merchandise retailing	96	91	82	44	100
Restaurants	92	104			100

1.   Average productivity of the European airline industry.
2.   Total factor productivity.
Source: Baily (1993).

With respect to the United States, the direction of the differences implied by the industry results in service and manufacturing broadly supports the findings obtained at the market GDP level in each country. However, the magnitude of the differences implied by the industry results would suggest somewhat larger productivity differences for Germany and France at the aggregate level. Part of this can be explained by industrial and sectorial composition effects, which in the case of Germany work in favour of aggregate productivity.[7]

Causes of cross-country differences in productivity

In the next step we examine the nature of the productivity differences in order to assess the actual changes companies and industries have to make. This, in turn, can help in assessing how far productivity could be raised by structural reforms.

We summarise the proximate causes for productivity differences. By proximate causes we mean differences in the mode of operation which appear to explain differences in output per hour worked across countries. In Baily and Gersbach (1995), a microeconomic framework is described for measuring the causes of productivity differences. How much output a worker produces, on average, in an hour's work depends on the following factors: 1) the type of output (product mix, variety and quality); 2) technology, plant, and equipment in use; 3) the scale of operations (plant, company etc.); 4) the ease of the production of goods and services (*i.e.*, "design for production"); 5) the parts, raw materials and energy; 6) the worker's motivation and skill; and 7) the detailed organisation of the many tasks (*i.e.*, "organisation of functions and tasks").

The framework departs from standard growth accounting techniques introduced by Solow (1957) and extends them in two respects. First, more and softer factors are taken into account, especially, how goods and services are designed for production and the organisation of functions and tasks. Obviously, both soft factors can involve the use of current information and communication technologies. Second, in evaluating the relative importance of all factors, the factors were ordered by their inclusiveness and considered in sequence. Hence, the framework may attribute productivity differences more to the first factors, output mix, physical capital, etc. However, this potential bias is well-suited for testing whether design for production and organisation of functions and tasks are independent causes of productivity differences.

The conclusion from this exercise is that the major share of productivity differences can be attributed to the way functions and tasks are organised and to the fact that some companies have designed their products and services so that they require less labour and material to manufacture or to deliver. A detailed account for the fourteen industries is shown in Table 4.[8] Differences in the mix of products and investments in new capital can also be a source of productivity growth. Moreover, in three out of four cases in manufacturing, differences in the capital used for production also implied scale differences, whereas economies of scale as an independent factor were not important. In two out of four cases in manufacturing in which differences in capital intensity and capital composition played a substantial role, "soft factors" such as the design of products for manufacturing and the organisation

Table 4. **Causes of labour productivity differences at the production process**

Industries	Causes of labour productivity differences	
	Design for production Organisation of functions and tasks	Remaining factors: Product mix, capital intensity and scale, skill of labour
Auto cars	•	
Auto parts	•	
Metalworking	•	•
Steel	•	•
Computer	•	•
Electrical consumer goods	•	
Detergents		•
Beer		•
Food		•
Airlines	•	
Telecommunications	•	
Retail banking	•	•
General merchandise retailing	•	

Notes: • indicates that no other factor did significantly contribute more to explain the productivity differences.
Source: Baily and Gersbach (1995); taken from McKinsey (1993 and 1994).

of functions and tasks were necessary simultaneous innovations to achieve the benefits of installing new machinery and equipment.

In short, we can interpret Table 4 as indicative of the persistence of an ongoing technology shock in the form of improved design for production and organisation of functions and tasks, partially depending on the use of information technologies. Traditionally, the key distinction between technological systems is geared to craft or mass production. In mass production, special purpose machinery is substituted for labour to produce identical components which are then brought together in a standardised assembly line. Craft production methods make use of skilled labour to produce output which, in general, is much more customised. In recent years a third paradigm emerged which includes the described causes of the observed productivity differences.[9]

Productivity growth in "reformed" industries

The most difficult task is to determine to what extent such productivity differences are caused by specific regulations in product markets and by how much productivity could be raised by structural reforms. We cannot directly infer from our findings, that the observed productivity differences can be eliminated by product market reforms, even in industries in which regulations play a major role in the functioning of these industries. The causes of the productivity differences indicate, however, that large improvements can be achieved by improving design for production and organisation of functions and tasks. This depends on the nature of competition in a particular industry, which, in turn, is affected by structural reforms.

Moreover, one needs to look at specific cases. There are a growing number of examples which show that deregulation led to productivity growth and an increase in product variety. Examples can be found in the manufacturing and service sector, as e.g. in the telecommunications industry (Baily, 1993), the automotive industry (Baily and Gersbach, 1995), and in the airline industry (Marin, 1995).

INTERACTION BETWEEN PRODUCT AND LABOUR MARKET REFORM

The clearly most challenging problem for Europe is the elimination of high unemployment. The economic and personal consequences of long-term unemployment are so serious that economically desirable and political feasible reforms are urgent. However, no single factor emerges which can fully explain why so many Europeans fail to find jobs. A lot of proposals for combatting European unemployment, including the OECD Jobs Study, call for extensive deregulation to move towards US-style flexible labour markets. Others are more cautious and only advocate the removal of some specific rigidities in an incremental way. Incremental reforms are considered to be crucial in the area of size and duration of unemployment benefits and active labour market policies, as well as with regard to the reduction of real wages for low-skilled people, either through reducing minimum wages or the tax wedge (e.g. Jackman, Layard and Nickell, 1996).

The independent effect of labour market rigidities for structural unemployment has been suggested in many studies and will be demonstrated in the next chapter by new data, which also incorporates regulatory changes. In this section we argue that there are economic and, potentially, also political interaction between incremental reforms in labour markets and the deregulation in product markets to lessen the unemployment problem.

International trends in employment

We first give an overall comparative picture of the compositional changes in employment across countries. We denote by $E(t_1, t_2)$ the change in employment on the aggregate or industry level between two different points in time $t_1 < t_2$. The employment changes are adjusted for working-age population growth in order to factor out the effect of these differences and to emphasise the ability to create employment relative to the potential supply of labour.[10] Hence:

$$E(t_1, t_2) = \frac{E(t_2)}{WA(t_2)} - \frac{E(t_1)}{WA(t_1)}$$

with $E(t_1)$, $E(t_2)$ representing the stock of employed people at t_1 and t_2, and $WA(t_1)$ and $WA(t_2)$ denoting the number of people between the ages of 15 and 64 at t_1 and t_2, respectively. A positive value for $E(t_1, t_2)$ thus means that net job growth exceeded the increase in the working-age population.

Aggregate trends

We begin with the well-known picture that countries that came closest to creating enough jobs to prevent a secular rise in unemployment, had larger than average labour force growth. The slow employment creation in Europe was in turn not caused mainly by the increase in labour supply as a share of the working-age population since participation rates and overall population grew slowly. In fact, shifting to an hours-worked measure would widen rather than reduce the employment difference between European countries and the United States and Japan.

We next distinguish between the market and non-market part of an economy, the latter including government, private and public education, and private and public health. This dichotomy reveals the strikingly different employment patterns in the five countries considered (Table 5). There are smaller differences in job growth in the non-market part of the economy than in the market part. Only, the United States and Japan exhibit job growth in the market economy.

Table 5. **Employment performance 1980-93**

Net jobs created per thousand working age population[1]

	Total	Non-market services[2]	Market economy
France	−44.5	22.9	−67.4
Germany	−16.6	19.6	−36.0
Italy	−41.3	8.3	−49.6
Japan	19.3	10.5	8.8
United States	47.5	17.1	30.4

1. Adjusted for growth in the working age population.
2. Including government, private and public education, and private and public health care.
Source: OECD Labour Force Statistics and OECD National Accounts; McKinsey Global Institute (1994).

An examination by sector (Table 6) sheds light on the causes of this pattern. As it is well-known, the United States has created significantly more market service jobs than any of the European economies. Japan retained its share of manufacturing jobs, while all other countries failed to increase these at anywhere near the rate of growth of the working-age population. The overall employment declines in France and Italy can be attributed to particularly rapid declines in manufacturing and construction and mining, and, in the case of Italy, in agriculture. Table 5 and Table 6 also reveal that differences in market services account for most of the differences in service sector employment. Differences in the development of non-market services are less pronounced. Table 7 exhibits the sectoral distribution of employment, revealing the strong manufacturing base in Japan and in Germany.

The overall picture is in line with the deindustrialization hypothesis, *i.e.*, the pattern of employment exhibits a relative decline in manufacturing. However, the

Table 6. **Employment performance – market economy 1980-93**

Net jobs created per thousand working age population[1]

	Market economy	Agriculture	Manufacturing	Construction[2]	Market services
France	−67.4	−24.7	−47.5	−14.3	19.1
Germany	−36.0	−15.3	−31.0	−17.4	27.6
Italy	−49.6	−40.4	−41.2	2.1	29.8
Japan	8.8	−30.0	4.2	−2.8	37.4
United States	30.4	−4.1	−27.0	−4.2	65.8

1. Adjusted for growth in the working age population.
2. Including mining and utilities.
Source: OECD Labour Force Statistics and OECD National Accounts; McKinsey Global Institute (1994).

Table 7. **Employment level, 1993**

Employment per thousand working age population

	Agriculture	Construction[1]	Manufacturing	Market services	Non-market services	Total
France	29.3	49.0	112.6	217.0	169.3	577.2
Germany	19.0	50.2	184.7	239.1	140.1	633.1
Italy	37.7	63.1	105.3	206.0	93.9	506.0
Japan	43.3	72.1	177.9	347.5	88.4	729.2
United States	19.3	51.4	118.5	355.4	161.7	706.3

1.   Including mining and utilities.
Source: OECD Labour Force Statistics; National Household Surveys, McKinsey Global Institute (1994).

sectoral picture is still highly incomplete. First, employment in almost half of the manufacturing industries grew as a percentage of total employment, even between 1980 and 1990. However, their growth was not sufficient to offset the decline experienced by more mature manufacturing sectors. In the service sector roughly 90 per cent of all industries are growing or stagnant in employment. Second, differences in the way companies and plants are operating are obviously not taken into account, as for instance, the increasing share of service-like tasks in manufacturing and the increasing outsourcing phenomena.

Labour reallocation has not only a sectoral dimension. Two other phenomena are important and related to the shifts in the industry mix: shifts in the mix of skill, including skill-biased technological change, and shifts in the mix of firms. The structural shift in the skill composition is best documented for the United States and invokes three explanations: skill-biased technological change, the relative decline in the number of high-wage blue collar jobs in industry, and the increased competition from low-wage economies (*e.g.* Drèze and Sneesens, 1994). Overall it

Table 8. **Employment creation by occupation, 1980-93**

Net jobs created per thousand working age population[1]

	Professional, technical and managerial	Clerical, sales and service	Production, transport and agricultural
France	20	−9	−55
Germany	22	9	−47
United States	49	26	−28

1.   Adjusted for growth in working age population; occupational split in 1980 and 1993 estimated using data from 1982-91 (France), 1980-92 (Germany) and 1979-92 (United States).
Source: ILO Statistical Yearbook; OECD Jobs Study (1994b); OECD Labour Force Statistics; McKinsey Global Institute (1994).

appears that the employment prospects for the low-skilled have deteriorated, both absolutely and relatively to the prospects of higher-skilled workers. Employment creation by occupation differs substantially among the three occupational classes compared in Table 8 (see also Layard *et al.*, 1991, Freeman, 1994), a phenomenon observed in almost all countries, but most prominently in European countries.

Industry trends

Let us also look at the development in specific industries. Table 9 shows the changes in employment in five countries for three manufacturing industries: auto-motive, computers, furniture, and software industry. The overall picture is consis-tent with the decline in manufacturing on average. The auto industry reflects partic-ularly well the general pattern of employment in manufacturing in a country. The results for the computer industry reflect the shift from hardware towards software and the strong growth of employment in software, which is even more pronounced in France than in the United States.

In the service and construction sectors, industries were chosen in which the United States had higher employment growth (Table 10), in order to assess the likely causes of these differential developments. Table 10 presents the aggregate picture. However, it also reveals that the more deregulated service industries in the United States, such as banking, retailing, as well as film, TV and video, had the highest growth in employment.

The preceding discussion suggests that reallocation difficulties play an essen-tial role in Europe, *i.e.*, structural rigidities inhibit the rapid transfer of workers from declining firms and sectors to growing firms and sectors. Standard mismatch exami-nations paint a different picture, however, as they suggest decreasing structural and

Table 9.   **Employment performance in manufacturing and computer services**

Net jobs created per thousand working age population[1]

	Auto 1980-92	Computer hardware[2] 1981-91	Furniture 1980-91	Manufacturing case total	Computer software 1981-91
France	−5.3	0.1	−1.4	−6.6	3.5
Germany	0.5	0.3	−0.4	0.4	n.a.
Italy	−3.0	0.1	−0.7	−3.6	n.a.
Japan	0.7	1.3	−1.2	0.8	4.4
United States	−0.6	−0.4	−0.2	−1.2	2.7

1.   Adjusted for growth in the working age population.
2.   Including semi-conductor manufacturing
Source: McKinsey Global Institute (1994).

Table 10. **Employment performance in market services and construction**

Net jobs created per thousand working age population[1]

	Banking	Retail	Film/TV/video	Service case total	Construction
	1982-92	1980-90	1980-92		1980-90
France	−0.5	−3.6	1.1	−3.0	−10.7
Germany	1.9	−2.1	0.9	0.7	−8.1
Italy	0.9	4.1	0.5	5.5	−6.3
Japan	1.0	−2.3	1.3	0.0	−1.3
United States	1.9	4.9	1.5	8.3	3.0

1.   Adjusted for growth in the working age population.
Source: McKinsey Global Institute (1994).

reallocation difficulties since 1974 and hence attribute shifts in the Beveridge curve to macro phenomena (*e.g.* Jackman *et al.*, 1990). These mismatch indicators do not capture the large variety of interrelated mismatch phenomena (regional, skill, sectoral, etc.), however, and they may suffer from classification problems. New examinations also suggest that mismatch stories are more complicated and econometric evidence for other mismatch indices appear to be inconclusive (*e.g.* Entorf, 1993).

Effect of product market reform on employment

The industry trends reveal that the more deregulated service industries in the United States, such as banking, retailing, as well as film, TV and video, had the highest growth in employment. This is suggestive, but it does not provide conclusive evidence that further product market reforms can reduce unemployment, even if they are combined with incremental labour market reform. Hence, in this section we consider arguments and evidence that product market reforms can enhance labour reallocation in Europe. The arguments remain tentative since they require a general equilibrium perspective with simultaneous rigidities in the product and labour markets. Such frameworks are rarely available (see Gersbach, 1996 for an example).

Subsidies to and protection of declining industries

We first consider government policies in Europe of subsidising declining industries to buffer employment shifts, *e.g.*, by government-financed early retirement schemes and direct firm subsidies. While there are a number of arguments for industrial policies to correct market failures (externalities, increasing returns, imperfect information, etc.), the arguments are difficult to justify for a lot of industries (see also Leonard and van Audenrode, 1993). The system of industrial subsidies is principally tailored to easing the adjustment of mature industries facing decline (OECD, 1992). Such subsidies can affect the labour market through two channels.

First, a subsidy to declining firms supported by a tax on growing firms is likely to reduce labour demand and, with rigid wages, increase unemployment. A decline in labour demand occurs if the elasticity of output in the taxed (expanding) sector is greater than that in the subsidised (mature) sector. The negative effects can be reinforced if potential growth sectors are themselves regulated, exhibiting, e.g., fix-price behaviour. Second, subsidies can contribute to excessive real wages by creating moral hazard problems for employers and unions in their bargaining process for wages. Overall, absolute and relative real wages are distorted, which leads to transition rigidities and overall employment decline. Hence, directional remedies in both product and labour markets interact to reduce unemployment. The overall effects obviously depend on elasticity considerations.

Developing the service sector

Generally, most of the job creation to reduce unemployment and to absorb further declines in the industrial or even in the public sector has to come from the private service sector and service-type activities. In the service sector, there are a number of important industries which have historically been regulated and still remain regulated today to some extent (see Baily, 1993, OECD, 1994a). A number of channels exist through which deregulation in the service sector increases employment: output growth, real wage moderation, and improved skill match.

As indicated in the preceding main section, regulated service industries often lead to low labour productivity which, in turn, can lead to labour shedding if deregulation is introduced. Hence, positive net employment effects from product market reforms have to come from general equilibrium effects yielding output growth in the deregulated and in other industries, and from real wage moderation via decreased rents. Moreover, employment growth should not be inhibited by capacity constraints.[11]

There is no general evidence of real wage moderation due to deregulation. However, current examples of deregulation in Europe certainly provide circumstantial evidence (see also Layard et al., 1991). Here, the need for complementary reform in product and labour markets to capture the employment gains is evident. Low relative real wages in job creating industries create incentives for wait unemployment (Burda, 1988), lengthening unemployment spells.

Output growth in the economy through product market reforms rests upon general equilibrium effects affecting all industries through aggregate demand externalities for given initial conditions, such as absolute and relative real wages. No

Table 11. **General merchandise retail employment by format, 1990**

Per cent, thousands of employees

	Individual stores	Department and variety stores	Discounters[1]	Speciality chains and franchises	Mail order	Total
France[1]	63	5	9	22	1	100 = 932
Germany[1]	59	10	5	23	3	100 = 1 421
Japan[2]	65	14	2	19	0	100 = 3 616
United States	44	16	12	27	1	100 = 8 184

1. Excludes food sales in hypermarkets and supermarkets.
2. 1991 franchises are included in the individual stores; discounters are negligible.
Source: McKinsey Global Institute (1994).

general evidence for such effects is available. However, the United States examples indicate, that despite the downsizing effects of deregulation, employment in the deregulated service industries does not decline, and even displays greater growth than more regulated industries in Europe. If deregulation also affects the availability of other complementary production factors such as land, whose use is limited by zoning laws, the positive effect on employment is immediate since marginal productivity of workers should increase, and relative and absolute real wages become less binding.

A further interesting aspect of the deregulation exercise is the evolution of product mix. Part of the job creating mechanism in the service sector in the United States is the more rapid expansion of product mix and variety, as illustrated in Table 11 for the retail industry. Even more pronounced effects can be seen in banking, film/TV/video.

Product market reform and political constraints

Proposed remedies are commonly not implemented because of strong political opposition. We review briefly some of the issues and then ask in which way product market reforms can help to ease current political constraints.

The irreversibility and the information problem

Political decisions in indirect democracies show a higher degree of irreversibility than private decisions (see *e.g.* Gersbach, 1993*a*, 1993*b*). Regulations once in place are hard to withdraw, even if their introduction today would fail. There is a tendency in democracies toward the status quo if there are uncertainties as to who will lose and who will win, *i.e.*, as to who will be in the majority *ex post*.

For example, equity and poverty concerns were used to argue for the extension of entitlement durations in Switzerland during recessions in the early eighties. However, no considerations were given to whether this measure should be lifted in the future and substantial irreversibility was created as a result (Blattner, 1994). Solving the irreversibility problem through temporary policy design (*e.g.*, conversion clauses) is a potential remedy, but suffers from the time-inconsistency problem.

Connected to the irreversibility problem is the information problem. If reforms do not get enough political support at a particular point in time, potential losers of reforms have an incentive to object research and the acquisition of information about the likely consequences of current regulations and reforms, since they are afraid that the chances for acceptance increase (see Gersbach, 1992).

The winner/loser paradox and the open window problem

Nearly all market reforms attack rents of formerly protected economic groups. If there are more losers than winners and winners cannot compensate for the smaller number through good organisation, reforms are difficult to implement. For instance, some of the labour market regulations may benefit a substantial part of the employed and are difficult to remove.

If there are more winners they may constitute a heterogeneous group and their incentives to invest in reforms suffer from the public good problem and from rational ignorance. For instance, deregulation in the service sector has been difficult to implement in Europe. Obviously, the threat of real wage moderation in an industry, declining mark-ups and initial downsizing creates substantial incentives for owners and workers in such an industry to resist reforms.

The timing of structural reforms in terms of overall conditions can be crucial. While in favourable economic conditions incentives to implement reforms are usually weak, in bad times the size of groups actually or potentially benefiting from regulation increases. Hence, there is no clearly optimal timing for structural reforms.

Reform design

Since almost all reforms attack rents accruing to specific economic groups, there are only three possible strategies open to governments who themselves have an incentive to implement reforms: get a majority of winners, compensate losers enough, or combine various reforms in order to get a majority which on average wins.

The first strategy may suffer from the irreversibility and winner/looser problem. Sometimes liberalising at the margin could help, *e.g.*, by a two-tier system which only includes liberalising new labour contracts (see Saint-Paul, 1995). The standard objection to the second strategy is that potential losers can not be sure that they get real compensation, and hence, that either a social contract or a simultaneous implementation is necessary. The third option poses the question as to whether combinations of measures or even full-fledged packages can help to overcome the political constraints. This is the fundamental design question which has received too little attention.

Broad packages of product and labour market reforms, as, *e.g.*, proposed in Lindbeck *et al.* (1993), internalise complementarities across reforms through a growth and employment programme function and do not rely on knowledge of the exact causes of high unemployment, which is often missing. However, such a programme remains unstable against coalition formation lobbying for specific exemptions and hence unstable in general.

Ease of political constraints for labour reform by product market reform

The combination of product reform and labour market reform could in principle exploit specific political complementarities. For instance, if deregulation shifts labour demand and can reduce congestion effects, *i.e.*, enhance the returns of the matching function, incentives for labour market reform could increase as well. Another example is the reduction of subsidies to declining industries, which is difficult, especially if potential job losses are concentrated and relatively low and dispersed actual or potential job creation in potentially job-creating industries is expected. Barring substantial wage-raising accommodation effects (*e.g.* Calmfors, 1995), the elimination of subsidies could be combined with a temporary active labour market programme (financed partially by the subsidies) for the people who will become unemployed in this industry.

New coalitions for joint market reforms are rarely observed, and if the labour market is very rigid to start with, no great support for whatever reform considered can be expected. Then ultimately only product market forces, transmitted through financial markets, can break vested interests. Circumstantial evidence suggests that product market reforms have become less difficult than labour market reforms and, hence, that the only viable method to change the political equilibrium supporting labour market rigidities is reform in the product market, including liberalisation of trade and foreign direct investment.

INTERACTION OF STRUCTURAL REFORMS AND MACROECONOMIC POLICY

We now turn to the question as to which way structural reforms and macroeconomic policy interact with respect to the European unemployment problem.

Scope for aggregate demand stimulation

We note that in the presence of major public sector imbalances the scope for aggregate demand stimulation through fiscal policies is extremely limited. Indeed, several European countries are not in a position to increase actual budget deficits without moving into unsustainable debt/GDP levels and most countries are facing the need to restructure their pension systems. Also, there is evidence that fiscal consolidation, at least at a certain level of debt in relation to savings and GDP, is neutral or can even have a positive effect on output and employment, *i.e.*, fiscal policy exhibits a zero or negative multiplier (*e.g.* Hellwig and Neumann, 1987, Giavazzi and Pagano, 1990, Alesina and Perotti, 1995). The offsetting effect to the short run contraction of aggregated demand rests on changes in expectations in a non-Ricardian world. A permanent cut of the public sector's share lowers the burden of government debt. The anticipation leads to a fall in the long-term interest rate as well as in taxation. With the initiation of the programme, permanent income and the marginal efficiency of fixed investment will rise while interest rates will begin to fall.[12]

Monetary policy could in principle substitute for tight fiscal policy. In Europe, monetary policy was primarily committed to the defence of pegged exchange rates, and only in those countries where this policy has failed in the face of speculative attacks has monetary policy been relaxed. Only recently, there are signs that the German monetary policy has become less tight. There are at least three potential interactions between monetary policy and labour market reform.

Macroeconomic policy and unemployment insurance

An unresolved puzzle in macroeconomic theory is the relationship between rigidities, *i.e.* departures from the Walrasian model, and the effectiveness of macroeconomic policies. Empirical results from the next chapter, summarised here, show that changes in UI regulations, in particular with respect to the length of benefit entitlements, can counteract the effects on unemployment of macroeconomic policy. Moreover, extending entitlements shifts the modal escape rate to the right and increases the share of long-term unemployed, whose chances of escaping unemployment are relatively insensitive to cyclical fluctuations in aggregate demand and, by extension, to countercyclical measures.

Monetary policy and real wage moderation

An expansionary monetary shock could enhance the downward pressure on real wages when labour market reforms are simultaneously introduced. Since real wage moderation cannot be expected immediately from labour market reforms, a temporary monetary shock could help to reap early employment gains. Moreover, the consequential decrease in real wages would be validated by the decline of the equilibrium unemployment rate.[13] Obviously, such strategies cannot be applied systematically and may lead to more restrictive policies later to fight inflation, even though the increase in inflation should be temporary. Moreover, since reforms are often introduced incrementally over time, standard fine-tuning objections apply.

Monetary policy and political constraints

Monetary policy support could also be justified on the grounds that it may serve to weaken resistance to reforms. *E.g.*, we might think of agreements among labour interest groups, governments, and central banks under which, simultaneously, future expansionary demand policies and regulatory changes are considered. Concerted action in the fiscal, monetary and wage policy area was part of an agreed recovery programme in Germany in 1978 and 1979 when expansionary demand policies and moderate wage policies were pledged (see Hellwig and Neumann, 1987). Monetary policy in such an agreement has to be committed in order to overcome shocks in terms of output or employment, with the agreement that wage policy does not react contrarily. Although such co-operative strategies promise a solution in times when no other policy is feasible, behavioural risks and time inconsistency problems in such a package are obvious as is the difficulty in following such an arrangement repeatedly.

CASE STUDY FOR SWITZERLAND

This chapter provides the econometric background to the interaction between unemployment insurance and macroeconomic policies. We focus on the Swiss labour market in the 1990s, concentrating on the development of the escape probabilities of the unemployed across the business cycle. There are two reasons for selecting Switzerland. First of all, the access to a unique data set (AVAM), which documents all individual spells of registered unemployment in Switzerland, permits an uncommonly precise estimation of escape probabilities. Secondly, Switzerland's unemployment insurance (UI) system experienced a number of regulatory changes in the sample period, providing us with a quasi experimental setting for disentangling UI effects and business cycle effects, the latter acting as a proxy for potential countercyclical policy effects on unemployment.

Historical background

As a historical backdrop to the following analysis, we first provide a short overview of the development of economic activity in Switzerland during the sample period. We start with demand. As Figure 1[14] indicates, economic activity in

◆   Figure 1.   **BAK industrial production index**
1980 = 100, seasonally adjusted

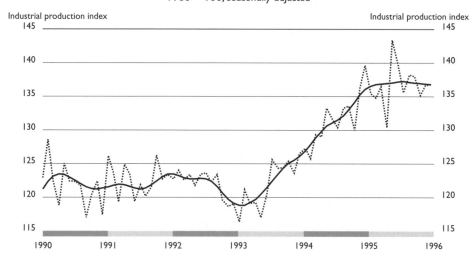

Source: BAK Economics, Basel.

◆   Figure 2.   **Registered unemployment**
Percentage of the labour force

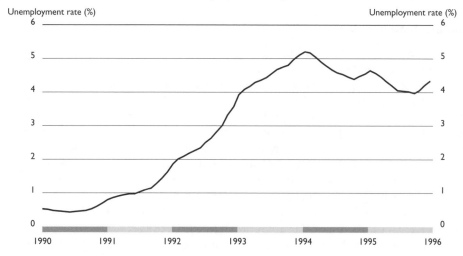

Source: Federal Office of Industry, Trade and Labour, Bern.

Table 12. **Changes in the length of UI entitlements**

Period	Maximum entitlement (weeks)
January 1990 – Q1 1992	17-34-50
Q2 1992 – Q1 1993	34-50-60
Q2 1993 – present	34-50-80

Switzerland showed no signs of growth from 1990 to 1993, marking the most prolonged economic slowdown in Switzerland since the Second World War.

This decline led, in turn, to the largest increase in unemployment in Switzerland in the 20th century (Figure 2). Beginning in the summer of 1990, the unemployment rate rose from 0.5 to 5.2 per cent, reaching its maximum in January 1994, the sharpest relative increase ever experienced in the OECD. Since 1994 the unemployment rate has been falling, reaching 4.3 per cent at the end of December 1995.

In answer to the mounting numbers of unemployed, the coalition government in Switzerland has extended the length of UI entitlements throughout the 1990s. Table 12 gives an overview of the changes and the dates of implementation. The different lengths of entitlement are linked to an individual's previous record of insured employment (see Sheldon, 1996 for details).

Empirical methodology

Our approach consists of modelling unemployment as an absorbing Markov chain in which employment and out-of-the-labour-force together serve as the absorbing state. Elapsed time in registered unemployment is subdivided into a set of discrete duration classes $\{(0, 1), (1, 2), ..., (T, T + 1)\}$, where T symbolises the longest possible completed spell of unemployment, which we take to be 48 months.[15] Process time t in unemployment is measured in calendar months, meaning that January and February represent equivalent lengths of time. Furthermore, we assume – in line with the Markov chain model – that all entries into and exits out of unemployment occur on the first of a calendar month, and that no entry and exit takes place within the same calendar month.[16] The duration class $(t, t + 1)$ thus encompasses all individuals in the stock of unemployed who have been jobless for t months, while the duration class $(0, 1)$ consists of the new entrants (unemployment cohort) in a given month who are still unemployed at the end of that month. In this setting, the following definitions hold:[17]

i) mean duration D of completed unemployment spells,

$$D = \sum_{t=0}^{T} \prod_{i=0}^{t} P(i) \tag{1}$$

ii)   risk R of long-term unemployment,

$$R = \prod_{i=0}^{11} P(i) \tag{2}$$

iii)   stock U of unemployed,

$$U = N(0)D \tag{3}$$

iv) share L of long-term unemployed,

$$L = \sum_{t=12}^{T} \prod_{i=0}^{t} P(i) / D \tag{4}$$

where P(t), the individual probability of remaining unemployed another calendar month, i.e., of passing into the next duration class, given that unemployment has already lasted t months, is calculated as

1 for t = 0,

$$P(t)_t = N(t)_\tau / N(t-1)_{\tau-1} \text{ for } t = 1, ..., 47 \text{ and} \tag{5}$$

0 for t = 48,

where t = January 1990, ..., December 1995. $N(t)_t$ represents the number of unemployed in the duration class (t, t + 1) on the last working day of the calendar month t. Note that $N(t)_t$ and $N(t-1)_{t-1}$ refer to the same cohort. Hence (5) bases the calculation of continuation rates on one minus the rate of cohort attrition or escape.[18]

The formulas (1) – (4) yield steady-state values. These correspond to the long-term equilibrium values the variables would assume if the labour market conditions that ruled in any given month t remained constant. In other words, they correspond to the steady-state values that the continuation rates and, in the case of the steady-state unemployment rate, the size of entering cohorts in any given month imply.

To separate the impact of UI on unemployment from that of cyclical fluctuations, we regress the above steady-state variables together with the rate of unemployment incidence[19] and the continuation rates pertaining to the duration classes 1 to 24 on i) a business cycle variable (relative deviation of the seasonally and shock-adjusted monthly index of industrial production from its trend), ii) a trend variable, iii) month-specific dummy variables and iv) two UI regime dummy variables (April 1992-December 1995 and April 1993-December 1995, respectively).[20] With the exception of the trend and dummy variables, all variables are measured in logs.

The use of steady-state values as left-hand variables has two advantages: *i)* it avoids the simultaneity problem inherent in the fact that UI regime changes can be both a cause and an effect of higher unemployment (see Atkinson and Micklewright, 1991, p. 1708), and *ii)* it permits a more precise identification of the time period responsible for measured cyclical and UI effects, since steady-state variables, unlike their observable counterparts, depend solely on the labour market conditions (continuation rates) that prevailed in a specific calendar month.

Our regression approach is also akin to the hazard function analysis common to microeconometric studies. Essentially, the microeconometric approach entails estimating the parameters of the escape rate

$$Q(t, z_{i\tau}) = Q_0(t) \exp(\beta_t^T z_{i\tau})$$
(6)

where z represents a column vector of regressors describing a person i and/or economic and institutional conditions at calendar time t, b a column vector of parameters, and $Q_0(t)$ the base hazard or escape rate for duration interval t. In contrast, our approach essentially assumes the following specification[21]

$$Q(t, z_{\tau}) = Q_0(t) \exp(\beta_t^T z_{\tau})$$
(7)

In other words, our approach differs from that of microeconometric studies in that the latter control for individual effects and ignore duration-class-specific effects, while we do the opposite. Figure 3 below suggests that ignoring interval-specific effects is inappropriate. Our approach also avoids the aggregation problem faced by microeconometric studies when they attempt to extrapolate their results to the level of the economy as a whole (see Atkinson and Micklewright, 1991, p. 1710).

Effects of regulatory change

Before we consider the regression results, it is instructive to examine the evolution of escape rates in Switzerland in the 1990s shown in Figure 3. As the figure indicates, each extension of the maximum length of entitlement, from 50 to 60 weeks (*i.e.*, from approximately 11-12 to 13-14 calendar months) in 1992 and from 60 to 80 weeks (approximately 18-19 calendar months) in 1993, has shifted the modal escape rate to the right by a corresponding number of months.[22] Although the evidence is surely suggestive of strong UI effects on unemployment, the picture is not complete. For one, no spikes appear at the other points of benefit exhaustion of 17 weeks (3-4 calendar months) and 34 weeks (7-8 calendar months). Regression analysis is required for more insight. Our results appear in Table 13.[23]

The moral hazard effect of the entitlement extensions should have been to increase the tendency of the unemployed in the duration classes from 4 to 7 months (reflecting the entitlement shift from 17 to 34 weeks), from 8 to 11 months

◆   Figure 3. **Escape rates from registered unemployment**

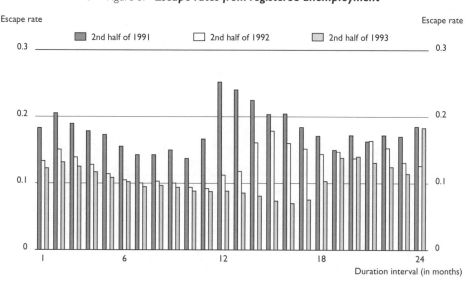

(reflecting the shift from 35 to 50 weeks), from 12 to 13 months (reflecting the move from 50 to 60 weeks), and from 14-18 months (reflecting the switch from 60 to 80 weeks) to remain unemployed. And indeed, this is exactly what the regression results for the continuation rates show. The coefficients of the UI dummy variable "UI 92" and "UI 93" are all highly significant in the appropriate duration classes (see shaded area) and imply increases in the continuation rates ranging from 1.9 to 11.9 per cent.[24]

Note, too, that the statistical significance of the UI regime variables rises as cohorts reach the threshold where UI benefits previously expired. This indicates that entitlement extensions also reduced the increased exit that normally occurs just before benefits lapse.

The lengthening of UI entitlements also shifts the various thresholds outwards where cantonal unemployment aid (UA), which can follow upon UI, lapses. These knock-on effects are reflected in the various positive signs in duration classes exceeding 60 weeks in the case of "UI 92" and exceeding 80 weeks in the case of "UI 93". UA benefits expire in any case, however, after a total of 24 months of unemployment, which explains the significant negative sign in the 24-month duration class.

The pattern of statistical significance clearly indicates that the UI regime variables capture the effect of entitlement extensions.[25] Turning to the effects of UI

Table 13. **Regression results**

Left- Hand Variable	Cycle	Trend	UI 92	UI 93	DW	adj. R2
ln (P1)	−1.26***	0.003***	0.016	−0.014	1.98	0.93
	(0.11)	(0.000)	(0.012)	(0.010)		
ln (P2)	−1.26***	0.003***	0.023*	−0.004	1.80	0.93
	(0.12)	(0.000)	(0.013)	(0.011)		
ln (P3)	−1.08***	0.002***	0.025**	−0.003	1.92	0.92
17 weeks						
ln (P4)	−0.97***	0.002***	0.035***	−0.003	1.93	0.88
	(0.12)	(0.000)	(0.013)	(0.011)		
ln (P5)	−0.82***	0.001***	0.042***	−0.002	2.06	0.91
	(0.10)	(0.000)	(0.010)	(0.009)		
ln (P6)	−0.68***	0.001***	0.040***	−0.006	1.90	0.87
	(0.10)	(0.000)	(0.010)	(0.009)		
ln (P7)	−0.63***	0.001*	0.042***	−0.002	1.81	0.80
34 weeks						
ln (P8)	−0.66***	0.001***	0.031***	−0.001	1.95	0.86
	(0.09)	(0.000)	(0.009)	(0.008)		
ln (P9)	−0.54***	0.000	0.033***	0.010	1.63	0.88
	(0.07)	(0.000)	(0.007)	(0.006)		
ln (P10)	−0.66***	0.001***	0.019**	0.001	1.92	0.84
	(0.08)	(0.000)	(0.009)	(0.007)		
ln (P11)	−0.58***	0.001*	0.049***	0.012	1.94	0.84
50 weeks						
ln (P12)	−0.77***	0.001	0.112***	0.039**	1.72	0.88
	(0.19)	(0.001)	(0.020)	(0.017)		
ln (P13)	−0.68***	0.001	0.097***	0.052***	1.90	0.86
60 weeks						
ln (P14)	−0.64***	0.001	0.037*	0.087***	2.02	0.81
	(0.20)	(0.001)	(0.021)	(0.018)		
ln (P15)	−0.37	0.001	0.041	0.083***	1.87	0.68
	(0.26)	(0.001)	(0.028)	(0.023)		
ln (P16)	−0.23	−0.000	0.069***	0.081***	1.86	0.86
	(0.15)	(0.000)	(0.016)	(0.013)		
ln (P17)	−0.49**	0.001	0.024	0.061***	1.82	0.67
	(0.21)	(0.001)	(0.022)	(0.018)		
ln (P18)	−0.51***	−0.000	0.032	0.050***	1.98	0.52
80 weeks						
ln (P19)	−0.75***	0.000	−0.005	0.013	1.99	0.13
	(0.26)	(0.001)	(0.027)	(0.023)		
ln (P20)	−0.22	−0.001	0.093**	0.009	2.12	0.14
	(0.37)	(0.001)	(0.039)	(0.033)		
ln (P21)	−0.45	−0.001	0.028	0.025	1.96	0.12
	(0.36)	(0.001)	(0.038)	(0.032)		
ln (P22)	−0.36	−0.001	0.021	0.024	1.67	0.01
	(0.27)	(0.001)	(0.029)	(0.024)		
ln (P23)	−0.10	−0.002	0.061***	0.044**	1.88	0.28
	(0.19)	(0.001)	(0.020)	(0.017)		
ln (P24)	−0.72*	0.002*	0.015	−0.100	2.24	0.26
ln (D)	−4.89***	0.005***	0.193***	0.111***	1.93	0.94
	(0.41)	(0.001)	(0.043)	(0.036)		
ln (R)	−9.24***	0.015***	0.337***	−0.012	2.03	0.92
	(0.90)	(0.003)	(0.096)	(0.080)		
ln (L)	−7.45***	0.010***	0.424***	0.179**	2.03	0.91
	(0.95)	(0.003)	(0.101)	(0.085)		
ln (U-risk)	−3.69*	0.019**	0.115	000	2.08	0.74
	(1.99)	(0.008)	(0.077)	(0.075)		
ln (U-rate)	−8.58***	0.024***	0.308***	0.112	–	–
	(2.03)	(0.008)	(0.089)	(0.083)		

changes on the steady-state variables, we see that the expected mean duration D of completed spells of unemployment increased by 35.5 per cent as a result of extending the length of entitlements in 1992 and again in 1993.[26]

The first extension of entitlements in 1992 increased the probability R of remaining long-term unemployed by 40.1 per cent. The second extension of entitlements in 1993, on the other hand, apparently had no effect on the risk of long-term unemployment, which is as it should be since the entitlement extension from 60 to 80 weeks applied only to individuals who were already long-term unemployed, *i.e.*, jobless for more than a year.

The lengthening of entitlements from 60 to 80 weeks can nevertheless still effect the proportion L of long-term unemployed, as it is shown to do. Both entitlement extensions together led to an 82.7 per cent increase in the share of long-term unemployed.

As the results further indicate, neither regime change had a statistically significant effect on the risk of unemployment, implying that these changes did not draw additional people into registered unemployment. With respect to the steady-state rate of unemployment, we find that only the UI regime change in 1992 had a statistically significant impact. This reflects the fact that the high duration classes, affected by the April 1993 UI regime change, contain but a small fraction of all unemployed. As a result of the 1992 entitlement extension, the steady-state unemployment rate lies 36.1 per cent higher than it otherwise would.

In summary, the extension of UI entitlements had a very pronounced effect on steady-state, *i.e.*, equilibrium unemployment in Switzerland. We now contrast these effects with those of trend and cyclical fluctuations in an attempt to assess the potential impact of counter-cyclical measures.

Limitations of aggregate demand

We judge the potential of aggregate demand management by the responsiveness of the left-hand variables to trend ("Trend") and cyclical fluctuations ("Cycle"). Note that "Cycle" measures the relative change in a given left-hand variable in reaction to a one percentage point increase in industrial production *vis-à-vis* its trend level. Hence, by implication, trend production growth has no effect on unemployment. In other words, macroeconomic policy measures that succeed in completely stabilising aggregate demand would hold unemployment constant, all else equal. Note that any secular effects, such as labour-saving technical progress, are captured by the trend variable.

The results pertaining to continuation rates indicate that they have been rising at a trend rate of 0.0 to 0.3 per cent per month throughout the 1990s. Of greater interest, however, is the relatively low cyclical elasticity of continuation rates in duration classes above 12 months. This indicates that the probability of escape for the long-term unemployed is relatively unresponsive to cyclical fluctuations,[27] implying that counter-cyclical policy measures would have little effect on the employment opportunities of the long-term unemployed. Elasticities in excess of one are observed only in the first three months of unemployment.

According to the estimate of the responsiveness of mean spell duration to cyclical fluctuations, a one percentage point increase in the relative deviation of industrial production from its trend level would decrease the average expected duration of completed spells of unemployment by roughly 4.9 per cent. An increase of that magnitude took, on average, three months to achieve in periods of sustained positive or negative growth in our sample period. Hence, at this rate it would take about a year of typical trend-exceeding growth to lower the mean duration of unemployment by about 20 per cent. However, the mean duration of unemployment increased at a trend rate of 0.5 per cent per month or 6.2 per cent per year in the sample period. Given this opposing force, a year of trend-surpassing growth in industrial production would shorten mean duration thus by just 13.4 per cent. These values along with those for the other components of unemployment appear in Table 14.

The column marked "Cycle" gives the potential impact of one year of counter-cyclical policy measures were they to succeed in increasing aggregate demand at the rate common to business cycles in Switzerland. According to the results, macroeconomic policy of the sort just described would have its greatest impact on the risk of long-term unemployment, lowering it by 36.7 per cent, followed by the rate of unemployment, dropping it by 34.3 per cent. Note, however, that a secular increase ("Trend") in both variables works against counter-cyclical measures, limiting their visible effectiveness.

It is interesting to observe that all steady-state variables (D, R and L) linked solely to escape rates are more responsive to cyclical fluctuations than to trend, whereas the opposite holds true for those variables exclusively (risk of unemployment) or additionally (unemployment rate) dependent on entry into employ-

Table 14. **Effects of a one-year cyclical upswing, a one-year trend and UI changes on various dimensions of unemployment**

Per cent

Variable	Cycle	Trend	UI change
Duration (D)	−19.6	6.2	35.5
Long-term risk (R)	−36.7	19.6	40.1
Long-term share (L)	−29.8	12.7	82.8
Unemployment risk	−14.8	25.3	0.0
Unemployment rate	−34.3	33.3	36.1

ment. This implies that important factors other than cyclical fluctuations are driving entry into unemployment, thus preventing the cyclical recovery from having a greater visible impact on the rate of unemployment in Switzerland.

Finally, we compare the impact of cyclical fluctuations on unemployment with that of UI regime changes ("UI Change").[28] Here it can be seen that it would take close to three years of trend-surpassing growth in manufacturing to neutralise the increase in the share of long-term unemployed that entitlement extensions engendered. In other words, UI entitlement extensions appear to place a large restriction on the effectiveness of counter-cyclical policy measures.

In short, extending entitlements runs the risk of creating a large stock of long-term unemployed whose chances of finding unemployment are impervious to counter-cyclical measures or to a general improvement in economic conditions. To avoid the vicious circle of extended entitlements, followed by increased long-term and structural unemployment, followed by further entitlement extensions *ad infinitum*, measures must be taken to ensure the quick reintegration of the unemployed in the employment process, if need be, at the risk of accepting low-paying work. A policy aimed at a quick reintegration of the unemployed calls for shortening entitlements, on the one hand, and implementing active labour market policy measures, on the other. Income distribution objectives can be dealt with better by adjusting after-tax income rather than intervening in the labour market with extended benefit entitlements.

CONCLUDING REMARKS

Policy making in Europe faces a variety of pressing issues. The twin objective of reducing long-term unemployment over the medium run while at the same time promoting productivity gains in product markets constitutes a formidable challenge for policy. The nature of technological progress has changed. Tackling the unemployment problem requires not only reforming labour market institutions and regulations, but also stimulating the labour demand schedules originating from product markets.

The allocative objectives discussed in this paper have, as a rule, distributional implications. Barring substantial negative incentive effects, it is clear that working towards allocative objectives while preserving some of the distributional achievements in Europe calls for wide-ranging policy reform measures. However, tailoring policy to objectives of flexibility and allocative efficiency faces enormous political feasibility constraints. The greatest challenge is choosing a policy mix that achieves the necessary allocative objectives while maintaining social cohesion among the main interest groups.

NOTES

1. We would like to thank Martin Hellwig, the discussant Richard Jackman, the editor Friedrich Klau and the conference participants for helpful comments.

2. For the mechanics and interpretation of inter-industry and inter-region wage differentials see Haisken and Schmidt (1996).

3. In recent years, there has been a real explosion in the detection of new transmission channels for monetary and fiscal policy (see e.g. Symposium, 1993, Phelps, 1994, Rotemberg and Woodford, 1992). Given the additional prominence of real business cycle theory, no consensus has yet emerged as to whether and by how much demand policies can be effective and as to which departures from Walrasian markets determine effectiveness. Although the reduction of some of the structural rigidities through structural reforms could fundamentally alter the effectiveness of macroeconomic policies, these effects are equally unclear.

4. The very low productivity in the German beer industry deserves particular remarks. In general, the productivity figures are based on product matches and need to be adjusted for quality differences if the product matches include high and low-quality products. For the beer industry only the physical measure litres per hours worked, adjusted for differences in vertical integration, was used. Adjusting for quality is impossible since German beer commands a price premium in the United States, but the same holds true for some American beer in Germany. Since the beer markets do only overlap in niche markets, price premiums for quality cannot be directly measured. Moreover, as large restructuring activities in the German beer industry have indicated, most of the beer sold in Germany can be made using large-scale production methods as in the United States. The quality argument has to be distinguished from differences in customer tastes. Clearly, German beer consumers have a preference for locally produced beer. But consumer taste differences, while being a reason for productivity differences, are not counted as quality differences.

5. Jorgensen and Kuroda (1992) remove taxes and transportation costs from the expenditure PPPs in order to correct for two methodological flaws. They also use gross output rather than value added to overcome the problem of input prices differing from output prices.

6. For more details on measurement see Baily (1993). For an overview of the measurement problems and some other case study results for individual countries see e.g. Grilliches (1992).

7. Composition effects in conjunction with measurement issues may also explain why overall growth rates for output per hour or multi-factor productivity in the United States remain substantially below that in other countries in the time period 1979-1992, although the United States shows a remarkable recovery in manufacturing (e.g. Gordon, 1995).

8. Note that it is also necessary to estimate the share of technical (in)efficiency and allocative (in)efficiency (see e.g. Caves and Associates, 1992). A lot of these productivity differences could be tied to differences in factor prices. This possible source of productivity differences can easily be refuted in most of the cases (see Baily and Gersbach, 1995).

9. For details and extended discussions see Baily and Gersbach (1995).

10. Relating employment changes to labour force participation changes, while conceptually preferable, is not suitable due to difficulties in measuring potential labour force participation.

11. Almost all studies on unemployment report that industrial capacity in Europe is insufficient to employ its people (e.g. Franz and Gordon, 1993). This is merely a consequence of the fact that most of unemployment is structural in nature and not due to cyclical demand deficiencies. Insufficient productive capacity is not eliminated, at least in the short term. However, capacity constraints are more fuzzy in the service sector and on average less binding than in manufacturing. Moreover, the removal of regulatory barriers can help to accelerate the increase in service capacity. A considerable job growth potential exists in the area of personal services where capacity constraints are virtually absent.

12. The composition of government budgets has to be taken into account. In particular, there is no clear justification why the share of public expenditures for infrastructure should decline as it has in the last decades (see e.g. Drèze and Malinvaud, 1994). In general, the positive arguments for fiscal adjustment suggest that consolidation should not go at the expense of public investments.

13. Gordon (1996) provides a more direct argument, based on a favorable short-run Phillips curve once structural reforms have been implemented.

14. Figure 2 displays the BAK monthly index of industrial production.

15. This assumption holds true on average for 99.8 per cent of the members of an unemployment cohort.

16. These assumptions are broadly supported by the data.

17. Proofs can be found in any textbook on Markov chains. See Snell (1988, pp. 421-438), for example. The same formulas can be found scattered throughout the literature on unemployment. However, it has apparently gone unnoticed that they stem from a common model viewing unemployment as an absorbing Markov chain.

18. Bowers and Harkess (1979), Sider (1985) and Budd et al. (1988) employ a similar method of calculation.

19. This is defined as $N(0)_t$, the size of entering cohorts, divided by the size of the labour force. We also divide U by the labour force to replace U with the steady-state rate of unemployment.

20. A similar regression methodology has been adopted by Björklund (1978), with respect to continuation rates, and by Sider (1985), with regard to continuation rates, D, U, and unemployment risk.

21. Taking logs of (7) produces our specification, yet applied here to escape rates rather than to continuation rates.

22. The accumulation of exits at the moment of benefit exhaustion is a commonly observed phenomenon in North America (Marston, 1975; Moffitt, 1985; Ham and Rea, 1987; Katz and Meyer, 1990), and can be explained within a search model framework as resulting either from the increase in the opportunity cost of unemployment due to the exhaustion of benefits or from an entitlement effect stemming from the need to enter insured employment in order to regain eligibility to UI benefits.

23. The results for the calendar-month dummy variables are not presented. Estimation included a correction for a first-order moving-average error when appropriate. The non-stationarity of the log of unemployment risk necessitated estimation in first differences in this case. The estimates for the steady-state employment rate were obtained by imposing the definitional restriction ln(unemployment rate) = ln(duration) + ln(unemployment risk). Asterisks indicate that a coefficient is significantly different from zero (two-tailed test) with a 10 (*), 5 (**) or 1 per cent (***) probability of error. The numbers in parentheses represent standard errors.

24. The coefficients of the dummy variables represent first differences of logs. Hence, exp(b)-1, not b, gives the percent change in the left-hand variable. Yet for values of b not much exceeding 0.1, both expressions are virtually equivalent.

25. As the continuation rates apply to registered unemployment, it is unclear to what extent these estimates are simply capturing reporting effects. Results from the Swiss Labour Force Survey (SAKE) however indicate that the proportion of surveyed unemployed not registered at the employment office has fallen continuously throughout the 1990s. In fact, the number of registered unemployed in Switzerland currently exceeds the surveyed number. Furthermore, an earlier study (Sheldon, 1993, p. 99) shows that the share of individuals exiting registered unemployment and known by the employment office to have found work fell merely from 71.2 per cent to 70.4 per cent from 1990 to 1993. In short, the reporting effect does not appear to be dramatic.

26. North American studies report the impact of entitlement extensions on unemployment in terms of the number of weeks of unemployment that a one-week increase in entitlements causes. In order to compare these findings with our results, we focus on the entitlement extension in April 1993 since it was of uniform length, i.e., 20 weeks. According to our estimates, the mean duration of unemployment rose by 11.7 per cent as a result of this increase. Applied to a mean duration of eight months or roughly 34 weeks, which held on average for the period 1993-95, the size of this relative increase in mean duration implies an absolute increase of four weeks. Hence, a 20-week increase in entitlements apparently increases the mean spell length by four weeks, thus

implying that a one-week increase would raise the mean duration of unemployment by 0.2 weeks. This fits well with the findings of North American studies, which report values ranging from 0.10 to 0.33 weeks (Moffitt, 1985; Ham and Rea, 1987; Katz and Meyer, 1990).

27. Whether this is due to duration dependence or unobserved heterogeneity (Heckman, and Borjas, 1980) is unclear.

28. We abstract from the effect that entitlement extensions may have on cyclical fluctuations.

BIBLIOGRAPHY

Atkinson, A., J. Mickelwright (1991), "Unemployment Compensation and Labour Market Transitions: A Critical Review", *Journal of Economic Literature*, 29, 1679-1727.

Alesina, A., R. Perotti (1995), "Fiscal Expansions and Fiscal Adjustments in OECD Countries", *NBER Working paper*, 5214.

van Ark, B. and D. Pilat (1993), "Cross Country Productivity Levels: Differences and Causes", *Brookings Papers on Economic Activity: Microeconomics*, 2, 1-69.

van Ark, B. (1995), "Manufacturing Prices, Productivity, and Labour Costs in Five Economies", *Monthly Labour Review*, July, 56-72.

Baily, M.N. (1993), "Competition, Regulation and Efficiency in Service Industries", *Brookings Papers on Economic Activity: Microeconomics*, 2, 71-159.

Baily, M.N., H. Gersbach (1995), "Efficiency in Manufacturing and the Need for Global Competition", *Brooking Papers on Economic Activity: Microeconomics*, 307-358.

Björklund, A. (1978), "On the Duration of Unemployment in Sweden, 1965-1976", *Scandinavian Journal of Economics*, 80, 421-439.

Blattner (1994), "Arbeitslosigkeit, Aufgaben für Wirtschafts- und Sozialpolitik", *WWZ Sonderdruck*, 17, University Basel.

Bowers, J., D. Harkess (1979), "Duration of Unemployment by Age and Sex", *Economica*, 46, 239-260.

Budd, A., P. Levine, P. Smith (1988), "Unemployment, Vacancies and the Long-Term Unemployed", *Economic Journal*, 98, 1071-1091.

Burda, M. (1988), "Wait Unemployment in Europe", *Economic* Policy, 393-425.

Calmfors, L. (1995), "Labour Market Policy and Unemployment", *European Economic Review*, 39, 583-592.

Caves, R.E. and Associates (1992), *Industrial Efficiency in Six Nations*, MIT Press, Cambridge Massachusetts.

Dollar, D., E.N. Wolff (1993), *Competitiveness, Convergence, and International Specialization*, MIT Press, Cambridge, Massachusetts.

Drèze, J.H., E. Malinvaud (1994), "Growth and Employment: The Scope of a European Initiative", *European Economic Review*, 38, 489-504.

Drèze, J.H., H. Sneesens (1994), "Technical Development, Competition from Low-Wage Economies and Low-Skilled Unemployment", *Swedish Economic Policy Review*, 1, 185-214.

Entorf, H., (1993), "Do Aggregate Measures of Mismatch Measure Mismatch? A Time-Series Analysis of Existing Concepts", Département de la Recherche, INSEE, Paris.

Franz, W., R.J. Gordon (1993), "German and American Wage and Price Dynamics: Differences and Common Themes", European Economic Review, 37, 719-754.

Freeman, R.B. (ed.) (1994), Working under Different Rules, National Bureau of Economic Research, Russell Sage Foundation, New York.

Gersbach, H. (1992), "Allocation of Information by Majority Decisions", Journal of Public Economics, 48, 259-268.

Gersbach, H. (1993a), "Politics and the Choice of Durability. Comment", The American Economic Review, 83, 670-673.

Gersbach, H. (1993b), "Environmental Preservation and Majority Decisions", Land Economics, 69 (2), 147-155.

Gersbach, H. (1996), "Unemployment and the Interaction of Product and Labour Market Rigidites", University of Heidelberg.

Giavazzi, F., M. Pagano (1990), "Can Severe Fiscal Contractions be Expansionary?" in Blanchard, O., Fischer, S, Macroeconomics Annual 1990, Cambridge, MA, MIT Press.

Gordon, R.J. (1993), "Comments on Baily, M.N., Competition, Regulation, and Efficiency in Service Industries", Brookings Papers on Economic Activity: Microeconomics, 2, 131-144.

Gordon, R.J. (1995), "Is there a Tradeoff between Unemployment and Productivity Growth?" NBER Working Paper, 5081.

Gordon, R.J. (1996) "Interactions between Structural Reform, Macroeconomic Policies and Economic Performance", this volume.

Grilliches, Z. (ed.) (1992), "Output Measurement in the Service Sector", NBER, 56, Chicago.

Haisken, J.P., C. Schmidt (1996) "Inter-Industry and Inter-Region Differentials: Mechanics and Interpretation", Review of Economics and Statistics, (forthcoming).

Ham, J., S. Rea (1987), "Unemployment Insurance and Male Unemployment Duration in Canada", Journal of Labour Economics, 5, 325-353.

Heckman, J., G. Borjas (1980), "Does Unemployment Cause Future Unemployment, Definitions, Questions, and Answers from a Contious Time Model of Heterogeneity and Time Dependence", Economica, 47, 247-283.

Hellwig, M., M.N. Neumann (1987), "Economic Policy in Germany: Was there a Turnaround", Economic Policy, 105-133.

Hunt, J. (1995), "The Effect of Unemployment Compensation on Unemployment Duration in Germany", Journal of Labour Economics, 13, 88-120.

ILO (recent issues) Statistical Yearbook, ILO, Genf.

Jackman, R., R. Layard, S. Savouri (1990), "Labour-Market Mismatch: A Framework or Thought", in Padoa-Schioppa, T., (ed.) Mismatch and Labour Mobility, Cambridge University Press.

Jackman, R., R. Layard, S. Nickell (1996), "Structural Aspects of OECD Unemployment", this volume.

Jorgensen, D.W., M. Kuroda (1992), "Productivity and International Competitiveness in Japan and the United States, 1960-1985", *The Economics Studies Quarterly*, 43, 313-325.

Katz, L., B. Meyer (1990), "The Impact of the Potential Duration Unemployment Benefits on the Duration of Unemployment", *Journal of Public Economics*, 41, 45-72.

Layard, A. *et al.* (1991), *Unemployment, Macroeconomic Performance and the Labour Market*, Oxford University Press.

Leonard, J.S., M. Van Audenrode (1993), "Corporatism Run Amok: Job Stability and Industrial Policy in Belgium and the United States", *Economic Policy*, 355-400.

Lindbeck, A. *et al.* (1993) "Options for Economic and Policy Reform in Sweden", *Economic Policy*, 219-263.

Marin, P.L. (1995), "Productivity Differences in the Airline Industry: Partial Deregulation versus Short Run Protection", *Discussion Paper, The Economics of Industry Group*, LSE.

Marston, St. (1975), "The Impact of Unemployment Insurance on Job Search", *Brookings Papers on Economic Activity*, 1, 13-48.

McKinsey Global Institute (1992), *Service Sector Productivity*, McKinsey & Co., Washington DC.

McKinsey Global Institute (1993), *Manufacturing Productivity*, McKinsey & Co., Washington DC.

McKinsey Global Institute (1994), *Employment Performance*, McKinsey & Co., Washington DC.

Moffitt, R. (1985), "Unemployment Insurance and the Distribution of Unemployment Spells", *Journal of Econometrics*, 28, 85-101.

OECD (1992), *Industrial Support Policies in OECD Countries*, Paris.

OECD (1993), *Employment Outlook*, Paris.

OECD (1994a), *Assessing Structural Reform: Lessons for the Future*, Paris.

OECD (1994b), *Jobs Study*, Paris.

OECD (1995), *Implementing the Strategy*, Paris.

OECD (recent issues), *Labour Force Statistics, National Accounts*, Paris.

Phelps, E.S. (1994), *Structural Slumps*, Harvard University Press, Cambridge Massachusetts.

Rotemberg, J., M. Woodford (1992), "Oligopolistic Pricing and the Effects of Aggregate Demand on Economic Activity", *Journal of Political Economy*, 100, 1153-1204.

Saint-Paul, G. (1995), "Some Political Aspects of Unemployment", *European Economic Review*, 39, 575-582.

Sheldon, G. (1993), "Konjunkturelle und strukturelle Aspekte des schweizerischen Arbeitsmarktes", *Bundesamt für Konjunkturfragen*, 16, Bern.

Sheldon, G. (1996), "Unemployment and Unemployment Insurance in Switzerland", Paper presented at the conference commemorating the 10-year anniversary of the Gerzensee Center of Studies.

Sider, H. (1985), "Unemployment Duration and Incidence: 1968-82", *American Economic Review*, 75, 461-472.

Snell, L. (1988), *Introduction to Probability*, New York.

Solow, R. (1957), "Technical Change and the Aggregate Production Function", *Review of Economic Statistics*, 47, 312-320.

Symposium: Keynsian Economics Today (1993), *Journal of Economics Perspectives*, 7, 3-82.

COMMENTS

by
R. Jackman

The Gersbach and Sheldon paper covers a wide range of issues and makes a number of interesting points. I support very strongly the paper's policy stance of regarding the objectives of curbing unemployment and of increasing productivity growth as complementary elements in raising economic welfare rather than as substitute inputs into some predetermined growth of output.

The paper starts by pointing out that structural reforms, insofar as they contribute to either increased flexibility of nominal wages and prices, or to the reduction of uncompetitive restrictions in product or factor markets, will not only enhance efficiency but tend to lessen the seriousness of macroeconomic problems. In the limit of perfect wage and price flexibility, for example, all markets will clear and there can then be no involuntary unemployment. However, as the paper rightly states, even if structural reforms are successful in removing some rigidities, others will remain, and then standard second-best arguments show that there is no necessary welfare improvement. I would argue that similar caution is appropriate on the macroeconomic side also – if some rigidities remain, some types of structural reform can do more harm than good. A standard result in the literature, for example, is that if there are long-term wage contracts, synchronisation of wage-setting can lead to greater aggregate wage flexibility, and a structural reform leading to desynchronisation of wage-setting could lead to more nominal wage rigidity as each group of workers would resist wage cuts when they had no assurance that other groups would follow.

The conclusion in the paper, however, is that many existing regulations cannot be justified on a cost-benefit basis but rather have to be understood in terms of political economic considerations. I think it would give more point to this discussion if the author could give a few examples of regulations which he feels have no economic justification, as against examples where second-best or other considerations may be important.

The next section of the paper looks at the scope for productivity improvements by comparing labour productivity by industry in different economies and over time. The differences are very large, both across industries and over time, but it is unfortunately not clear to what extent these differences are attributable to regulation, or how far productivity could be raised by structural reforms. The detailed discussion of the causes of productivity differentials concerns itself with questions of product mix, design, internal organisation and the like which have no very obvious bearing on government policy. Nor is it clear from, e.g. Table 1, that industries where productivity in Germany is relatively high compared to the United States (metalworking) are less regulated than those where productivity is relatively low (beer). Indeed taken at face value these figures suggest that labour productivity in beer is so low that it is remarkable that the German beer industry is able to survive, let alone to export, and one can only suspect that there are important differences in quality which are not recorded in the data.

Table 2 shows a sharp relative improvement in labour manufacturing productivity in the United Kingdom since 1980 relative to the United States and France with over the same period a significant decline in labour productivity in Germany. This table might be taken as an example of the possible benefits of structural reform, which has clearly been pursued more vigorously in the United Kingdom than in Germany. Again, however, one might worry about quality – is it not often argued that while UK firms have become more competitive by cost cutting including cutting the number of jobs, German firms have responded to competition by improving product quality? Concerns recently surfacing within Germany over foreign direct investment by German companies suggest that quality improvements have not saved the day. Even allowing for the high quality of the product, unit labour costs in Germany are too high and this in part reflects the slowness of structural reform in the German economy.

The paper goes on to look at the changes in the pattern of employment by industrial sector across countries, and concludes that "reallocation difficulties play an essential role (in explaining the growth in unemployment) in Europe". More light on this subject could be provided if this section were to examine a wider range of countries. Data is taken from the United States and Japan and in Europe for France, Germany and Italy. It would be particularly interesting in this context to contrast the experience of these countries with countries following different approaches – in Europe with the United Kingdom or Sweden or Switzerland, or outside Europe with Australia or New Zealand. (Clearly, the availability of comparable data is a serious problem here, but much is available from the Jobs Study and other OECD sources.)

I would also be interested in the way in which the author would model the impact of structural change on aggregate unemployment. Demand shifts do not of themselves create unemployment. Relative wages may adjust, but even if they do not, the aggregate wage level in the economy might be expected to adjust to equate the rate of job loss in the declining sectors to the rate of new job creation. It is necessary to focus on the aggregate economy, rather than on partial equilibrium analysis of individual sectors (such as the discussion of demand elasticities).

The section concludes with a brief review of some "political economy" explanations of the resistance to economic reform. I think the literature on this subject, though thought-provoking, has yet to produce any robust conclusions. Clearly nearly all reforms create some losers, yet a lot of reforms go ahead, and the theory does not seem able to predict when opposition to reform will be successful and when not.

The final section of the paper looks at the impact of the changes to the unemployment benefit system in Switzerland over the last five years, in particular the extension of the duration for which unemployment benefits can be paid, from 12 to 15 months in mid 1992 and from 15 to 20 months in May 1993. The paper shows rather strikingly (in Figure 3) how the "spike" in the outflow rate has moved almost exactly in line with the duration of benefit entitlement. The author concludes from this evidence that unemployment insurance regulations have a "very pronounced effect on steady-state, i.e., equilibrium unemployment". But it has to be said that the Swiss data refers to registered unemployment and irrespective of their labour force status, or of any change in it, people may simply not bother to register if they are no longer entitled to benefit. One's concern is perhaps not so much with those who leave the register when benefits run out (many of whom perhaps should never have been paid unemployment benefit in the first place), but with the rather larger number who remain on the register, still looking for work but with no income support (at least from the unemployment insurance system). It would make life very much easier if we could be confident that unemployed people would all find work quickly if their benefits were cut off, but I do not think the evidence presented here permits such a conclusion.

MACROECONOMIC POLICY IN THE PRESENCE OF STRUCTURAL MALADJUSTMENT

by

Robert Gordon[1]
Northwestern University

INTRODUCTION

Perhaps the most important single economic issue in Europe today can be linked to the topic of this paper, macroeconomic policy and structural maladjustment. Is it possible for Europe to pursue the macroeconomic policies needed to achieve monetary union despite the existence of structural maladjustments, such as excessive fiscal debt and deficits, underfunded state pension and welfare programmes, state subsidies of inefficient firms, and over-regulated product and labour markets? What are the connections and feedbacks between macro policy and structural reform? Do these connections suggest any new avenues for policy in countries like France that are currently struggling to resolve the conflicts among fiscal stringency required on the route to monetary union, monetary tightness required to maintain a fixed exchange rate, and the political strife with interest groups resisting structural reform?

The paper begins by examining data on major aspects of macroeconomic performance in Europe and the United States. It then turns to a theoretical section that interprets the interactions between macro policy and structural maladjustment in terms of aggregate demand and supply analysis. In this view, the task of macro policy is to control the growth rate of nominal aggregate demand, while structural maladjustment can be viewed as an adverse supply shock, and successful structural reform as a beneficial supply shock. We shall analyse the similarities and differences between the effects of structural maladjustment and adverse supply shocks, such as oil price shocks.

The supply shock model forces us to distinguish between the level and rate of change of structural maladjustment. Structural reform may be viewed as analogous to a negative change in the degree of structural maladjustment. On closer examination some types of structural reform are just as likely to reduce the rate of productivity growth as to raise it. The analysis of demand and supply shocks forces us to distinguish as well between two leading models of aggregate supply – the natural rate hypothesis and the hysteresis model – and a hybrid that combines them. How does the outcome of alternative policy interventions depend on knowing the right model in advance?

The next section of the paper examines feedback from reform to macro policy: countries with more flexible markets may have a more favourable short-term inflation-unemployment trade-off. This is particularly important from the perspective of the hysteresis hypothesis, which implies that a reduction in unemployment may be achieved at the cost of only a finite increase in the inflation rate, the amount of which depends on the slope of the short-run trade-off curve. There is also feedback from macro policy to reform: a policy that leans in the direction of expansion may make it possible to create a political deal with interest groups that resist reform. An expansionary policy also reduces the impact of transition costs from reform.

Most of our discussion of macro policy revolves around monetary policy and exchange rate policy. There is still the need to determine where fiscal policy fits in. Is there still a role for fiscal policy in managing aggregate demand? The theory of the monetary-fiscal mix states that monetary policy mainly controls aggregate demand; fiscal policy mainly influences the real interest rate and hence the rate of long-run capital accumulation and growth.

Should monetary policy be conducted differently in nations that have relatively high ratios of public debt to GDP? When fiscal deficits exceed the level consistent with a stable debt-GDP ratio, the need to run a budget surplus becomes an imperative and requires a stimulative monetary policy to compensate, with the implication that exchange rate stability may not be consistent with fiscal convergence.

The empirical section of the paper examines data on the experience of selected European countries since the 1992 breakdown of ERM, which provides a controlled experiment of the consequences of expansionary aggregate demand policy. We examine the behaviour of nominal GDP growth, as well as the "split" of nominal GDP growth between inflation and real GDP growth, in those countries that experienced major effective exchange rate depreciations in 1992-93 as compared with some of those that did not depreciate. We conclude by developing the implications of the empirical results for future macro policy within Europe and exploring the desirability of a continued push toward monetary union.

THE PRIMARY PUZZLES IN MACROECONOMIC BEHAVIOUR

Inflation, unemployment, and labour's share

We begin by comparing basic macroeconomic indicators for Europe and the United States, in order to identify the puzzles to be explained. Figure 1 displays the well-known divergence in the time series of unemployment rates in Europe and the

United States. In 1995 the unemployment rate for the current members of the European Union (labelled "Europe" in Figure 1) was 11.0 per cent, compared to roughly 2 per cent for the same countries in the early 1960s. The 1995 unemployment rate in the United States was 5.7 per cent, exactly the same as in 1963. The upsurge of European unemployment relative to United States unemployment occurred primarily between 1975 and 1985, suggesting that the search for an explanation should begin with major structural changes that occurred within Europe during that decade.

The major theories that describe the interrelation between the unemployment and inflation rates are the natural rate hypothesis and the hysteresis hypothesis. Inflation rates for the United States and the same set of European countries are displayed in Figure 2. Here we see that the average inflation behaviour of "Europe" has been remarkably similar to that of the United States since the late 1960s, with the European inflation rate exceeding that for the United States by one or two percentage points per year in most years. Given the similarity of the inflation performances, the natural rate hypothesis is consistent with the data only if the natural rate of unemployment was roughly stationary in the United States over the last three decades but increased by roughly as much as the actual unemployment

◆   Figure 1.   **Unemployment rate in the United States and Europe**

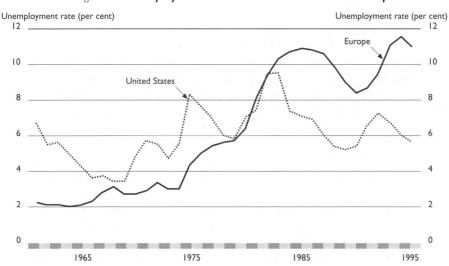

Unemployment rate (per cent)

Unemployment rate (per cent)

Source: Standardised unemployment rates for EU and US from *OECD Economic Outlook*, various issues.

◆   Figure 2.   **Inflation rate in the United States and Europe**

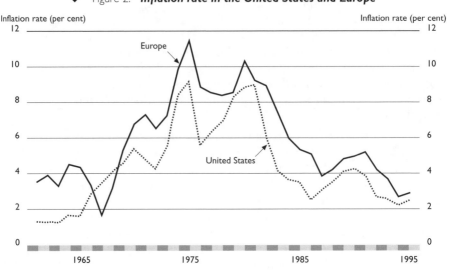

Source: GDP deflator for EU (*OECD National Accounts*, Vol. 1: 1960-1992, Table VI.31) and Chain-Weighted GDP deflator for US (NIPA).

rate in Europe over the same period. This leaves the causes of the increase in the European natural unemployment rate unexplained.

During the early 1980s a popular explanation for the divergence of European and United States unemployment rates was a contrast in labour-market behaviour. The seminal work of Branson-Rotemberg (1980), Sachs (1979), and Bruno-Sachs (1985), emphasised the contrast between real wage rigidity in Europe and real wage flexibility in the United States. Following the early-1970s slowdown of productivity growth shared in common by all industrialised nations, real wage flexibility in the United States allowed the growth of real wages to decelerate in tandem with productivity growth, while real wage rigidity in Europe prevented such a deceleration.

It is easy to assess the validity of this hypothesis by examining data on labour's share in national income. By definition, labour's income share *(S)* is equal to the real wage *(W/P)* divided by output per hour *(Q/H)*. Using lower-case letters for logs, this definition implies that the growth rate of the real wage is equal to the growth rate of productivity plus the growth rate of labour's share:

$$\Delta w - \Delta p = (\Delta q - \Delta h) + \Delta s \qquad (1)$$

Thus any tendency of the growth rate of real wages $(\Delta w - \Delta p)$ to exceed the growth rate of productivity $(\Delta q - \Delta h)$ would be reflected in positive growth in labour's share (Δs). In consequence, the real-wage rigidity hypothesis leads us to expect that labour's share in Europe would have increased relative to that in the United States during 1975-85, the period of the rising relative European unemployment rate. As the cost of labour increased relative to its marginal product, profits would have been squeezed, the demand for labour would have decreased, and unemployment would have increased.

The real-wage rigidity hypothesis regarding Europe has as its counterpart a substantial United States literature on the failure of real wages to grow over the past two decades, despite a positive (albeit small) growth rate of output per hour. In the American view, structural features of United States labour markets account for the failure of real wages to keep pace with productivity. According to equation (1), this common perception implies that the United States wage share must have declined substantially. For zero real wage growth to have been consistent with a 1.0 per cent annual rate of productivity growth, labour's share should have declined at 1.0 per cent per year, for instance from 70 per cent in 1973 to 53 per cent in 1993.

Both the real-wage rigidity hypothesis for Europe as well as the common United States perception of stagnant real wages appear to be the reverse of the truth, as shown by the display of wage shares in Figure 3. These wage share series, constructed by the OECD, include in wage income an imputation for the labour income earned by the self-employed. Far from declining rapidly, the wage share series for North America (dominated by the United States) has remained roughly constant, falling only from 68 per cent in 1973 to 66.5 per cent in 1993. The wage share series for Europe did increase relative to North America during 1974-81, which coincides with the period when the European unemployment rate began its relentless ascent. But since 1981 the European wage share has declined much more, from a 1981 value of 69.3 per cent to 63.4 per cent in 1993.

Thus any effect on unemployment of the high European wage share during the late 1970s should have been more than reversed by the declining wage share during the 1980s and early 1990s. The absence of such a reversal in the natural unemployment rate casts doubt on the original rigid-real-wage hypothesis as a convincing cause of persistently high European unemployment. The difficulty in this explanation is parallel to that in linking the world-wide post-1973 productivity slowdown in the industrialised countries to the oil price shocks of the 1970s, since the oil shocks have now been completely reversed in real terms, while the productivity slowdown has not been reversed in most countries.

Competing with the view that the increased natural rate of unemployment was structural in origin is the hysteresis hypothesis, which postulates that the natural rate is "state dependent," automatically following in the path of the actual unemployment rate like the tail of a dog.[2] The hysteresis hypothesis can explain the

◆ Figure 3. **Wage shares by region, 1970-93**

Source: The OECD Jobs Study (1994), Chart 13, p. 22.

evolution of actual unemployment in Europe by a combination of events that raised the actual unemployment rate, especially adverse supply shocks (*e.g.*, higher oil prices and a temporary increase in labour's share) accompanied by restrictive demand policy. In turn, through hysteresis the natural rate followed in the path of the actual unemployment rate. Because the actual unemployment rate was above the natural rate during the transition process, the inflation rate declined, as shown in Figure 2. To reverse the process, some combination of beneficial supply shocks supported by expansionary demand policy must bring the actual unemployment rate below the natural rate, *i.e.*, the unemployment gap must become negative, in order to "drag down" the natural rate.

As we shall see in Figure 4, none of the major European countries is close to having a negative unemployment gap. The consequence of such hypothetical expansionary policies would be to raise the inflation rate until the economy stabilises at a new equilibrium with a lower actual and natural unemployment rate, and a more rapid rate of inflation. A key issue in evaluating the merits of expansionary policy is to determine the trade-off between inflation and unemployment in the transition to the new equilibrium. The divergent experiences of those countries that dropped out of the ERM in 1992-93 highlight the recent behaviour of the trade-off.

◆   Figure 4.   **Unemployment gaps, 1995**

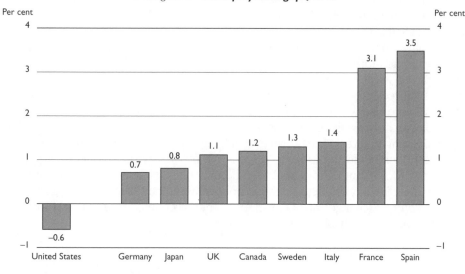

Source: Giorno et al. (1995), Table 1.

Unemployment gaps, structural deficits, and the stabilising deficit ratio

Studies are available for many different countries which provide estimates of the natural rate of unemployment, and of the gap between the actual and natural rates of unemployment. 1995 unemployment gaps for the G7 countries, plus Spain and Sweden, are shown in Figure 4. The source is Giorno et. al. (1995), which uses a method developed by Elmeskov and MacFarlan (1993). The natural rate of unemployment is estimated by solving an equation in which the rate of change of wages is related simply to the unemployment gap; thus the natural unemployment rate is equal to the actual unemployment rate in any year in which wages are neither accelerating nor decelerating. The unemployment gaps in Figure 4 are arrayed between the United States, which in 1995 had a negative unemployment gap and was assessed to be producing actual real GDP in excess of potential real GDP, and at the other extreme France and Spain, with estimated unemployment gaps in excess of 3 per cent. The average gap for Europe is about 2 per cent, and subtracting this from the actual unemployment rate of 11 per cent (Figure 1) implies that the natural unemployment rate for Europe in 1995 was about 9 per cent, much higher than the estimate of 6 per cent for the United States.[3]

Using a version of Okun's law to translate unemployment gaps into gaps between actual and potential output, Giorno *et. al.* (1995) also compute structural budget deficits, *i.e.*, the budget deficit that would be incurred if the economy was operating at potential output instead of at actual output. Figure 5 displays the 1995 estimates for the same set of countries covered by Figure 4 and shows that most of the fiscal problems of the high-deficit European countries are structural rather than recession-induced. None of the European countries have actual deficits that are more than double their structural deficits. Of course, if the natural rate of unemployment were lower in these countries, the structural deficits would be correspondingly lower. This provides a link between the hysteresis hypothesis and the fiscal dilemma facing Europe. There is the possibility that monetary expansion could pull down both the actual and natural rates of unemployment, and thus reduce the structural deficits without politically difficult budget-cutting. But this would require exchange rate depreciation, the acceptance of additional inflation, and the abandonment of monetary union.

◆ Figure 5. **Actual and structural budget deficit, 1995**
As a per cent of GDP

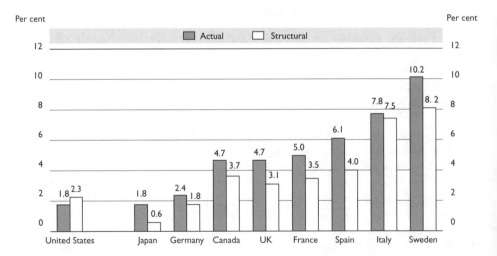

Source: Giorno *et al.* (1995), Table 6.

The consequence of large fiscal deficits is, of course, an increase in the ratio of government debt to GDP. Currently for the major European countries this ratio ranges from 52 per cent for France to 125 per cent for Italy, as shown in Figure 6. A standard relation states that stability of the debt-GDP ratio requires that the deficit-GDP ratio be equal to the growth rate of nominal GDP times the debt-GDP ratio. Table 1 compares the actual and structural deficits for the same countries included in Figure 6 with a computed "stability value" of the deficit-GDP ratio. The stability ratio is the current debt-GDP ratio from Figure 6, multiplied by the "warranted" growth rate of nominal GDP, which in turn is set equal to the rate of potential output growth plus the current rate of inflation.[4] As shown in the first column of Table 1, for the United States, in which nominal GDP growth of 5.0 per cent is consistent with steady inflation and steady output growth at the potential rate, the required deficit-GDP ratio is 2.3 per cent (.46 times .05 equals .023), a bit above the 1995 actual deficit and exactly equal to the 1995 structural deficit. Hence the figure displayed on line 5 for the United States is –0.5, indicating that the actual deficit is smaller than the stability value, implying a slight shrinkage in 1995 of the debt/GDP ratio, while the figure displayed on line 7 is 0.0, indicating that the structural deficit is exactly equal to the stability value.

◆   Figure 6.   **General government gross debt, 1995**
Per cent ratio to GDP

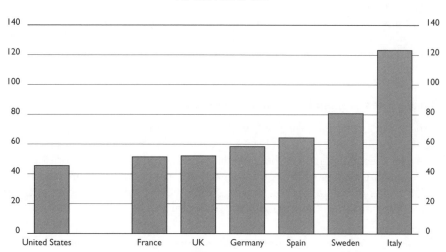

Note: United States is net debt while European countries are gross debt.
Source: European Commission.

Table 1. **1995 gaps between actual and structural deficit/GDP ratios and deficit/
GDP ratio required to stabilise debt/GDP ratio**

	US	France	UK	Germany	Spain	Sweden	Italy
Debt-GDP ratio [1]	46.0	51.5	52.5	58.8	64.8	81.4	124.9
Warranted nominal GDP growth [2]	5.0	4.1	4.2	5.0	7.9	4.9	7.1
Stability value of deficit/GDP ratio [3]	2.3	2.1	2.2	2.9	5.1	4.0	8.9
Actual deficit [4]	1.8	5.0	4.7	2.4	6.1	10.2	7.8
Actual deficit minus stability value	−0.5	2.9	2.5	−0.5	1.0	6.2	−1.1
Structural deficit [4]	2.3	3.5	3.1	1.8	4.0	8.2	7.5
Structural deficit minus stability value	0.0	1.4	0.9	−1.1	1.1	4.2	−1.4

1. Figure 6.
2. 1995 Potential Output Growth from Giorno *et al.* (1995), Table 2, plus 1995 rate of change of GDP deflator, from IMF World Economic Outlook, October 1995, Table A-9.
3. Line 1 times line 2, calculated as per cent.
4. Figure 5.

Table 1 includes similar calculations for the other European countries covered by Figures 4-6. Line 5 shows that all but Germany and Italy have actual deficits well in excess of the stability value, implying continued growth in the debt-GDP ratio. The surprising inclusion of Italy in the stability group results from a combination of a huge debt/GDP ratio and relatively rapid inflation (and hence high warranted nominal GDP growth). The list of countries with structural deficits in excess of the stability value on line 7 is the same as the list of countries with positive gaps on line 5, although of course the debt/GDP ratio would grow more slowly if these countries adopted expansionary policies to eliminate their output and unemployment gaps.

Exchange rates, demand growth, and inflation

The macroeconomic policy discussion within Europe over the past few years has been dominated by the Maastricht conditions for monetary union, and the debate over the significance of the breakdown of the ERM in 1992. Figure 7 plots the effective exchange rates of the four largest European countries from 1981 to 1995. The history has three stages: convergence from 1981 to 1987, the ERM period from 1987 to 1992, and then the breakdown period starting in 1992.

Subsequently we will return to the recent period and ask how the post-1992 divergence of exchange rates influenced nominal GDP growth and the split of nominal GDP growth between real GDP growth and inflation. A preview for the four largest countries is provided in Figures 8 and 9. Many different factors influence nominal GDP growth, and we can focus on several major episodes. The major events

◆ Figure 7. **Nominal effective exchange rates**
1981: Q1 – 1995: Q2 (1990 = 100)

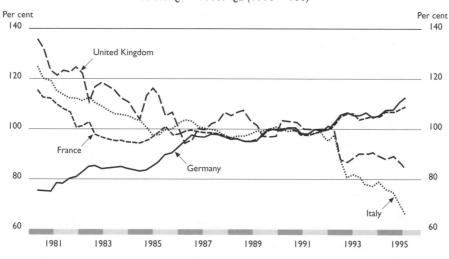

Source: European Commission.

◆ Figure 8. **Nominal gross domestic product**
1981: Q1 – 1995: Q2
Four quarter moving average rate of change

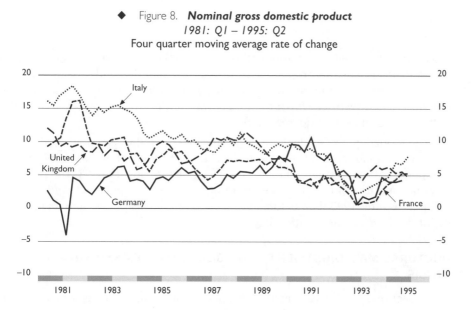

Source: European Commission.

◆ Figure 9. **GDP implicit price deflator**
1981: Q1 – 1995: Q2
Four quarter moving average rate of change

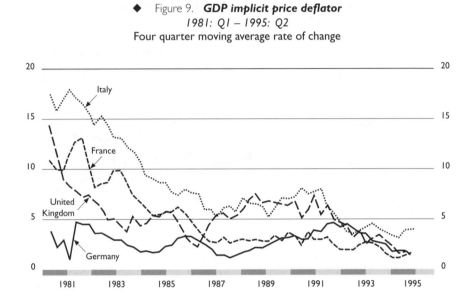

Source: European Commission.

that occurred after 1987 were the British boom of 1987-89, the German reunification boom of 1990-91, and the divergence of British nominal demand growth from the French rate after 1992. Italy presents a puzzle, with the appearance of convergence of nominal GDP growth closer to the French rate rather than divergence after the 1992 Italian exchange rate depreciation.

Further puzzles are evident in the behaviour of inflation rates in Figure 9. French and German inflation rates were relatively close together after 1987, except for the period of the German reunification and its aftermath, 1991-93. The puzzle is that British and Italian inflation rates were much closer to the French and German inflation rates after 1992 than before. We shall return to this puzzle, and its implications for demand management policy.

STRUCTURAL MALADJUSTMENT AND AGGREGATE DEMAND-SUPPLY ANALYSIS

This section links the two main topics of the paper, macro policy and structural maladjustment, to several simple analytical tools and theories. These include the distinction between demand and supply shocks, the natural rate hypothesis, the hysteresis hypothesis, and the response of demand-management policy to supply shocks.

Demand shocks and the natural rate hypothesis

We begin with the familiar expectational Phillips curve diagram in Figure 10, which plots the inflation rate against the unemployment rate. If the natural rate hypothesis is valid, the long-run Phillips curve (LP) is a vertical line rising above the natural unemployment rate (U*). The initial short-run Phillips curve (SP₀) is drawn on the assumption that the expected inflation rate is p^e_0, which in turn is equal to the actual inflation rate (p_0), the point in the vertical dimension at which the SP curve intersects the vertical LP line. The SP curve shifts whenever there is a change in the expected inflation rate (p^e). The SP curve can also shift upward in the case of an adverse supply shock, and down in the case of a beneficial supply shock. We will shortly link the concept of structural maladjustment to that of supply shocks.

The influence of aggregate demand is shown by the DG (for Demand Growth) schedule. The position of the DG schedule is determined by the excess of the rate of nominal GDP growth over potential output growth, or "excess nominal GDP growth" (x), as well as the previous period's unemployment rate. When x is equal to the inflation rate, then by definition actual output growth is equal to potential output growth, and the unemployment rate is fixed. When x exceeds the inflation rate, then

◆ Figure 10. **Expectational Phillips Curve**

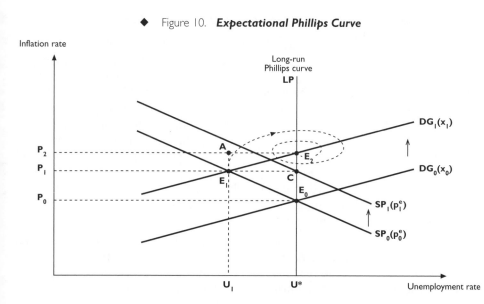

actual output growth exceeds potential output growth, and the unemployment rate declines.[5]

Consider the effect of a permanent acceleration of excess nominal GDP growth from x_0 to x_1. The DG line shifts upward as shown, and the economy initially moves to point E_1. With adaptive expectations and an adjustment coefficient of unity, the expected inflation rate is equal to last period's actual inflation rate. Hence in the subsequent period the SP line shifts upward to cross the LP line at a point (marked C) directly to the right of point E_1. In the subsequent period the DG schedule shifts to intersect the long-run rate of inflation directly above the initial equilibrium point (at the point marked A).[6] If the rate of excess nominal GDP growth is maintained at x_1 permanently, the economy will go through the loop shown by the dashed spiral line.

This diagram summarises the basic results implied by the natural rate hypothesis. A permanent acceleration of excess nominal GDP growth causes a permanent acceleration of inflation of the same amount after a transition period in which the inflation rate oscillates above and below its long-run equilibrium value. Maintaining an unemployment rate (U_1) below the natural unemployment rate (U^*) requires a steady acceleration of excess nominal GDP growth and results in a steady acceleration of the inflation rate. The process is symmetric if the short-run Phillips curve is linear, as shown in Figure 10. A deceleration of inflation requires a permanent deceleration of excess nominal GDP growth, results in oscillating inflation, and a temporary period of unemployment above the natural rate.

Supply shocks and the interpretation of structural maladjustment

Figure 11 uses the same model to examine the effects of an adverse supply shock. The shock is viewed as shifting the SP schedule upwards without changing its slope. If the shock is an agricultural crop failure, the relative price of farm products will temporarily increase, and the initial SP_0 schedule will shift upward to SP'. But after the cause of the agricultural problem is over and normal conditions return, the relative price of farm products will decline. The economy will temporarily enjoy a beneficial supply shock due to the relative price decline, and the SP curve will shift down to SP'' during the transition period back to normal prices. The OPEC oil shocks of 1974-75 and 1979-81 raised the relative price of oil for a substantial period. In this case the upward shift of the SP curve to SP' is followed by a return to the initial position (SP_0) when the transition to the higher relative price is complete, ignoring the impact of shifting inflation expectations.

A central case useful for the analysis of supply shocks is a situation in which excess nominal GDP growth remains unchanged at x_0, and so for the initial transition period the DG schedule remains fixed. Then with an adverse supply shock the economy would go initially to point L, with higher inflation and higher unemploy-

◆ Figure 11. *Impact of an adverse supply shock*

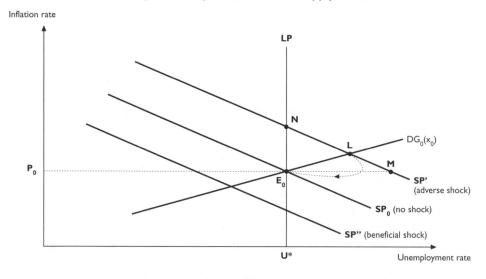

ment. Even if in the subsequent period the supply shock goes away, the *SP* schedule will stay above its initial position if expectations are formed as we assumed previously in Figure 10, reflecting the response of expected inflation to the higher actual inflation caused by the supply shock. Gradually higher unemployment will push down the inflation rate, and the economy will slide back to the initial position by the route shown by the dashed line.

But policymakers will be tempted to fight the unemployment caused by the supply shock. If they accelerate nominal demand growth sufficiently, *i.e.*, pursue a policy of "accommodating" the supply shock, the economy will avoid an increase in unemployment but at the cost of a permanent increase in inflation. The economy will arrive at a point like N, with both actual and expected inflation equal to the permanently higher rate of excess nominal GDP growth. The shift from a point like E_0 to a point like *N* provides a realistic description of the process by which the United States made a transition from 5 per cent inflation in the early 1970s to 10 per cent inflation in the late 1970s.

The opposite extreme is a policy of "extinguishing" the supply shock. Nominal GDP growth is dropped sufficiently to push the economy rightward to a point like *M*. Because inflation does not accelerate, there is no adjustment of expectations. Eventually, when the initial transition is completed (*i.e.*, the relative price of oil settles down to its new higher level), the *SP* curve will shift back to its initial position. However, excess nominal GDP growth has been diminished, and if this reduction is maintained, there will be a permanent reduction in the rate of inflation in the subsequent transition. In short the policymakers face a trade-off in reacting to supply shocks, with a neutral (point *L*) or extinguishing (point *M*) policy implying a temporary increase in unemployment, but an accommodating policy (point *N*) implying a permanent increase of inflation. The contrast between the effects of accommodating and extinguishing policies helps to explain why Germany did not experience an increase in its inflation rate in the late 1970s, whereas the United States and several other European countries did experience an acceleration of inflation that persisted until the major monetary restriction of the early 1980s began.

Numerous events can be fit into the framework of supply shocks and demand responses. In particular, Franz-Gordon (1992) show that a change in labour's share, such as that implied by the real-wage rigidity hypothesis discussed in Part II, shifts the inflation-unemployment relation in exactly the same way as a change in the relative price of oil. The *SP* schedule shifts upward during the period when labour's share is increasing. Whether or not it returns to its original position depends on the degree of accommodation, if any, and the adjustment of expectations of inflation.

Thus far the analysis does not allow for a permanent increase in unemployment, simply because the natural rate hypothesis is maintained and we have not allowed for an increase in the natural rate of unemployment. This could occur in two ways. First, the nature of the structural maladjustment could be to impair the functioning of the labour market sufficiently to increase the natural rate. Second, there could be a hysteresis mechanism in place which automatically translates a period of high actual unemployment into an increase in the natural rate of unemployment.

Krugman (1994) asks whether generous European welfare policies, combined with a relatively high reservation wage (or legal minimum wage) could explain the rise in the natural unemployment rate in Europe. Such policies could explain high unemployment but not *rising* unemployment, as was observed between the early 1970s and late 1980s, unless the benefits had increased significantly. But European welfare states were already generous back in the early 1970s when unemployment was relatively low. Instead, he argues that the facts are consistent with a twist in the demand for labour, combining a decrease in the demand for low-productivity workers and an increase in the demand for high productivity workers. If reservation wages do not change, or if there is a minimum wage that does not change, then the decreased demand for low-productivity workers will be translated into higher unemployment rate than reduced relative wages. This hypothesis is consistent with the facts that long-term unemployment of young people has increased significantly in many European countries, while in the United States the same demand twist has emerged in the form of an increase in the inequality of wage rates. In searching for explanations of the demand twist, Krugman rejects international competition from low-wage countries, which he argues would change the sectoral mix of high skill relative to low skill employment. Instead, he favours the explanation that there has been a generalised skill-biased shift in technology that has affected all industries.

Krugman places his emphasis on skill-biased technology shifts by comparing the evolution of European and American labour markets. In contrast, Bean (1994) argues that no one factor appears significant enough fully to explain the increase in European unemployment and concludes that there must be multiple causes, rather than a single cause. Gordon (1995), like Krugman, uses the differing performance of the American and European economies as a criterion to assess the plausibility of a long list of potential causes of a rising natural unemployment rate in Europe in contrast to a stable (and recently declining) natural rate in the United States. He centres his analysis on a standard labour market diagram in which, following Layard *et. al.* (1991), short-term equilibrium occurs at the intersection of a labour demand curve with a positively sloped "wage setting curve" which displays the wage that emerges from the bargaining process at alternative levels of labour input. What factors could have caused the European wage-setting curve to shift upwards or the United States wage-setting curve to shift downwards?

- An increase in the tax wedge. Since firms pay pre-tax wages but workers receive after-tax wages, any increase in payroll or income taxes can shift up the wage-setting schedule. The tax wedge in the Europe is both higher and increased more than in the United States between the late 1960s and late 1980s (Bean, 1994, p. 586).

- The rigid real wage hypothesis seems consistent with the observed bulge in the European labour share between 1974 and 1982 (Figure 3 above), which coincides with the period of most rapid increase in the natural rate of unemployment.

- A leading candidate for causing divergent behaviour across the Atlantic is the marked decline in United States trade union membership, from 26.2 per cent in 1977 to 15.8 per cent in 1993 (union members as a fraction of wage and salary workers).

- The real minimum wage has fallen sharply in the United States while rising in some European countries, particularly France.

- Both legal and illegal immigration of unskilled workers into the United States has added substantially to the supply of unskilled labour and plausibly added to downward pressure on the United States wage-setting schedule.

- Product market regulation in Europe, particularly German shop-closing hours, reduce the demand for unskilled labour as contrasted to the demand that would emerge with an unregulated product market.

These six factors are complementary to Krugman's skill-biased demand twist and provide a convincing set of microeconomic phenomena that can be summarised by the phrase "structural maladjustment". We will return below to the interactions of structural maladjustment and reform with demand management policy and with the evolution of productivity growth.

The hysteresis hypothesis

The second approach to explaining a permanent rise in the natural rate of unemployment is the hysteresis hypothesis. It can be shown formally that the hysteresis hypothesis is equivalent to replacing the *level* of the unemployment gap as the driving variable in the inflation equation by the *change* of the unemployment rate.[7] It contradicts the basic implication of the natural rate hypothesis that demand-management policy cannot permanently alter the unemployment rate. Instead, it revives the original Phillips trade-off between inflation and unemployment. A demand-induced recession boosts unemployment, which in turn boosts the natural rate. Inflation stabilises at a new lower level when the new higher natural rate converges to the new higher actual unemployment rate. In reverse, the hypothesis implies that demand-management policy always is faced with the choice of achieving a reduction of unemployment at the cost of a finite, not ever-accelerating, increase in the inflation rate. But, unlike the original stable Phillips trade-off, the trade-off schedule available to policymakers at any given time depends on all of past history. The experience of high unemployment implies that European policymakers cannot push the unemployment rate as low as they could were they taking the same policy actions as fifteen or twenty-five years ago.

If hysteresis is present in fact, this calls for a theoretical explanation.[8] The insider-outsider model of wage determination shows how employed insiders are able to convert a favourable demand or supply shock into wage increases for themselves rather than into new jobs for the unemployed. The target real-wage bargaining model goes in the same direction. In addition to total unemployment in the Phillips curve approach, nominal wage increases are influenced in addition by the deviation of real wages or of labour's income share from target levels. If the target level of labour's share responds hysteresis-like to its actual level, then any pressure on wages stemming from deviations of the actual share from the target share gradually disappears.

Implications of structural maladjustment and hysteresis

How can the structural maladjustment and hysteresis hypotheses be interpreted in the diagrammatic framework previously introduced? In Figure 12 we consider a possibility that might have occurred in the 1970s and early 1980s, the conjunction of a temporary adverse supply shock caused by higher oil prices and/or an increase in labour's income share, with a permanent increase in the natural rate of unemployment caused by Krugman's labour demand twist toward more highly skilled workers, together with some combination of my previous list of supply-side impediments, including an increase in the real minimum wage and an increase in the tax wedge. In Figure 12 the temporary shock is indicated by the upward shift in the *SP* curve, and the permanent increase in the natural rate by the rightward shift in the *LP* line.

What choices are open to policymakers? If the growth rate of nominal GDP relative to potential output growth *(x)* remains unchanged, the economy initially moves to point *L*, just as in Figure 11. Once the source of the supply shock is removed *(e.g.*, the relative price of oil or labour's share stabilises at a new level), in Figure 11 inflation and unemployment returned to their original levels. But in Figure 12 there no longer is a positive unemployment gap at point L. Inflation is higher than excess nominal GDP growth, and so output must grow more slowly than potential output, and the unemployment rate must rise relative to the new higher natural rate. The economy goes through the disinflationary loop shown by the dashed line in Figure 12, initially experiencing a further rise in unemployment and then a partial recovery to the equilibrium level U_1^*.

Both the structural maladjustment approach and the hysteresis approach can explain the observed increase in Europe's natural rate of unemployment. Can they be distinguished? One approach is to estimate wage and price equations to determine the validity of the condition for "pure hysteresis", namely the absence of a "level" effect of the unemployment gap. In one such attempt, Franz and Gordon

◆ Figure 12. ***Temporary shocks and structural maladjustment***

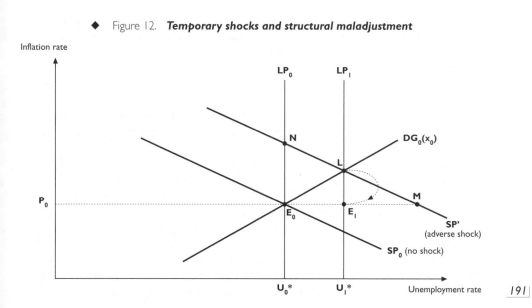

(1992) found that hysteresis was partial rather than full in both Germany and the United States, since both level and rate of change effects are highly significant in both countries. Because the German and United States coefficients are so similar, yet the evolution of unemployment in the two countries is so different, there appears to be little potential through this route for explaining that evolution. If hysteresis is partial (*i.e.*, inflation depends on both the level and change of the unemployment gap), it provides no explanation of a permanent increase in unemployment, since the equilibrium properties of the economy are the same as with a straightforward natural rate model in which inflation depends only on the level of the unemployment gap.

The structural maladjustment approach as depicted in Figure 12 has the appeal of realism. Oil shocks, an increase in labour's share, and a skill-biased demand twist, all began to occur in the 1970s. By the time the oil shocks and the increase in labour's share had been reversed, the natural rate of unemployment had been increased by aspects of the European welfare system that prevented the demand twist from being translated into greater inequality of wages, as it was in the United States and to some extent in the United Kingdom.

INTERACTIONS BETWEEN MACRO POLICY AND STRUCTURAL MALADJUSTMENT

Responses of demand management to successful structural reform

We can now discuss interactions between structural reform and macro demand-management policy. If the sources of structural maladjustment are identified and microeconomic policy reform begins to reverse their effects, how should demand management policy respond?[9] Our previous framework is easiest to interpret if, as in Figure 13, we assume that successful structural reform instantaneously shifts the LP line leftward. We have relabeled the points on the diagram, so that the economy's initial high level of the natural rate is at U_0^* and moves leftward suddenly to U_1^*. Because the unemployment gap is now zero at point E_1 there is a new SP_1 schedule that has shifted to the left at the initial inflation rate and expected inflation rate. However, the economy does not move instantly from point E_0 to E_1. Instead, it moves to point A, which is at the intersection of the new SP_1 line with the initial DG_0 line, which holds fixed the initial rate of excess nominal GDP growth (x_0). At point A inflation has declined below the initial value of x, and this allows actual output growth to rise above the rate of potential output growth. Successive periods in which inflation remains below x_0 allow a temporary acceleration of output growth, which in turn allows the actual unemployment rate to decline to the new equilibrium point E_1. An alternative policy could achieve the same output path by temporarily raising excess nominal GDP growth by enough to maintain a constant

◆ Figure 13. **Structural reform and demand management**

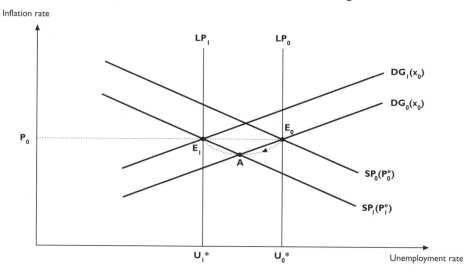

inflation rate, thus allowing the economy to move straight left from E_0 to E_1 rather than following the curved dashed path drawn through point A.

How can such a policy procedure be carried out in practice? The United States Federal Reserve Board appears to follow a policy procedure that could be interpreted as targeting the unemployment rate consistent with steady nonaccelerating inflation, *i.e.*, adjusting interest rates to keep the actual unemployment rate as close as possible to the natural unemployment rate (U^*). Since the Fed believes that the effects of its immediate instrument, the Federal Funds rate, take roughly one year to influence the unemployment rate, it leans toward raising the Federal Funds rate when its best forecast of the actual unemployment rate one year from now is below its estimated value of U^*. Symmetrically, it leans toward reducing the Federal Funds rate when its best forecast of the actual unemployment rate one year from now is above its estimated value of U^*.

Although U^* may not move around as much as the actual unemployment rate, but it is not immutably carved in stone as a single precise number. When inflation turns out to be lower than the value forecast by the Fed's staff or a consensus of private forecasters, as in much of 1995, the Fed concludes that U^* has declined from the value previously assumed by forecasters. This makes it more likely that the Fed will reduce interest rates and less likely that it will raise them. Accordingly, a low realised value of inflation or a high realised value of unemployment can both lead to lower long-term interest rates as speculators guess that the Fed's next move will be to reduce short-term interest rates.

The Fed appears to act as if it is operating in a closed economy environment, and it does not appear to adjust its operation of this policy procedure in response to movements of the exchange rate of the dollar. It would therefore appear that an attempt by an individual central bank within Europe to emulate the Fed's procedure could lead to exchange rate fluctuations sufficiently large to compromise the movement toward Monetary Union. A policymaker in Europe attempting to reduce the actual unemployment rate in response to a lower natural unemployment rate (achieved by a successful microeconomic reform policy) would notice first that inflation is turning out to be below forecast, and would react by reducing interest rates to stimulate the domestic economy in order to push down the actual unemployment rate. The central aspect of this policy is taking the good news on inflation to be a signal that stimulative policies should be adopted to reduce the unemployment rate, rather than just "accommodating" the lower inflation rate by maintaining the existing unemployment rate.

Structural reform and productivity growth

The analysis of Figure 13 did not take into account any effect of structural reform on the growth rate of potential output, which would reduce x (the excess of nominal GDP growth over potential output growth) if actual nominal GDP growth were to remain unchanged. Uncertainty regarding the effect of structural reform on potential output growth stems from the conflict between two forces. Pure efficiency gains should raise productivity growth. But reforms in labour markets that make labour less expensive for employers to hire, such as the reduction or elimination of the minimum wage, may raise the demand for labour at a given level of output and reduce productivity. The same effect would be expected of particular product market reforms, especially a loosening of German regulations on shop-closing hours that would trade consumer convenience for an increase in the labour requirements needed to achieve a given total of real retail sales.

The interactions between changes in the degree of structural maladjustment, both in an adverse and beneficial direction, are explored in Gordon (1995b). The evolution of European unemployment is portrayed as resulting from a set of adverse wage-setting shocks (e.g., an increase in the real effective minimum wage) which initially raises unemployment and, by shifting the economy Northwest up a labour demand curve, also boosts the marginal and average products of labour. This is then followed by a profit squeeze and a period of disinvestment, which eliminates the productivity gain but further increases the unemployment rate. Reversing this process by achieving a beneficial wage-setting shock (e.g., a reduction in the real effective minimum wage) would initially reduce unemployment and both the marginal and average products of labour. This would then be followed by a profits boom and an increase of investment, which would offset the initial productivity loss and further reduce the unemployment rate.

Feedback from macro policy to structural reform and *vice versa*

The analysis of Figure 13 emphasises the opportunity for macro policy to respond to a reduction in the natural rate of unemployment achieved by structural reform. A policy response that stabilises inflation and responds to a reduction in the natural rate as an opportunity to accelerate nominal demand growth differs from a passive policy in which excess nominal GDP growth *(x)* is stabilised.

This policy choice may influence the likelihood and magnitude of structural reform. When there is strong political opposition to such reform measures as reducing the minimum wage and reducing government subsidies, the willingness of central bankers and finance ministers to respond aggressively to successful reforms may make those reforms more likely. There is potential for a political deal in which the demand-management authorities promise to lean toward lower interest rates and faster nominal demand growth, in trade for the willingness of political interest groups to support those reform measures that appear to have the greatest change of reducing the natural unemployment rate. Demand expansion, by creating jobs, may also reduce the transition costs of reform policies which create temporary unemployment through the required restructuring of a particular industry that, for instance, has been overstaffed as a result of previous state ownership and subsidies (the "olive-belt" airlines come to mind).

Another related feedback is from monetary policy to fiscal policy. Demand expansion which reduces the unemployment gap brings the actual government budget deficit closer to the structural deficits displayed in Figure 5. A successful deal in which demand expansion goes hand in hand with structural reform may succeed in reducing the natural rate of unemployment and hence the structural deficits themselves. Reducing the deficit then raises the potential for using the fiscal dividend to reduce tax rates and hence the tax wedge, at least in those countries which are not on an explosive track for the debt-GDP ratio.

There is feedback in the reverse direction as well. Countries with more flexible labour markets may have a more favourable inflation-unemployment trade-off, *i.e.*, a flatter *SP* schedule in Figures 10-13. This is particularly important from the perspective of the hysteresis hypothesis, which implies that a reduction in unemployment may be achieved at the cost of only a finite increase in the inflation rate, the amount of which depends on the slope of the short-run trade-off curve. The United States, with its flexible labour market, has a very flat short-run trade-off. Current estimates show that a one-year sustained reduction of the actual unemployment rate by one full percentage point below the natural unemployment rate raises the inflation rate by only 0.35 of a percentage point after one year (Gordon, 1995a, Table 1).

POLICY LESSONS FROM THE 1992-93 ERM BREAKDOWN

An important controlled experiment was carried out in Europe in 1992-93 when several important countries, particularly Italy, Portugal, Spain, Sweden, and the United Kingdom, broke away from the ERM and achieved substantial depreciations of their currencies against the countries which remained aligned with the Deutsche mark, including France, the Benelux countries, Austria, and Switzerland. Some European analysts have previously believed that depreciation by any individual country is futile, since any transitory output gains soon would be eroded by an acceleration of inflation that will soon cause the competitive gains from the exchange depreciation to evaporate. In its most extreme form, this view holds that countries do not have any control, past a transition period of a year or two, over their real exchange rates.

A pessimistic interpretation of the outcome of the 1992-93 divergence is provided by some authors. DeGrauwe (1995, p. 9) focuses on the two cases of Italy and Spain. He points to the temporary nature of the competitive gains. While initially the sharp depreciations "did not affect inflation very much in these countries (mainly because of the recession), since 1994 inflation differentials with Germany have started to increase significantly". He concludes that in order for Italy and Spain to guide their inflation rates to the differential prescribed by the Maastricht Treaty, a new policy of "painful disinflation" would have to begin. Since he views the prospect of success of such policies as low, he thinks that "the door to monetary union will be shut for a long time for these countries".

DeGrauwe's treatment is misleading, for numerous reasons. He focuses only on two depreciating countries. He greatly exaggerates the acceleration of inflation in those countries by comparing their inflation rates only with Germany, failing to note that the German inflation rate was temporarily high in 1992-93 as a result of the aftermath of the reunification boom. A more balanced appraisal would look at a set of countries that depreciated and compare them with a set of countries *other than Germany* that did not depreciate. The omission of Germany is crucial, because the time path of its disinflation in 1994-95 makes the inflation differential of any other country with Germany a misleading indicator of the inflation differential of that country with all countries other than Germany.

The results of the analysis are summarised in Table 2. The five appreciating countries (not including Germany) are Austria, Belgium, France, Netherlands, and Switzerland. On average these countries experienced a nominal effective appreciation of 10.2 percentage points, from exchange rate indexes of 99.5 in 1992:Q2 to 109.7 in 1995:Q2. In contrast the depreciating countries – Italy, Portugal, Spain,

Sweden, and the United Kingdom – experienced an average depreciation of 22.2 points, from an average index value of 99.1 in 1992:Q2 to 76.9 in 1995:Q2. All of the average values in Table 2 are weighted across the five countries in each group using Summers-Heston 1985 PPP weights. Thus among the appreciating countries, the weight of France is 59 per cent. Among the depreciating countries, the respective weights of Italy, Spain, and the United Kingdom are 36.2, 17.0, and 37.2 per cent.

Both groups of countries enjoyed an acceleration of nominal GDP growth, a deceleration of inflation, and thus an even greater acceleration of real GDP growth. But there the similarity stops. The acceleration of nominal GDP growth in the depreciating countries exceeded that in the appreciating countries by 1.3 percentage points. *Yet none of this was absorbed by inflation; inflation actually decelerated more in the depreciating countries than the appreciating countries.* And as a result

Table 2. **Change in effective exchange rates, and growth rates of nominal GDP, real GDP, and GDP deflator, 1992-95**

Five appreciating countries and five depreciating countries

	Appreciating countries	Depreciating countries	Difference, between depreciating and appreciating
Effective nominal exchange rate			
1992: Q2	99.5	99.1	−0.4
1995: Q2	109.7	76.9	−32.8
1995-1992	10.2	−22.2	−32.4
Per cent change in nominal GDP			
1992	4.2	5.0	0.8
1995	4.6	6.7	2.1
1995-1992	0.4	1.7	1.3
Per cent change in real GDP			
1992	1.7	0.2	−1.5
1995	2.7	2.9	0.2
1995-1992	1.0	2.7	1.7
Per cent change in GDP deflator			
1992	2.5	4.8	2.3
1995	1.9	3.8	1.9
1995-1992	−0.6	−1.0	−0.4

Notes: Appreciating countries are Austria, Belgium, France, the Netherlands and Switzerland.
Depreciating countries are Italy, Portugal, Spain, Sweden and the United Kingdom.
All data are aggregated using 1985 Summers-Heston GDP weights.
Source: Nominal and real GDP deflator growth rates are from IMF World Economic Outlook, October 1995, Tables A2 and A9.

the acceleration of real GDP growth in the depreciating countries exceeded that in the depreciating countries by 1.7 percentage point.

It is implausible that this favourable outcome for the depreciating countries could continue forever, but the IMF forecasts for 1996 (from the same source as used for Table 2) show no acceleration of inflation to be predicted for the same average of five depreciating countries. Thus it appears that the depreciating countries have discovered a "macroeconomic free lunch", an improvement in competitiveness and a route to macroeconomic expansion without inflation. The implication is that there is substantial room for individual nations in Europe to reduce their unemployment gaps and their actual budget deficits through expansionary monetary policy. The inevitable depreciation in the nominal exchange rate will translate into a durable depreciation in the real exchange rate and an improvement in competitiveness.

With inflation in Germany at only 2 per cent, some of which doubtless reflects the well-known upward bias in price indexes, there is ample room for Germany to lead the remaining nations tied to its exchange rate into a further expansion of nominal GDP growth. The experience of the depreciating nations suggests that the "split" of additional nominal GDP growth between output growth and inflation is highly favourable under present conditions. Stated another way, the benign behaviour of inflation in Europe suggests that the natural rate of unemployment has begun to decline, just as the Federal Reserve believes has occurred within the United States.

CONCLUSION

The management of demand policy interacts with structural maladjustment, both when maladjustment is getting worse, as in the 1970s and early 1980s, and when successful structural reforms reduce the influence of structural maladjustment and allow a decrease in the natural (i.e., constant-inflation) rate of unemployment. In our interpretation a combination of structural factors, rather than a single "silver bullet", explains the substantial increase in Europe's natural unemployment during the decade 1975-85 and the divergence of that natural rate from the stationary or even declining natural rate in the United States. In the 1970s two supply shocks, in the form of higher real oil prices and an increase in labour's share in national income, pushed European economies in the direction of higher inflation and higher unemployment. Reactions of central banks varied, with monetary accommodation in some countries – but not others – leading to a substantial divergence of inflation rates in Europe by the early 1980s.

These two supply shocks, both of which were temporary and had their influence reversed in the mid-1980s, combined with more deeply entrenched structural maladjustments to boost the European natural unemployment rate from low single digits in the early 1970s to nearly 10 per cent by 1985. While real oil prices and labour's income share declined subsequently, the natural rate did not. This reflects the role of other longer-lasting maladjustments, especially inflexible real wages for the unskilled who were harmed by skill-biased technical change, and this inflexibility in turn reflects three dimensions along which Europe (on average if not for every country) differs from the United States – high and rising tax wedges, more powerful unions, and a higher and (in some countries) rising real minimum wage.

This account does not place much emphasis on hysteresis. Empirical research does not support the "pure hysteresis" view that requires the absence of level effects of the unemployment gap in dynamic wage and price adjustment equations. The most plausible channel by which hysteresis operated was through feedback from the other sources of maladjustment to low capital accumulation, with the result that the capacity utilisation rate in Europe has been roughly stationary despite the rise in the natural unemployment rate. Stated differently, Europe no longer has sufficient capital to employ fully its existing labour force.

The paper stresses two-way interactions between structural reform and macro policy. With flexible labour markets, the short-run inflation-unemployment trade-off is likely to be favourable, providing an incentive for policymakers to expand aggregate demand. The benign effect of the British depreciation in 1992 on the inflation rate provides one example of the potential payoff of more flexible labour markets. In turn, the promise by policymakers that they will encourage a decline in unemployment in response to good news on inflation can be used to strike a political deal with political interests opposed to the introduction or extension of structural reform. Expansionary monetary policy also provides relief on the fiscal front, both by reducing the unemployment gap and bringing the actual budget deficit closer to the structural budget deficit, but also, by encouraging structural reform, potentially reducing the natural unemployment rate and therefore the structural budget deficit itself.

In 1992-93 several European countries dropped out of the ERM to pursue more expansionary monetary policies. The difference in the performance of these countries and those countries which maintained a peg between their currencies and the Deutsche mark provides an important test case of the consequences of expansionary monetary policy. Not surprisingly, the depreciating nations by 1995 enjoyed a substantial acceleration of nominal GDP growth relative to the nations that did not depreciate. But, surprisingly, they enjoyed an even greater deceleration of inflation, so that their growth rate of real GDP accelerated more than their growth rate of nominal GDP.

This augurs well for a favourable outcome of expansionary demand policy. It may be that the natural unemployment rate has begun to decline significantly in Europe, and that this explains why inflation has continued to decelerate in countries which have depreciated their exchange rates significantly. Job creation in those countries creates an environment favourable to continued success in structural reform.

The set of issues addressed in this paper seems a long way from the depressing litany of contractionary demand decisions currently being made in numerous European countries in the name of the Maastricht criteria. Some countries are on an explosive path for the debt-GDP ratio and need to bring their fiscal house in order. An important lesson can be drawn from the traditional textbook discussion of the fiscal-monetary mix, that a shift toward tighter fiscal policy need not reduce output or raise unemployment if accompanied by a shift toward easier monetary policy. A shift toward a mix of tighter fiscal policy and easier monetary policy can occur in two ways. First, the Bundesbank could adopt easier policies, allowing other countries to expand while maintaining a fixed exchange rate with Germany. Second, if the Bundesbank does not adopt easier policies, other countries have the option of abandoning the path to monetary union and adopting expansionary monetary policies that would bring down both the actual and natural rates of unemployment with a minimal acceleration of inflation.

NOTES

1. The research has been supported by the National Science Foundation. I am grateful to Martin Cohan and Tomonori Ishikawa for help with the data and graphs.

2. See the recent book edited by Cross (1995a), especially his own essay (Cross, 1995b).

3. In Gordon (1995a) I have recently estimated the United States natural rate of unemployment as a time-varying parameter and have found it to have decreased gradually from about 6.4 per cent in 1981 to about 5.8 per cent in 1995.

4. For countries with positive unemployment gaps in Figure 4, the natural rate hypothesis predicts that inflation is decelerating. Thus the warranted nominal GDP growth rate allows the rate of real GDP growth to accelerate *pari passu* with the deceleration of inflation until the unemployment gap is eliminated.

5. When this analysis is done on a diagram with the output gap on the horizontal axis, then the DG schedule is a negative 45 degree line. If the Okun's law coefficient linking the unemployment gap to the output gap were unity, then the DG schedule in Figure 10 would be a positive 45 degree line. If the Okun's law coefficient is 2 (an output gap of 2 corresponds to an unemployment gap of 1), then the slope of the DG line is 2, indicating that a shortfall of inflation below x of one percentage point corresponds to an unemployment gap of minus 0.5.

6. Imagine a DG_2 line drawn through point A. This indicates that the unemployment rate would be unchanged if the inflation rate at that point (p_2) equalled the value of excess nominal GDP growth (x_1) at the same point.

7. Our discussion here refers to a "linear" version of the hysteresis hypothesis in which the equilibrium unemployment rate "like an elephant" remembers all past shocks. Cross (1995b, p. 190) distinguishes this from the nonlinear version in which the memory of past shocks is selective.

8. A wide variety of theoretical and empirical papers on hysteresis is found in Cross (1988).

9. A detailed evaluation and chronology of structural reform efforts is provided in OECD (1994b).

BIBLIOGRAPHY

Bean, C.R. (1994). "European Unemployment: A Survey", *Journal of Economic Literature*, 32 (June), 573-619.

Branson, W.H. and J.J. Rotemberg (1980), "International Adjustment with Wage rigidity", *European Economic Review*, 13 (May), pp 309-32.

Bruno, M. and J.D. Sachs (1985), *Economics of World-wide Stagflation* (Cambridge MA: Harvard University Press).

Cross, R. (ed.) (1988), *Unemployment, Hysteresis, and the Natural Rate Hypothesis.* Oxford and New York: Basil Blackwell.

———— (1995a), The Natural Rate of Unemployment: Reflections on 25 Years of the Hypothesis. (Cambridge UK: Cambridge University Press).

———— (1995b), "Is the Natural Rate Hypothesis Consistent with Hysteresis?" in Cross, ed. (1995a), pp. 181-200.

DeGrauwe, P. (1995), "The Economics of Convergence towards Monetary Union in Europe", CEPR discussion paper 1213, July.

Elmeskov, J. and M. MacFarlan (1993), "Unemployment Persistence", *OECD Economic Studies* (No. 21, Winter), pp. 57-88.

Franz, W. and R.J. Gordon (1993), "Wage and Price Dynamics in Germany and America: Differences and Common Themes", *European Economic Review*, 37 (May), pp. 719-54.

Giorno, C., P. Richardson, D. Roseveare, P. van den Noord (1995), "Potential Output, Output Gaps, and Structural Budget Balances", *OECD Economic Studies* (No. 24), pp. 167-209.

Gordon, R.J. (1995a), "Estimating the NAIRU as a Time-varying Parameter", paper presented to Panel of Economic Advisers, Congressional Budget Office, November 16.

———— (1995b), "Is There a Trade-off between Unemployment and Productivity Growth?" NBER working paper 5081, April. Forthcoming in Dennis J. Snower and Guillermo de la Dehesa, eds., *Unemployment Policy: How Should Governments Respond to Unemployment?* Cambridge UK: Cambridge University Press for CEPR.

Krugman, P. (1994), "Past and Prospective Causes of High Unemployment", *Federal Reserve Bank of Kansas City Economic Review* (fourth quarter), pp. 21-43.

Layard, R., S. Nickell and R. Jackman (1991), *Unemployment: Macroeconomic Performance and the Labor Market* (Oxford: Oxford University Press).

OECD (1994a), The OECD Jobs Study: Unemployment in the OECD Area, 1950-95 (Paris).

——————— (1994b), Assessing Structural Reform: Lessons for the Future (Paris).

Sachs, J.D. (1979), "Wages, Profits, and Macroeconomic Adjustment: A Comparative Study", *Brookings Papers on Economic Activity,* 10 (No. 2), pp. 269-319.

COMMENTS

by

R. FORD

I found myself agreeing with most of Professor Gordon's interesting paper, and so my comments mainly emphasise points which seem to me of particular importance. The paper can be thought of as asking, and answering, three essential questions.

First, has the increase in the unemployment rate since 1970 reflected structural or cyclical factors? The answer is that structural unemployment has risen substantially in Europe, but that in the United States it is more or less at the same level now as it was 25 years ago. At the same time, there is now some cyclical unemployment in Europe.

The second question is, what has been responsible for the increase in the natural rate in Europe? This is obviously a difficult question.

Structural rigidities have probably not gotten much worse in either Europe or the United States over the past 25 years. However, changes in the economic environment may have interacted with structural rigidities. That is, institutions in Europe were fine in the 1950s and 1960s, but may have become increasingly maladapted in the last 25 years.

The two leading candidates for the change in the economic environment are competition from low-skill low-wage countries, and a twist in the production function. Either would reduce the marginal product of unskilled workers and reduce their wages. Arguably, this has occurred in the United States. But if the lower end of the wage distribution were prevented from falling, then firms would shed workers, moving back up the labour demand curve until the marginal product of remaining employees matched the high real wage. One result would be higher unemployment, as in Europe.

I would like to digress here on the question of real wages. Professor Gordon argues, on the basis of labour shares, that real wage rigidity is unlikely to be a problem in Europe. This way of putting the matter may lead to confusion, although I hasten to add, not on the part of Professor Gordon. Extracting information from labour's share is very difficult. If real wages were pushed up exogenously, by labour market rigidities, for example, the marginal product would rise to match and firms shed labour. Depending on the elasticity of substitution, labour's share might rise or fall.

To return to the main story line, Professor Gordon identifies several structural factors that differ between Europe and the United States and that could have interacted with the changing economic environment. I agree with his list, but would add a few more, including:

  - Restrictions on hiring and firing are common in Europe, although in recent years the trend has been to relax them. A firing restriction increases the discounted present value of the cost of hiring a worker, because separation will be costly if the worker proves unsuitable or if business conditions change. Since this cost is likely to be only weakly related to wages and productivity, its impact will fall particularly heavily on the unskilled. Since business conditions seem to be changing more rapidly these days, the cost may have risen over time.

  - Restrictions on temporary, seasonal and part-time work have much the same effect, since full-time workers normally have greater legal job security and generate larger social charges for the firm.

  - Generous unemployment and other social benefits raise wages by raising the opportunity costs of employment, again especially at the bottom end of the wage distribution. Some of these factors could be reflected in low labour-force participation as well as in high unemployment. The two tend to be related, even in the longer run across countries (see Elmeskov and Pichelmann: "Interpreting Unemployment", OECD Economic Studies No. 21, 1993).

  - Wage compression, either through centralised bargaining or administrative extension of wage bargains, creates a more even distribution of wage income, but also tends to cut off the bottom of the wage distribution.

It is equally interesting to consider factors that do not differ much between Europe and the United States. Two that are particularly prominent in the European unemployment debate are:

  - Disinflation. Both areas disinflated in the 1980s. This undermines the case for hysteresis, but it is not decisive. The sort of structural factors highlighted by Professor Gordon could have interacted with the disinflation process to raise unemployment in Europe.

  - Capital shortage. As the IMF pointed out in its May 1995 World Economic Outlook, since 1970 real GDP and the capital stock have grown at almost exactly the same rate in the United States and Europe, and the capital-labour ratio by much more in Europe. This is a powerful argument against capital shortage. However, since real wages also grew much more in Europe, it is plausible that European capital is suited to capital-intensive production. I would emphasise three points consistent with this view. First, high real wages are a symptom, or perhaps a transmission mechanism, not a root cause, of unemployment. Second, Europe does not need more capital, but different capital. And, third, it will get different capital after the root causes of unemployment have been eliminated.

Other factors that don't differ much between Europe and the United States, or that go the wrong way, include:

– Active labour market policies, including training. These are not especially important in the United States, and so cannot explain the relatively good employment record there.

– Wage or employment subsidies. Again, these are not common in the United States, although the Earned Income Tax Credit, which provides negative marginal tax rates for some low-paid workers, should be mentioned.

– Reductions in hours worked. Average hours worked in the United States is among the highest in the world. Thus, relatively low unemployment there cannot plausibly be explained by restrictions on labour supply.

I would say parenthetically that these lists of differences and similarities accord quite well with the econometric evidence presented by Jackman, Layard and Nickell in their paper at this conference. The two major discrepancies are the tax wedge, mentioned by Professor Gordon but dismissed by Jackman *et al.*, and active labour market policies, the expansion of which forms the core of the policy advice of Jackman *et al.*

The third question is, what is the appropriate policy response? When it comes to structural policy, the answer follows from the answer to the previous question: the structural rigidities that are interacting adversely with the economic environment should be relaxed or eliminated. But this may be too facile an answer, for two reasons. First, Europeans may not want an American-style labour market, because the outcome may conflict with social or distributional objectives. From this perspective, policy suggestions such as Active Labour Market Policies and employment subsidies could be seen as second-best policies to offset the employment distortions of rigidities. The difficult question is whether such second-best policies will actually work, especially in the context of tight government budgets and already very high tax burdens. Second, there is likely to be a long period of adjustment following the elimination of structural rigidities. For example, firms' adjustment of the capital stock to lower real wages and more labour-intensive production is bound to take time.

As to macroeconomic policy, Professor Gordon seems to argue that expansionary monetary policy can pave the way for structural reform, because social partners will then accept structural change in return. Although he does not stress it, a hysteresis effect would also help here. This is significantly riskier than a policy of simply responding to structural reforms after their consequences have become clear. The danger is that inflation will rise if the structural reform part of the bargain does not work out as expected. And as we know, lowering inflation again will be costly. So, I will finish my remarks by making four cautionary points:

- First, it is difficult to assess how structural reform will affect potential output and the natural rate, especially during the transition period.
- Second, given the potential costs, a government would want to be very sure about the existence and importance of hysteresis before it embarked on an inflationary policy in the hope of permanently reducing unemployment.
- Third, in Italy and the United Kingdom, the monetary expansions in 1992 were not in exchange for future structural reforms, but instead came after reforms.
- Finally, in contrast to the successes in these countries, one could point to the dash for growth in France in the early 1980s as an example of how expansionary policy can go wrong.

SUBSTITUTABILITIES VS COMPLEMENTARITIES BETWEEN STRUCTURAL AND MACROECONOMIC POLICIES

Professor of Economics, Institut d'études politiques, Paris

INTRODUCTION

Since the end of World War II, social justice in European societies has been based upon the tacit agreement that State-designed mechanisms had to provide everyone "from womb to tomb" with security (see *e.g.* Shonfield, 1982). While the feasibility of this social contract has been ensured by rapid growth until the mid-1970s, the slowdown that European nations have experienced since then, along with the rise of mass unemployment in the 1980s, has led to its unravelling.

To put things bluntly, unemployment is probably the greatest challenge to the post World War II European social contract. This explains the considerable attention that not only policy makers and economists, but the public at large, have paid in European democracies to finding ways towards a solution of the unemployment problem. Three questions have dominated the debate: How did we get there? Why do traditional solutions (*i.e.* macroeconomic policies) appear unable to reduce the size of the unemployment problem in Europe? And finally, in the absence of macroeconomic policies what can structural policies do?

Obviously, it is no place here to provide a full and detailed answer to these quandaries. Instead, our goal in this paper is the following: first, we would like to explain why, in recent debates, macroeconomic and structural policies have gradually appeared as substitutes; in other words, why is it that interest has shifted from attempts to boost output to attempts to carry on structural transformations, mostly aimed at providing labour markets with more flexibility as a solution to the unemployment problem. Second, we want to demonstrate that the range of structural policies available to policy makers is probably much wider than usually thought and is not limited to fostering flexibility. In particular, we claim that there is scope for structural reforms of the socio-economic system which would also produce several of the effects that are traditionally associated with macroeconomic policies. Our basic message is that structural and macroeconomic policies, far from being perfect substitutes, might exhibit complementarities.

The remainder of this paper is organised as follows. In the next section, we describe the extent of Europe's unemployment problem as well as the main recipes that have been proposed to moderate it. In the second main section, we review the forecasts relating to the evolution of unemployment over the next decade, and show that no autonomous reduction of Europe's unemployment is to be expected as long as the current policy framework remains unchanged. In the final section, we provide a theoretical discussion of the relative merits of increased flexibility and of an alternative structural reform based on employment subsidies. We argue that the latter is probably the most capable of contributing to a solution of Europe's unemployment problem that would be consistent with the spirit of European social contracts as they have existed for about half a century.

THE RISE OF MASS UNEMPLOYMENT: PAVING THE WAY FOR STRUCTURAL REFORMS AS A SUBSTITUTE FOR SOUND MACROECONOMIC POLICIES

Today and yesterday

In the past twenty years unemployment has risen to unprecedented levels. By many aspects, this situation (which is accompanied with financial disorder, and more recently deflationary pressures), seems reminiscent of the crisis of the 1930s. In other ways the current situation is very specific because today's system differs so radically from yesterday's capitalism. Social protection and national budgets are powerful stabilisers for economic activity because they help maintain demand during recessions.

In the thirties by contrast, adjustment by the market could not operate because of the very absence of an adequate social protection system. However, economists who supported *laissez-faire* policies, like Jacques Rueff, thought at the time that the market was capable of automatic adjustment and that the existing rudimentary social protection, (such as unemployment benefits in the United Kingdom), were the real obstacles to full employment. Indeed, deflation was seen as part of a mechanism which contributed to the adjustment towards equilibrium. But far from bringing about a return to equilibrium, deflation in the thirties had the opposite effect. Keynes held that price decreases could not provoke an automatic increase in demand, *because the unemployed have no income*. This was the distinctively modern ingredient of the Keynesian diagnosis.

It could be argued however that today, adjustment by market forces relies on social protection, thus ruling out the need for discretionary intervention by governments. As a result, economic policies have to be *active* only where the social protection system is insufficient to maintain the consumption levels of the less wealthy (*i.e.* in the United States), and *passive* where the system is thought to be too generous (*i.e.* in Europe). This is the origin of the real contradiction we now face in the latter region.

Unemployment is developing here up to levels which it would have been difficult to imagine even a few years ago, precisely because it can develop without, as yet, provoking a major crisis of under-consumption. If this had not been the case, action would have been taken without hesitation. In earlier times it would have led automatically to deflation. Our societies now continue to become richer, in living standards and particularly in personal wealth, while this was not the case in previous periods of mass unemployment. But this is partly a result of the normal functioning of social protection, which permits the unemployed – even those who no longer receive unemployment benefits – to have an income and therefore contribute to demand. The functioning of the system prevents demand from collapsing in periods of crisis. But recession obviously makes the system more expensive by increasing expenditure while limiting receipts at the same time. A curious inversion of logic then blames the system itself for unemployment. But the truth is that its very existence prevents recessions from becoming major crises of under-consumption. If social protection did not exist, economic policies would have to be much more active and none of the current objectives of economic policy could be pursued.

This makes the architecture of the current problem clearer. Macroeconomic policy is becoming unidimensional, *i.e.* only seeks to meet one single objective: price and/or exchange rate stability. It can therefore no longer be mobilised to promote employment. The abnormally high level of interest rates to which it leads, worsens recessions while weakening recovery at the same time. Expansionary shocks, where they appear, will be softened to prevent the emergence of inflationary surges. Trends towards employment imbalance can therefore only increase, with phases of expansion never being sufficient to wipe out the employment consequences of previous recessions. But this tendency can make itself evident without provoking a major crisis because the public sector acts as a shock-absorber. It is carrying most of the burden of adjustment (*i.e.* it pays unemployment benefits), and is consequently in deficit. It is only too tempting to present deficits as the very source of the problem, thus pointing an accusing finger at the system itself.

In a way, the European economic system has become structurally keynesian, through its social protection system. Some kind of macroeconomic policy is automatically activated when the activity level is too low. The paradox is that this expansionary macro-policy is put in motion whenever traditional macro-policies (fiscal and monetary) are too timid. If, then, the social protection system is disactivated, one has to have a terribly strong faith in market economics, to think that restrictive macro-policies will lead to increased employment, in a world where initial conditions are an historically low rate of inflation, mass unemployment and excess saving.

Technocrats dream of a different world, where each problem has a single solution and where what is needed is merely to break up an inherited structure or fabric of society in order to reduce economic imbalances. Economists have long known that in an open economy it is often possible to reduce unemployment by lowering wages. This basic solution is as old as the economy itself. However, they have never stopped looking actively for alternative solutions because they know that wage reduction (even if it were viable), could bring about much more serious imbalances than the ones it is supposed to combat, both at the societal level and for international relations. Competition through wage reduction or reduction in social protection coverage is just as dangerous as competitive devaluation: today's winners can be tomorrow's losers. Keynes was able to identify solutions which corresponded to the problems of his time. Today's economists have to find new ones. Otherwise they are faced with the task of justifying, in political and social terms, the fact that our societies continue to enrich themselves while asking their most vulnerable members to accept increased poverty.

It is of course true that the road to hell is paved with good intentions and that there are painful realities with which we are sometimes confronted; but why not try out other solutions before surrendering? Rueff was perhaps wearing the logician's cap when he argued that suppressing unemployment benefits would cure the unemployment problem in the UK during the twenties; but so was Keynes when he recommended abandoning the policy of overvaluing the pound:

> "The policy of gradually raising the value of a country's money to (say) 100 per cent above its present value in terms of goods amounts to giving notice to every merchant and every manufacturer, that for some time to come his stock and his raw materials will steadily depreciate on his hands, and to every one who finances his business with borrowed money that he will, sooner or later, lose 100 per cent on his liabilities (since he will have to pay back in terms of commodities twice as much as he has borrowed). Modern business, being carried on largely with borrowed money, must necessarily be brought to a standstill by such a process. It will be to the interest of every one in business to go out of business for the time being; and of every one who is contemplating expenditure to postpone his orders so long as he can. The wise man will be he who turns his assets into cash, withdraws from the risks and the exertions of activity, and awaits in country retirement the steady appreciation promised him in the value of his cash. A probable expectation of Deflation is bad enough; a certain expectation is disastrous. For the mechanism of the modern business world is even less adapted to fluctuations in the value of money upwards than it is to fluctuations downwards."

John Maynard Keynes[2]

And once logic has spoken, we must turn to welfare criteria to assess the relative merits of alternative proposals. It does seem that Keynes' solution was superior to Rueff's and, as it turned out, it was more effective, too.

This episode of economic history has perhaps something to teach us today, and it may be useful to review it in more details, especially today where decentralised monetary union has a deflationary bias of which the unemployment rate may be a systemic measure (Fitoussi and Flandreau, 1994). This deflationary bias may be exacerbated if the leader country experiences a shock which implies a tightening of its monetary policy, as was the case with German unification. If, in spite of this shock, external stability of the value of money is given priority, it will be at the expense of the stability of the price level, and strong deflationary pressures will emerge. The only option then which is left to cope with the unemployment problem is structural reform. Structural remedies appear as the only way out, thus representing a substitute to macroeconomic policies (for instance because the social protection system prevents deflation to be fast enough to compensate for the overvaluation of the currency). It may well be that in certain circumstances, structural reforms are badly needed. But we have before to make sure that they are not mainly needed to compensate for bad macroeconomic policies.

The unemployment problem: theoretical notes

The various theories that seek to explain the unemployment problem may be interpreted as different diagnoses of a single illness. Each provides its own analysis of the rise of unemployment and offers remedies that are related to the assumed nature of the disease.

In the framework of a general equilibrium model, which describes a set of *interdependent* markets, there is no reason why the origin of the disequilibrium arising in one given market should be found in that market where the disequilibrium has appeared. The price vector may differ from its equilibrium level for a number of reasons of which only a few may have to do with a disfunctioning of the labour market. It remains true that the sheer existence of (involuntary) unemployment implies that some prices are false in the hicksian sense, but this does not mean that the price of labour has to adjust downwards or that it is the only one that should adjust.

The search for efficiency often leads to reallocation of resources in *several* markets (Malinvaud, 1977). Consider for instance inefficiencies arising from asymmetric information or market imperfections. In this case, equilibrium prices will generally not lead to an efficient allocation of resources. For instance, this may lead to a situation where real wages are high and some agents are unemployed. This does not mean, however that real wages cause unemployment, since both variables are endogenous (Solow, 1986). Alternatively, if prices and wages both exhibit downward rigidities, unemployment and high real wages might result from restrictions upon money supply. Indeed, one may argue that such a situation was probably responsible for the recent deterioration of employment prospects in Europe (GIPE, 1994).

More generally, the very nature of problems associated with information asymmetries suggests that it is precisely in those markets which are in charge of co-ordinating intertemporal decisions that rigidities and inefficiencies are most common. Equilibrium interest rates might not coincide with full employment: since investment decisions (which in turn determine labour demand by firms) are made on the basis of signals sent by these typically inefficient markets, it is only too natural to expect that they lead to distortions. As a result, the burden of adjustment will fall upon *other markets*. For instance, a high rate of interest, by generating a reduction in profitability, will in turn produce a contraction of real wages if full employment is required.

This basic insight was spelt out in Fitoussi-Phelps (1988). The Fitoussi-Phelps monograph focused on the impact of the interest rate upon labour demand in several kinds of models, each of them exhibiting a negative effect (on labour demand) of real interest rate hikes.[3] While the exact channel through which the real interest rate affects labour demand may vary, all go in the same direction. And their implications are important because they point to a neglected short-run as well a long-run supply effect of the real rate of interest. Taking this effect into account may serve two purposes:

- The new transmission mechanism through which the real rate of interest affects supply may constitute the building block of a new structuralist theory of unemployment (Phelps, 1994).

- Alternatively it could be added to existing standard economic theory, say the Keynesian-neo-classical model, to weaken or even reverse its main conclusions regarding employment.

The basic insight is the following: consider for instance a customer market whose distinctive feature is that informational frictions on the buyer's side lead each firm to consider its market share as an asset (*i.e.* it will provide the firm with a future flow of purchases that are partly irresponsive to price changes).[4] In such a market, it is obvious that prices are not fully competed down to cost level. A firm's mark-up policy makes each firm's selling price a function of the price of other firms and of the real interest rate. As a result, the amount supplied at a given price by a given firm is a decreasing function of price rises in other firms (since this acts in a way that increases the monopoly power of that firm). Similarly, an increase in the real interest rate, by lowering the present value of attracting more customers from other firms, leads managers to reduce their current output.

Hence the capital market is the essential transmission mechanism, since asset prices are inversely related to interest rates. A high level of interest rate lowers the price of assets and thus reduces the demand for labour. This produces an increase in the equilibrium rate of involuntary unemployment. The reasoning is consistent with standard profit maximisation in an imperfectly competitive environment. In such a setting there is a trade-off between present profits and market shares, or equivalently between present profits and future profits, which is controlled by the real rate of interest. Quite importantly, this mechanism is activated by the structure of the policy mix at work. Consider for instance the effects of an expansive budgetary policy along with monetary tightening. While fiscal expansion tends to rise nominal interest rates, monetary tightening keeps prices down. As a result, real interest rates rise (Fitoussi and Phelps, 1988, p. 60). Firms thus modify their time arbitrage towards current profits, raise prices, reduce output and increase unemployment.

If we believe in such a theory the policy conclusion is straightforward: in the presence of unemployment, the policy mix should never imply a too expansionary budgetary policy, nor a too restrictive monetary policy since both will lead to an increase in unemployment. This finding is quite important, especially in view of the policies adopted in Europe during the 1980s, where expansionary budgetary policies and very restrictive monetary policies dominated. The situation has further deteriorated since German unification. From that date on, the policy mix in Europe was exactly the reverse of what was required: short-term real interest rates have been historically high, as well as budget deficits. As a result, the prospects for potential growth have deteriorated, and income inequalities have increased.

A clear and strong inversion of the policy mix in Europe will undoubtedly ease the burden which is put on structural reforms, even this would not suffice to solve the unemployment problem.

The unemployment problem: current proposals

The previous theoretical considerations have suggested that while it is certainly on the job market that the pathology of European economies is most clearly observed, nothing can lead us to reject that the source of the disequilibrium can be traced to other markets. Such a conclusion seems to deserve particular attention: indeed, the rise of mass unemployment in the 1980s has been paralleled by a second striking event, i.e. the shift, since 1980, of world real interest rates to historically high levels. This observation fits very well with the previous conclusion that high real interest rates might be the cause of the rise of unemployment rates in Europe, and of the depreciation of certain categories of labour elsewhere.

Of course, other authors have come to a quite different conclusion. They have argued that labour market imperfections have been to some extent responsible for the unemployment problem. According to them, minimum wage arrangements are the main inefficiency that contributes to rationing on labour markets. In this view, such arrangements should be removed as part of a general solution to Europe's unemployment problem.

Finally, there is quite a range of opinion relative to what should be done. The menu of recommendations that are most often debated range from enhancing flexibility in the labour market to activating passive expenditures on social protection. A more active employment policy is desirable *per se*, but the evaluation of the effects of these kind of policies in the countries where they are pursued leads to mixed feelings. The results that can be expected do not match the dimensions of the problem of mass unemployment which has been building up progressively for two decades. This even seems to be true for employment-cost reduction policies, particularly for the unskilled, upon which several countries have placed high expectations. Does this mean that governments are heading for a dead-end? Of course there are grounds for thinking that it is still too early to reach this conclusion, but what is really missing when it comes to resolving the problem of employment in Europe is time. We can no longer put off the solution to a problem which threatens the very foundation of our societies. Mass unemployment changes the behaviour of the actors involved and leaves permanent scars on both social cohesion and economic efficiency.

GLOOMY PROSPECTS

What are the prospects for the spontaneous evolution of unemployment in the coming years? These can be assessed under the assumption that the international framework shaping national economic policies remains unchanged. This seems a reasonable assumption: the persistence of these policies, throughout the 1980s and early 1990s suggests that no major change is in sight. In particular, one should expect that the basic features of current macroeconomic policies in Europe – internal and external monetary stability, and strict controls on budget deficits and public debt according to Maastricht's convergence criteria – will be kept in force. Such an exercise will provide a useful benchmark that will allow us to derive the most likely evolutions, if no change occurs in the current stance of economic policy.

With this in mind a group of economists from OFCE and CEPII[5] has attempted to determine what would be the "natural" evolution of the world economy until 2002. Their predictions draw quite gloomy perspectives for the unemployment front – especially in Europe. Table I as well as Figures I and 2 summarise the evolution of unemployment prospects for a number of countries (Germany, France, Italy, United Kingdom and United States) as they emerged from the MIMOSA study.

The profiles result from the combination of a number of factors affecting both labour supply and labour demand. On the supply side, the growth of the population

Table 1. **Recent and projected rates of unemployment**

	1990	1994	1995	1996	1997	2002
West Germany	6.2	8.3	8.4	8.4	8.2	5.9
Germany	..	9.6	9.6	9.8	9.8	7.5
France	8.9	12.4	12.0	11.9	11.9	11.1
Italy	11.5	11.3	11.1	10.4	9.4	8.4
United Kingdom	5.5	9.4	8.5	7.8	7.6	7.2
EU North	8.3	9.8	9.4	9.2	9.1	9.5
EU South	12.6	18.3	18.0	17.4	16.7	17.2
United States	5.5	6.1	5.2	4.8	4.8	5.8
Japan	2.1	2.9	3.1	3.2	3.0	2.0

Source: MIMOSA model, CEPII-OFCE.

willing to work will be quite rapid in the US (1 per cent), more moderate in France (0.5 per cent) and Japan (0.4 per cent) and relatively limited in Germany (0.3 per cent), Italy and the United Kingdom (about 0.25 per cent).

Productivity gains on the other hand will be quite small. They range between 2 per cent per year (Japan) and 1 per cent (United States). In the long run, potential

◆ Figure 1. **Unemployment rate**

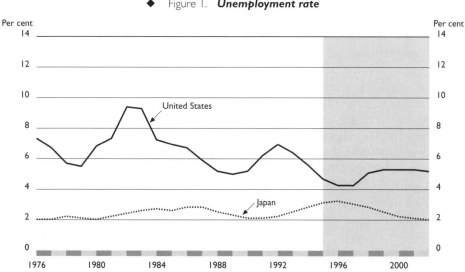

Source: MIMOSA model, CEPII-OFCE.

Figure 2. **Unemployment rate**

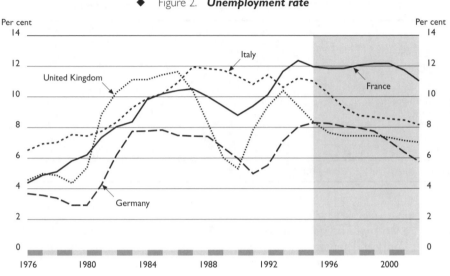

Source: MIMOSA model, CEPII-OFCE.

economic growth is of about 2 per cent only. As a result employment will increase at a 0.6 per cent annual rate in Germany, France, and the United Kingdom, and perhaps slightly quicker in Italy (0.8 per cent) and in the United States (1.2 per cent).

The combination of these various factors imply that the United States will experience a relatively low unemployment rate, hovering around 5.5 per cent in 2002. Similarly, Japan will experience a decreasing unemployment rate, down to 2 per cent by 2002. It is in Europe that prospects are much less encouraging. The German unemployment rate will move down to 5.9 per cent in West Germany (8 per cent for unified Germany), to 7.2 per cent in the United Kingdom, and to 8.3 per cent in Italy. In France, the unemployment rate will remain a two digit number (down to 11 per cent).[6]

Obviously, there is nothing in these conclusions that should lead us to be overly optimistic. This is quite worrying especially in light of the fact that the hypotheses upon which the previous predictions are based are relatively favourable.

Part of these disappointing results reflect the sluggishness of demand which appears to be the weak side of the market. Indeed the supply side seems comparatively healthy, with high profits that represent in some countries like France a very large fraction of national income compared to earlier years. Similarly, the fraction of investment financed out of retained earnings is everywhere pretty high.

On the other hand, the high rate of unemployment, by pushing wages in European countries down, acts as a break on aggregate consumption, which in turn checks any acceleration of investment. The result is that unemployment exhibits a high degree of persistence.

The previous analysis, while quite pessimistic, may raise some afterthoughts. After all, from a theoretical point of view, it is much easier to cure (through macroeconomic policies) demand side problems than supply side difficulties. This is in turn highlights the fact that the full thrust of Europe's unemployment problem comes from the constraints upon budget deficits and public debts: these constraints arise from markets asking for credibility, or from Maastricht asking for convergence criteria, at a time where monetary policy remains extremely restrictive.

Indeed, in a recent study by Cornilleau *et al.*, it was shown that if France would slightly relax its budget deficit constraint, this could lead to a reduction of its unemployment by about 250 000. And it is likely that a similar result would also hold for Europe at large. Such a claim was at the heart of the Drèze-Fitoussi-Malinvaud proposal, about a year ago.[7]

The overall conclusion seems pretty simple. Firms find themselves more willing to invest, but their incentives are counteracted by sluggish demand. On the other hand, macroeconomic solutions to pump up aggregate demand seem to be outside the considered options of European policy makers, who find themselves severely bound by budgetary constraints. The outcome is that it is very hard to get out of the European unemployment trap.

But since there does not seem to exist any way to increase the size of the cake, it becomes more and more likely that the forthcoming years will be devoted to debating on how to share it. In fact, some authors have argued that this might be a way to increase the size of the cake. Among proposals aimed at generating a more favourable evolution of the unemployment rate, some authors – especially in France – have argued that reducing the number of hours worked of wage and salary earners would be a great step towards solving the unemployment problem with the existing work being shared among more people. By reducing the financial burden of unemployment benefits, this would in turn stimulate aggregate demand and thus lead to a further reduction of unemployment. While the economic validity of such a reasoning may be debated, we believe that its practical implementation raises considerable difficulties. Indeed, it means that employed individuals will have to accept a short term reduction of their income, to be compensated in the long run by increased wages generated through higher growth and a reduction of unemployment.

This of course requires a quite substantial level of solidarity, which seems a bit at odds with current evolutions. As argued later, high interest rates and a riskier future renders co-operative behaviour (even when Pareto superior) rather hard to implement. While it seems obvious that given the current constraints upon budgetary and monetary policies, any solution to Europe's unemployment problem has to go through a reallocation of incomes, the exact way through which these reallocations should be implemented remains undecided. This is why we now turn to a theoretical assessment of the comparative properties of various structural policies.

STRUCTURAL UTOPIAS

As argued in the introduction, structural remedies to European unemployment problems may appear at first sight as an obvious challenge to the European model of Social Contract as it emerged after World War II. From an economic point of view, this contract developed upon the agreement that a pure market economy was unable to deliver equity and efficiency at once, and that a system of transfers was necessary to complement the forces of competition and to correct the income consequences of these forces. It is obvious that the sirens advocating structural remedies are the heralds of the unravelling of the European Social Contract. Hence time may be ripe for a re-examination of the foundations of traditional structural policies: this will lead us to restate their limits as well as to argue that alternative structural policies (that would leave the basic core of Europe's social pact unharmed) should be considered.

Traditional structural policies

As we know, Europe's unemployment problem does not affect the work force homogeneously. Instead, it tends to fall disproportionately on the less qualified or the unqualified workers. According to the pure walrasian theory, the price of factors such as labour should equal their marginal productivity. In this view, minimum wage arrangements may be considered as obstacles to full employment, for they may raise real wages above less qualified workers' productivity. The seemingly logical conclusion of this analysis is thus that minimum wages and unemployment benefits represent obstacles to solving Europe's unemployment problem.

This apparently reasonable inference is a bit oblivious however of a deeper theoretical problem that was hotly debated a few decades ago. While we know since Walras that the general equilibrium of a perfectly competitive economy does exist *under some assumptions*, it is not obvious that this equilibrium has a system of prices that guarantees a minimum standard of living to all agents – or even a *survival* standard of living.

The problem was brushed away by Arrow and Debreu[8] in a classic paper. If the agents' initial endowments are such that they have enough resources to survive without working, then any equilibrium wage is admissible. Of course this solution did not address the heart of the matter – namely what would happen if agents do not have the required initial endowments.

Carrying on this line of thinking raises additional questions. While it is possible to argue that a narrowly defined concept of "survival level" corresponds to a rather low minimum wage, a more properly defined concept would include items relating to the building and amortisation of human capital, such as training (or re-training in case of knowledge obsolescence due to technical progress). It is clear that these basic necessities, which are especially substantial for less skilled workers who might find themselves unable to get a new job after having been laid off, adds to support costs, thus raising the minimum survival level. Hence the minimum survival level is a social concept, which varies with time and space and which refers to the requirements of social stability rather than biological survival.

This is what the founders of the European social pact had in mind when they thought of providing all agents with minimum wages and unemployment benefits: the market solution may not be sustainable. It is thus necessary to amend it, and to make it sustainable.[9]

Realising this crucial fact sheds light on the most basic rationale for social contracts involving minimum wage provisions. The key issue is of course not to subsidise idleness as the classical view would have it, but rather to rule out equilibria that would leave part of the nation on the side of the road. This suggests that the *exact* form of the post World War II social contract is no holy cow. Any other arrangement that would deliver the same features (*i.e.* that would eliminate equilibrium incomes below the minimum level) would do just as well, and perhaps better.

This is why we now turn to the formal discussion and comparison of various institutional regimes.

The minimum wage, and employment subsidies regimes

In what follows we discuss the respective properties of the free market equilibrium, of a minimum wage cum unemployment benefits equilibrium, and of an employment subsidies equilibrium.

Our goal is to show that the market solution is not the only "structural reform" that may help Europe out of its unemployment problem. Actually, it is probably even the worst solution because of the poverty it may generate. On the other hand, we show that the current minimum wage regime is clearly inferior to the employment subsidies solution.

The model below is an aggregated version of a general equilibrium model analysed by Dehez and Fitoussi (1993).[10] In the more general version, there are several categories of labour each characterised by an inelastic labour supply and a specific level of productivity; a minimum wage is also explicitly introduced. Two results of that model are relevant for the present discussion.

First, an increase in the minimum wage will always cause an increase in unemployment; it will lead to a decrease in the real wage of the more highly skilled labour categories when the types of labour are complementary and to an increase when they are substitutes.[11]

Second, nothing guarantees the uniqueness of the solution in terms of unemployment and the real wage level, unless a very strong condition is imposed, namely, whenever there is unemployment in one category (even a high-skill one), the real wage in that category equals the minimum wage. Even if one accepts this stringent assumption, full employment can still be obtained through a wage-subsidy scheme if, and only if, the minimum net income received by a wage earner is strictly less than the weighted average of marginal productivities.

Such a solution may be spontaneously achieved if the wage structure is such that the degree of inequality in the wage distribution is smaller than the degree of inequality in marginal productivities. Social norms may impose such an implicit system of subsidies: in effect, the set of relative wages is as much the result of social conventions as the result of spontaneous economic forces, as great economists like John Maynard Keynes and J.R. Hicks have pointed out. A sense of fairness cannot be totally absent from the process of income distribution. Hence a move toward a great degree of individualism, with each category trying to strictly maximise the quasi-rent from its human capital, can lead to an increase in unemployment in the low-skilled segment of the labour market. Whether the minimum wage is binding or not may depend in this case on social conventions. This implies that increased inequality and unemployment may go hand in hand, and that curing the second may require reducing wage inequality.

Hence, to reach full employment, a wage-subsidy scheme may have to be imposed explicitly through taxation, and it will achieve its aim if the high-skilled workers do not reduce their labour supply by a critical amount (as assumed in that model) because of the increased taxation.

The latter result may explain why different patterns of wage distribution across countries are consistent with a similar evolution in the structure of unemployment. On the basis of the former result, one should expect, *ceteris paribus*, a smaller increase in inequality of wage distribution in countries characterised by a binding system of minimum wages.

Let's consider a simple macro-model of the economy that allows to compare the outcomes of minimum wages with those of employment subsidies schemes. The model has three sectors: production, consumption and government.

The production sector

We consider the equilibria of an economy populated by two types of workers (skilled and unskilled, S and U respectively); workers may be either employed or unemployed. They produce one consumption good and hold money which will be used to implement transfers. The consumption good is produced through a technology of a Cobb-Douglas production function type.[12] Q stands for output.

$$Q = S^{\alpha_1} U^{\alpha_2} \quad 0 < \alpha_1 < 1 \quad 0 < \alpha_2 < 1 \quad \alpha_1 + \alpha_2 \leq 1 \tag{1}$$

The producer maximises:

$$\Pi = pQ - w_1 L - w_2 N \quad \text{with} \quad w_1 = p\omega_1 \quad \text{and} \quad w_2 = p\omega_2 \tag{2}$$

Where p is the price level, w_1 and w_2 are the nominal wages of skilled and unskilled workers respectively. Moreover we assume that the supply of labour is price-inelastic.

The consumer sector

The consumer maximises the following utility function (s refers to employee's status *i.e.* either employed: E or unemployed: N)

$$\text{Max}W(c_{i,s}, m_{i,s}) = \log(c_{i,s}^{\beta} m_{i,s}^{1-\beta}) \quad 0 < \beta < 1 \quad i = S,U \text{ and } s = E,N \tag{3}$$

under the budget constraint: $pc_{i,s} + m_{i,s} = m_i + e$

where $c_{i,s}$ denotes per head demands of employed and unemployed skilled and unskilled workers, $m_{i,s}$ stands for their demand for money, m_i denotes their initial money stock, and e stands for the per head income. Profits are distributed at the end of each period; hence m_i includes the profits from the last period.

It follows that per head consumption is:

$$c_{i,s}(p,e) = \beta(m_i + e)/p \quad i = S,U \text{ and } s = E,N \tag{4}$$

Finally, we assume that the government taxes the economy with a tax rate t. These taxes will be used to finance transfers when desired.

The first run with this model is aimed at providing us with the "market" benchmark, *i.e.* we assume that markets clear in a walrasian way: there is no unemployment. The model is then solved in (5) – (8).

Free market benchmark

Exogenously given labour supply determines the real wage for both skilled and unskilled labour, as well as output and the price level.

$$L = \alpha_1 / \omega_1 (\alpha_1 / \omega_1)^{\alpha_1/(1-\alpha_1-\alpha_2)}(\alpha_2 / \omega_2)^{\alpha_2/(1-\alpha_1-\alpha_2)} \tag{5}$$

$$N = \alpha_2 / \omega_2 (\alpha_1 / \omega_1)^{\alpha_1/(1-\alpha_1-\alpha_2)}(\alpha_2 / \omega_2)^{\alpha_2/(1-\alpha_1-\alpha_2)} \tag{6}$$

$$\hat{Q} = (\alpha_1 / \omega_1)^{\alpha_1/(1-\alpha_1-\alpha_2)}(\alpha_2 / \omega_2)^{\alpha_2/(1-\alpha_1-\alpha_2)} \tag{7}$$

$$\hat{\omega}_1 = \alpha_1 \hat{Q} / L \quad \hat{\omega}_2 = \alpha_2 \hat{Q} / N \quad \hat{p} = \beta M / (1-(\alpha_1 + \alpha_2))\hat{Q}$$

The aggregate net income is then: $\quad \hat{Y} = (\alpha_1 + \alpha_2)\hat{Q}$

and the government budget surplus is: $\hat{G} = 0$ since there is no tax at that stage.

Minimum wage

Let's now assume that there does exist a minimum level of subsistence defined by a positive quantity μ expressed in terms of the aggregate consumption good. Assume further that the equilibrium real income for unskilled workers falls below the minimum level. A minimum wage $\hat{\omega}_2$ has to be introduced.

As a result, a fraction of the unskilled workers will be unemployed (and will then get the unemployment compensation ω_2.

The demand for unskilled workers is:

$$\bar{N} = N(\hat{\omega}_2 / \omega_0)^{\alpha_2/(1-\alpha_2)} \tag{9}$$

Output is then:

$$\bar{Q} = \hat{Q}(\hat{\omega}_2 / \omega_0)^{\alpha_2/(1-\alpha_2)} \tag{10}$$

The real wage of skilled workers, and the price level are:

$$\bar{\omega}_1 = \hat{\omega}_1 (\hat{\omega}_2 / \omega_0)^{\alpha_2/(1-\alpha_2)} \quad \bar{p} = \beta M / \left[(1-\beta(1-t)\alpha_1)\bar{Q} - \beta\mu N\right] \tag{11}$$

The net income is: $\quad \bar{Y} = (1-t)\alpha_1 \bar{Q} + \mu N$

and the budget surplus is: $\quad \bar{G} = \left[t(\alpha_1 + \alpha_2) + (1-t)\alpha_2\right]\bar{Q} - \mu N$

Employment subsidies

To ensure full employment of unskilled workers whose marginal productivity is less than the minimum of subsistence, the government induces firms to employ all unskilled workers by providing them with a subsidy that makes up for the difference between the walrasian wage and the minimum wage.

Since: $(1-t)\hat{\omega}_2 < \mu < (1-t)\hat{\omega}_1$

It follows:

$\bar{\bar{\omega}} = \hat{\omega}_1, \quad \bar{\bar{\omega}}_2 = \mu/(1-t),$ and $\bar{\bar{p}} = \beta M/\left[\left(1-\beta(1-t)\alpha_1\right)\hat{Q} - \beta\mu N\right]$

The net income is then: $\bar{\bar{Y}} = (1-t)\alpha_1\hat{Q} + \mu N$

and the budget surplus is: $\bar{\bar{G}} = \left(t\alpha_1 + \alpha_2\right)\hat{Q} - \mu N$

It is now time to summarise the conclusions of the previous analysis. When the existence of a minimum level of subsistence is taken into account, the free market solution is no longer feasible because it leads to the "death", (at least the social death) of the unskilled population, and thus to the collapse of output. Society at large has an advantage in finding a way to help the unskilled out.

Let's now turn to the comparison of cases (2) and (3). It is obvious that employment subsidies lead, by construction, to full employment and therefore to a higher level of production. What about real net income and real budget surplus? Obviously, the same intuition holds because with a higher level of production more resources can be shared between agents and thus a higher level of welfare is reached. Finally it is obvious that employment subsidies are clearly superior to unemployment compensations.

Towards a new social contract?

What emerges from the previous discussion is that it is possible to draw a one-for-one correspondence between economic regimes and implicit social contracts.

The implicit contract embedded in the free market regime is obviously one where *any* equilibrium price vector is considered as acceptable. The implicit contract embedded in the minimum wage regime is one where society values the fact that every agent is provided with resources above the socially accepted survival level. The implicit contract embedded in the employment subsidies regime is one where society values the fact that every agent is provided with both minimum resources *and* a job. Intuitively, this regime is one where the basic payroll system is supplemented by a set of transfers going top down, from the highest pay jobs to the lowest ones, thus reducing their spread. Such a system might appear quite reasonable, especially because wage distribution within a firm or industry always include element of arbitrariness. It is well known that individual productivities are difficult to measure leading managers to focus on the global outcome of team (or firm) effort. While it is possible to rank jobs in terms of productivity, it is never easy to assign to each agent a precise cardinal measures of productivity. Again, this suggests that every system for assigning shares of aggregate income to individual jobs is to a certain extent a matter of social convention. And indeed even today the actual systems that we do observe in Europe differ quite substantially from country to country.

Since we have argued that a case can be made to show that the implicit contract embedded in the employment subsidies regime dominates that embedded in the minimum wage regime, we will restrict our attention to comparing employment subsidies (ES) to free market type (FM) solutions. Our claim is that there are strong reasons to believe that the employment subsidies regime is preferable.

Most of the advantages accruing to the ES solution can be related to the externalities that it generates in terms of human capital. The first and most obvious externality arises from the benefits associated with providing everybody with a job. While no free human capital accumulation can take place for agents that are unemployed, economic activity goes along with skill acquiring, training, and knowledge building, at a rate at least comparable to the free market solution and perhaps even larger, since it goes along with a better standard of life.

Moreover, employment subsidies, by reducing the risk of becoming unemployed, favours the development of long term job relations. Agents are more willing to invest larger resources in collective action and in counterpart, firms are ready to provide them with long run contracts.

This has several effects. First, it leads firms to devote larger resources to workers' training and education, because they know that they will be able to derive benefits from their employees' improved abilities. Again, it is obvious that human capital accumulation is favoured.

A second effect relates to the fact that the cross-sectional transfers associated with employment subsidies have dynamic effects as well. The existence of long run relations provides a way to introduce built-in incentives to work efficiently precisely because income increases along with the stock of achievements. This also eases intergenerational transfers because young workers subsidise old retired ones, before being themselves subsidised by a new generation. Finally, in the ES solution, both firms and employees can derive all sort of externalities that cannot be achieved as efficiently through the walrasian solution.

Of course, the trend that has developed in the past 20 years has pushed towards a quite different direction. Rising unemployment, along with high real interest rates have led to the unravelling of long run economic relations. Faced with an increased risk of being laid off and with a more discounted future, agents have asked for higher pay whenever possible, and have been drawn away from intertemporal contracts. To protect themselves against economic risks they have saved more. Young and less qualified workers have been laid-off. This has tended to increase competition for lower pay jobs. In turn, the situation of older and now "overpaid" workers has been contaminated.

Some have advocated to go further along the same path by increasing flexibility. But the increased flexibility might only increase discrepancies between agents, further dissolving the glue which has bound together European societies since 1945. The emerging social contract is such that reduced solidarity is less and less perceived as an evil. Instead of changing our societies, we change our norms.

By contrast, our claim is that an explicit system of employment subsidies between categories and between generations might be part of an efficient solution to Europe's unemployment problem.

CONCLUSION

In this paper, we surveyed the rise of Europe's unemployment problem, its prospects, and discussed several of its proposed solutions.

We demonstrated that among the various options, the employment subsidies scheme should retain some attention. The basic insight that motivates the desirability of such arrangements is that it is always better to provide people with a job rather than providing them with income compensations. This arises for two reasons. First any economic activity somehow contributes to improving GNP. Second, there is a number of externalities that are derived through being employed, for economic activity is always favourable to human capital building.

Moreover, it should be emphasised that such solutions might receive relatively wide political support. First, it is obvious that compared to the job-sharing-with-payroll-reductions solution, employment subsidies could be more easily accepted by employees, because it is a pure State policy that does not require active co-operation. Second, it must be remarked that a dose of employment subsidies has received favourable review even by proponents of structural policies.[13]

Obviously, both the choice and the actual implementation of such schemes will raise a number of difficulties. As pointed out in the OECD Report, several questions will have to be examined to help forming a view about which specific form of employment subsidy would be the most efficient: Do these programmes generate enough human capital accumulation for the newly employed (or re-employed) so that their employment prospects will improve? Do these programmes reduce aggregate unemployment rather than prompting companies to substitutions that would offset part of the initial benefits? Equally important, would the country's macroeconomic performance be improved?

It is never easy to answer such questions, and the road to full employment in Europe will be a rocky one. Nevertheless we believe that the suggestions spelt out here might go some way towards solving Europe's unemployment problem.   227

NOTES

1. The author is grateful to Marc Flandreau for his help and his suggestions concerning this chapter.

2. John Maynard Keynes (1923): *A tract of monetary reform*, page 144. MacMillan and Co. Ltd., London.

3. These models include: 1) the customer-market model in which a firm's market share – or customer base – is considered to be an asset, 2) the model of turnover of employees, with current trained workers being the asset and 3) the two-sector model in which firms invest in physical capital, the production of which is labour-intensive, in order to reduce the costs of producing the consumer good.

4. Consumer markets may be taken as emblematic of other transmission mechanisms (from real interest rates to unemployment) that are developed in Fitoussi-Phelps (1988).

5. MIMOSA team. See "Une projection de l'économie mondiale à l'horizon 2002"; Observations et diagnostics, *Revue de l'OFCE*, No. 55, 1995, pp. 95-150.

6. A similar pattern is observed for Spain and other South European countries, but figures are not reported here.

7. Similar conclusions were reached by Gordon in his contribution to this Conference volume where he shows that the French unemployment rate is well above the NAIRU.

8. Arrow; K.J. and G. Debreu (1954), "Existence of an Equilibrium for a Competitive Economy", *Econometrica*, 22, p. 265-290.

9. For a classic statement of this well-known but too often forgotten problem, see *e.g.* N. Georgescu-Rogen, "Limitationality, limitativeness and economic equilibrium" in Georgescu-Rogen, *Analytical Economics*, HUP (1967).

10. Rahim-Loufir was of great help in the design of this aggregated version.

11. Two types of labour are complements when the productivity of one category increases when the other category is used more intensively. They are substitutes if the converse is true.

12. Note that the analysis could also be conducted with a constant elasticity of substitution between the two kinds of labour close to one.

13. See for instance the 1995 OECD Jobs Study, which advocates "active labour market measures" to fight unemployment.

COMMENTS

F. Larsen[1]

The key policy recommendation in Professor Fitoussi's paper is that employment subsidies would help to combat structural unemployment in Europe while safeguarding Europe's social fabric. The proposal is both unorthodox and likely to be viewed by many as a logical solution to the problem of unemployment. It may be helpful, therefore, to consider its merits from the perspective of the following two quotes:

"Although it is true that economists disagree about economic policy, almost all agree about the framework within which the argument should be conducted. Economists disagree about the effect of a minimum wage on unemployment, for instance, but they agree about the kinds of theory and evidence that would settle the issue... One test of the value of an unorthodox idea is therefore the extent to which it understands, however much it may disagree with, the orthodoxy."

The Economist, 1996

"Depuis de nombreuses années déjà, les prophètes abondent qui, inlassablement, disent leur foi en l'application d'une mesure particulière, d'un principe d'organisation. Chacun a trouvé le *deus ex machina*. La solution unique succède à l'objectif unique. Heureusement, face à des recettes qui relèvent plus de l'arithmétique élémentaire que de l'analyse sociale, les gouvernements gardent leur scepticisme. Ce fut d'abord le marché, l'autre partage salaire-emploi, le partage du travail, le développement des emplois de "proximité", la flexiblité, etc. Certains, avec raison, concevant qu'il n'est pas de solutions miracles, préconisent qu'il faut faire de tout un peu. Pour les gouvernements, en tout cas, le temps des promesses inconsidérées paraît bien révolu."

Jean-Paul Fitoussi, 1995

In accordance with the first quote, I will discuss Professor Fitoussi's proposal from the perspective of how well it "understands" what I believe is the consensus diagnosis of the unemployment problem among "orthodox" economists. Let me say immediately that Professor Fitoussi's analysis of the root causes of persistently high unemployment is very similar to that of the orthodoxy. From the perspective of the second quote, I will not claim to pass a definitive judgement on the question of whether employment subsidies might be helpful. I certainly do not believe that the proposal is, in Professor Fitoussi's own words "promise inconsiderate", but his paper nevertheless leaves a number of important questions unanswered. As an indirect way of addressing these issues, I discuss a modified proposal more closely in accordance with orthodox prescriptions, yet consistent with Professor Fitoussi's primary concern.

WHY HAS EUROPEAN UNEMPLOYMENT RISEN SO MUCH?

In order to examine this issue, it is useful to compare the experience of Europe with that of the United States displayed in the accompanying figure. This comparison also allows one to reject some common fallacies.

Similarities and differences between Europe (the data refer to the European Union, excluding Greece, Portugal, and Luxembourg) can be summarised as follows.[2] During the past quarter century, the increase in real GDP in the United States and Europe has been remarkably similar. So has the growth of the capital stock. However, employment and real wages have developed quite differently. In the United States, real wages rose by only 5 per cent over the period while employment rose by about 60 per cent, enough to absorb the rapid growth of the labour force and keep the level of unemployment essentially unchanged (abstracting from cyclical influences). In Europe, by contrast, real wages rose by over 40 per cent while employment went up by only slightly more than 10 per cent – almost the opposite proportional changes compared with the United States. Although the labour force increased much less in Europe than in the United States, the modest increase in employment was insufficient to prevent the unemployment rate from rising by a staggering 8 to 9 percentage points, most of which appears to have been structural.

This combination of developments suggests that Europe's poor employment performance, relative to the United States, cannot be blamed on insufficient demand (real GDP growth was similar). Nor can it be attributed to capital shortage (the expansion of the capital stock was also similar). One can also reject the notion that the amount of work to be carried out is fixed. This implies, I believe, that work sharing – i.e. reductions in the number of hours worked – is unlikely to reduce unemployment, but will tend to reduce labour supply and, hence, activity; if workers are compensated for the loss of income, work sharing may even lead to a rise in structural unemployment.

Instead, the evidence seems to point to the rapid increase in real wages, together with the rise in capital intensity, as the principal reason for the modest rise in European employment. Rapid real wage growth encouraged capital deepening, which raised labour productivity by substituting increases in the capital stock for

◆ Figure I. **The European Union and the United States:**
output, capital, employment, and wages
(1970 = 100, unless noted otherwise)

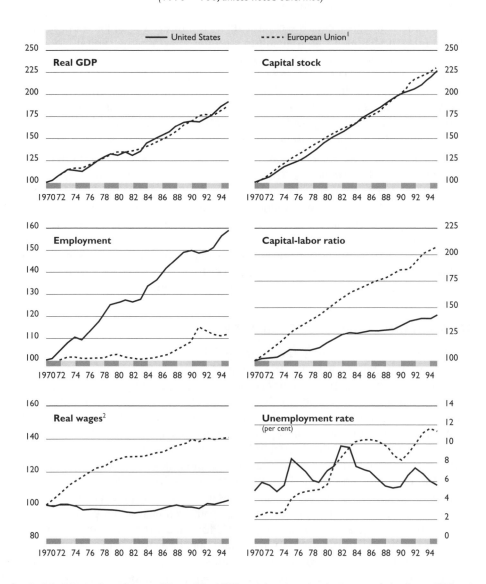

1. Excluding Greece, Luxembourg and Portugal. Real GDP, capital stocks, and real wages are calculated using PPP-based weights.
2. National accounts compensation per employee deflated by the GDP deflator.
Source: OECD, analytical data base; and IMF staff estimates.

increases in employment. In the United States, investment was more capital widening in nature, generating much less of an increase in the capital-labour ratio but permitting significant job creation.

With the same growth of the capital stock, the modest expansion of the labour force in Europe obviously had to result in stronger growth in the capital-labour ratio and, in the absence of a significant difference in technology, stronger growth in labour productivity. This should, in principle, have permitted stronger growth of real wages in Europe than in the United States, without raising the unemployment rate. However, the problem is that real wages in Europe have been rising, on average, in excess of the "warranted" growth rate, i.e. in excess of the rate that would have been consistent with the maintenance of unemployment at reasonable levels.

This analysis does not necessarily imply that real wages in Europe have risen too much for all skill categories. There are many reasons to believe, however, that real wages have risen too much for unskilled workers with low productivity, including youth with little practical experience: many low-skilled jobs have effectively disappeared in Europe and it is in these categories that unemployment is heavily concentrated. The much smaller increase in average real wages in the United States reflects the fact that much, but not all, of the rise in employment was in jobs that paid relatively low wages. As a result, wage inequality has increased, with a growing number of workers joining the ranks of the "working poor".

SAFEGUARDING EUROPE'S SOCIAL FABRIC

Professor Fitoussi rejects the US model as a workable solution for Europe because of the implications for the living standards of low skilled workers. He particularly emphasises the importance of safeguarding Europe's social consensus. This is a legitimate objective for economic policy that many, including myself, regard as one of the most important. Indeed, concern over the implications for the social fabric is warranted, I believe, by the signs that technological developments and global competitive forces particularly seem to benefit higher skill groups. These factors may be contributing both to the growing phenomenon of the "working poor" in the United States and to the high levels of unemployment in Europe, which can be viewed as different manifestations of essentially the same economic forces. Because society as a whole benefits so much from technical progress and increased globalization, there is clearly an obligation for those that benefit the most to compensate the less fortunate or to help them benefit as well. The question is what form should the compensation take to minimise undesirable side effects.

While he rejects the US model, Professor Fitoussi clearly agrees with the vast majority of economists that the present European model of "social compensation" is badly in need of reform. Not only does it not work as intended, but it is increasingly obvious that it has serious adverse implications for growth, for financial stability, for employment, and even for economic welfare, which it was supposed to protect. To put things a little bluntly, how can you maintain a system that forces enterprises to adjust to high labour costs by reducing employment, leaving it to governments – or rather, present and/or future taxpayers, or the beneficiaries of other expenditure that has to be foregone – to pick up the tab for growing numbers of unemployed? A system where social entitlements are financed in part by government borrowing and therefore by future generations, who will have to service the public debt? And a system where well-intended social benefit programmes and labour market regulations are affecting incentives to work and to create jobs, thereby aggravating the problem of social exclusion? The obvious answer to these rhetorical questions is that the present European system needs rethinking!

HOW TO WEAKEN THE LINK BETWEEN WAGES AND DISPOSABLE INCOMES

Professor Fitoussi acknowledges that the achievement of distribution objectives in Europe occurs at present at tremendous economic and social costs. It is therefore natural to explore whether it is possible to weaken the link between wages and disposable incomes. To renew and strengthen Europe's social consensus, he proposes the introduction of employment subsidies as an alternative to traditional structural policies that emphasise deregulation and flexibility. By reducing the cost of employing low-skilled labour, he hopes that more low-skilled jobs will be created, permitting a reduction in structural unemployment without jeopardising distribution objectives.

At first glance, Professor Fitoussi's proposal is a logical answer to a difficult dilemma and the proposal merits careful consideration. Before it can be implemented, however, a number of questions will need to be addressed. Critics would argue, for example, that employment subsidies would further distort price signals in the labour market rather than improving them. There is also a danger that employment subsidies might be shifted into higher wages, leaving labour costs and employment unchanged, particularly in the absence of greater flexibility in the labour market. By increasing the wage received by the employee, employment subsidies may also reduce incentives to acquire education and training. And employment subsidies may be a relatively inefficient and expensive way to achieve distribution objectives since not all low-wage workers are poor (e.g. young workers), particularly when compared with a system of income transfers.[3] A particularly serious omission is the lack of discussion of how employment subsidies should be financed. In all fairness, Professor Fitoussi has suggested elsewhere[4] that employment subsidies should be financed through higher taxes on non-wage income. But this might well introduce new distortions with adverse effects on capital formation, saving, and employment.

As a somewhat modified version of Professor Fitoussi's proposal, I believe that fundamental reforms of tax and transfer systems will be necessary in order to better meet social objectives while permitting greater labour market flexibility without sacrificing social objectives. For example, in some countries it would seem sensible to substantially reduce the level of social security contributions for low-wage workers, with higher-income groups financing a larger share of universal health and pension insurance systems. Such a restructuring of social security contributions would of course need to be accepted by the social partners in order to reduce the risk that changes in contributions are shifted into wages. In other countries, transfers or negative income taxes might have a greater role to play to achieve distribution objectives, although they obviously would need to be fully financed, preferably through expenditure reductions.[5]

At the same time, it is important to recognise that such reforms are unlikely to be very effective unless they are accompanied by increased labour market flexibility in order to allow market forces to play a greater role in wage determination. This is perhaps my biggest disagreement with Professor Fitoussi: unless governments reduce the generosity of unemployment insurance schemes, lessen the many other restrictions that hamper the functioning of European labour markets, and strengthen education and training as opposed to passive income support, I do not believe that structural unemployment is likely to diminish significantly. The positive message from the US experience is that markets do have the ability to create jobs for a much larger proportion of the labour force than presently is the case in Europe.

THE INTERDEPENDENCE BETWEEN LABOUR MARKET REFORMS AND MACROECONOMIC POLICIES

Professor Fitoussi is concerned about the risk that labour market reform be viewed as a substitute for macroeconomic policies in the fight against unemployment. However, I would not only stress the complementarity between structural reform and macroeconomic policies but also their interdependence. This is because Europe seems to be facing a vicious circle in which the same forces that generate high levels of structural unemployment are contributing to excessive growth of public expenditures, large structural fiscal imbalances, and a policy mix that is biased toward lax fiscal policy and, consequently, relatively tight monetary conditions. Fiscal consolidation and a lowering of long-term interest rates are unquestionably important for Europe's longer-term growth and employment prospects. But the necessary degree of improvement in fiscal positions and in labour market conditions will be very hard to achieve simultaneously without fundamental labour market and public expenditure reforms that tackle the roots of the present problem.

NOTES

1. The views expressed are those of the author and do not necessarily represent those of the Fund.
2. See IMF, 1995.
3. See Saint-Paul, 1994.
4. See Fitoussi, 1995.
5. The achievement of distributional objectives does not necessarily require a very large share of public expenditures in GDP, as convincingly argued by Tanzi and Schuknecht, 1995.

BIBLIOGRAPHY

The Economist (1996), "Economics Focus", January 13.

Fitoussi, J.P. (1995), *Le Débat interdit – Monnaie, Europe, Pauvreté*, Arléa, Paris.

International Monetary Fund (1995), *World Economic Outlook*, Washington, May.

Saint-Paul, G. (1994), "Do Labour Market Objectives Fulfill Distributive Objectives? Searching for the Virtues of the European Model", *IMF Staff Papers*, Vol. 41, No. 4, Washington, December.

Tanzi, V. and L. Schuknecht (1995), "The Growth of Government and the Reform of the State in Industrial Countries", *IMF Working Paper*, 130, December.

LONG-RUN MACROECONOMIC EFFECTS
OF FISCAL CONSOLIDATION
AND INCREASED COMPETITION IN EUROPE

by

Werner Röger[1]
European Commission

INTRODUCTION

Two goals currently rank high on the policy agenda for Europe: consolidation of government budgets with the aim of eventually reducing the tax burden, and structural reforms in the markets for goods and services. The first task has become increasingly urgent, since continued fiscal deficits through many years have led to a sizeable public debt which is now considerably narrowing the scope of economic policy. Also ranking high on the policy agenda are structural reforms aiming at opening up markets to foreign companies and also to increase competition among domestic firms. This is achieved by changing and harmonising regulations, removing entry barriers, privatisation etc. Both types of policies were initiated in the 1980s in Europe in an attempt to restore and stimulate growth and employment in the European Union.

The fiscal policy targets set by many European countries coincide more or less with the Maastricht criteria each member state of the European Union must fulfil in order to qualify for Monetary Union in Europe. However, even without these criteria it is clear for many policy makers that reducing debt and deficits will be inevitable. Nevertheless, fiscal consolidation has since then provoked a lot of discussion both among economists and policy makers. Indeed there seems to be little consensus about the short-term gains of such policies, because these depend on many factors over which economists can strongly disagree, like, for example, the size of adjustment costs, the severity of short-term price and wage rigidities, the relevance of forward looking behaviour of households and firms, the credibility of policies, etc. Indeed, the position one adopts on any of these issues strongly shapes the conclusions one reaches about the short-term costs of the adjustment. Some of the crucial questions that can be asked in this context are the following:

— How quickly will private consumption and investment fill the gap left by a reduction in public spending? The answer to this question depends strongly on whether households and firms are basing their consumption and investment decisions on future net earnings and profitability, or whether they tend to a more backward looking or adaptive mode of behaviour.

— How easily will workers — which are laid off because of restructuring, new technologies, etc. — be able to find employment in new or expanding sectors of the economy? This depends strongly on the flexibility of the labour market and the efficiency of training and retraining programmes.

Instead of contributing to this discussion the aim of this paper is more modest. I will concentrate on more longer term issues and ask whether it is worth undergoing these adjustments for European countries, in view of what traditional models of growth will predict concerning the order of magnitude these reforms might have for employment, output, consumption and investment in a longer term perspective. More precisely, the following questions will be addressed in this paper. How large are the long term quantitative impacts, given realistic orders of magnitude of relevant policy impulses? How strongly will this outcome depend on how governments use the proceeds of fiscal consolidation to increase net income of households and/or firms? In other words, how strongly does the outcome depend on the type of taxes that will be lowered after a successful fiscal consolidation attempt? And finally, how strongly does wage behaviour affect the outcome? Or, put differently, could a change in wage behaviour in Europe make a substantial difference to the outcome of these reforms?

A second set of policies currently pursued in Europe consist of many programmes, initiated both at the national level as well as the level of the Community, — most prominently among them the Internal Market Programme for example — to open up markets and increase competition in the markets for goods and services. It would be far too demanding for this paper and for an analysis that is confined to the macroeconomic level to trace out the many consequences these reforms may have on various sectors of the European economy. Instead, I want to confine myself to the following narrow question. Suppose the regulatory reforms implemented in Europe were successful in stimulating competition in the relevant markets for goods and services, i.e. monopoly rents would actually be reduced as a consequence of these reforms, what would be the effect of increased competition for investment, employment, output and real wages in Europe?

How do these two separate issues fit together? One of the most important strategic issues concerns the ability of European countries to sustain their system of social protection or what is sometimes called the "European Model". Both policies, if implemented successfully may contribute towards securing this model. Fiscal reform may have some positive impact, since lowering the tax burden in the long run will enable European countries to increase the wedge between net wage income and unemployment benefits or the value of leisure more generally, without being forced to cut benefits below existing levels. Structural reforms in commodity markets, on the other hand, could both stimulate real economic activity but also lower rent sharing in labour markets and thus have beneficial effects for employment in this way. As we will argue below, goods market reforms could also increase the wedge between net wages and unemployment benefits in the long run. Both policies are similar in precisely this respect, they allow an increase in net wage income, and thus provide incentive effects without lowering social protection. They can therefore also be seen as an alternative to policies which try to create incentive effects by cutting social benefits. How strong these former effects could be in a longer run perspective is the question asked in this paper.

The paper is organised as follows. We first present the model and discuss the major assumptions underlying our analysis. This is followed by the presentation of our results and some sensitivity analysis. The final section concludes.

MODEL DESCRIPTION

The model underlying this analysis is a four region model of the OECD area, comprising EUR15, the United States, Japan and the rest of the OECD as separate blocks. This model is a condensed version of the Commission's new QUEST model that is currently finalised. It is based on the following assumptions. Goods in each region are produced by monopolistically competitive firms. Production technology is given by a neo-classical production function exhibiting constant returns to scale and exogenous technical progress. More specifically, a Cobb Douglas production function is assumed. Output per worker (y) is thus given by

$$y = k^{(1 - \alpha)} \qquad (1)$$

where k is the capital labour ratio and denotes the output elasticity of labour. For expositional purposes, the technology constant is ignored. Household behaviour is characterised by the life cycle hypothesis. Firms try to maximise the present value of their cash flow subject to a capital accumulation and cost of adjustment constraints for both labour and capital. The goods produced in each region are imperfect substitutes for goods produced elsewhere. Capital is assumed to be freely mobile among regions and exchange rates and interest rates are linked across regions via standard interest arbitrage conditions where we assume risk neutrality. So far the analysis is standard. Concerning the labour market, we depart from the standard neo-classical assumption emphasising intertemporal substitution of leisure, and instead adopt a search theoretic hypothesis as suggested by Pissarides (1990). As will be shown below, this model has many advantages for our present purpose. First of all, it is based on the more realistic assumption that workers usually work a fixed time schedule and do not individually adjust working time to economic conditions. Second, it allows to characterise "involuntary unemployment". Third it leaves us with a specification of wage equations which are known from many mainstream empirical studies and it allows us to give a straightforward structural interpretation for the coefficients of this equation. Moreover, Pissarides (1995) has demonstrated the near observational equivalence of this formulation to alternative specifications like, for example, trade union bargaining models or efficiency wage models. Finally it also allows us to look at the neo-classical labour supply hypothesis as a special case.

Why the neo-classical model of growth? Recent years have experienced a revival of growth analysis in general and the neo-classical growth model in particular. Notwithstanding serious measurement problems, numerous empirical studies have shown results which are broadly consistent with the prediction of this model. Among these are the results of Mankiw, Romer and Weil (1992) on the impact of the level of saving and population growth on steady state income, the results of De Long and Summers (1991) on the role of equipment investment and recent results by Mendoza, Milesi-Ferretti and Asea (1995) on the role of taxes. See, for example, Mankiw (1995) for a recent discussion of the record of this model concerning major stylised facts of economic growth.

Before laying out the main mechanisms that we regard as important for evaluating the long term consequences of policies, one important feature of our analysis must be stressed, namely the fact that we explicitly introduce open economy considerations into our analysis. This has serious consequences for the effects of fiscal policy in particular. Many economists would regard a reduction in real interest rates as the main positive effect of fiscal consolidation. This mechanism will largely be absent in our analysis for two reasons. Though Europe is a large region within the OECD, it is not a closed economy, but can borrow on the world financial market. A change in public saving will therefore only have a limited impact on OECD savings and therefore real interest rates. Second, since we adopt the life cycle hypothesis, changes in public savings will, to a large extent, be compensated by private saving, thus interest rate reactions are unlikely to be an important channel transmitting the fiscal impulse into the economy. It is especially this latter feature which may bias our result towards underestimating the full impact of fiscal reforms for both Europe and the OECD as a whole. In the theoretical discussion which follows we will heavily exploit this feature of our model and assume that steady state real interest rates will not be affected by the policies which we are discussing. Of course, our simulations will not be run under this assumption, but the results will largely confirm our assumption of a constant real interest rate.

The assumption that real interest rates are unaltered in the long run allows us to confine our theoretical discussion of the policy implications of the proposed reforms to only the factor markets for labour and (real) capital.

The labour market

Only a very small segment of the labour market corresponds to the Walrasian notion of a spot market, where employers and employees meet to negotiate a new labour contract with a market clearing price every day. Also, labour services offered and demanded in each segment of the labour market are certainly not homogenous. Many highly differentiated skills and abilities are traded. Neither for firms nor for workers is the type of work required or the quality of labour that is offered completely transparent. Also, both workers and firms may have an interest in longer term employment contracts due, for example, to training or mobility costs, or simply as insurance against unemployment. All these different aspects taken together render the services traded in labour markets rather complex and neither for firms nor for workers is it easy to achieve an optimal match. This is the central idea of search theoretic models. Trade in the labour market must be regarded as highly uncoordinated, time-consuming and costly for both workers and firms. In specifying labour market interactions between workers and firms we therefore adopt a model suggested by Pissarides (1990) and augment it slightly by assuming that firms are operating under imperfect competition in the goods market. Pissarides (1995) has shown that alternative models of the labour market like, for example, bargaining models or efficiency wage models, would lead to similar specifications of the wage formation process.

The basic incentives for search activities in the labour market by both workers and firms are the profit opportunities in present value terms which are associated with a successful job match for workers and firms. The net return a worker can get from a successful match is the difference between his permanent income if employed in the current period (h^e) and his permanent income if unemployed (h^u). These two processes can best be described in terms of arbitrage conditions.

$$rh^e = (1-t_l)wc + s(h^u - h^e) + d(h^e)/dt \qquad (2a)$$

$$rh^u = (ben + leis) + p(.)(h^e - h^u) + d(h^u)/dt. \qquad (2b)$$

The left hand side of equation (2a) is the return from the human capital of an employed person and is composed of the net wage rate $[(1 - t_l)wc]$, the risk of losing the job, characterised by a constant separation rate s and any other changes which result from future expected changes in the wage rate and job security. Similarly, the left hand side of equation (2b) is the return for an unemployed worker which consists of unemployment benefits (ben) and the imputed value of leisure (leis), an expected capital gain from moving into employment with probability p(.), which depends on labour market tightness. Also any changes in h^u associated with any future changes in benefits or job prospects will affect current human wealth of an unemployed worker.

The net return a firm can obtain from employing an individual worker (under the assumption that all other workers are employed under the same conditions) is the pure after tax profit per worker in present value terms (J). In calculating the present value the firm also takes into account the positive separation probability s. The profit term in the squared brackets consist of the marginal revenue of the worker plus the monopoly rent minus wage costs.

$$J = \int_0^\infty [\alpha k^{1-\alpha} + \eta(1-\alpha)k^{1-\alpha} - wc]\exp(-\int_0^t (r+s)dz)dt \tag{3}$$

The actual labour demand decision of a firm departs slightly from the conventional first order condition which equates the marginal product of labour to real gross wages. The firm also has to cover adjustment costs for labour which are a function of vacancy costs (vc) and the probability of filling an existing vacancy (q(.)). Since labour is a fixed factor of production it is an asset for the firm, therefore interest rates (r) also play a role in the labour demand schedule. Finally, the absolute value of the price elasticity of demand (η) which determines mark-ups in this model restricts the demand for labour. The marginal condition for employment is given by

$$(1-\eta)\alpha k^{1-\alpha} = (wc + r^*vc/q(.)). \tag{4}$$

Under the assumptions that both parties know about the profit opportunities of their respective partners, firms and workers solve the following Nash bargaining problem by setting wages such as to maximise the product

$$\text{Max } (h^e - h^u)^\beta J^{(1-\beta)}$$
$$\{wc\} \tag{5}$$

where β denotes the bargaining strength of workers, thus it essentially determines the fraction of total profits from a successful job match going to workers. As a solution of this bargaining problem the following wage equation can be derived.

$$wc = (1-\beta)/(1-t)(ben +leis) + \beta[\alpha k^{1-\alpha} + \eta(1-\alpha)k^{1-\alpha} + vc^*p(.)/q(.)] \tag{6}$$

It is interesting to notice the generality of equation (6). It encompasses the neo-classical labour supply hypothesis – based on consumption leisure choice – and formulations of wage equations known from the bargaining literature which identify productivity, benefit levels and labour market tightness as major determinants of wage claims by workers. Which feature dominates in this formulation depends crucially on the parameter β characterising the bargaining strength of workers. Some theoretical insights can be gained by specifying alternative institutional details. Consider first the oldest solution of the pricing problem which is due to Diamond (1973), where employers post wage offers and workers search among them randomly without recall. In this situation it is optimal for firms to set wages equal to the reservation wage since this will be the lowest wage workers are willing to accept. As Mortenson (1987) has pointed out, the assumption that employers post wage offers is sufficient to ensure full bargaining power of firms. Since workers are indifferent in this situation between work and unemployment in this equilibrium, unemployment can under this assumption be termed "voluntary". Recently some other models have been suggested to explain "involuntary" unemployment, especially in Europe. Most prominent among these is the insider-outsider model of Lindbeck and Snower (1987). Under this hypothesis incumbent workers have bargaining power, since replacing them would be costly for the firm because of search costs. Consequently they can extract a share of the rents from the firm. Notice also, since under the assumption of some bargaining strength of workers the wage exceeds the reservation wage, this hypothesis can therefore explain the existence of "involuntary" unemployment.

Gross wages are positively indexed to labour productivity, with a coefficient depending on the bargaining power of workers. More precisely, in the case of perfect competition in the goods market, wages are linked to the marginal product of labour, while in the case of imperfect competition ($\eta > 0$) and positive β there exists some rent sharing between workers and firms. Wages also depend on the reservation wage which is composed of unemployment benefits and the value of leisure. Provided workers have market power, they can demand real wages which exceed their reservation wage. Finally, real wages depend on labour market tightness.

This formulation of the wage equation also exhibits how the two reforms we are discussing will impact on wage behaviour and it shows clearly the impact structural characteristics of labour markets may have on the policy outcome. Before going into an explanation of how taxation affects wages and employment in this model, some differences to the neo-classical labour supply hypothesis should be stressed at this point. In the neo-classical model taxation has its major impact on the supply of hours an economic agent is willing to work for a given gross wage rate, given his marginal utility schedule for both consumption and leisure. In this analysis these considerations are unimportant since we assume that hours of work are institutionally fixed. Therefore the mechanism by which taxation can influence labour market outcomes must be based on different principles. The intuitive economic explanation for tax effects in this model is the following: the two parties in the labour market share profits between each other and they are implicitly playing against a third player, namely the government which tries to extract taxes in the case of a successful job match. Given the fact that wages are taxed it is in the interest of both parties to minimise their "common" tax burden by lowering the net wage, or in other words by reducing the share of workers in total surplus, if taxes are increased, and vice versa if they are reduced. The sensitivity to which the share of workers in total surplus reacts to tax changes varies positively with the bargaining strength of workers.

It is equally important to notice, however, that taxes per se do not have an effect on real wage costs but only in conjunction with the benefit system that we have left unspecified so far. In many OECD countries unemployment benefits are indexed to the wage rate, but it is unclear whether they follow gross or net wages. While statutory rates are likely to be more strongly linked to gross wages it may still be the case that occasional reforms of the benefit system realign benefit payments with the net wage rate. Within this model this institutional feature will have far reaching consequences for the effects of labour taxation on wage costs. Consider the following general unemployment benefit scheme

$$\text{ben} = (1\text{-}t) \; \phi \; b_0 wc \qquad\qquad (7)$$

where b_0 denotes the replacement ratio and the parameter ϕ indicates whether unemployment benefits are linked to gross ($\phi = 0$) or net wages ($\phi = 1$). If unemployment benefits are in fact indexed to net wages then the effect of taxation on wage costs would be rather limited. The impact would only come via the imputed value of leisure which is not taxed.

To summarise our discussion of tax effects, what we would expect from this model therefore is the following. Small reactions of wages to changes in tax rates and therefore small incentive effects should be expected if either of the following conditions is met:

– unemployment benefits are indexed to net wages;
– the bargaining strength of workers is high.

Thus, changes in labour income taxes or social security contributions will generally not lead to proportional changes in wage costs for firms. This will only occur in the special case of zero bargaining strength of workers and indexation of unemployment benefits to gross wages. The fact that zero bargaining strength of workers will be associated with strong tax shifting into wage costs may appear counterintuitive. However, in this case wages are already at a low level such that firms must compete with a reservation wage which is not taxed, *i.e.* a tax increase in a situation where workers have been indifferent to working or remaining unemployed will induce them to switch to non-work activities unless the firm is increasing wages such that their take home pay is unaltered. Of course this situation corresponds closely to the neo-classical model of labour supply.

Notice either of these two conditions could also partly explain why it is so difficult to firmly establish an empirical link between labour tax and/or benefit reforms and unemployment in OECD countries. It clearly suggests that the impact of taxation and unemployment benefits on wages must be looked at simultaneously. At this point it should, however, be emphasised that for the policy experiments conducted in this paper the question of how unemployment benefits have historically been indexed to wages (gross or net) is of minor importance, since we will implicitly assume in our experiments that governments will lower taxes (*i.e.* increase net wages) but will not increase unemployment benefits at the same time. Indeed we will present results for two alternatives: first we will assume that unemployment benefits remain linked to gross wages, *i.e.* they will change to the extent to which gross wages adjust to the fiscal and structural reforms. In a second set of simulations selected results will be presented with unemployment benefits fixed at the current level.

As presented so far, the model is able to encompass many different hypotheses on wage formation. Combining this wage equation with a standard neo-classical labour demand schedule can moreover explain two basic stylised facts of many European labour markets, namely a strong positive contemporaneous correlation between real wages (productivity) and GDP over the business cycle, but a zero or even slightly negative correlation between real wages/labour productivity and employment. This phenomenon can be captured in this model, since for sufficiently high values of the bargaining strength of workers (β), the replacement ratio (b_0) and/ or monopoly rents (η), it implies a downward sloping wage curve at least in the short run. As is shown in the Figure 1, this, together with a downward sloping labour demand equation, results in wage increases associated with an increase in demand but a decline in employment.

The intuitive theoretical explanation for this phenomenon goes as follows. Consider a monopolistically competitive firm which is experiencing a positive unit shock to technology (*i.e.* disembodied technical progress). For given real wages the firm would be willing to expand employment by $(1 - \eta)\alpha$, *i.e.* by less than the marginal product of labour since it expects a downward sloping demand curve for

◆ Figure 1. ***Equilibrium in the European Labour Market***

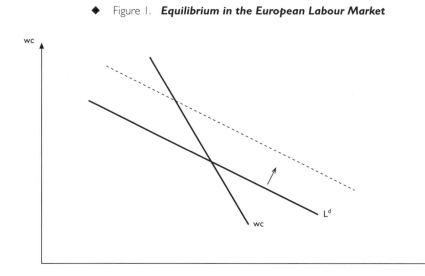

Note: For definition see text.

its products. (Incumbent) Workers on the other side want to participate in the productivity increase by demanding wage increases which do not only cover the marginal product (which the monopolistically competitive firm would not be willing to grant without a reduction in employment), but they also aim at extracting a fraction of the monopoly rent from the firm and thus may demand more than the marginal product of labour. The conflict between a firm which would be willing to grant wage increases which are smaller than the increase in marginal product of labour and workers wanting their share in monopoly profits is resolved by reducing employment. It should, however, be stressed that a downward sloping wage curve is not the automatic outcome of the bargaining model; it only occurs if the replacement ratio (b_0), the bargaining strength of workers β and/or mark-ups (η) are sufficiently high. In the current version of the model we have selected a value of .4 for the replacement ratio, a value of .5 for the bargaining strength of workers and a value of .12 for η. The appendix to this paper describes how these parameters have been selected for aggregate Europe.

The estimates of β largely determine the degree of tax shifting in this model. This allows us to contrast basic policy implications of this model with other studies. Our preferred estimate for Europe is .5 for β which implies that roughly 50 per cent of the change in labour income tax is shifted forward into wage costs. This estimate is at the lower end of available estimates. It is not inconsistent with estimates obtained by the OECD. Results cited in the Jobs-Study (Tyrväinen, 1995) show some variation over Europe, implying a very high degree of tax shifting for Germany (100 per cent) but substantially smaller values for other European countries such as 40 per cent for France and Italy and 25 per cent for the United Kingdom. The results obtained for Japan, implying tax shifting of 50 per cent and for the United States implying 100 per cent are also roughly in line with our estimates, since we assume similar parameters for Japan (but a higher elasticity of wages to the unemployment rate) and a bargaining strength of .2 for the United States.

The capital market

Equilibrium in the market for real capital is established along conventional lines. In order to determine their optimal capital stock firms equate the marginal product of capital, adjusted for a mark-up factor to the capital cost, which consist of the real interest rate, the rate of depreciation (δ) and the effective corporate tax rate (t_c)

$$(1-\eta)(1-\alpha)k^{-\alpha} = (r+\delta)/(1-t_c). \qquad (8)$$

For the theoretical discussion we neglect adjustment costs for capital. In the model it is assumed that investment is subject to rising marginal cost of installation. The unit installation costs are assumed to be a linear function of the investment to capital ratio. The supply of funds is perfectly elastic for a given level of the real interest rate.

THEORETICALLY EXPECTED EFFECTS

Notice now equations (4), (6), (7) and (8) fully describe the long term adjustment of the economy under the assumption that interest rates are entirely fixed in the long run and the value of leisure is exogenous. The analytical results which can be derived from this set of equations serves therefore as a good first approximation for the effects that we expect from the simulations. Both fiscal reforms and goods market reforms will have an impact on the economy only to the extent in which they influence factor markets. First we consider fiscal consolidation. The effect of fiscal consolidation within this framework is entirely confined to a reaction of the private sector to changes in taxation induced by the reform. Both a cut in expenditure and a debt reduction will eventually make room for tax cuts which can be handed over to the private sector in various forms: as a reduction in lump sum taxes, labour income taxes or corporate taxes. Let us consider the three options in turn.

Lump sum taxes:

They will not have any impact on factor markets and therefore their effects on employment and GDP will be negligible in the long run. Their main effect is likely to be a switch in demand from public to private consumption.

Labour income taxes:

A decrease in labour income taxes has clearly identifiable effects as long as the level of unemployment benefits remain constant or are fixed to gross wages. First notice the long run capital output ratio remains unaffected. From equation (4), this implies that real wage costs will also remain constant. However, since the ratio between net take home wage and unemployment benefits has changed, the wage curve shifts downwards and a new equilibrium with higher employment and higher net wages will eventually be established. Formally this can be shown by inserting (4) into (6) to substitute for wc. Notice this long run effect on net wages is quite independent from the wage rule, indeed the same increase of net wages will occur for any parametrisation of the wage rule. The wage equation in the long run only determines the level of employment. This suggests an intertemporal trade off. A wage rule which implies a strong short run indexation of wages to productivity will be associated with a lower response of investment to an initial corporate tax impulse and therefore will lead to a new equilibrium with a smaller level of employment. On the other hand, a less strong indexation of real wages will be associated with a stronger corporate tax multiplier and thus lead to an equilibrium with more employment. Notice, however, real wages over the transition path to the new steady state will be higher in the case of strong productivity indexation of real wages.

Corporate income taxes:

Reducing corporate taxes will lead to an increase in capital intensity of production and will thus increase the marginal product of labour. Eventually real wages will increase until the new marginal condition for labour holds. Again, by inserting the first order condition for labour into the wage curve shows that in this case the level of employment may be largely unaltered. This conclusion does, however, strongly rest on the assumption that unemployment benefits will also increase with wage costs. Under the alternative assumption of fixed unemployment benefit levels, the productivity increase generates an incentive effect for labour since it drives a stronger wedge between net wages and the value of leisure.

Mark-up ratio:

An increase of competition will have the most comprehensive effects on labour markets and employment in the neo-classical growth model. As can be seen from equations (4), (6) and (8) it will affect labour demand, investment and wage claims simultaneously in the desired direction. For given wage and capital costs, firms will demand more labour and capital. Also possibilities of rent sharing between workers and firms have declined thus putting downward pressure on wages. Given the magnifying effects of these reactions a new equilibrium with higher levels of output and higher levels of both employment and real wages is likely to be established in the longer term.

THE LONG TERM EFFECTS OF FISCAL ADJUSTMENT IN EUROPE

According to the latest forecasts (autumn 1995), the EU is running a government deficit of 4.7 as a per cent of GDP in 1995 and the debt to GDP ratio is now 71 per cent. Given the Maastricht criteria this situation calls for a substantial fiscal tightening in the coming years. Fiscal tightening can of course be achieved either by increasing government receipts or by lowering expenditure. Both economic theory but also some recent empirical studies (see, for example Alesina and Perotti, 1995) suggest that successful fiscal consolidations have mostly been associated with a strategy of cutting expenditure. To show the long run benefits of a cut in government expenditure over an increase in taxes we will compare two possible developments with each other. In a first base line scenario it is assumed that governments will actually not succeed in reducing the debt to GDP ratio and are also not able to cut government spending. This development will be contrasted to a situation where it is assumed that European governments will manage a cut in (primary) spending as a share of GDP by about 2 percentage points permanently, and in addition reach the desired government debt target of 60 per cent. In order to avoid discussions on how government services should be treated in national accounts, we think of the fiscal reform as a reduction in the share of government purchases of goods and services and a cut in government transfers by roughly similar absolute amounts. In this simulation we think of transfer cuts which are unrelated to unemployment compensation such as spending on health, education and pensions. This is largely done for technical reasons since we want to show the effects of a cut in government spending and not a combined effect of a cut in spending together with a cut in benefits.

Our perspective in this paper will be on the long term consequences of such policies. That means we are ignoring possible short term adjustment problems and concentrate fully at the effects which will occur after all mechanisms involved had their time to work themselves out within the new economic environment. As mentioned above, this perspective has the advantage that from a theoretical and political perspective the effects are possibly less controversial and we can fully exploit the comparative advantage a growth model offers for the analysis of long term reactions.

In order to make a proper long term comparison one has to ask: how would major macroeconomic aggregates evolve in the long run, if governments continued with the current level of spending as a share of GDP and made no effort to reduce the debt to GDP ratio but instead increased lump sum taxes of households to the extent required to prevent an increase in the debt to GDP ratio? This scenario is our baseline case.

Table I contrasts the current economic situation in Europe with the long run behaviour under the baseline assumption of fiscal policy in the European Union. The long run solution is calculated on the assumption that labour saving technical progress and population grow at a constant rate of 1.7 and .3 per cent p.a., i.e. with growth rates roughly comparable to the trend growth observed over the 1980s. The second line shows the costs of maintaining the current government shares in terms of the losses incurred on private consumption. The increase in lump sum taxes associated with maintaining the government share at the current level would require a reduction in private consumption of slightly more than 2 percentage points. Since households bear the costs of financing the government, investment would roughly remain at its historically given level. Our assumptions on wage behaviour also imply that unemployment would be stabilised at the current level. The share of government expenditure and government debt remain at their given levels in the long run.

To this scenario we compare a steady state solution where governments manage to reduce their spending by 2 per cent of GDP permanently and cut the debt to GDP ratio to 60 per cent. Alternatively, they adjust lump sum taxes, payroll taxes or

Table 1. **Baseline projection (EUR15)**

	1981-84	1995	Long-run projection
GDP (per cent, per annum)	2.0	2.7	2.0
C/GDP	61.1	61.4	57.1
I/GDP	19.8	19.3	20.0
LUR	9.3	10.7	10.1
G/GDP	47.7	51.9	51.9
DEBT/GDP	57.7	71.0	71.0

Note: GDP = gross domestic product.
C = private consumption.
I = total investment.
LUR = unemployment rate.
G = total government expenditure.
DEBT = government debt.
Source: European Union and own projections.

corporate income taxes to achieve sustainability of the budgetary situation. The long run beneficial effects of a cut in the government share (g) and/or the debt to GDP ratio (b) can clearly be seen from the government budget constraint which implies the following relationship between the interest payments and the primary surplus when variables are expressed as ratios of GDP

$$(r-\pi)b = (t_d + t_{ls} - g).\tag{9}$$

Here t_{ls} and t_d denote lump sum and distortionary tax rates respectively and π is the long run growth rate of the economy. From this formulation it is fairly obvious that for a given level of the government debt, any permanent change in government expenditure share must be accompanied by a permanent change in the share of government revenue in the same order of magnitude and in the same direction. Because both r and π will be largely unaltered by fiscal reforms in the long run a cut in the share of government expenditure (g) by 2 percentage points will allow a reduction in the overall tax burden of about 2 percentage points in the long run. The relationship between taxation and government debt seems less obvious and will depend crucially on the difference between the real rate of interest and the growth rate of the economy. Though dynamic efficiency implies that interest rates will exceed the growth rate, as is the case in our model solution, Ball and Mankiw (1995) argue on empirical grounds that this relationship does not hold for the US economy, for example. If this were correct it would allow the US government in principle to roll over debt. A real growth rate exceeding the rate of interest automatically insures that the economy grows its way out of the debt.

To disentangle the economic effects of the debt reduction from those of a spending cut, we first look at the long term gains of a policy which has achieved reducing government debt by 11 per cent but has left the expenditure share of the government untouched. Under the permanent income hypothesis under which "Ricardian Equivalence" does approximately hold, the level of debt should not have an effect on economic activity. Private and public saving would just compensate each other. Since we are adopting the life cycle hypothesis under the assumption that the forward-looking horizon of households is approximately over the range of one generation, we expect some small positive effects from reducing the debt to GDP ratio alone, since under these conditions households regard government debt partly as net wealth. A reduction in government debt could therefore slightly increase the private savings rate.

However, results indicate the wealth effect of public debt on private consumption must be regarded as extremely small under the life cycle hypothesis. Reducing the debt to GDP ratio by roughly 11 percentage points would lead to a long run increase of real GDP by around .09 per cent, if the proceeds from smaller government interest payments would be given to private households in the form of lump sum taxes. Handing over the proceeds to the private sector in the form of lower distortionary taxes would slightly increase the positive effect to around .2 per cent in the long run. It can safely be concluded that large positive effects from fiscal consolidation are unlikely to come from reductions in government debt as long as we assume that private households largely discount future tax payments associated with government debt. If we expect substantial gains from fiscal consolidation those must then come from a reduction in the share of government spending in current GDP, to which we turn next. Now we look at the combined policy of both a reduction in the debt to GDP ratio and a cut in government spending of 2 per cent as a share of GDP.

We turn to the discussion of the long term effects of a cut in government spending. Since this paper is mainly concerned with the possible long term effects of a cut in government expenditure, the short term adjustment will be largely neglected in our discussion.[2] The results in the tables reported below refer to level differences between the non-consolidation and the various consolidation scenarios after a period of roughly 10 years i.e. when the economy has settled down on a new long run growth path.

Given the previous theoretical discussion it is important how the government returns the consolidation gains to the private sector, i.e. the tax revenue that is no longer needed to finance the (smaller) government primary expenditure share and the (reduced) debt service burden. Consider first the case with our given estimates of the wage equation listed in columns (1) to (3) of Table 2. If lump sum taxes (TLS) for households are lowered, then the effect of a fiscal consolidation are largely limited to a switch from public to private consumption expenditure with nearly zero positive effects on GDP and employment. The results also confirm the previous conjecture that the most positive employment effects should result from a reduc-

Table 2. **Effects of fiscal consolidation in Europe**

	High bargaining strength[1]			Low bargaining strength[2]		
	(1) TLS	(2) TL	(3) TC	(4) TLS	(5) TL	(6) TC
GDP	0.05	0.31	2.37	0.05	1.68	2.73
C	1.83	2.07	2.03	1.85	3.34	2.38
I	0.09	0.35	7.38	0.12	1.73	7.80
L	0.01	0.28	0.03	0.02	1.75	0.43
W	0.04	0.02	2.31	0.03	−0.06	2.28

Note: Results are percentage deviation from baseline levels.
       GDP = gross domestic product.
       C = private consumption.
       I = private investment.
       L = employment.
       W = wage costs.
       All results refer to EUR15 aggregates.
1. Value for β of 0.5.
2. Value for β 0.25.

tion in labour income taxes (TL). A reduction in corporate taxes yields the highest benefits in terms of GDP growth which is generated by substantial increases in investment.

In columns (4) to (6) of this table we list results obtained with an alternative wage rule. This experiment is conducted for two reasons. First, in the theoretical section of the paper it was conjectured that the wage rule would not so much determine the level of real wages itself in the long run, but rather the level of employment. Second, the wage equation in the model is, of course, calibrated to meet certain moment conditions in the historically observed data. Given the severity of the European unemployment problem it cannot be excluded that there will be changes in wage behaviour in Europe in the coming years, with trade unions putting much more emphasis on employment creation than before. Recent suggestions of the German trade union leadership of decoupling wages from productivity, at least temporarily, are one important indication in this direction.

In the alternative wage rule it is assumed that β is reduced to .25, which is a value that is estimated for the US wage equation. In order for the theoretical economy to reach a baseline steady state with 11 per cent unemployed, we compensate this change by introducing a positive exogenous value of leisure. As can be seen from column (5), now the labour tax experiment gives substantially higher increases in employment with only slightly smaller real wages. Also a less strong contemporaneous response of real wages to productivity increases the investment response to tax changes considerably. This largely confirms our theoretical conjecture.

Though there emerges a clear ranking of policies with respect to GDP and employment objectives, it seems nevertheless surprising that in the case of lump sum taxes private consumption increases nearly as much as in the other cases. Larger differences between the various tax options can only be seen in the case where we allow for stronger incentive effects by reducing β. Another interesting feature of these results concerns the relative gains from a change in corporate taxes versus a change of labour income taxes. Our results so far would clearly favour a labour tax reduction over a decrease in corporate taxes. Here it must, however, be noted that due to the strong increase in productivity and real wages with the corporate tax experiment we are implicitly looking at a combined shock of a decrease in corporate tax rates and an increase in unemployment benefits. Notice, an increase in unemployment benefits does not occur in the other two experiments, since in these cases real wages remain roughly constant. The results for the corporate tax experiment with constant unemployment benefits are shown in Table 3.

The employment effects from this policy are now increased, but still they only amount to about 50 per cent of the employment effect that could be achieved with lower labour income taxes. This policy would yield the highest increase in GDP, and would likely be the most optimal solution from a simple welfare theoretic point of view, since it allows an increase in consumption in the order of magnitude of the labour tax reform with less labour input. If, however, employment is a goal in itself for policy makers and private households, then the labour tax reform is clearly preferred.

How do these simulation results relate to other recent empirical findings on the relationship between taxation and growth? In recent years various studies, mostly using a combination of cross section and time series data, test growth model predictions concerning the effects of income tax rates. Easterly and Rebelo (1993), for example, got somewhat mixed results. While they find a rather strong negative correlation between tax rates and growth for OECD countries, they also notice that by controlling for initial income this effect is substantially weakened and

Table 3. **Effects of corporate taxes with benefits fixed**

	High bargaining strength	Low bargaining strength
GDP	2.52	3.18
C	2.15	2.75
I	7.68	8.39
L	0.17	0.85
W	2.35	2.30

Note: Results are percentage deviations from baseline levels.

they find it difficult to disentangle the effects of fiscal variables from those of the initial level of income. However, in a dataset covering both industrial and developing economies they obtain statistically significant negative effects of income tax rates for both the growth rate per capita and the ratio of private investment to GDP, even after controlling for initial income and various human capital indicators. Recently, Mendoza *et al.* (1995) have presented cross section and time series results with effective tax rates for consumption, labour and capital used separately in the regressions. Even after controlling for variables like initial income per capita, human capital and terms of trade, they find significant negative effects of both labour taxes and capital taxes on the investment to GDP ratio. Their empirical results suggest that a reduction of the labour income tax or the capital tax by 10 percentage points would increase the investment rate by 1.8 and 1.3 percentage point respectively. Our results differ in that respect from their results since we do not get an increase in the investment to GDP ratio with the labour tax experiment. Our corporate tax experiment gives results which come close to these estimates. Here we get a reduction of the corporate tax rate of about 5 percentage points and an increase of the investment to GDP ratio of about 1 per cent. Empirical results obtained concerning the growth rate of GDP itself are generally less robust, in the light of the traditional growth model. However, this is not surprising since it would not predict a permanent increase in the growth of income per capita but only a level effect. As already mentioned above, our results concerning the degree of tax shifting in Europe are not inconsistent with estimates obtained by the OECD, using very different methodologies.

LONG TERM EFFECTS OF INCREASED COMPETITION IN EUROPE

The first question to be asked for this sort of exercise is, of course, what reduction in price cost mark-ups could be expected from successful structural reforms in European markets for goods and services? This question is difficult to answer for at least two reasons. Available estimates differ strongly concerning the size of mark-ups, and depend heavily on the methodology adopted for estimating them. For example, Hall (1988) finds very high mark-ups for US manufacturing. In subsequent work, various authors using refinements to both the data (see, for example, Norrbin, 1994) and the methodology (see, for example, Röger, 1995) find much lower mark-ups. But even if reliable estimates could be obtained there still remains a problem of interpretation. Do these estimates reflect pure monopoly rents or do they to a large extent only cover existing sunk costs or other fixed costs for firms? In this paper, we deal with these issues in a rather pragmatic way. The existing empirical evidence (see, for example, OECD, 1995) seems to suggest that mark-ups in European countries are indeed somewhat higher than in the United States. The estimated mark-up of prices over marginal cost for US manufacturing, obtained by the OECD, is at around 10 per cent. Corresponding results for European countries are generally higher with an average value between 13 and 14 per cent. Given the similar industry structure and technologies adopted in both economies it seems reasonable to assume that this difference actually reflects to a large extent differences in the level of protection of firms and not so much differences in industry and cost structure. This difference may be regarded as a lower bound for a possible reduction in monopoly rents that could be achieved in Europe as a result of structural reforms. In the results presented in this section we therefore look at the impact of a reduction in European mark-ups of 3 per cent.

The results of this exercise shows (see Table 4) that indeed some beneficial effects for employment can be expected. The effects seem to culminate in a strong increase in investment activities by firms. The induced increase in labour productivity allows for higher real wages in the long run, despite the fact that rent sharing between workers and firms may initially lead to a decline in wages relative to a baseline with higher monopoly rents. That these reforms may be associated with serious distributional consequences can be seen from the change in private consumption. Private consumption increases significantly less than GDP, despite the strong increase in wage income, thus profit income of households is significantly reduced in this case. Also, the outcome of the structural reform is somewhat dependent on the wage curve. Here one could conjecture that since in the case of higher bargaining strength the direct rent sharing effect on wages from a reduction in mark-ups would be higher, the overall expansionary effects should also be stronger. This conjecture is, however, not borne out by our results, which suggest that the expansionary effects may again be stronger with smaller indexation to labour productivity.

Looking at the strong increase of real wages associated with this policy, which is caused by the increase in labour productivity, there is some room available for policy to increase the wedge between net income and unemployment benefits in this scenario, by keeping real unemployment benefits at baseline level. The results

Table 4. **Effects of increased competition (with benefits indexed)**

	High bargaining strength	Low bargaining strength
GDP	2.91	3.82
C	1.01	1.81
I	6.44	7.38
L	1.31	2.27
W	5.19	5.13

Note: Results are percentage deviations from baseline levels.

Table 5. **Effects of increased competition (with benefits fixed)**

	High bargaining strength	Low bargaining strength
GDP	3.30	4.79
C	1.29	2.61
I	7.02	8.51
L	1.64	3.22
W	5.25	5.14

Note: Results are percentage deviations from baseline levels.

presented in Table 5 correspond to such a policy regime. The employment effect of increasing the wedge will be rather limited in the case of our historically given value for β, but they could be substantial for a wage rule with smaller indexation to productivity.

CONCLUSIONS

This paper has looked at the long run quantitative effects associated with substantial fiscal and structural reforms in Europe. It appears that though these reforms will certainly not be sufficient to solve the European unemployment problem, they nevertheless seem to go quite a long way in alleviating it. If, as assumed in this analysis, the major impact of the fiscal reform is not so much a reduction in real interest rates, because of open economy and life cycle considerations, then the permanent positive impulse generated by the fiscal reforms will rest largely on the incentive effects that will arise from the room of manoeuvre available to governments to lower taxes.

Most of these policies will be employment creating, to the extent to which they increase the gap between net wages and unemployment benefits. Though they will not be associated with a cut in unemployment benefits, they will nevertheless have distributional consequences, since they will increase net wage rates between 4 and 6 per cent while the level of unemployment benefits will largely be unaffected. These results also heavily rest on the assumption concerning the wage rule that will prevail in the future.

Our results of the macroeconomic effects of structural reforms show that these could be sizeable. Goods market imperfections in the order assumed in this analysis can cause output losses which are similar in size to gains expected from future fiscal reforms. It is especially the combined effect of an increase in factor demand and a reduction in rent sharing which leads to these employment outcomes. The distributional effect in this case would of course mainly concern shareholders and workers.

Appendix

SELECTION OF PARAMETER VALUES
FOR EUROPEAN WAGE RULE AND THE MARK-UP

The estimation of wage equation poses substantial methodological difficulties. Especially if terms like labour productivity appear as an explanatory variable, problems of identification are not avoidable. Estimation of an aggregate European wage equation poses even more problems to the econometrician. Our strategy, therefore, has been to select as much information as possible from existing labour market studies in order to parameterise the model and the wage rule in particular. To fix the wage response to unemployment and vacancies we draw on recent results from Burda and Wyplosz (1994) who have recently estimated the elasticity of matches with respect to unemployment to vary between .5 and .7 for major European countries. Layard *et al.* (1990) provide some information on "equilibrium separation rates" from data on gross labour market flows. According to their figures the inflow rate into unemployment fluctuates between one and two per cent for the reported European countries per quarter. Given this information and information of vacancy rates, the average rate in which firms can fill existing vacancies could be determined. Unfortunately, vacancy statistics are highly unreliable and nearly incomparable across countries within Europe. (For a detailed discussion see OECD Employment Outlook 1992). On vacancy durations specifically we could only find data for Germany (Erdmann 1990). According to these figures the average duration of vacancies over the period 1974 to 1990 was about two months. We take this figure as roughly representative for Europe and assume that firms can fill existing vacancies within a quarter. Also, internationally comparable figures on unemployment compensation are not easy to obtain, since countries do not only differ with respect to the replacement ratio but also with respect to benefit duration and coverage. To cover all these different aspects, Layard *et al.* have calculated expenditures on unemployment benefits per unemployed person as a per cent of output per worker for major OECD countries for the year 1987. According to these figures the ratio is highest for Denmark (42 per cent) and lowest for Italy (4 per cent) and no calculations are presented for Portugal and Greece. The European average is slightly below

20 per cent. We therefore assume that unemployment benefits amount to roughly 40 per cent of gross wages.

The crucial question that remains to be answered is how strong is the bargaining strength of workers. It is needless to say that this is a hard question to answer empirically. There have been numerous attempts to pin down such a coefficient by using observable characteristics of labour markets such as degree of unionisation, days lost due to strikes, etc. Here we are pursuing an entirely different strategy. The parameter β and the value of leisure (which we set equal to a constant for the purpose of this exercise) together with some other parameters, are determined by exposing the model to exogenous shocks to supply (shocks to total factor productivity) and demand (shocks to government consumption and money shocks) and selected parameter values in such a way that the model replicates an average European unemployment rate of roughly 11 per cent, a standard deviation of employment relative to GDP of 60 per cent and a zero contemporaneous correlation between labour productivity and employment. Putting the bargaining strength of workers to .5 and the exogenous value of leisure to zero allows the model to replicate these observed moments.

Another parameter for which estimates are not readily available is the average mark-up ratio for Europe and the US. Here we have selected a parameter of .12 for η which gives a mark-up ratio between prices and marginal cost of roughly 13 per cent, a value which does not seem entirely out of line with empirical evidence, given the recent findings obtained by the OECD. The estimate obtained for the US is 9.5 per cent.

NOTES

1. The views expressed in this paper are entirely those of the author and should not be attributed to the European Commission.

2. In recent work (see Int'Veld and Röger, 1995) we have analysed the short-term response extensively under alternative assumptions on the speed in which spending cuts are implemented. Our conclusion is that even if fiscal consolidation is perfectly credible to the private sector, such a policy will generally be accompanied by short-term output losses. This result occurs especially if the cut in government spending is phased in over a period of five to ten years. If the policy can be implemented as a one shot reduction, the so called "Non-Keynesian effects" (see, for example, Giavazzi and Pagano, 1990) of fiscal policy, with a short run negative fiscal multiplier can arise. The reason why the fiscal multiplier is positive in the short run in general, even under neoclassical assumptions is simple. A credibly announced gradual reduction in government spending will lead to a rise in private consumption, exceeding the decline in public expenditure in the short-term and will thus crowd out investment via higher interest rates. The short run multiplier is, however, below one. After a period of 3 to 5 years (depending on tax policy) the output effects of a fiscal consolidation become positive.

BIBLIOGRAPHY

Alesina, A. and R. Perotti (1995), "Fiscal Adjustment: Fiscal Expansions and Adjustments in OECD Countries", *Economic Policy*, 205-48.

Ball, L. and N.G. Mankiw (1995), "What Do Budget Deficits Do?", *Federal Reserve Bank of Kansas City Symposium on Budget Deficits and Debt*.

Burda, M. and C. Wyplosz (1994), "Gross Worker and Job Flows in Europe", *European Economic Review*, 1287-1315.

De Long, J.B. and L.H. Summers (1991), "Equipment Investment and Economic Growth: How Strong is the Nexus?", *Quarterly Journal of Economics*, 157-99.

Diamond, P. (1973), "Aggregate Demand Management in Search Equilibrium", *Journal of Political Economy*, 881-94.

Easterly, W. and S. Rebelo (1993), "Fiscal Policy and Economic Growth: An Empirical Investigation", *Journal of Monetary Economics*, 417-58.

Giavazzi, F. and M. Pagano (1990), "Can Severe Fiscal Contractions be Expansionary? Tales of Two Small European Countries", *NBER Macroeconomics Annual*, 75-116.

Hall, R.E. (1988), "The Relation Between Price and Marginal Cost in US Industry", *Journal of Political Economy*, 921-47.

Inet'Veld, J. and W. Röger (1995), "Non-Keynesian Effects of Fiscal Contractions in a Forward Looking Model", mimeo, European Commission, Brussels.

Layard, R., S. Nickell and R. Jackman (1991), *Unemployment*, Oxford University Press, Oxford.

Lindbeck, A. and D. Snower (1988), *The Insider-Outsider Theory*, MIT-Press, Cambridge, MA.

Mankiw, N.G. (1995), "The Growth of Nations", *Brookings Papers of Economic Activity*, 275-326.

Mankiw, N.G., D. Romer and D.N. Weil (1992), "A Contribution to the Empirics of Economic Growth", *Quarterly Journal of Economics*, 407-73.

Mendoza, G.E., G.M. Milesi-Ferretti and P. Asea (1995), "Do Taxes Matter for Long-Run Growth? Harberger's Superneutrality Conjecture", Board of Governors of the Federal Reserve System, *International Finance Discussion Papers*, No. 511.

Mendoza, G.E., A. Razin and L.L. Tesar (1994), "Effective Tax Rates in Macroeconomics: Cross Country Estimates of Tax Rates on Factor Incomes and Consumption", *Journal of Monetary Economics*, 297-323.

Mortensen, D.T. (1989), "The Persistence and Indeterminacy of Unemployment in Search Equilibrium", *Scandinavian Journal of Economics*, 347-70.

Norrbin, S.C. (1993), "The Relation between Price and Marginal Cost: A Contradiction", *Journal of Political Economy*, 1149-64.

OECD (1994), *The OECD Jobs Study*, Paris.

OECD (1995), *Competition, Regulation and Performance*, Paris.

Pissarides, C.A. (1990), *Equilibrium Unemployment Theory*, Basil Blackwell, Oxford.

Pissarides, C.A. (1995), "The Modelling of Employment Taxes in Labour Market Equilibrium", unpublished manuscript, London.

Röger, W. (1995), "Can Imperfect Competition Explain the Difference between Primal and Dual Productivity Measures? Estimates for US Manufacturing", *Journal of Political Economy*, 316-30.

Tyrväinen, T. (1995), "Real Wage Resistance and Unemployment: Multivariate Analysis of Cointegrating Relations in 10 OECD Countries", *The Jobs Study Working Paper Series*, 10, OECD.

COMMENTS

by

P. Andersen*

I would like to start my comments on Mr. Röger's paper with a short quotation from the *Wall Street Journal*.

"Since the early 1990s, the European Union has pitched fiscal crackdown with the fair-weather promise that deficit reduction over the longer term will yield faster growth, more jobs and a single European currency as a bonus.

Nobody could argue with that, and few did. But after economic growth collapsed and joblessness soared last year, it is clear that Europe's fiscal adjustment will be more difficult, hurt more people and last longer than many thought."

Wall Street Journal, 15 April, 1996, page 1

I have a few problems with this paper, but in my remarks I shall try to be constructive. To this end I have structured my comments into three parts: Theoretical/Technical; Empirical Results and General Observations.

THEORETICAL/TECHNICAL COMMENTS

Model

The general model is presented as a "growth model", which might give some readers the impression that the simulation results refer to the effects of fiscal consolidation on steady-state growth rates. However, the actual model used is a very traditional neo-classical model and it is well known that in such models changes in investment and consumption ratios do not affect steady-state growth rates but only steady-state income levels. It is also well known, however, that the transition between alternative steady states are very long and can take up to 35 years (Mankiw *et al.*, 1992) and I interpret the tables as showing effects on transitional growth rates (on which I have more to say further below). Now, growth

---

* The following comments are my own views and are not necessarily shared by the BIS.

effects of the magnitude shown in the tables for several decades are high enough to impress me, but the precise definition should be clarified.

Policy variables

Another well known feature of the neo-classical growth model is that it is silent with respect to the influence of policies. Extensions to the neo-classical model, incorporating human capital and different types of capital goods (see, for instance, de Long and Summers, 1992, Mankiw *et al., op. cit.* and Mendoza *et al.*, 1995) provide a link to policies, so that we do not need to enter the uncertain area of endogenous growth models. Röger's model does not, however, have these extensions. Instead it includes demand and supply equations for the labour market. This is a neat and novel idea, but it is not clear to me how these equations, which are essentially short term, are integrated with a neo-classical growth model and the paper would gain in clarity if this integration was more formally explained.

Labour supply or wage setting equation

Precisely with respect to the short-term part of the model I had some trouble reconciling the downward-sloping wage setting equation in Figure I with what we normally see in the empirical literature, including numerous papers by the first speakers at this Conference and several of their colleagues at the LSE. Although I can see how, on certain assumptions, the wage-setting equation obtains a negative slope, I do not find this result convincing. At the very least, the author should provide an alternative set of simulations based on a slope of the wage-setting equation which is consistent with the consensus view.

Role of supply-side parameters

The rather important role which the model assigns to supply-side parameters also leaves me with a feeling of unease. From my own experience with estimates of wage-setting equations I know how difficult it is to identify significant and stable parameters for tax and benefit variables and to determine whether changes in such variables have a permanent or transitory effect on the level of wages. Perhaps the author has managed to obtain satisfactory results but until I have seen more specific evidence I remain sceptical.

EMPIRICAL RESULTS

Transition path

How are we to interpret the results reported for the simulations of fiscal consolidation? As far as I can make out, the simulations are done in two stages. In a first stage, public expenditure and debt ratios are reduced; then, at a second stage, it is assumed that by some magic trick enough room has been created to allow governments to reduce taxes and the simulations then refer to this second stage. I can easily believe that tax reductions will have the effects shown in the paper and it is plausible and consistent with other results in this area that lower corporate taxes have stronger output effects than lower labour and lump-sum taxes. I also share the view that fiscal consolidation has become increasingly urgent and is needed in virtually all industrial countries to secure long-run sustainability.

However, as illustrated by the above quote, it is equally clear that fiscal consolidation is becoming increasingly difficult and that, for quite a while, the transitional problems will dominate the long-run gains. Consequently, the paper appears to provide us with a picture of what the promised land of fiscal consolidation looks like, while the far more interesting and policy-relevant problems concerning the transition path to the promised land are conveniently ignored.

I also find it unconvincing to ignore the transitional uncertainties on the grounds that too much depends on various assumptions made. Indeed, in addition to the issues already alluded to in the above quote, there are at least two more that would be worth considering:

- could Europe phase the risk of a self-reinforcing recessionary spiral when all EU members simultaneously adopt more restrictive fiscal policies in an attempt to meet certain targets within a very short time period? I hope not, but given the close trade links in Europe, we should not ignore this issue;
- in what shape will the EU countries arrive at the gate to the promised land? Considering the current problems and the fiscal rigour required I am not at all sure that the baseline projections give a realistic picture of the initial conditions; or, to put it differently, to satisfy the baseline conditions the transitional period could be quite long and is likely to differ in length between countries.

Real interest rates

While the previous remarks throw some doubt on the positive growth effects, the assumption of unchanged real interest rates following fiscal consolidation seems to me unnecessarily restrictive. First, the assumption of Ricardian equivalence strikes me as unrealistic and inconsistent with the general consensus of empirical estimates. Though dependent on whether fiscal consolidation is obtained through tax increases or expenditure cuts, the empirical literature suggests that only one-half of a rise in public saving will be offset by lower private saving. Secondly, the EU area is certainly large enough to have a non-negligible effect on world real interest rates. Hence, on both accounts we can expect fiscal consolidation in EU to have a sizeable effect on world real interest rates. Thirdly, though less directly relevant to the question of real interest rates, the simulations in the paper ignore the operational target of the future European Central Bank. Of course, we all know that price stability is going to be the primary target, but will monetary policy be based directly on the price stability target or is the ECB more likely to pursue an intermediate monetary aggregate target?

Increased competition

I do not have much to say on the results shown in Tables 3 and 4. I can believe that mark-ups are higher in Europe than in the United States, but it would improve the paper if it contained more on how mark-ups were estimated. Are they based on level or first-difference equations and do lower mark-ups imply a one-time change in the level of prices or the rate of inflation? How are the cost-terms for the mark-ups defined? Are they unit labour costs (which are hard to measure across countries) or just labour costs and are import prices and costs of capital included?

GENERAL OBSERVATIONS

I shall confine myself to just three remarks:

- What is the role of the United States, Japan and "other" countries in the model simulations?

- The author poses the very important question as to how the issues of fiscal consolidation and increased competition fit together. However, I was not able to find the answer in the paper. Of course, if the model is largely linear, I could just aggregate the simulated effects, but is this really how the two issues fit together?

- Although the author provides some evidence of substantial cross-country differences in parameter values, he prefers a model for Europe as a whole. I think a lot might be gained by a more disaggregated approach which could also allow for country differences in the degree of fiscal consolidation and/or increases in competition.

BIBLIOGRAPHY

De Long, J.B. and L.H. Summers (1992), "Equipment Investment and Economic Growth: How Strong is the Nexus?", *Brookings Papers on Economic Activity*, 2, pp. 157-99.

Mankiw, N.G., D. Romer and D.N. Weil (1992), "A Contribution to the Empirics of Economic Growth", *Quarterly Journal of Economics*, 107(2), pp. 407-37.

Mendoza, E.G., G.M. Milesi-Ferretti and P. Asea (1995), "Do Taxes Matter for Long-run Growth?: Harberger's Superneutrality Conjecture", Board of Governors of the Federal Reserve System, *International Finance Discussion Papers*, No. 511.

GENERAL DISCUSSION OF SESSION II

The general discussion at the end of the second half-day session was centred on three issues, which had been more or less explicitly addressed in the four papers presented in this session:

- the need for structural adjustment and the scope for macroeconomic policy change;

- the sequencing of structural reforms;

- the interactions between macroeconomic policies and structural reform, and the questions of "deals", *i.e.* negotiated policy packages.

There was fairly general acceptance of the view expressed in the Gersbach and Röger papers, that both fiscal and monetary policies should be geared to the attainment of medium-to-longer term targets and that the scope for discretionary short-term macro policy changes was extremely small. On the fiscal side, the need was to reduce public sector claims on both private savings and private incomes so as to reduce the relative size of public debt as well as the burden of taxation with its distortionary consequences. Monetary policy, in turn, should be aimed at creating and sustaining a non-inflationary climate.

Opinions differed, however, about the seriousness and duration of the negative short-term consequences for the level of real demand from fiscal consolidation and the persistence of still relatively high real interest rates. There was much opposition to the view expressed in the Gordon and Fitoussi papers, that high interest rates were a major factor behind high European unemployment levels. It was also felt that in the light of demographic changes it was misleading and dangerous to use current deficits and debt levels as a measure of sustainable fiscal policy. On the other hand, it is unrealistic to think that a reduction of public sector claims on real and financial resources would be immediately made up by induced higher private claims. On exchange rate policies most participants rejected the idea of competitive devaluations as a means of supporting output and employment. The 1992 devaluation experience of some European countries should therefore not be considered as a model case for other countries.

There was a lively debate on optimal sequencing of structural reforms and the appropriate macroeconomic environment. From a theoretical point of view, it was suggested that deregulations should start with the labour markets, then the product markets and completed with the financial markets. It was noted, however, that no OECD country has been able to follow such a blue-print for reform. Instead, opportunities had to be seized as they arose. A related observation was that pressure for reform has typically been strongest when macroeconomic conditions were unfavourable, *i.e.* not conducive to absorbing the initial shock and the associated costs smoothly.

Given that the strength and duration of transition costs of reform processes and the occurrence of the expected positive results depended in an important measure on prevailing macroeconomic conditions, and noting at the same time that structural reforms are meant to improve overall economic performance, the question naturally arose whether "deals" could not be struck between micro and macro policymakers. Efforts have been made on occasions in the past to trade-off wage increases against fiscal or monetary relaxation but opinions differ as to how successful these deals were. More importantly, it was pointed out that macro and structural policy instruments are not commensurable and have very different and uncertain time-lags as to their effects.

While scepticism about negotiated linkages between reform measures and macroeconomic policy commitments was widely shared, there was, however, agreement that any extra scope for a non-inflationary expansion of demand, provided through a successful implementation of structural reform, should be fully and timely utilised. A close empirical observation and identification of the non-acceleration inflation rate of unemployment (NAIRU) was therefore required. There was a strongly emphasised view that monetary policy should be targeted to real activity indicators, like unemployment, which, by United States experience at least, move much faster in response to monetary policy changes than inflation.

Session III

THE KEY CHALLENGES AND PRIORITIES
FOR THE OECD IN PURSUIT
OF IMPROVED STRUCTURAL REFORM

LABOUR MARKET IMPLICATIONS OF CHANGING CORPORATE GOVERNANCE IN JAPAN

by

Masaru Yoshitomi

Vice-President, Research Institute of Long-Term Credit, Bank of Japan

INTRODUCTION – IDENTIFYING MAIN ISSUES

This paper highlights new and key challenges for the Japanese economy by analysing factors responsible for changes in corporate governance and their implications for labour and financial markets. The following subsection gives some background information, while the main issues to be addressed in this paper are presented thereafter.

What has shaken corporate governance in Japan?

The extraordinary asset price inflation ("bubble") in the 1980s (for example, see Kahkonen, 1995) cannot only be attributed to the easy monetary policy, prolonged after the Plaza accord and the Black Monday. Such macroeconomic monetary policy is simply a necessary, but not a sufficient condition for a bubble. Sufficient conditions can be established only by taking account of the declining role of the main-bank system in the 1980s as well as markets' strong confidence in near-perpetual excellent industrial performance of machinery industries and home electronics based on then-going innovations.

The order of priority in which the stakeholders in a Japanese company have been placed starts with employees, followed by a main bank, then by the company's managers, and finally by stockholders. This priority order is exactly the opposite to that in the United States *i.e.*, first, stockholders, followed by managers, and then by banks and, finally, by employees (for this comparison, see for example Binder, 1991 and 1992).

It has been the main-bank system that governs the Japanese firm which would otherwise have suffered from soft budget constraint and managerial inefficiency due to its strong employee-orientation. The main bank 1) monitors the performance of Japanese borrowing firms as the delegated monitor; 2) finances risky and bold

Schumpeterian innovation based on such monitoring; and 3) engages in rescue operation of troubled borrowers through restructuring their management and providing financial assistance. The main-bank system has been a solution to agency problems and associated costs under the separation between ownerships and management of a modern company. Agency problems tend to arise from conflicts between management (agents) who may not maximise stockholders' profits, on the one hand and short-sighted stockholders (principals) who may not sufficiently evaluate long-term business strategy of management, on the other. In Japan, this solution has been strengthened by intercorporate cross shareholdings in a business group in which a main bank plays a key role not only as the largest, not necessarily predominant, lender to member company but also as its large shareholder.

Main-bank relationship should be distinguished from the loose forms of corporate groups of large firms known as financial keiretsu (affiliated group). This is a group of large major corporations from diverse industrial, financial and commercial sectors, connected by cross shareholdings, a common main-bank relationship, and common membership in a presidential club for core firms. There are at least seven or eight such business groups, among which market competition is quite fierce horizontally. While member firms of financial keiretsu have affiliated city banks in the same group as their main bank, even those firms not affiliated with any keiretsu, including small-scale firms, normally maintain a main-bank relationship with one of the principal banks. This last point is important since more than 55 per cent of Japan's value added has been produced in the small business sector with 300 or less employees in the case of manufacturing.

In the 1980s, the aforementioned three functions of main banks considerably weakened for essentially two reasons. First, capital markets have been extensively liberalised, to which major clients of main bank have turned for raising external funds. Second, such major clients as large-scale enterprises have increasingly become able to self-finance their own physical business investment. Main banks were forced to find new outlets for lending where they had not experienced sufficient monitoring. Furthermore, the banks whose profits were squeezed by liberalisation of interest rates on deposits searched for high-risk, high-return projects. A result was the extreme concentration of bank lending in the real estate and commercial building construction sectors. At the same time, the banks heavily relied on land as collateral to secure their little-monitored loans. In other words, this peculiar sectoral concentration of bank lending cannot be explained just by monetary aggregates (credit and money), the supply of which was indeed excessive compared with their underlying demand but not sufficient enough to account for triple asset price inflation (see Hoffmaister and Schinasi, 1995).

The bursting of the bubble in the 1990s has considerably impaired banks' capital, enabling them to rescue troubled borrowers and smaller insolvent financial institutions. In the past, the latter operation was conducted through purchases of their assets and assumptions of their deposits, administered by the regulatory authorities. Now that the capital-impaired large banks are hardly in such a position. The policy of "no failure of any bank" has collapsed in the 1990s, indicating the emergence of a great stress on the relationships between regulatory authorities and the depository banking industry.

Main banks were guaranteed rents until interest rates were liberalised on loans and deposits, which could be utilised for compensating for the costs associated with the above-mentioned rescue operation as well as the delegated monitoring. The rigid control over new entry to city bank status and bank branch licenses generated such rents. Under this corporate governance structure, the banks were managerially almost autonomous. Who, then, has monitored such monitors (*i.e.*, the main banks)? The Banking Bureau of the Ministry of Finance (MOF) and the Credit and Management Department and the Supervision Department of the Bank of Japan (BOJ) have been in charge of detecting violations of the Banking Law and the Securities and Exchange Law, by inspecting the books of banks and conducting on-site examinations. If a bank was in need of drastic restructuring of its organisation and balance sheets, the MOF has usually sent a retired high-ranking MOF bureaucrat as a director or even as the president. This is very much like the main banks' rescue operation of a troubled firm which has to accept bank-dispatched managers. The regulatory authorities have kept strong leverage over the banks with the help of, say, the aforementioned bank license permits by the MOF and the extension of emergency loans by the BOJ (Aoki, Patrick and Sheard, 1993).

But, who has then monitored such regulatory agencies? It has been the incentives of the bureaucrats to contribute, through monitoring, to the steady growth of the banking industry whose prosperous development ultimately provided bureaucrats with better post-retirement jobs. Bureaucrats with these incentives have been in general well disciplined and extremely clean.

In the 1980s, however, this corporate governance structure began to be shaken. As mentioned earlier, the main banks have lost such major clients as large-scale enterprises under liberalisation, which in turn induced banks to concentrate their new lending into the real estate sector, causing asset-price inflation. The regulatory authorities have failed to monitor such banks, reflecting a lack of understanding the full consequences of liberalisation or failure to strengthen prudential measures or depository insurance schemes. What is worse, the MOF has failed to monitor seven housing loan corporations ("jusen"), where ex-MOF officials have occupied major managerial positions.

What are new challenges for financial and employment systems in Japan?

The shaken corporate governance in Japan has serious implications for both its financial and employment systems. The following questions can be raised.

275

First, who would monitor the firm? To answer this basic question, we will have to identify which firms have really loosened ties with main banks by moving away from bank borrowing. Some firms, if they are financially excellent, may not need to be monitored through bank borrowing. Yet, these firm may want to keep bank ties not through bank borrowing but through other functions of bank ties, including cross shareholding. The following main section discusses these issues.

Second, who would more suitably finance Schumpeterian innovations when the consequences of undertaking innovations and managerial strategies have become much more uncertain to Japanese firms as they move to more sophisticated industries and even go beyond the international frontier of technology. Is financing innovations through the capital market rather than the banking industry more suitable to highly uncertain economic environments? Is there any basic weakness in the functions of the main banks as the delegated monitor and their long-term relationship with firms? The next section will also deal with these issues.

Third, what are the implications of the shaken corporate governance for the priority order placed on stakeholders in a Japanese company? Will the highest priority placed on employees quickly decline? Long-term employment and seniority wage systems have contributed to nourishing firm-specific skills for core employees over time. This is one of the strong reasons why the performance of the Japanese labour market has been good by international standards, as will be discussed further below. Why should this employment system be changed? Now that the main-bank system has weakened its functions, will the takeover mechanism guided by the capital market not immediately replace the way how to control Japanese firms? However, the core part of cross shareholding will remain unchanged, so long as such shareholding is not aimed at maximising return on stocks (dividends + capital gains) but at supervisory function and long-term transactions relationship with partner companies by preventing hostile take-over. Under these circumstances what new forms of corporate governance will emerge?

Fourth, from the view point of the labour market, what new challenges now confront the Japanese employment system (penultimate section)? One challenge is changing labour force structure by age and sex. The pyramidal, male-based hierarchy will be less dominant in Japanese firms. Another challenge is changes in the industrial structure or the technology paradigm, from one based on strong components and machinery industries toward one based on information technologies and new industrial and technological areas at which the Japanese firms are not strong. Both changes require Japanese firms to adopt new personnel management by embracing more professional and independent-minded persons available on the open labour market. The key question is, therefore, whether these new challenges can effectively be coped with in a manner which will be consistent with making full use of still important functional merits attached to long-term employment and seniority wage system for core employees. Such systems maintain employees' strong incentives and loyalty as well as nourish firm-specific multi-intellectual skills over time. After analysing these issues, the penultimate section will also discuss what is actually happening to the Japanese labour market and where it appears to be heading for.

IMPLICATIONS FOR THE MAIN-BANK SYSTEM OF FINANCIAL LIBERALISATION

What determines the firm's choice between bank borrowing and bond financing?

As stated earlier, the combination of liberalisation, deregulation and internationalisation of the Japanese financial market and increasing self-finance by large enterprises have resulted in the relative contraction of bank financing. The proportion of bank borrowing by the large firms covered by the BOJ's Annual Financial Statements of Principal Enterprises fell from 39.5 per cent in the late 1960s to only 8.0 per cent in the late 1980s. At the same time, however, it should be clearly noted that not all the large enterprises have simultaneously reduced bank borrowing. Even among those firms which have been given similar opportunities for bond financing, the financing patterns and the bank debt ratio have significantly varied, depending upon the firm. Some firms have not much reduced bank borrowing, while others have taken full advantage of deregulation by moving away from banks (Kashyap, 1994: the following analysis in this section relies heavily on this paper).

What determines the choice of firms between bank and bond financing? A key question in this regard is whether the lenders monitor the firm or not. If the financial ties with the banks through monitoring are beneficial, there would be no strong reasons why the firms should loosen the ties. If the costs of maintaining the ties outweigh the benefits, however, the firms would loosen the ties. The main bank can monitor the borrowers' activity. In contrast, bond holders who buy corporate bonds in the open capital market do not usually monitor, since they do not have either capacity to monitor through multi-faceted relationship with customers unlike the main bank or strong incentives to monitor due to expensive monitoring costs compared with their relatively small individual stake.

Monitoring is necessary because lenders cannot automatically observe all the decisions made by the managers of the company. Without monitoring, the creditors will not be in a position to tell whether their money is effectively utilised for most productive projects. By monitoring closely the actions of the manager and the daily performance of the company, a lender can force firms to choose productive and profitable projects. Since monitoring is costly, the monitoring bank will charge a higher interest rate than bond holders to the same borrower. The cost of bank financing will be, therefore, higher than the cost of bond financing. Instead of costly monitoring, bond holders will charge different interest rates, depending on the performance of the company which is in turn influenced by the type of investment projects the management staff of the company favours.

How does a firm choose between bank borrowing and bond financing, given these interest rate differentials? The firm whose possibility of using borrowed money for unproductive purpose is judged very small even in the absence of a bank monitoring will choose bond financing to take advantage of lower interest rate of bonds. The conditions of these firms must be financially excellent, characterised as constantly high profitability and a large amount of collateralisable assets compared with a relatively small amount of existing debt. The possibility of default should be very low for these firms, allowing them to benefit from lower bond interest rates. The firms with low profitability and a small amount of collateralisable assets net of existing debt may also want to choose bond financing over bank borrowing in order simply to avoid bank monitoring. In this case, however, these firms will end up with being penalised by higher interest rates on bonds.

Another important question is whether keiretsu-firms (*i.e.*, firms tied with a particular business group through cross shareholdings) have a preference for strong bank ties or not. Cross shareholding between a main bank and a borrower under the same business group may suggest stronger ties of keiretsu-firms. On the contrary, however, the importance of bank borrowing alone is smaller for keiretsu firms, so long as they benefit from the overall main-bank relationship and cross shareholdings.

The overall main-bank relationships have five important aspects of the relations between a firm and its main bank (Aoki, Patrick and Sheard 1993): 1) bank loans; 2) bond-issue related services such as legally required trustee administrator for domestic bond issues and co-lead management for Euro-issues; 3) stockholdings; 4) payment settlement accounts and 5) information and investment banking services and supply of management resources such as the introduction of potential business partners as well as acquisition of business assets. The aforementioned financially excellent companies have main-bank relationships mainly through shareholdings and payment settlement accounts, whereas financially normal companies maintain traditional bank ties through bank borrowing and banks' rescue operation in addition to other relational aspects. In fact, a study suggests (Hoshi, Kashyap, and Scharfstein, 1993) that keiretsu-firms with high values of Tobin's q are predicted to reduce the bank borrowing ratio and to use more bond financing. If so, who monitors keiretsu firms? Because of mutual monitoring among member firms the same business group through cross shareholdings, the managers of group firms may more greatly stress the importance of high profits and good performance of other member firms. Furthermore, if a main bank engages in the rescue operation of a troubled borrower and hence reduces the cost of its financial distress, the benefit of group membership should be higher for financially normal companies and lower for the financially excellent companies. In this case, the financially excellent keiretsu firms may have more reason to weaken the need of bank borrowing and monitoring as compared with non-keiretsu firms with equally excellent financial conditions.

As the financially excellent keiretsu-firms are weakening their ties to the main banks, traditional Japanese corporate governance and monitoring systems are bound to be affected. It is indeed true that Japan's corporate governance and monitory systems are changing and in a phase of transition, but it is equally true that they are not crumbling in terms of functions. First, high-performance firms just shifted to a new stage of main-bank relationship, focusing more on cross shareholding, bond issue services and other non-bank loan businesses. More explicitly, bank borrowing has alone become less important as a monitoring channel, but other channels such as cross shareholdings will continue to monitor business performance. Furthermore, since these firms are virtually all multinational, global competition should continue to discipline them. Second, the share of financially excellent companies in the Japanese economy is still limited and financially less independent companies account for more than 60 per cent of total companies. Hence, bank loans will remain important as a key function of the main-bank system for the majority of Japanese corporations, even though other functions will become increasingly more important. For these reasons, it can be concluded that, indeed, corporate governance has seriously been challenged in Japan in the 1980s and 1990s but that monitoring systems are not crumbling in the presence of cross-shareholding, global competition and the declining but still dominant share of financially normal (but not excellent) companies.

We now turn to the following question: which financing can better accommodate Schumpeterian innovations under greater risks and uncertainties? Is it bank lending or capital market financing? This question highlights the nature of needed changes for Japanese financial systems in transition. This question will in turn lead us to the issue of new challenges for the Japanese labour market, as will be described below.

Determinants of advantages of a particular financial system

The important difference in financial systems between the United States and Japan is that the capital markets (both stocks and bonds) predominate in the United States, whereas in Japan banks predominate and the capital markets have been less important. This difference can imply very different dynamic properties for capital allocation systems. There is a wide spectrum regarding uncertainties about both production technologies and the consequences for managerial strategies. At one end of the spectrum, there are economic conditions where production technologies are reasonably well known internationally and the consequences of managers' strategies are largely predictable. An example is labour-intensive, technologically less advanced industries, including agriculture. In these industries, the available body of accumulated experience, technology and managerial strategies is already so rich that there is little scope for new, fundamental discoveries and innovations. In this case, there will be a fair degree of managerial consensus on how firms should be run for these less sophisticated industries.

At the other end of the spectrum, however, there are newly emerging industries where technology is rapidly changing, so that it takes a great deal of lead time before the benefits of new actions show up and can be fully assessed. Under these conditions, much greater uncertainties associated with new activities will make it much more difficult to arrive at a consensus on how a firm should be run in the face of such uncertainties. In a very new industry there has been no actual experience on the consequences of innovation and associated new managerial strategies. An example would be life sciences.

Between the two ends of the spectrum, there is still a wide range of industries with regards to uncertainties of technological innovations and associated managerial strategies. As an economy matures, its industrial structure will change, moving away from less sophisticated industries towards completely new industries which typically are full of uncertainties about technological and market developments and the consequences of managerial decisions. At the early stage of industrial development, the incremental type of process innovation of how to produce internationally known products more efficiently and productively will be more important for improving total factor productivity. The more developed the industrial structure becomes, the closer the economy will approach the international frontiers of technologies and the increasingly more important the breakthrough type of product innovation will become as compared with process innovation. The breakthrough innovation will completely replace an older generation of technology. In between, there are intermediate stages of industrial development when technology fusions will be important. This is the innovation of producing marriage of existing different technologies of different industries. Innovation of technology fusion combines existing technologies into hybrid technologies (Kodama, 1991 and 1995). In Japan, notable examples are mechatronics in the 1970s (i.e., fusion of mechanics and electronics such as N.C. machine tools and industrial robots) and optoelectronics in the 1980s (i.e., the marriage of electronics and optics such as optical fibre communication systems).

Depending on the degree of uncertainties about the consequences of technological innovation and managerial strategies, a particular type of financial system can be more suited for optimal allocation of capital compared with other types. Banks can be more suited for financing innovations and new managerial strategies whose consequences are less uncertain. In contrast, the capital markets, particularly stock markets, can be more suited to financing more innovative and riskier industries which stand at and/or go beyond the international frontier of technologies.

There are at least two main advantages in bank financing. First, banks act as delegated monitors of firms (Diamond, 1984). Second, in contrast to stock markets, banks engage in long-term relationship and commitments (Shleifer and Summers, 1988). As mentioned earlier, the main banks in Japan have exhibited these two advantages. A main-bank monitors a borrowing firm to ensure that its management acts in the interest of the lenders to the firm, so as to avoid wasting resources. Moreover, the monitoring needs to be done by just one bank for two reasons. First, duplication will not improve monitoring due to costly repetition of monitoring. Second, each investor would want others to bear the costs of monitoring, *i.e.*, a free-rider problem. By holding a large portfolio of loans to different firms and undertaking the delegated monitoring, the main bank can guarantee and promise good stable return to its depositors.

However, this monitoring theory appears to rely on the assumption that the probability of distribution of returns on bank loans is reasonably well known so that banks can guarantee returns to the depositors who would not be in a position to evaluate the bank's monitoring. This assumption can be satisfied more easily when banks finance innovations in less sophisticated industries.

Long-term relationships and commitments between the main bank and the firm encourage employees and suppliers to acquire firm-specific skill and capital which will contribute to steady improvement in productivity and quality. However, if hostile takeovers through the stock market cease such long-term commitments, the associated advantages would not be realised. Here again, however, this theory of long-term relationships appears to rely on the assumption that the consequences of actions based on such long-term commitments are more or less predictable and hence that the parties' expectations about the consequences may not be widely different, which, in turn, helps reaching consensus. This advantage of long-term relationships and commitments will, therefore, be more assured when banks finance less uncertain technological innovation and less sophisticated industries.

By mobilising a great number of people to undertake research and analysis about highly uncertain developments, stock markets can provide the better way of scrutinising newly emerging, much riskier projects and undertakings. People buy and sell shares on the basis of this information. The profits people make will compensate them for the expenses incurred in undertaking researches. The diversity of views and opinions can play an important role in checking the newly emerging risky projects and the associated actions of managers. Even in industries where there have been few firms and little experience, this checking process through mobilising a great number of analysts in the stock market will result in finding out more effectively which innovation, which managerial strategies and which firms would be most promising.

In contrast, banks are not equipped with equivalently broad-based checking devices and instruments. Moreover, the number of bank officers overseeing loan operations and monitoring the firm managers is very limited. The greater the uncertainties about the consequences, the more diversified views and opinions tend to be. This will make it even more difficult for the limited number of bank officers to reach a consensus based on a limited set of judgements. Moreover, the lack of information to the public and the paucity of disclosure will cause little open public debate to develop as to the evaluation of emerging projects and various managerial strategies. The firm may be better informed about its own prospects than any single investor. However, the point is that the stock market as a body or place of aggregated opinion can be better informed (Allen, 1993).

This changing nature of innovation and industrial development leads us to new challenges for the Japanese employment system as well, to which we now turn.

DIFFERENCES IN THE NATURE OF UNEMPLOYMENT ISSUES BETWEEN JAPAN AND OTHER OECD COUNTRIES

General characteristics of unemployment in OECD

The problem of high structural unemployment or widening income disparity in OECD countries includes a common issue of how to respond to fewer job opportunities available for low-skilled workers in the face of rapid changes in the technological and industrial structure.

The unemployment rate for low-skilled workers is several times higher than for highly-skilled workers in OECD countries, when skills are measured by levels of education. Furthermore, the gap in the unemployment rate between low- and high-skilled workers has been widening in many advanced countries over the past 20 years (OECD Job Study). In the United States, however, the rate of unemployment is not particularly high for low-skilled workers, due to flexibly adjusted real wages, which has, in turn, caused widening income disparity (measured by dividing the 9th decile by the 1st one).

In the United States there is high risk of losing a job, but re-entry into employment is relatively swift, so that unemployment with a duration of less than one month is rather high by international comparison, while long-term (longer than one year) unemployment is comparatively low. The United States labour market can, therefore, be said to be characterised by high labour mobility. In Europe, in sharp contrast, short-term unemployment is relatively low, while long-term unemployment is generally uncomfortably high. Thus, the European labour market is characterised by rigidity with relatively low risks of losing a job but also low chances of finding a job. The long-term unemployment in 1993 accounted for 31-37 per cent of total unemployment in France, Germany and the United Kingdom, compared with 10.5 per cent in the United States.

In Japan, long-term unemployment accounted for 16.7 per cent of total unemployment in 1993, lying somewhat in between the United States and Europe, with the overall unemployment rate being, however, the lowest among the three regions. In Japan, as elsewhere, the demand for jobs which require sophisticated professional and technical abilities has been expanding relative to total labour demand, in contrast to job openings which require lower skills such as clerical and related work. However, Japan has not yet suffered either from high long-term unemployment or from widening income disparity.

Japan's overall rate of unemployment has been on a long-term rising trend, mainly reflecting increased joblessness among young age groups (both sexes at 15-24 age), females in the 25-34 age bracket and higher age males (at 60-64 age), as will be discussed below in greater detail. However, even these age- and gender-specific rates have remained low by international standards during the current prolonged recession after 1992 (Figure 1). What accounts for this generally good performance of the Japanese labour market?

Basic characteristics of the Japanese labour market, both internal and external

The Japanese labour market appears extremely "fixed" (rather than "rigid") under the corporate governance structure. In particular, both low rates of labour turnover due to long-term employment practice and the institutionalised wage structure as reflected in seniority salary scale appear to be inconsistent with an efficient allocation of labour and low levels of unemployment to be attained through competitive labour markets.

However, what is most responsible for better allocation of labour and lower unemployment is not apparent fixity or flexibility of the labour market per se but actual functions of the internal labour market and macroeconomic adjustments of real wages. In particular, what is really responsible for the good performance of the labour market are two features: first, the way how workers' skills are formed and how such skills can continuously be adjusted and upgraded to changing economic circumstances; second, the way how workers' real wages are kept pro-cyclical in the business cycle and thus consistent with macroeconomic conditions. The interactions of these micro- and macroeconomic functions of the internal and external labour market are also important, since they are not independent of each other. As described below, the institutionally "fixed" but "functionally flexibly adaptable" labour market reflects an important element of corporate governance in Japan.

The way the skills of workers are formed in Japan stands in sharp contrast to most of other OECD countries. First, the wide range of job rotation is designed to produce multi-skilled workers, both blue- and white-collar, over the long run who are more productive than single-skilled workers.

◆ Figure I. **Trends in unemployment rate by age group**

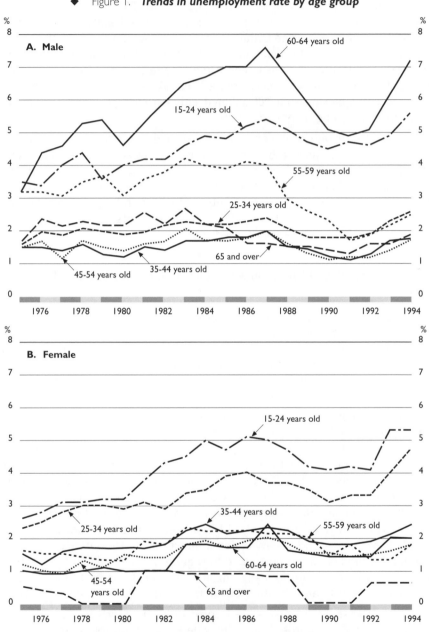

Source: Statistics Bureau, Management and Co-ordination Agency, *Labour Force Survey.*

Second, a large stock of multi-skilled workers can make intra-firm (internal) reallocation of labour easier over the business cycle. Furthermore, this system of shifting occupations for a worker under enterprise-based labour unions in Japan can also contribute to less frictional structural adjustment of employment over the long-run, particularly compared with occupation-based labour union system in other OECD countries. High intra-firm mobility in Japan thus accompanies occupational shifts for a worker.

Third, the on-the-job skill formation process involves "joint investment" in human capital formation by both employers and employees. While younger workers accept lower wages than their productivity, older workers receive higher-than-productivity wages as a (delayed) return to such investment. Employees thus become almost stockholders of their own company. Moreover, skills formed in a firm are so firm-specific that once middle-aged and older workers move to other firms, they will lose their benefits and hence have to accept lower salaries. For instance, if a university graduate male worker switches firms at the age of 40, his lifetime income may well decline by as much as 27 per cent in manufacturing and 13 per cent in total industries as reported in a recent official survey (The Ministry of Labour, 1995).

Fourth, the seniority promotion system applies not only to employees but also to management staff. In Japan, more than 80 per cent of total companies have more than 60 per cent of executives promoted from their own staff, compared with less than 35 per cent of US companies. In terms of stakeholders' interests in a company, there is great harmony rather than conflicts between management staff and labour union. This is a reason why executives cut down their own salaries when their company falls under financial distress or recession.

Fifth, there must be intense competition mechanisms at work among workers so as to avoid the risk that, under job security supported by long-term employment practice and largely automatic salary increases, free riders may attempt to benefit from others' contributions to the firm. On the contrary, however, through the job rotation by assigning an employee to various types of occupations, he or she will be screened by many supervisors over the long-run. A result is a widening, albeit gradually, gap in wages among employees at similar ages or similar length of services. But, a major difference in earnings emerges at the age about 50 and above. Those judged superior in performance can have a chance to be promoted to management staff of the company or one of its subsidiaries. Those judged average receive a lump-sum retirement payment from the company but find a new job in other companies with lower salaries. Others may not be able to find a job and be forced to withdraw from the labour force. This differentiation in earnings toward the end of long-time employment, therefore, places employees under almost lifetime, continuous competition among colleagues at similar age.

WHERE IS THE JAPANESE LABOUR MARKET GOING?

Nature of five new challenges

Five new challenges may now impinge on the traditional way of skill formation in firms which so far have contributed to achieving low unemployment and containing mismatches in the Japanese labour market.

The first challenge is labour hoarding which has become as large as open unemployment under the protracted recession after 1992 and subsequent sluggish recovery.

Labour hoarding in a recession has both positive and negative aspects. With regards to beneficial aspects, labour hoarding can, first of all, reduce the costs of laying-off and re-recruiting workers, while at the same time avoiding job searching costs for the workers. Second, firm-specific skills accumulated over time will not be lost for the firms. Third, labour hoarding facilitates intra-firm retraining and education from the long-run strategic view point. Fourth, as compared with "revealed" unemployment caused by lay-off, labour hoarding can contribute to maintaining employees' high incentives to work and loyalty to their company.

On the other hand, however, labour hoarding also has several negative features. First, labour costs remain high during a recession, possibly delaying economic recovery due to slow improvements in corporate profit rates. Second, the age structure of employees tends to worsen, in particular in companies which are forced to reduce the number of employees. These companies will have to rely on the natural attrition of incumbent employees and will be limited in their possibility of recruitment of young graduates. Third, labour hoarding may hamper skills – and productivity-raising inter-company labour mobility, particularly when it is associated with the long-term employment and seniority salary system.

Two ways are available to reduce the costs of labour hoarding. One is the downward flexibility of real wages per person during a recession. Bonus payments, accounting now for nearly one-third of annual salaries, have been helpful for this downward adjustment in Japan. The other is the flexible adjustability of the internal labour market. Intra-firm temporary occupational transfers and secondment to subsidiaries contribute not only to enabling workers to change workplace without resorting to open unemployment or reducing lifetime income but also to providing opportunities to help multi-skills formation.

However, there are limits to these two avenues or practices. As to adjustments of real wages per person and per hour, the scope for downward flexibility does not only depend on the existence and the size of bonus payments but also on the extent to which extra-hours worked can be cut in order to maintain the number of the employed. As to internal labour market adjustments, intra-firm temporary occupational transfers, unless they are organised in a more systematic way through well planned career development programmes, can result in wasting human resources particularly when such transfers become large in number. On the part of the receiving companies of outplaced workers, the reception of aged workers, increased personnel costs and widened gap in required types of human resources between sending and receiving companies have made internal labour market adjustments increasingly more difficult. In the meantime, the excess supply of incumbent white-collars at age 45 and above has continued.

The second challenge is the increasingly larger proportion of middle-aged and older employees in the labour force due to longer life expectancy and higher, i.e. prolonged, education. This has been increasingly incompatible with seniority salary scale as well as long-time employment practice. Companies maintaining proportionately greater middle-aged and older employees incur higher labour costs associated with seniority salary system. At the same time, the relatively short supply of young labour causes higher salaries for the young. These changes in the relative labour demand and supply situations by age group will certainly cause the slope of seniority salary scale to be increasingly less steep, undermining the seniority salary system.

The third challenge is a decline in the role played by firm-specific skills nurtured through the internal labour market within a firm, compared with the role of general professional skills acquired outside the firm which are mobile and transferable in the external open labour market. This is because changing industrial structure headed toward information technologies and sophisticated software development will enhance the role of new type of innovations which can not simply be achieved through firm-specific skill formation under long-time employment-cum-seniority salary scale. Moreover, management staff should be able to develop independently new ideas and to take strategic decisions in the uncharted water of a new technology paradigm. Japanese employment system and corporate governance have blurred the functional distinction between employees and management staff. Management staff can hardly develop new managerial strategies independently of general employees' ideas and opinions. Under the new circumstances of greater uncertainties and risks of innovations, the nourishing of firm-specific skills may become more expensive and less efficient in relation to the recruitment cost and efficiency of more professional skills from the general open markets.

The fourth challenge is that the greater participation of women in workplace, particularly in the service sector, will enforce firms to alter the hitherto male-based long-time employment and seniority salary system. This is because married women of child-bearing age (25 to 40 years) are now more actively participating in the labour force (*i.e.*, the flattening of the M-shaped labour force participation by age) and they have increasingly higher education and want to work on a part-time basis. An important reason for higher unemployment of females at 25-34 age is less withdrawal of (or less discouraged) females from the labour force participation than in the past once they become unemployed (The Ministry of Labour 1995). Furthermore, many jobless women have been voluntarily unemployed, which appears to be caused for domestic reasons such as child care or care for elderly parents and other family members.

In this regard, an important question is associated with the state of the discouraged workers in Japan. In the United States, the short-term duration of unemployment can be ascribed not only to the aforementioned high escape rate from unemployment but also withdrawal from the labour force and entry into the non-labour force. A key question is why some of those who are not in the labour force but wish to work are not seeking jobs. In the United States, nearly 70 per cent of both males and females reply "tried hard to find a job in vain" and "no job available in my neighbourhood". They are discouraged and have withdrawn from the labour force. In Japan, such discouraged workers account for 2.08 per cent of total male labour force and 12.48 per cent of total female labour force, compared with 0.75 per cent and 1.03 per cent, respectively, in the United States. Discouraged female workers account for 80 per cent of total discouraged workers in Japan, compared with 50 per cent, in the United States. In Japan, 50 per cent of discouraged females responded "Duty hours not suitable". This indicates some shortcomings of the employment system for females in Japan which cannot provide job opportunities compatible with household keeping (The Ministry of Labour, 1995).

The fifth (last) challenge is that an important feature of structural unemployment can be seen in the UV curve, namely, the relationship between the unemployment/employment rate and vacancy rate (i.e., the gap between job openings and job placements divided by total of employees and job openings not filled). For the old age group (at 55 and above), the vacancy rate is always lower but the unemployment/employment rate is higher than that in the active middle age group (at 25-54 age) (Figure 2). This is due essentially to lower demand for the old age group.

In the young age group, however, both the vacancy and unemployment/employment rates are high, reflecting a failure of enterprises to satisfy the job demand by the young as well as their voluntary unemployment. Young age groups, including "junior baby boomers" born between 1971 and 1974, are entering the labour market, together with their changing attitude toward jobs. The high rate of mobility from employment to unemployment, especially to voluntary unemployment, is a major cause of higher unemployment for the young. Personal reasons for getting unemployed account for 83 per cent of the 20-24 age and for 80 per cent of the 25-29 age group of males (The Ministry of Labour 1995).

In the midst of the further ageing of the Japanese population, the number of older persons is growing along with an increase in labour force participation. Getting unemployed can be divided into two aspects: 1) unemployment from employment (the rate of unemployment from employment); 2) unemployment from non-labour force (the rate of transition from non-labour force to employment). The

◆ Figure 2. **Trends in employment and vacancy rates by age group**

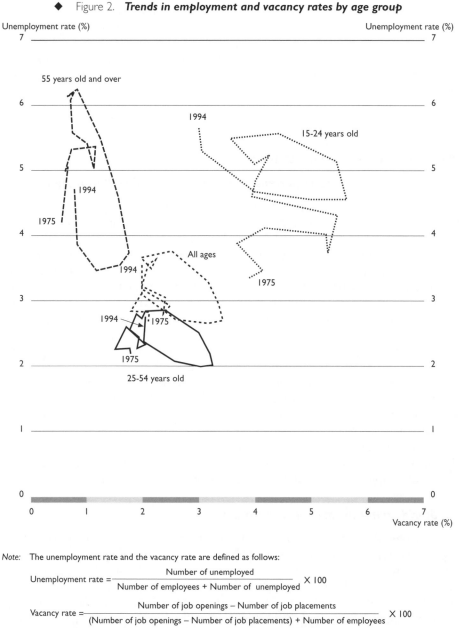

Note: The unemployment rate and the vacancy rate are defined as follows:

$$\text{Unemployment rate} = \frac{\text{Number of unemployed}}{\text{Number of employees} + \text{Number of unemployed}} \times 100$$

$$\text{Vacancy rate} = \frac{\text{Number of job openings} - \text{Number of job placements}}{(\text{Number of job openings} - \text{Number of job placements}) + \text{Number of employees}} \times 100$$

Job openings and placements refer to regular workers in October of each year.

Source: Ministry of Labour, *Report on Employment Service*; Statistics Bureau, Management and Coordination Agency, *Labour Force Survey*.

former is due to the fact that aged males are involuntarily out of work for such reasons as "mandatory retirement", "expiration of a contract period", and "management reasons". The latter is due to in the process of re-entry to employment, which in turn largely reflects the process of final retirement to a great degree. Out of total males in the old age group (at 55 and above) in non-labour force, 9.1 per cent want new jobs, as compared with only 1.0 per cent for the 25-54 age group in non-labour force. This difference is, in turn, due to fewer job opportunities available for the older age group.

What is actually happening to the Japanese labour market?

What is becoming more important, internal or external skill formation?

Real wages per employee can be positively influenced by 1) the duration of tenure within a firm (internal experience); 2) the duration of experience in other firms (external experience); and 3) the level of education. An interesting study indicates that in the course of the 1980s, the effect on real wage of the duration of internal experience, which is responsible for the firm-specific skill formation has declined in Japan (Yashiro, 1995). This is consistent with the flattening of the former steep salary profile by age due to the increased excess supply of older employees and firms' weaker incentives to train them. This is particularly so in the case of university graduate males. In contrast, the effect of external experience on real wage has become the greater, the higher the level of education. This may suggest that firms tend to pay higher salaries for skills developed in the open external labour market rather than for those acquired in the relatively closed internal labour market within firms. It is still true, however, that the effect of the level of education on real wage has remained positive despite greater supply of high-education employees. As a result, there has been some widening of the gap in wages between university and high school graduates. This is probably because the higher the level of education, the greater the trainability viewed by a firm, resulting in crowding out of low education employees from opportunities for on-the-job-training.

Greater demand for high-skilled workers

In Japan, it is clearly observed that some service sectors, which are expected to expand more rapidly relative to the overall economy, are equipped with high-level education workers and that such manufacturing industries as electrical machinery and chemicals which are also expected to expand relatively rapidly require high-education workers. Furthermore, even at the factory floor, conventional craftsmen will increasingly be replaced by machinery as well as more qualified labour. Regarding middle-level engineers who need to be equipped with wide-ranging professional and technical knowledge, nearly half of total Japanese enterprises make efforts to raise their quality level and shift labour demand towards highly skilled workers.

◆ Figure 3. **Trends in share of job openings and job seekers by occupation in all job openings and job seekers**

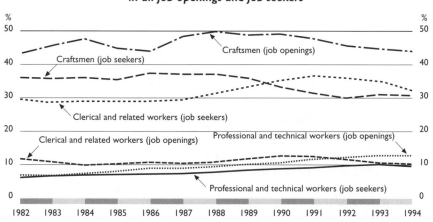

Notes: 1. Number of job openings and job seekers refer to new regular workers excluding part-time workers in August of
              each year.
              2. Craftsmen include two groups: craftsmen and labourers in mining and quarrying, manufacturing and construction.
Source: Ministry of Labour, *Report on Employment Service.*

In fact, the share of job openings for professional and technical workers has consistently exceeded that of job seekers in the 1980s. Furthermore, excess demand for such workers has been growing, even in the face of the stagnant economic situation after 1992. For general clerical workers, in contrast, the share of job seekers has increasingly exceeded job openings. The same pattern has emerged for craftsmen, with excess demand for skilled workers even during the slowdown of economic activities after 1992, and excess supply of unskilled and low-skill workers (Figure 3).

Employment in the distribution system?

The distribution system in Japan has been confronted with challenges in the wake of changing consumers' taste towards low-priced, yet high-quality products and services, and with intensifying competition following the liberalisation of the Large-Scale Retail Store Law. The number of owner-run shops, small-size shops and traditional-type stores has declined, whereas new types of operations such as convenience stores and speciality supermarkets have been conspicuously expanding in the retail sector. The number of self-employed persons in the former categories of shops declined by 5.2 per cent in the three years to 1994 and 11.0 per cent in the three years to 1991, while that in the latter category of shops increased by 10.3 per cent and 11.9 per cent, respectively. The number of employed persons in convenience stores, speciality stores and other supermarkets expanded by 2-3 per cent, respectively, more than offsetting the decline in department and "other" stores. A result was a 5.5 per cent increase in the total number of employed persons in the retail sector as a whole in the three years to 1994. At the same time, the number of non-regular workers such as part-time workers, has increased as a result of the above structural changes, accounting for 53-55 per cent of the staff in convenience stores and supermarkets (The Ministry of Labour, 1995).

In the wholesale sector, too, the number of self-employed persons in unincorporated shops declined by 11.8 per cent and 11.0 per cent in the three years to 1991 and to 1994 respectively. The number of employees in incorporated companies also declined by 2.1 per cent in the three years to 1994 because of the recession, after having increased by 12.3 per cent in the preceding three years. As a result, the total number declined by 2.7 per cent between 1991 and 1994, after having increased by 10.2 per cent in the preceding three years.

CONCLUSIONS

Given the above mentioned specific characteristics of both labour and financial markets and the new challenges that have arisen on both markets after the bursting of the financial market bubble, the question is how this will affect the basic structure of corporate governance in Japan? I offer the following considerations: no enterprise system will remain unchanged having to respond to changes in both the technology paradigm and the domestic and international market environment. Thus, the enterprise system has to evolve over time in order to survive global competition. My hypothesis is that the Japanese enterprise system is clearly in transition during which both the labour management policy and the enterprise finance policy will run on two tracks as follows.

As the Japanese industrial structure further advances towards the international frontier of technologies, and even goes beyond, capital markets will become more important than the banking industry so as to facilitate Schumpeterian innovation more effectively and efficiently. The Japanese financial systems are clearly in transition. During the transition, the Japanese financial systems will run on two tracks, namely, the main-bank system and capital-market financing. There are essentially three reasons for this. First, the majority of Japanese companies is financially in a normal, but not excellent position, so that these companies will continue to rely on bank loans and banks' rescue operation. Second, even the financially excellent companies will utilise other functions of long-term relations with banks, including cross shareholding, administrative trust of bond issues, and settlement accounts. Third, Japanese industries, too, will run on two tracks during a transitional period.

On the one hand, Japanese industries will continue to be strong at technology fusion as well as highly-sophisticated assembly know-how (e.g., semi-conductors and flexible manufacturing), nanotic micro-processing technologies such as electric devices and non-organic advanced materials (e.g., structural ceramics, displays and silicon). These sophisticated products are indispensable as "hardware" for information technology. On the other hand, however, Japanese industries are weak at biotechnology, software development and gigantic system technologies which require a small number of independent and highly creative scientists as well as highly strategic management. Japanese industries will advance into those areas.

What can be said about the direction of changes in the Japanese labour market?

After the first oil crisis, the annual growth of real GDP has been just above 4 per cent, down from above 10 per cent in the preceding two decades. Under this medium growth path, machinery and components industries flourished, supported by innovations, particularly technology fusions such as mechatronics (e.g., N.C. machine tools and industrial robotics), optoelectonics (e.g., optical fibres) and liquid crystal displays. In particular, automobiles and home electronics industries developed most handsomely. The lean production system embodying just-in-time, design-in, and development of multi-skill workers enjoyed its heyday in the 1980s. These were all the benefits obtained from long-term labour and business relationships. In the 1990s, however, information technologies have enhanced the importance of software development, at which the Japanese firm system is not strong. Japanese industrial and comparative advantage structure should be upgraded by overcoming this weakness. Under this rapidly changing technology paradigm, the Japanese labour market will change in the following directions.

First, there will be a declining trend of the share of the core workers who are equiped with firm-specific skill formation under the long-time employment system, whereas the number of outsourced, non-regular, professional and technical workers will increase over-proportionately. The latest severe recession has demonstrated that Japanese firms have made strenuous efforts to strike a sound balance between the merits attached to maintaining such core-workers through large-scale labour hoarding, on the one hand, and the immediate need of the Japanese enterprise system or corporate governance to drastically reduce regular employees for a limited period, on the other. It is clear, however, that Japanese firms will increasingly rely on more mobile and transferable professional and technical works in the open external market, as compared with multi-skill formation for core workers within the internal labour market.

Second, the profit-sharing mechanisms between a firm and employees will remain still solid. However, firms will rely increasingly more on part-time and outsourced work in the face of greater uncertainties and greater labour force participation of women. The growing imbalance between the increasing labour supply of older people and the weaker labour demand for them should result in lower real wages of older people. Salary profile by age will, therefore, further flatten.

Any particular firm system does not have an absolute advantage, but only a comparative advantage, which is, in turn, determined by characteristics of market conditions and the technological paradigm. Changes in market conditions caused by financial liberalisation and the bursting of the bubble and concomitant changes in the technology paradigm are the driving forces for altering Japanese corporate governance. Thus, the financial system will run on two tracks to finance innovations: bank loans and capital markets. The monitoring function will be performed by both the main bank and intercorporate cross share-holding. This double track system in financing Schumpeterian innovations and monitoring enterprises will be paralleled by a double track system in the Japanese labour market: the formation of multi-skills for the core employees in the internal labour market and greater reliance on the external labour market for more professional expertises in response to the changing technology paradigm.

BIBLIOGRAPHY

Aoki, M., H. Patrick, and P. Sheard (1993), "The Japanese main-bank system: An Introductory Overview", in Masahiko Aoki and Hugh Patrick eds., *The Japanese main-bank system: Its Relevancy for Developing and Transforming Economies*.

Aoki, M., and D. Dore, eds., 1994 and 1995, The Japanese Firm – Sources of Competition Strength 1994 (in English) and 1995 (in Japanese, translated by NTT Data Communication and System Science Research Institute).

The Bank of Japan, 1993, "On the Japanese Employment System", Monthly Report, March, pp. 13-45

Blinder, A.S. (1991), "Profit Maximization and international Competition", in R. O'Brien ed., *Finance and the International Economy 5*, The AMEX Bank Review Prize Essays, Oxford University Press, pp. 40-53.

Blinder, A.S. (1992), "Should the Former Socialist Economies Look East or West or a Model?", Center for Economic Policy Studies, Working Paper (August 1992), Princeton University

Diamond, D. (1984), "Financing intermediation and delegated monitoring", *Review of economic Studies*, 51, pp. 393-414.

Franklin, Allen (1983), "Strategic Management and Financial Market", *Strategic Management Journal*, Vol. 14, pp. 11-22.

Hoffmaister, A.W. and G.J. Schinasi, "Asset Prices, Financial Liberalization, and Inflation in Japan", in Ulrich Baumgartner and Guy Meredich, eds., *Saving Behavior and the Asset Price "Bubble" in Japan – Analytical Studies*, IMF Occasional Paper, April, pp. 63-77.

Hoshi, T., A.. Kashyap and D. Scharfstein (1990), "Bank Monitoring and Investment: Evidence from the Changing Structure of Japanese Corporate Banking Relationships", in Glenn Hubbard ed., *Asymmetric Information, Corporate Finance, and Investment*, Chicago, IL; University of Chicago Press, pp. 105-126.

Hoshi, T., A. Kashyap and D. Scharfstein (1993), "The Choice Between Public and Private Debt: An Analysis of Post-Deregulation Corporate Financing in Japan", manuscript.

Kahkonen, J. (1995), "Movements in Asset Prices Since the Mid-1980s" in U. Baumgartner and G. Meredich, eds., *Saving Behavior and the Asset Price "Bubble" in Japan – Analytical Studies*, IMF Occasional Paper, April, pp. 51-62.

Kodama, F. (1995), *Emerging Patterns of Innovation – Source of Japan's Technological Edge*, Harvard Business School Review, Boston, Massachusetts.

Kodama, F. (1991), *Analyzing Japanese High Technologies*, Printer Publishers, London.

Ministry of Labour, 1995, *White Paper on Labour 1995*, Tokyo.

Nelson, R. (1991), "Why do firms differ and how does it matter?", *Strategic Management Journal*, Winter Special Issue, 12, pp. 61-74

Nonaka, I. and H. Takeuchi (1995), *The Knowledge-Creativity Company – How Japanese Companies Create the Dynamic of Innovation*, Oxford University Press.

OECD, 1995, *Employment Outlook*, July.

Shleifer, A. and L. Summers (1988), "Breach of trust in hostile takeovers", in A. Auerbach ed., *Mergers and Acquisitions*, NBER, University of Chicago Press.

Yashiro, N. (1994), "Changes in the Japanese Labour Market: Population Aging and Technological Progress", in Mihaly Simai ed., *Global Employment – An International Investigation into the Future of Work*, UNU/WIDER, Zed Books and United Nations University Press, pp. 131-153.

Yashiro, N. (1995), "Recession and Labour Hoarding", JECR Discussion Paper No. 37 (in Japanese), Tokyo

Yashiro, N., A. Oishi, and W. Suzuki (1995), "Economic meanings of liberalization of employment practices", manuscript (in Japanese).

COMMENTS

by

Y. Imai

Professor Yoshitomi's paper discusses specific structural reform challenges to Japan but also raises some interesting general issues. It is a useful piece in that it talks about the forces that are behind the structural changes that are currently taking place in Japan.

I agree with much of his analysis. Contrary to the claim of the author, however, the paper is not about how the changes in corporate governance are affecting the Japanese employment practices. Rather, it is about the changes in both areas which are concurring in response to three, more or less, exogenous forces: 1) Deregulation and internationalisation of financial markets, weakening the role of bank loans in corporate finance; 2) Greater technological uncertainty as the Japanese firms are increasingly faced with the need to be a generator of new technology, rather than adapting existing technology imaginatively to commercial needs; and 3) A substantial slowdown in the trend growth rate of the Japanese economy, the factor which is only implicit in Yoshitomi's paper.

As the paper makes it clear, financial liberalisation – by providing large firms direct access to capital markets – reduced the role of main banks as a "stakeholder". The need to be technologically more innovative has raised the desirability of both funding through capital markets – thereby affecting corporate governance – and recruiting skilled workers more from external labour markets – thereby impacting on employment practices. And slower overall economic growth too affected corporate governance as well as employment practices. For large successful firms slower growth has resulted in cashflows in excess of their investment requirements – thus no need for bank loans (Toyota, *e.g.*). Slower growth has led to excess labour hoarding and pressure on the middle-aged and above to quit. The extent of labour hoarding has clearly become excessive. This has raised doubts in the mind of workers about the validity of the implicit contract of so-called life time employment.

The distinction between labour market implications resulting from changes in corporate governance and from other changes is important. Indeed, the conclusion of the paper that corporate governance will remain more or less intact cannot be taken to mean that employment practices will also remain unchanged. Professor Yoshitomi himself cites several recent and ongoing changes in employment practices. As long as fundamental forces are pushing for change in employment practices they will eventually occur. The crucial parameter is the value of firm-specific human capital. The author cites some evidence that this factor is losing importance. If this continues, then changes of significant scale cannot be excluded.

The paper stops short of discussing reforms required by the changes in the Japanese governance and employment systems. What they should be is not obvious since the changes foreseen are gradual, and the Japanese economy has sufficient flexibility to accommodate gradual changes without much difficulty. Nonetheless, one can identify priority areas of reform for Japan. In the jobs-related area it is possible to anticipate problems associated with higher unemployment or reduced employment opportunities for certain groups, notably women and middle -aged and old men. The current system of unemployment insurance and social assistance along with the adequacy of placement service would have to be reviewed. One area where reform is clearly necessary is the governance of the public sector, which is unlikely to respond to market pressures. A series of post-bubble scandals revealed the weakness of financial supervision, and reform is in order in many areas to ensure that tax money is well spent and existing regulations have not outlived their usefulness.

Let me now turn to broad policy issues and challenges. To me the biggest contribution of Professor Yoshitomi's paper is that it gives a clear illustration of how some of the systemic characteristics of the Japanese economy are changing in response to larger forces operating in the world economy. Why is this important? First, it bears on the issue raised in this conference about the choice of a model or system. The very first question that needs to be asked in designing any reform is "Do we have a choice?" (Mr. Fitoussi asked "Reform towards which model?").

In the case of financial markets there seems to be no choice but to adapt to the exigence of increasing internationalisation and financial innovation. On the other hand, in labour markets the answer is not straightforward. There is the US model, which combines flexibility and working poor. The continental European model provides extensive social protection but also is characterised by rigidity and high unemployment. And, there is the Japanese (or Swiss) model, which combines flexibility and other mechanisms to deal with excess labour – hoarding in Japan and adjustment through foreign workers in Switzerland. It is also possible that there may be no choice, and all models converge over time. The United Kingdom today points to such a possibility as she found a middle way combining American-type flexibility and well-designed assistant programmes for those in need. It is not a pure coincidence that rising income disparity is observed there and the United Kingdom natural rate of unemployment falls between that in the United States and continental Europe.

The second reason why it is important to have a better grasp of systemic characteristics is that emerging areas for international co-operation require such knowledge. For example, in competition policy there is tension between different legal/institutional set-ups in individual countries on the one hand and the increasing need to deal with collusion on an international scale on the other. As well, the trade disputes between the United States and Japan vividly illustrate the crucial importance of such knowledge in resolving trade frictions, which now arise more often as a result of alleged non-tariff barriers, in turn closely linked to systemic characteristics of an economy.

TAX REFORM IN THE UNITED STATES: PROSPECTS AND POTENTIAL EFFECTS

by

Alan Auerbach
University of California, Berkeley and NBER

INTRODUCTION

At first blush, the current United States Congressional debate about tax reform bears little relationship to the macroeconomic problems the United States and other OECD countries face. For example, consider the most discussed option, the flat tax originally proposed by Hall and Rabushka (1995) and now supported by various politicians. While potentially unsustainable government budgets and maturing social welfare systems have been viewed by many as the central fiscal problem facing these countries (Auerbach 1995a), the flat tax and commonly discussed alternatives aim to keep revenues constant (with considerable dispute about whether even this would be achieved) and are largely silent on questions of government expenditure and social insurance.

How can one reconcile this attention to tax reform at a time when other fiscal issues seem more pressing? As discussed below, the questions of tax reform and fiscal balance are not as unrelated as might first appear. First, a major macroeconomic effect associated with large fiscal imbalances is their impact on national saving; all tax reform proposals under serious discussion in the United States would shift the tax burden toward consumption and away from income, thereby attempting to encourage saving. Second, the tax reforms generally would sacrifice progressivity in favour of a simpler and more efficient tax system. If the solution to present fiscal imbalances must come, in part, through higher tax collections, this shift can be seen as a logical first step to an attempt to extract more revenue from the economy without unacceptably high economic distortions and compliance problems.

In this paper, I analyse the impact of the flat tax on United States macroeconomic performance, and then return to consider the implications for the longer run fiscal problems that the United States shares with other OECD countries.

A FRAMEWORK FOR ANALYSIS

One can break the question of how the flat tax would affect behaviour into three parts. First, how large is the tax wedge imposed by the current United States tax system on labour supply, saving and investment? Second, how would the flat tax alter these distortions? Third, how would these changes be expected to alter economic behaviour?

The analysis presented below can be understood in reference to the budget constraint facing an individual household which, in the absence of taxes, may be written:

$$C = W + R - S$$

where C is current consumption, W current wage income, R current *net* (of depreciation) capital income, and S current *net* (of depreciation) saving. An income tax would be levied on W + R; a consumption tax on W + R − S; a wage tax on W.

As we are interested in how the tax system treats different types of assets, it is useful to disaggregate the right-hand side of expression (1) by asset type, 1, ..., N:

$$C = W + (R_1 - S_1) + (R_2 - S_2) + ... \pm (R_N - S_N)$$

Broad asset categories distinguished by major differences in tax treatment include corporate assets, non-corporate assets, housing, and net financial assets. In each case, we look at the ultimate household claims on assets, with the intervening financial assets and liabilities of financial intermediaries, and associated tax provisions, subsumed. Thus, net financial assets represented in (2) include claims on federal, state and local governments.

An important observation is useful at the outset. A wage tax and a consumption tax differ primarily in their treatment of existing assets, with the consumption tax including a cash-flow tax on assets (the R-S term) that imposes what essentially is a capital levy on existing assets.[1] Although both taxes may be neutral with respect to the choice between current and future consumption, the consumption tax reduces the wealth of current asset holders through the capitalisation of this implicit capital levy. The wealth effect of this capitalisation thus arises from inframarginal tax differences between new and existing capital.

THE CURRENT UNITED STATES FEDERAL INCOME TAX

The current tax reform debate centres around reform or replacement of the federal income tax. Several elements of the existing tax structure complicate the analysis of its effects.

Investment incentives

As discussed in Auerbach (1996), effective tax rates facing corporate equipment and structures are now 28 and 33 per cent, respectively (with an average of 31 per cent). But these calculations also suggest that the existing corporate fixed capital stock should carry a discount of approximately 8 per cent, because of the differential tax treatment of new and existing capital arising from the structure of nominal accelerated depreciation allowances. In terms of the framework laid out in the previous section, we can think of the current corporate tax as imposing a nearly uniform tax of 31 per cent, plus a cash-flow tax of 8 per cent.

Financial policy and individual taxes

The actual burdens imposed on corporate investment differ from those just presented, because of the additional taxes paid at the individual level and the deductibility of interest at the corporate level. In Auerbach (1996), I conclude that these additional factors contribute essentially no added burden under the traditional view of dividend taxation. However, it is important to recognise the fact that pension fund assets face cash-flow tax treatment, so that existing pension fund assets should (from the point of view of their ultimate beneficiaries) incorporate the capitalised value of future tax payments on withdrawals.

The corporate-non-corporate distinction

There are several margins over which the allocation of capital may be distorted. As suggested above, the distortions within the corporate sector are now rather insignificant. A second margin is the allocation of capital between the corporate and non-corporate sectors. My calculations under current tax rules, paralleling those reported above for the corporate sector, yield an overall tax rate of 18 per cent for non-corporate investment, with a corresponding market discount due to the differential treatment of new and existing assets of 6 per cent.

Thus, non-corporate investment faces an average marginal tax rate of approximately 18 per cent, compared to a range of 26 to 31 per cent on corporate investment. Still, this is not a very large gap, and does not alter the conclusion that business assets face a fairly uniform tax rate. It seems reasonable to conclude that the main distortion of the taxation of non-residential fixed investment under the present tax system is the overall taxation of capital income. My calculations put this tax rate at 26 per cent, with an associated capitalisation of nearly 8 per cent.

Other investment decisions

Aside from corporate and non-corporate fixed investment, the other major investment in the United States is housing. Most of this housing – 76 per cent – still is owner-occupied.[2] Given that the imputed rent on housing is not taxed, we can conclude that the effective tax rate on housing investment is very low, overall.

Finally, I have yet to touch on the complicated rules governing foreign investment, including the foreign tax credit, the different classes of income, and the rules for allocating interest and research and development expenses. I will discuss these issues, where relevant, in the process of analysing the flat tax.

TAX REFORM: THE NEW PROPOSALS

Most tax reform proposals currently being discussed involve some version of a consumption tax. The one being discussed most seriously is the flat tax.

As originally proposed by Hall and Rabushka (1995) and supported by Representative Armey and Presidential candidate Forbes, the flat tax differs from a traditional European-style VAT in a few respects. First, it imposes the tax on the wage component of value added at the individual level, rather than the business level. Second, and more importantly, maintaining a personal tax permits the preservation of certain aspects of the present individual income tax. As under present law, the Hall-Rabushka individual tax base includes pension benefits, rather than following the pure sales tax or VAT approach of including pension contributions in compensation. Thus, the flat tax imposes two layers of cash-flow taxation on pension returns: a cash-flow tax on the returns to capital at the business level, and a cash-flow tax on pension contributions and benefits. Put another way, we can imagine the personal tax under Hall-Rabushka as being a hybrid of a wage tax and a consumption tax, with the effective tax rate on labour supply equal to the flat tax rate. Also like the present individual income tax, the flat tax provides personal exemptions and a standard deduction that make the tax more progressive, but also require that the marginal tax rate be higher.

Third, Hall-Rabushka differs from the VAT in that it is an origin-based tax, not exempting export sales or taxing import sales. Given the identity that current and capital accounts must sum to zero, taxing imports and giving a deduction for exports is equivalent to providing cash-flow treatment for net foreign investment. Thus, the difference between this approach and the origin-based approach is one not of incentives, but of wealth effects, equal to the capitalised value of cash-flow taxes on net foreign assets. Given that the United States is now a net debtor nation, the origin-based approach provides a *broader* tax base.[3] This distinction has nothing to do with "competitiveness" as it is usually understood in the debate about value-added taxes, which appears to derive from an assumption that real exchange rates would be different under otherwise equivalent tax systems.

Finally, some (*e.g.* Hall 1995) have argued that the flat tax would have a different impact on the price level than a VAT. This argument hinges on a difference in national income accounting convention having real effects. Indirect business taxes, which would include a standard sales or value added tax, are subtracted from output before factor incomes are calculated; direct taxes, including the current income tax and, arguably, both the business and individual components of the flat tax, are not. Thus, a Fed monetary policy based on maintaining nominal wage levels (gross of direct taxes but net of indirect taxes) would lead to an increase in nominal output – a price level increase – under the introduction of an indirect tax, but no such increase under the introduction of a direct tax.

THE IMPACT OF TAX REFORM ON INTEREST RATES AND ASSET VALUES

A tax reform can affect asset values in three ways. Two already discussed are the distinction between new and existing assets associated with cash-flow taxation, and the impact of price-level changes on existing nominal assets. Both of these effects relate to the values of existing assets relative to cost of new assets.

The third potential impact of a tax reform on asset values is one that affects new and existing assets alike, through changes in the incentive to save and invest. Consider first the case of a closed economy. The flat tax would lower the income tax wedge facing new investment. We should expect such changes to reduce consumption and increase saving and investment, and to alter the mix of investment away from housing, which receives no added benefits relative to the current tax system, and toward business plant and equipment. In a world of homogeneous output and instantaneous adjustment of the capital stock, no changes in the value of new capital goods would result.

However, more generally, as in a "q" model of investment, we should expect at least a temporary increase in asset values overall in response to the increase in demand, with a decline in the values of those assets, such as housing, that become relatively less attractive. Accompanying these changes should be a rise in the after-tax rate of return on investment, a fall in the before-tax return on business assets, and a rise in the before-tax (and after-tax) return on housing. How much these relative returns will change in the short run depends not only on the technology of adjustment, but also individual responsiveness to the altered incentives.

The impact on interest rates is still more complicated, because of the distortions of the existing income tax among different assets, different forms of organisation and different methods of finance. If all corporate investment were financed by debt, then the interest rate would exceed the before-tax return to capital, as the combination of accelerated depreciation and the deductibility of nominal (rather than real) interest payments would result in a negative corporate tax liability. Thus, the total tax wedge between the before-tax and after-tax returns would be somewhat smaller than the personal tax rate. Moving to a consumption tax would reduce this wedge to zero, pushing up the after-tax return and, with the added saving and capital accumulation, pushing down the before-tax rate of return. The interest rate would fall even more than the before-tax rate of return, as the two would now be equal. Thus, under pure debt finance, the decline in the before-tax return would understate the decline in the interest rate.

However, tax reform would reduce the combined corporate and personal tax wedge facing equity investment even more, encouraging investors to purchase less debt and more equity, thereby moderating the decline in interest rates. This effect would cause interest rates to fall less than the before-tax rate of return.

Thus, depending on the relative importance of the two effects just considered, the interest rate could fall more than the before-tax return, or less. Indeed, as Feldstein (1995) shows, the interest rate could well rise even as the before-tax return falls. The simulations presented below, which do not distinguish among types of finance, equate the projected declines in before-tax returns and the decline in interest rates. Without a more specific model of relative asset price determination, it is difficult to translate, say, the extent to which this overstates or understates the decline in interest rates.

Relaxing the closed-economy assumption could temper the estimated drop in interest rates still further. The key issue is the extent to which foreign investors in the United States are faced with the same change in incentives as United States investors. If they are not (as would be the case if they lend to United States businesses and face only home country taxation), the effect may be to reduce sharply the increase in domestic investment and decline in interest rates, as foreign capital inflows are reduced by the less attractive (to foreigners) rates of return in the United States. This intuition underlies the "open economy" simulation presented below, which assume a fixed United States interest rate.[4]

But other types of inbound investment might be encouraged by the tax reform. Foreign investors that do pay taxes in the United States, such as those engaging in foreign direct investment in United States subsidiaries, would have their United States taxes reduced. To the extent that these investors do not face offsetting tax increases in their home countries (as they would under a tightly applied "world-wide" or residence-based tax system), they would wish to invest more in the United States at the pre-reform, before-tax rate of return. Whether they would invest more even at the lower rate of return induced by added United States household saving is less clear. If household saving were relatively unresponsive, capital inflows could result, *reinforcing* (rather than mitigating) the rise in United States investment. Again, a more complicated model than is used here would be necessary to trace out the changes in relative asset prices and investment.

SIMULATING THE EFFECTS OF TAX REFORM

To simulate the effects of tax reform proposals on saving, investment and growth in the short run, I use the Auerbach-Kotlikoff dynamic simulation model, described in detail in Auerbach and Kotlikoff (1987). The model has certain limitations for present purposes, most notably the lack of sectoral disaggregation. Thus, I cannot consider the impact of the shift away from housing investment that most of the proposals would encourage, nor can I account for the reduced wedge between corporate and non-corporate activities. Therefore, the efficiency gains identified will understate the full impact of the reforms.[5]

The model, described in more detail in the Appendix, does permit a fairly general specification of the tax system, with a payroll-tax-based social security system and separate taxes of variable progressivity on total income, labour income, capital income and consumption and, under the income and capital income tax bases, fractional expensing of new investment that can proxy for a range of investment incentives that apply only to new capital. It also permits one to set the level of adjustment costs facing new investment, and the "open economy" option of keeping the interest rate fixed.

The current tax system

I begin with a parameterisation of the present tax system, based in part on the material presented above in Section 3. Table 1 provides relevant parameters for this and other simulations. Starting with a figure .26 for the marginal effective tax rate on non-residential capital, I combine this with the an assumed low effective rate of .06 on residential capital and equal shares of residential and non-residential capital in the total capital stock to arrive at an effective marginal rate of .16. I assume that the non-residential capital stock bears a discount of .08 due to depreciation provisions, and hence the total fixed capital stock a discount of .04. This implies a statutory capital income tax rate of .2, with a fraction .2 of investment expensed.

To take account of the current treatment of pension contributions and benefits, I treat the remaining taxes as a hybrid of wage and consumption taxation. That is, I assume that some wages, and the associated saving, qualify for wage tax treatment (aside from the capital income taxes already considered), with the remainder qualifying for consumption tax treatment (deductible wages and taxable benefits). Given that household pension reserves equal about one-fourth of household wealth, I set the average consumption rate set at one-third the average wage tax rate. To account for the progressivity of the income tax, I set the average marginal wage tax rate higher than the average wage tax rate, with the average wage tax rate determined by the overall revenue target and the average marginal rate set so that, in combination with the consumption tax rate, it yields a total effective marginal tax rate on labour income equal to .236, an estimate of the current value for the United States based on the NBER Taxsim model.[6] This procedure yields an average wage tax of .075, an average consumption tax rate of .025, and an average marginal wage tax rate of .217.

Table 1. **Simulation parameters**

Parameter	Current System	Flat Tax
Wage Tax		
marginal rate	0.217	0.181
average rate	0.075	0.117
Capital Income Tax		
rate	0.200	0.056
fraction expensed	0.200	1.000
Consumption Tax		
marginal rate	0.025	0.025
average rate	0.025	0.025

In the initial steady state based on these tax parameters, and other parameter choices discussed in the Appendix, the before-tax rate of return to capital is 9.5 per cent, and the national saving rate is 4.1 per cent, both realistic numbers given the various simplifications of the model.[7] I normalise the average wage rate to 1.0 in this initial regime.

The flat tax

Next, I consider the flat tax, as proposed by Hall and Rabushka (1995). To model the basic Hall-Rabushka (HR) flat tax, I begin with their estimate of a 19 per cent marginal tax rate for those subject to taxation.

As a tax on all consumption purchases, excluding purchases of investment goods, the flat tax would approximate a consumption tax – a tax on labour income plus the cash flows from different assets. However, as designed, there would be certain deviations from this general result. First, unless the tax applied to the sales of existing homes, the cash-flow component associated with existing residential real estate would be left out of the tax base. Second, the treatment of government bonds would depend on the aggregate price level response to the tax shift. If the price level rose by the extent of the tax, then all existing nominal assets would decline in value. From the federal government's perspective, this would amount to the imposition of a cash-flow tax on existing federal debt. On the other hand, if the tax were absorbed through a decline in nominal wages, consumption out of existing federal debt would not be taxed. Third, consumption of imports is not taxed, but there is a tax on exported consumption goods. As discussed above, this imposes a cash-flow tax on net domestic assets held by foreigners.

As housing represents about half of the capital stock in the United States, I allow for this treatment of housing by setting the cash-flow tax at half the rate of the labour income tax, or .095. To take account of the fact that not every taxpayer will face the positive marginal tax rate on labour supply, I must translate the assumed 19 per cent flat rate into an average marginal tax rate. Based on aggregate tax return data, using the methodology described in Auerbach (1996), I arrive at an estimated average marginal tax rate on wages of .179.

As discussed above, the treatment of pensions under the flat tax further reduces the share of compensation that is taxed immediately by subjecting pension contributions and benefits to consumption tax treatment instead. This has the effect of lowering the wage tax and introducing a consumption tax, holding fixed the effective overall tax rate on labour income that takes the two taxes into account. For simplicity, I use the same consumption tax rate, .025, as derived for the current system to account for this treatment of pensions. The associated adjustment of the marginal tax rate on labour income brings that rate down from .179 to .158.[8] Then, the average tax rate on wages is derived as a residual of the equal-revenue requirement.

Before performing the simulations, I make one more adjustment. The Hall-Rabushka estimate of a 19 per cent tax rate holds for the original Hall-Rabushka plan, which offers no transition relief for existing assets. In particular, assets acquired before the tax change receive no depreciation deductions. However, Hall and Rabushka (1995, pp. 78-79) do recognise that it may be politically necessary to grant such relief. Without knowing the details of such relief, I assume that all assets are allowed to continue receiving depreciation allowances. This is roughly equivalent to allowing half of the value of such assets to be expensed, which I model by halving the effective cash-flow tax rate, to .048.[9] This reduction in revenue is then made up by raising the cash-flow tax rate and the average and marginal tax rates on labour income, keeping them in the same proportion to one another, as would occur if the flat rate were raised to make up the lost revenue. The effects of these assumptions yield the tax parameters presented in the second column of Table 1. They indicate that the flat tax would raise the average tax rate on labour income, to make up from the revenue lost by providing an immediate write-off for investment. But the reduced progressivity of the marginal rate schedule would still permit a reduction in the average *marginal* tax rate on labour income.

The first column of Table 2 presents the simulation for this base case, indicating that the wage rate would actually fall slightly in the short run, due to the decline in marginal tax rates on labour supply. However, over the longer run, the very large increase in the national saving rate would cause capital deepening that would increase the capital-labour ratio. After ten years, the reform is predicted to increase output by 5.0 per cent.

The effects on utility, as measured by the equivalent variation of the gain or loss as a share of lifetime resources, reflect the fact that this move to consumption taxation is modified by its transition relief for existing assets. Older generations

Table 2. **Simulation results**

Parameter	Base case	Adjustment costs	Open economy
Wage rate			
Year 0	1.000	1.000	1.000
Year 2	0.996	0.997	1.000
Year 5	1.007	0.999	1.000
Year 10	1.020	1.007	1.000
Year ∞	1.045	1.037	1.000
Interest rate			
Year 0	0.095	0.092	0.095
Year 2	0.096	0.103	0.095
Year 5	0.093	0.086	0.095
Year 10	0.089	0.086	0.095
Year ∞	0.083	0.088	0.095
Saving rate			
Year 0	0.041	0.033	0.041
Year 2	0.082	0.054	0.104
Year 5	0.075	0.047	0.099
Year 10	0.067	0.045	0.092
Year ∞	0.047	0.038	0.056
Output per capita (relative to year 0)			
Year 0	1.000	1.000	1.000
Year 2	1.033	1.017	1.055
Year 5	1.041	1.022	1.059
Year 10	1.050	1.030	1.065
Year ∞	1.063	1.056	1.093
Utility (% change; by year of birth)			
−60	+0.03	+0.08	+0.03
−40	+0.32	+0.32	+0.48
−20	−0.33	−1.03	−0.32
0	+0.72	+0.05	−0.64
∞	+0.64	+0.33	−0.41

gain, as their business assets are spared the full capital levy but still benefit from higher after-tax rates of return. Unborn generations also gain, as a result of the higher real wages generated by the reform's induced capital accumulation. But those who are 20 years old at enactment lose, as they have no assets to benefit from the wealth transfer but suffer from the higher average wage taxation and, unlike members of future generations, do not benefit very much from the higher real wages that prevail after several years.

Sensitivity analysis: adjustment costs, capital flows, and behavioural response

As discussed above, the impact of any tax change on the economy depends on the speed of adjustment and the openness of the economy. The remaining columns of Table 2 present alternative simulations to those in the first. Column 2 introduces adjustment costs. These assumed adjustment costs are moderate – that a one-percentage point increase in the investment-capital ratio increases the cost of investment goods to the firm by 10 per cent. This chosen value represents a compromise. While it is well below many estimates in the literature (e.g. Summers, 1981), recent research (Cummins et al., 1994) has offered evidence that adjustment costs are even lower than those assumed here. Because I have not altered any other parameters, some of the other characteristics of the initial steady state are slightly different. Most notable is that the national savings rate is initially 3.3 per cent rather than 4.1 per cent.

The impact of adjustment costs is to slow the rate of capital accumulation and temporarily increase the value of existing assets as the increased demand for investment goods is only partially satisfied by quantity adjustments. The national savings rate in year 2 rises by substantially less. The initial jump in asset values raises the welfare of older generations, who benefit most from this jump. With slower capital accumulation, output per capita grows more slowly. The delay in adjustment reduces the welfare gains of younger generations.

As discussed above, modelling the impact of international capital flows is complicated because reforms may encourage investment by some investors and discourage it by others. For purposes of illustration, the third column of Table 2 presents a simulation done under a very simple and extreme "open-economy" assumption – that the domestic before-tax return to capital is not affected by tax reform. This would be the case if foreign investors' tax liabilities were unaffected by tax reform, all assets were perfect substitutes, and international capital flows instantaneously eliminated all differences in after-tax returns. Now, the national savings rate nearly triples by year 2, and stays very high, as capital flows out of the country and creates a large current account surplus (which was assumed initially to be zero).[10] Because of this, output per capita (measured in terms of *national* product, rather than *domestic* product) also rises more substantially than in the base case. These assumptions have offsetting welfare effects. Older generations gain, as their capital can earn the higher, world-wide return to capital. Younger and future generations lose by not being able to benefit from real-wage growth.

As a final evaluation of the sensitivity of the basic results (not shown in the table), I consider the impact of changing a key behavioural parameter in the Auerbach-Kotlikoff model, the elasticity of substitution between goods and leisure. This parameter, which determines the labour supply elasticity to changes in the after-tax wage, equals .8 in all the simulations presented thus far. While .8 is a reasonable value for this parameter, it is also quite plausible that a lower elasticity of substitution would be more appropriate. To see how critical this parameter is, I redid the base case simulation using a very low goods-leisure elasticity of .3. The change in assumption reduces estimated output growth by about one-third, to 3.2 per cent after ten years, and reduces welfare gains accordingly.

Alternative proposals

There are a variety of other variants of the flat tax currently under discussion. Some would provide a higher standard deduction, in order to make the tax system more progressive over the lower part of the income distribution. However, by its nature, the flat tax is not as progressive as the current income tax. For example, a recent evaluation by the United States Treasury (*Tax Notes* 1996) of the "Armey-Shelby" flat tax, which, by its estimate, would require a 21 per cent marginal tax rate to make up the revenue lost by a more generous standard deduction, finds that this plan still would result in a net tax reduction for families with incomes over $200 000 per year and a net tax increase for all other income categories. As discussed in Auerbach (1996), the only consumption tax proposal currently under review which aims to maintain distributional neutrality, the so-called "US" tax system, would lead to a negligible gain in output. Under this proposal, maintaining progressivity entails a worsening of labour supply distortions. This is because the higher average tax rates on labour income necessitated by the removal of capital income from the tax base result in higher *marginal* tax rates on labour income as well. As a result, the increased incentive to save would be roughly offset by the reduction in labour supply.

In short, while a considerable amount of focus has been placed on the added saving generated by a shift to a flat tax, this added saving translates into a significant increase in output only if the reduced distortion of saving does not reappear as an increased distortion of labour supply. In practical terms, it appears that this trade-off can be avoided only through a decline in tax progressivity.

CONCLUSIONS

As the preceding simulations show, a flat tax has the potential to increase saving substantially, and to increase output as well, by reducing not only the tax wedge facing saving, but also that facing labour supply. In addition, the tax brings with it the potential for a simpler tax system. But there is a cost to such reform, in the form of reduced tax progressivity.

Other than a change in social preferences regarding the trade-off between equity and efficiency, can one justify adopting such a plan? Although this argument has not been put forward by the sponsors of the flat tax, there is justification if one views the current tax reform process as a part of the overall process of fiscal adjustment, which will likely require raising additional revenue in the future. Then, standard optimal tax arguments remind us that the price of progressivity, measured as the dead-weight loss from raising an additional dollar of revenue to be transferred to lower-income individuals, grows with the amount of revenue collected. Thus, the same preferences for equity, in the face of a worsened equity-efficiency trade-off, would lead to a smaller amount of redistribution. In short, redistribution would be partially crowded-out by simple revenue needs.

A similar argument holds with respect to promoting tax simplification. If the costs of administration rise with the tax burden, as taxpayers spend more resources to avoid and evade taxation, then the social benefits of a system that is easy to administer and enforce grow with the amount of revenue collected.

Thus, while the United States, and other OECD countries, may have relatively little reason to adopt a flat tax or another, similar reform, there may be logic in viewing such a step as complementary to other necessary fiscal reform measures.

NOTES

1. This follows from the fact that the value of an asset equals the present value of its cash flows. Thus, a tax on all future cash flows is equivalent to a tax on the asset value itself.

2. At the end of 1994, according to the Board of Governors (1995), there was $5.856 trillion in residential structures, of which $4.448 was owner-occupied housing.

3. See Auerbach (1995).

4. Actually, if all investment were debt-financed and the interest rate stayed fixed, the before-tax return to capital would have to *rise*, given the current negative corporate tax on debt-financed investment. However, the simulation model does not distinguish between the before-tax return to capital and the interest rate.

5. The model also does not incorporate any additional efficiency gains that might result from induced growth in technology spurred by capital deepening. See, for example, Stokey and Rebelo (1995).

6. The effective marginal wage tax, t, taking account of both wage and consumption tax effects, is defined by the expression $(1 - t) = (1 - t_w)/(1 + t_c)$, where t_w is the average marginal wage tax rate and t_c is the consumption tax rate.

7. Because there is no risk in the model, there is only one rate of return, typically calibrated to correspond to the observed return to capital, rather than a safe rate of interest.

8. The calculation is based on the expression given in footnote 6 above.

9. That is, under current law (and the current rate of inflation), the present value of remaining depreciation allowances per dollar of net nonresidential capital is approximately .5. Permitting these depreciation allowances to be taken has the same impact as forgiving half of the cash-flow tax on existing assets.

10. The implausibly high values of the current account surpluses offer clear confirmation that the simple open-economy assumption being imposed is too extreme to be realistic.

Appendix

THE AUERBACH-KOTLIKOFF
SIMULATION MODEL

The paper uses the Auerbach-Kotlikoff simulation model, described in Auerbach and Kotlikoff (1987), to simulate the macroeconomic effects of tax changes. This is a dynamic model which, at each date, has 55 overlapping generations of individuals who save and supply labour to maximise lifetime utility. Unless otherwise reported, all simulations reported in the paper use the base case parameter assumptions of the 1987 book, including a pure rate of time preference of .015, a population growth rate of .015, an inter-temporal elasticity of substitution of .25, an intra-temporal elasticity of substitution (between leisure and goods) of .8, a relative weight of 1.5 for leisure in each period's utility sub-function, and a Cobb-Douglas production function.

The initial steady state is calibrated so that the payroll tax rate is .153, the sum at present of employer and employee contribution rates. I assume that one-quarter of this tax rate is viewed by households as being offset by associated marginal social security benefits. The initial level of the national debt equals 55 per cent of one year's net output (roughly its current level), and federal revenue (excluding social insurance contributions) equals 13.5 per cent of net output, also roughly in line with its current level.

The model incorporates tax progressivity by allowing the marginal rate structure for each type of tax to be quadratic. While this does not precisely replicate the type of progressivity under a flat tax, it does allow a reasonable approximation, in that one can determine separately the average tax rate and the average marginal tax rate. The choice of tax parameters is described in the text and Table 1.

BIBLIOGRAPHY

Auerbach, A.J., 1995*a*, "Budget Deficits and Debt: Solutions for Developed Economies", paper presented at a symposium sponsored by the Federal Reserve Bank of Kansas City, September.

Auerbach, A.J., 1995*b*, "Flat Taxes: Some Economic Considerations", Testimony before the Committee on Finance, United States Senate, April.

Auerbach, A.J., 1996, "Tax Reform, Capital Allocation, Efficiency and Growth", paper presented to a conference on fundamental tax reform at the Brookings Institution, February.

Auerbach, A.J. and L.J. Kotlikoff, 1987, *Dynamic Fiscal Policy*.

Board of Governors, Federal Reserve System, 1995, *Balance Sheets for the United States Economy*.

Cummins, J., K. Hassett and G. Hubbard, 1994, "A Reconsideration of Investment Behavior Using Tax Reforms as Natural Experiments", *Brookings Papers on Economic Activity*.

Feldstein, M., 1995, "The Effect of a Consumption Tax on the Rate of Interest", NBER Working Paper No. 5397, December.

Hall, R., 1995, "The Effects of Tax Reform on Prices and Asset Values", in J. Poterba, ed., *Tax Policy and the Economy* 10, forthcoming.

Hall, R., and A.Rabushka, 1995, *The Flat Tax* (2nd ed.)

Stokey, N. and S.Rebelo, 1995, "The Growth Effects of Flat-Rate Taxes", *Journal of Political Economy*, June.

Summers, L., 1981, "Taxation and Investment: A Q-Theory Approach", *Brookings Papers on Economic Activity*.

Tax Notes, 1996, "'New' Armey-Shelby Flat Tax Would Still Lose Money", January 26.

STRUCTURAL REFORM IN OECD COUNTRIES: CRITICAL INTERACTIONS WITH THE REST OF THE WORLD

by

Alan Winters

International Trade Division, International Economics Department, The World Bank[1]

OECD accounts for a significant share of world population and a predominant share of its economic activity. Any fundamental reform it undertakes is bound to affect the non-OECD world in a dramatic and direct way. This paper starts, therefore, by outlining very briefly what those spillovers might be for developing countries. It argues that in some respects OECD structural reform has been more timid than developing countries would wish.

The causation is not just one way, however: developing countries are now sufficiently important economically that their actions have material effects on OECD. In the last decade or so, developing countries as a group have undertaken massive reforms which have generally strongly benefited OECD countries. The second main section of the paper outlines these. OECD countries now have an economic as well as a moral and political interest in the health of the developing world. This should sharpen their interest in seeing the evolution of healthy market-friendly policies in the developing world and will, one hopes, result in constructive dialogue and mutual support between rich and poor countries.

The final main section of the paper looks at the evidence of one particular interaction between OECD and developing countries – the effect of their mutual trade on the farmers' wages and employment of unskilled workers. It considers the analytical basis of worries that such trade is undermining wages and reports some pieces of evidence. Overall, it concludes, the concern is substantially overstated.

OECD ADJUSTMENT AND DEVELOPING COUNTRIES

The proposition that economic performance in OECD affects developing countries is sufficiently commonplace to require no justification. This section, therefore sketches only very briefly the effects of OECD countries' structural reforms on the developing world. It treats the latter as a bloc, but it should always be remembered that certain linkages – e.g., US-Latin America or Europe-Africa – are far stronger than others. I consider four channels of causation through which OECD structural adjustment (or lack of it) could affect the developing world, and I organise the discussion around mechanisms rather than policies. The four are:

– the structure of OECD-developing country trade given levels of income;

– financial flows, in terms of both assets and factor and interest payments;

– the level of OECD demand for developing country goods and services; and

– migration and remittances.

All of these mechanisms have elements of reverse (i.e., developing to industrial country) linkage which I treat in the next main section. I consider here, therefore, only the direct impacts of OECD adjustment policies rather than their final (global general equilibrium) consequences.

OECD trade policies

Developing countries depend heavily on industrial countries both as markets for their exports and sources of their imports. Nearly 60 per cent of their merchandise exports and imports are with industrial countries and the proportions for manufactures are nearer 70 per cent and 65 per cent, respectively. These flows with OECD are growing less rapidly than intra-developing country trade, but still outstrip GDP growth for the bulk of developing countries. With an average trade/GDP ratio of 43 per cent in 1993, developing countries are thus likely to be sensitive – and increasingly so – to factors that disturb or distort their trade with OECD countries.

Manufactures

Trade liberalisation in OECD countries has proceeded only very slowly since the early 1970s, and some would argue that it has actually gone into reverse so far as imports of developing country manufactures are concerned. Thus over the last two and a half decades we have witnessed increasing restrictiveness in the MFA – at least for suppliers outside the various OECD countries' preferred blocs – with lower growth rates for quotas and a greater readiness by importing countries to resort to restrictions at low levels of imports – for example, US actions against Kenya. Trade in iron and steel products is inhibited by VERs supported by price controls and, more recently, draconian anti-dumping measures, which carry the implicit but clear threat that attempts to enter new markets will be resisted. VERs have persisted in sectors such as footwear, and leather trade is also managed to a significant extent, see Low and Yeats (1995). Anti-dumping actions became more frequent through the 1980s (Finger, 1993), especially in the steel and basic chemicals sectors.

The process of negotiating of the Uruguay Round over 1986-93 helped to slow the spread of these trade restrictions and its final agreement in 1994 offered some prospect of future liberalisation. But the outcome was hardly spectacular. VERs are to be phased out, but safeguards have been made easier to implement. Anti-dumping procedures have been tightened up, but major loopholes have been left open and perhaps even enlarged by being officially recognised in the agreement. The abolition of the MFA is a major achievement and a significant liberalisation; however, some commentators fear that it will be replaced with equally restrictive GATT-consistent measures and everybody recognises that effective liberalisation will be delayed by seven or even ten years. Thus while one might take some comfort from the outcome of the Round, one is hardly confronted with evidence of an overwhelming OECD enthusiasm for liberalisation and adjustment in its trading relations with poor countries.

That said, however, it is easy to make too much out of the restrictions on developing countries' exports of manufactures; after all, some strong new exporters have emerged – e.g., Bangladesh and the Czech Republic – and developing country exports to OECD have expanded rapidly in aggregate – at about 12 per cent per year over 1970-90 (UNCTAD, 1995), albeit from a very low base. However, there is no doubt that OECD reluctance to accept imports does reduce developing countries' gains from comparative advantage (e.g., de Melo and Winters, 1993), discourage entrepreneurship and hinder the process of industrialisation.

The failure of OECD countries to embrace wholeheartedly the advantages of comparative advantage also restricts developing countries' access to manufactured and service imports from OECD. Since imports are the more direct link between trade and welfare and are the source of much technological improvement (e.g., Romer, 1994, and Coe, Helpman and Hoffmaister, 1995), this is no small matter. Indeed, it is probably the principal cost to developing countries of the lack of OECD adjustment, although it has so far evaded quantification.

Agriculture

Agricultural protection has been very high and very costly nearly everywhere in OECD for at least three decades. Moreover, although levels of protection are currently low by recent historical standards, the stratospheric tariff bindings committed to under the Uruguay Round indicate little determination to tackle this problem in the near future.[2] This failure imposes costs on many developing countries – not only those that actually export the temperate products most affected (e.g., the developing country members of the Cairns Group), but also the much larger set of those that would do so under free trade – see Falvey and Tyers (1989). The costs are difficult to calculate with any confidence, but Tyers and Anderson (1992) suggest

$11 billion (in 1985 prices) in 1992, while studies of the partial liberalisation agreed in the Uruguay Round suggest substantially more (Martin and Winters, 1995).

Whether these costs will grow or shrink in future is difficult to forecast: future levels of protection are so hard to predict because they depend in part on changes in the world economy. At current rates of technical progress and of shrinkage in the level of resources devoted to agriculture, growing demand for food, particularly in East Asia, seems likely to mop up excess capacity and thus to reduce OECD protection levels and therefore the costs of protection. However, if technical advance and the outflow of mobile factors respond endogenously to prices it is plausible to think that supply will keep up with demand, and prices will remain low and protection high.

Financial flows

Financial flows from OECD to developing countries are an important factor for the latter, even if they have not always been wisely spent in the past. The returns to investment – both private and public – are high in the capital-poor developing world and anything that curtails them is, at least potentially, damaging. Not all the damage is done to developing country residents, however, for foregone asset flows entail foregone income flows to OECD – see section on "Gains from greater financial integration".

The flow of private capital to the developing world is partly explained by the developing countries' policies.[3] It also has "supply-push" elements, however, reflecting the balance between savings and competing opportunities in OECD. Thus the early 1990s recession saw OECD investors seeking developing country outlets more actively than, say, the late 1980s and led some commentators to conclude that the flow would soon reverse.

For the future this view translates into fears of a capital shortage as growing investment and public sector deficits collide with falling savings in OECD countries, raising interest rates and cutting flows to developing countries. World Bank economists have argued that apart from the dangers of fiscal laxity, this is not a major threat (*Global Economic Prospects*, 1995, Box 1.1). Most investment in developing countries will be financed locally as increased incomes and lower dependency ratios boost savings. Moreover, OECD savings are not likely to fall for demographic reasons for a decade.

Over the next decade it is estimated that net private investment in industrial countries financed through capital markets could account for up to $5 trillion of the increase in net household financial savings. After allowing for a net capital flow to developing countries of $1.5 to $2.0 trillion (based on balance of payments projections) that would leave roughly another $5 trillion for financing government deficits. On current policies the aggregate borrowing requirements of governments in industrial countries could appreciably exceed $5 trillion over a ten-year period. Governments are responding to these fiscal challenges, but this is an area where failure to adjust could have serious spillover effects on developing countries.[4]

A major area of reform will be social security: the present value of unfunded public pension liabilities in several major industrial countries already exceeds 150 per cent of GDP. That means that the implicit social security debt is a multiple of an already large explicit public debt – in gross terms, the latter now averages about 70 per cent of GDP in industrial countries, having jumped from about 40 per cent only 15 years ago (World Bank 1994). Moreover, around 2010 the share in industrial country population of those over 65 years old will start to rise rapidly while the share of those aged 40-64 years will fall, tending to depress private savings rates once again. The rising proportion of retirees in the work force will add to public pension liabilities, which could start to rise exponentially unless pension systems are reformed.

The implications of an investment squeeze for developing growth are of concern, but so too are those of an interest rate hike on the cost of existing stocks of debt. With short-term and variable rate debt accounting for nearly half of developing countries' debt and approaching 20 per cent of their GDP, an increase in real interest rates of 100 basis points is roughly estimated to reduce developing country medium-term growth by 0.2 per cent per annum (*Global Economic Prospects*, 1991, Box 4.3).

One casualty of OECD countries' attempts to regain fiscal control has been their official development assistance. This has fallen from 0.35 per cent of GNP over 1986-89 to 0.33 per cent in 1992 and 0.30 per cent in 1993 (*World Debt Tables*, 1994, 1995). To the extent that an inability to control other elements of public expenditure or to stimulate faster growth have led to these declines (from already low levels), OECD countries' adjustment failures have impinged directly upon developing countries. To the extent, however, that reduced ODA reflects OECD countries' intended long-run priorities (perhaps because private flows have increased), it may be taken as evidence of successful adjustment and an example of where the latter is harmful to developing country interests.

OECD demand

In the longer run it is economic growth that matters. The trade links between OECD and developing countries ensure a direct and immediate link between their growth rates, 1 per cent on OECD growth allowing 0.7 per cent on developing countries. If the OECD growth in question is cyclical, part of the 0.7 per cent is offset by the effects of rising interest rates, but if it is based on structural reform it is largely unfettered by such considerations. The growth impulse is transmitted via extra demand for developing country exports[5] and increased supply of OECD exportables.[6] The former increases incomes if trade generates surpluses (e.g., if prices exceed marginal costs or if supply curves slope upwards) and stimulates investment. Both factors potentially improve developing country terms of trade, which will raise incomes and increase incentives for economic activity.[7]

Migration and remittances

Migration has traditionally been one of the major equilibration mechanisms of the world economy. For example, around 1900 immigration increased the US population by over 1 per cent per annum; current immigration is absolutely as high and accounts for about one quarter of total population growth, but adds only about 0.35 per cent per annum to the existing population stock (Friedberg and Hunt, 1995). Germany saw huge immigration after the war and, with France and the United Kingdom, significant flows in the 1950s and 1960s. After that inflows declined, but have recently increased in Germany to 2.5 per cent of population in 1989 and a further 5.4 per cent over 1990-92 (Zimmermann, 1995). For OECD as a whole, however, migration has fallen as a percentage of population since 1970 (World Development Report, 1995).

Migrants remittances have been important sources of income for several developing countries, for example, 8 per cent of GDP for Pakistan in the mid-1980s and 15 per cent of GDP for Egypt in 1990. If OECD countries fail to address their unemployment and/or skill differential problems successfully, and if this failure is manifest – as seems evident at least in the rhetoric – in anti-immigration policies, the effects on developing countries will be felt fairly rapidly in terms of falling remittances. Although the level of remittances depends on the stock of migrants, the latter's propensity to remit falls with the duration of their host country residence and possibly also as the chances of their bringing their (extended) families to join them fall. Also the stock of migrants will start to diminish fairly rapidly as returnees are not replaced.

Closing off opportunities for migration to OECD countries will also affect the composition of developing countries' labour forces. Since emigration is slightly biased towards higher skill groups,[8] curtailing it is likely to increase average developing country skill levels. Where governments severely distort labour markets such an enforced skill upgrading could have significantly beneficial effects on the home economy. Taken as a whole, however, the evidence probably supports the view that most developing countries do not suffer from such brain drain problems because the wedges between private and social costs are not so large (World Development Report, 1995).[9]

Immigration has generally benefited host economies – indeed, many migrants have been actively encouraged to move in order to meet skill shortages or fill jobs that local workers reject. Migrants do probably put some pressure on low-skilled wages, however, and so to the extent that this is seen as a problem in OECD countries, they might be unwelcome on distributional grounds.[10] Overall, therefore, to the extent that adjustment in OECD countries can address skill differentials through policies such as training local workers, and can relax immigration rules, developing countries (and indeed OECD countries) are likely to gain. Policies that address differentials by artificially raising low-skill wages will also strongly benefit migrants and their home countries if migration continues, but are more likely to lead to further restrictions on immigration. This would be a case where an inability to treat distribution effectively would have precluded policy stances that are desirable on efficiency grounds.

DEVELOPING COUNTRIES AFFECT OECD COUNTRIES

While it is clear that adjustment in OECD countries is an important issue for developing countries, it is also true that the reverse link is important.[11] One might identify three major channels of effect from developing to industrial countries: the gains from greater integration into the world economy, basically trade liberalisation; the gains from greater integration into capital markets, basically financial liberalisation; and the gains from enhanced economic growth in developing countries, which arise from general policy and regulatory issues.

Gains from greater trade integration

Since 1986, international trade in goods and non-factor services (exports plus imports) has risen as a proportion of developing countries' GDP from 33 per cent to about 43 per cent. Developing countries took part in the Uruguay Round to a greater extent than any previous Round, and there are now over 100 developing country members of the World Trade Organisation or the GATT. In the seven years since the Uruguay Round was launched in 1986, developing countries have been responsible for 58 of the 72 autonomous liberalisation actions reported to the GATT. Average tariffs, while still higher in the developing world than the industrial world, have fallen very significantly in the former. Figure 1 shows the distribution of average tariffs for 42 countries for which data were available in both the early eighties and early nineties. While tariff averaging is a dubious business and not all the averages included in these distributions will be precisely comparable, the general trend towards liberalisation is quite clear. Moreover, given that the majority of trade liberalisations within the developing world stressed the removal of quantitative trade restrictions, and frequently permitted their replacement by tariffs, the shift indicated in the figure understates the degree of progress made.

In the Uruguay Round developing countries agreed to reduce their tariffs by an average of about 30 per cent. While this was a smaller proportionate cut than industrial countries', it actually represented a larger decline in the internal prices of

◆ Figure I. **Distribution of average tariffs for 42 developing countries**
(unweighted average)

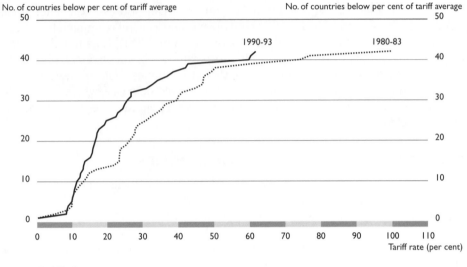

Source: World Bank.

imports because it was applied to a higher base. In that sense, it represents a greater liberalisation and adjustment. Developing countries enlarged the coverage of their tariff bindings dramatically from 13 per cent before the Round to 61 per cent of imports after it. The gains to industrial countries from these liberalisations in developing countries are an important part of the Uruguay Round agreement. In fact, offers by developing countries to reduce tariffs under the Round were more important to the United States than those of either the European Union or Japan, and more important than those of the United States to Japan and the European Union (Martin and Winters, 1995).

One indicator of potential gains from trade integration between industrial and developing countries is the price difference for similar products. The larger is the price difference, the greater is the potential gain from specialisation through trade. The differences in prices are much larger between industrial and developing countries than between industrial countries. A piece of transport equipment costs 2.5 times more in the Philippines than in the United States or the United Kingdom. But clothing and footwear cost four times more in the United States than in Bangladesh – five times more in Japan. The latest available price data show differences in consumer prices between industrial countries to be only about half as big on average as those between industrial countries and developing countries.[12]

If trade in services, especially such long-distance services as information processing and other clerical services, grows as fast as expected, the gains to industrial countries from trade integration with developing countries could be even larger. For example, in 1994 the gross dollar income of clerks in Bombay was about one-fortieth that of their counterparts in Zurich (Table 1). Small wonder that the Swiss national airline carries out a sizeable part of its back-office functions in India.

It is difficult to place precise figures on the benefits that accrue to OECD countries as a result of past or future trade liberalisations in the developing world, but for all the well-known reasons, they are likely to be of some significance. One very direct calculation that is of interest to governments, if not to students of economic welfare, is to look at the increases in OECD exports resulting from liberalisation. In one exercise, World Bank economists have attempted to assess the consequences of a World Bank policy-based lending.

Since the World Bank's policy-based lending began in 1981, 238 loans, totalling over $35 billion of lending, have included conditions for disbursement that are related to import policy, export policy, or foreign exchange allocation policy. These loans, made to 75 different countries, have specified over 2 000 such reforms as conditions for borrowing, and about 80 per cent of these reforms have been substantially implemented.

This policy-based lending went to countries that imported about one-seventh of industrial countries' and one-fourth of developing countries' merchandise exports – in 1993 dollar values, about $402 billion from industrial countries and $120 billion from developing countries (Table 2). Over the periods covered by the

Table 1. **Gross incomes of bank credit clerks, 1994 (US dollars)**[1]

	Annual income
Zurich	78 100
Tokyo	63 400
Abu Dhabi	47 800
Paris	42 000
New York	29 000
Bangkok	14 200
Tel Aviv	15 800
Rio de Janeiro	7 600
Jakarta	3 900
Bombay	1 900
Nairobi	1 600

1. Gross income of clerks with completed bank training, ten years of bank experience, and who are around 35 years old, married, with two children.
Source: Union Bank of Switzerland. Cited in the World Bank *Global Economic Prospects*, 1995.

Table 2. **World Bank lending to support trade or foreign exchange policy reform: amount of lending and number of policy conditions (by region); borrowing countries' imports from the world and from the United States**

Region[1]	World Bank lending to support trade or exchange rate policy reform			Imports from industrial countries		Imports from developing countries		Imports from United States	
	Amount of lending ($ millions)	Number of policy reform conditions	Percentage implemented[3]	Value, 1993 ($ millions)	Annual percentage increase[2]	Value, 1993 ($ millions)	Annual percentage increase[2]	Value, 1993 ($ millions)	Annual percentage increase[2]
Africa (33)	8 917	754	83	18 913	1.5	11 768	8.8	2 194	3.0
Asia (12)	6 295	297	75	167 452	6.3	145 833	9.5	35 752	7.3
Latin America (18)	11 434	634	79	119 400	12.2	41 647	6.4	71 685	15.5
Middle East and Northern Africa (6)	5 285	253	76	47 472	6.6	14 620	9.1	8 324	8.8
Transition Economies (6)	3 515	95	71	49 178	15.2	14 125	-1.5	2 507	8.2
All countries (75)	35 446	2 033	80	402 414	8.3	227 993	6.6	120 461	11.8
Memorandum item:									
Non-recipient developing countries (65)[4]				147 760	3.6	77 447	6.4	33 187	3.7

1. Number of countries in brackets.
2. Average annual rate of growth from before the first to after the last policy-based loan. See the text for the details of the calculation.
3. For the trade policy conditions coded for implementation, this percentage is the ratio of conditions with "substantial implementation" or better to the total number of trade policy conditions.
4. Growth between 1981-83 and 1991-93.
Sources: PSD data base and Direction of Trade Statistics, IMF; ALCID data base, World Bank.

reform process, the reforming countries' imports grew rapidly – on average 8.3 per cent per annum from industrial countries and 6.6 per cent per annum from developing countries. These rates compare with growth rates over the reform decade of 3.6 per cent and 6.4 per cent, respectively, in the imports of developing countries not receiving Bank policy-based lending (group excludes Hong Kong, Iraq, Taiwan, Singapore, and former USSR).

The growth of markets overseas is clearly an incentive to increase research and development and thus might generate genuinely new technical advance. But developing country liberalisation offers another route for increasing the rate of technical progress – the transfer of technology to developing countries. As developing countries have liberalised their arrangements for licensing technology and for foreign direct investment (FDI), new opportunities for OECD firms have emerged. Fifteen years ago, Mansfield, Teece and Romeo (1979) showed that a significant proportion of the return to new invention came from overseas applications and developing countries could clearly account for some of these. Relatedly, Coe, Grossman and Hoffmaister (1995) have shown that developing countries gained significantly from research and development undertaken in OECD. Where the channel of causation is trade in industrial products, as Coe *et al.* assume, or licensing or investment, it is unlikely that all these gains take the form of externalities. Thus part of the increase in productivity in developing countries that is attributable to OECD research and development is likely to accrue to OECD firms.

Gains from greater financial integration

During 1992-94 developing countries accounted for about 40 per cent of global FDI inflows, up dramatically from 23 per cent in the mid-1980s. Their share of portfolio investment flows also increased, from around 9 per cent in the late 1980s to 16 per cent in 1993. It is impossible to quantify the degree of financial liberalisation that has occurred in the developing world, but both from the frequency with which the financial reform is reported and these figures on outcomes, one can conclude that it is significant.

FDI flows are clearly an important part of the output-supply response to successful trade liberalisation. They also, however, influence the distribution of the benefits from such liberalisations, allowing part of it to accrue directly to firms in industrial countries. The evidence suggests that returns to FDI in developing countries considerably outstrip those on other opportunities available to such firms. For example, returns on US FDI flows to the rest of the G7 have averaged around 8 per cent over the past three years while returns on FDI to the eight largest developing country recipients have averaged about 21 per cent (*Global Economic Prospects*, 1995). Clearly there are differences in riskiness between the two destinations of investment, but if these are similar for FDI as for portfolio investment, the risk-adjusted return to FDI is still appreciably higher in developing countries than in G7. This difference probably reflects both ignorance and excessive caution by western investors on the one hand and remaining policy restrictions in the developing world on the other. Either way, the data make clear that the increases in FDI flows that have been observed in recent years have generated significant returns for investors.

Increasing flows of portfolio capital from industrial to developing countries also offer the prospect of significant gains for savers in industrial countries, for two reasons. First, as with FDI flows, expected risk-adjusted rates of return are generally much higher in developing countries. Second, the expected rates of return in emerging markets show a low, and sometimes negative, correlation with those of industrial countries, providing scope for gains from portfolio diversification.

Underlying the higher risk-adjusted average returns in developing countries are their improved growth prospects, the result of wide-ranging structural reforms of recent years, including capital market reforms. Between January 1989 and December 1994 the annualised nominal total return of emerging market stocks averaged 19 per cent, compared with 10.5 per cent on the Standard and Poor's (S&P) index. At the same time, the improving creditworthiness of many developing countries is beginning to reduce the riskiness of investments in their capital markets. Despite the Mexico crisis, average risk-adjusted rates of return in emerging markets remain higher than those in industrial countries. In theory, in an efficient market the price of emerging market equities should reflect the expected risk-return trade-off, so risk-adjusted expected returns would not differ from those of industrial countries. But because of the lack of familiarity with these markets, emerging market stocks should continue to outperform those of industrial countries for some time (Wadhwani and Shah 1994).[13]

Because the integration of developing countries into world financial markets is still at an early stage, expected returns in emerging markets continue to show a low correlation with those in industrial countries. Between January 1989 and December 1994 the correlation between the International Finance Corporation's (IFC) composite "emerging market total investible returns" and Standard and Poor's indices was 0.44, with some developing country regions showing considerably lower correlations. With increasing integration, emerging market returns will no doubt become progressively more closely correlated with those in industrial countries. But the scope for gains from portfolio diversification seems likely to remain significant because of continued differences in vulnerability to real and financial shocks and the addition of new developing countries to the emerging market portfolio.

The typical US pension fund currently holds no more than 1 to 2 per cent of its portfolio in emerging market stocks, and institutional investors in other industrial countries tend to hold even smaller shares. Compare these small shares with developing countries' share in world stock market capitalisation of around 10 per cent. If the average US pension fund is taken as representative of industrial country investors, typical investors could maintain the same risk in their portfolios and yet raise their annualised expected return by almost 2 percentage points by increasing their holdings of emerging market stocks to around 20 per cent of their portfolios, assuming that stock prices in these markets did not rise.

What would the higher risk-adjusted rates of return associated with portfolio and FDI flows to developing countries mean for gains to industrial country savers? Even allowing for both a rising correlations between industrial and developing countries' assets and a narrowing difference in risk-adjusted returns, the gains could be equivalent to a 0.4 per cent permanent increase in GDP.[14]

As is the case for trade integration, greater financial integration with growing emerging markets could have dynamic effects over time (Obstfeld, 1992). The premise is that stronger growth requires investments in new activities characterised by rapid productivity increases but also entailing significant sunk costs and risks. By including developing country assets in their portfolios, savers in industrial countries can reduce the overall risk associated with high-yielding investments since asset returns for developing countries and industrial countries show low correlation. This reduction in risk can lead savers in industrial countries to allocate more of their total savings to higher-yielding, faster-productivity-growth investments in both groups of countries, contributing to higher growth. Purely as an illustrative calculation, in Obstfeld's framework, which makes the extreme assumption of full global mobility of capital and labour, the higher growth spurred by financial integration could produce a permanent increase in industrial country GDP of about 4 per cent.[15] If the higher risk-adjusted returns from financial integration raise the saving rate in industrial countries, the gains could augment those from improved allocation of savings.

Gains from rapid growth in the developing world

By contributing to greater trade and investment integration with industrial countries, rapid growth of developing countries can generate first- and second-round gains for industrial countries similar to those from trade integration. Indeed, over time, growth could be more important than trade liberalisation as a source of gains from trade integration. Roughly half the increase in developing country imports from industrial countries since 1985 is attributable to growth in developing countries. In 1991-93, when most of the industrial world was stuck in a recession, developing countries provided markets for about three-quarters of the increase in world exports, making them an engine of growth in the industrial economies. Over the same period US exports to developing countries grew at an average annual rate of 10 per cent – five times the growth in exports to other industrial countries.

The rising share of developing countries in world output and trade could dampen cyclical swings in industrial countries and in the global economy because of the broader country and geographic distribution of world economic activity. Higher growth in developing countries can also improve industrial countries' terms of trade, although this result is not inevitable. Since developing countries tend to grow faster than industrial countries, the supply of their exportables will tend to grow faster than that of industrial countries. The demand for exportables will also tend to rise more for those of industrial countries than those of developing countries because industrial countries tend to produce goods with higher income elasticities.

TRADE AND THE SKILLS WAGE DIFFERENTIAL

Structural adjustment has tended to be interpreted recently in OECD countries largely in terms of policies to enhance employment and/or real wages. This focus is natural given current policy concerns although it should not blind us to other objectives of economic activity. I conclude this note, therefore, with a brief discussion of the consequences of the interactions between OECD and developing countries in the former's labour markets. Specifically, I address the question of whether increasing trade with the developing world has reduced employment and/or real wages for lower-skilled workers in OECD countries.[16] I concentrate on the case of the United States in which flexible labour markets have kept unskilled employment up but at the expense of falling real wages. The European phenomenon of rising wages but falling employment may be analysed in a related fashion.

This issue now sports a substantial literature which has been more than adequately surveyed elsewhere, *e.g.*, Bhagwati and Kosters (1994), Burtless (1995) and *The Journal of Economic Perspectives*, Summer 1995. Despising "make-work" schemes, I shall not attempt to replicate these surveys, but will merely select a few headlines from them and add a few new results from work carried out for the World Bank – McDougall and Tyers (1995), Falvey (1996), Tyers and Yang (1996) and Falvey and Tyers (1996).

The story so far

Since 1980, most OECD countries have experienced falling wages and/or rising unemployment for unskilled workers while the wages of skilled workers have increased strongly. These movements have been quite significant quantitatively; for example, the lowest paid workers experienced a fall of 11 per cent in real wages in the United States over the eighties, while in Germany the unemployment rate among low-skilled workers increased by 11 percentage points – see Revenga (1995). There has been a vigorous debate about whether the rapid growth of developing country trade has been responsible for this or whether it is due to technological change. That debate has recently begun to converge, at least in principle. Everyone recognises that it is ultimately a quantitative issue that can only be resolved by careful empirical work. That is, no one seriously maintains any more that trade has had absolutely no effect on low-skill wages and employment nor that it is the only cause of change over the last two decades. Rather the issue is whether or not it has been a significant factor.

A second general point should also be made. The processes under consideration here are large and operate over significant periods of time over which adjustment is feasible, at least unless it is frustrated by specific policy. The correct model, therefore, is a general equilibrium one with considerable flexibility – essentially the neo-classical trade model much beloved by trade theorists. The model allows us to consider trade and technology shocks together, and leads in its pure form to the rather strong conclusion that relative wages (employment if wages are rigid) can be explained solely by reference to factor intensities, which are given *ex ante* for any wage vector, and changes in relative product prices and sectoral total factor productivities (Richardson, 1995). At least within the cone of diversification (*i.e.*, when countries do not wholly specialise) changes in factor supplies, factor augmenting technical progress, and changes in the factor content of trade add no further information. Moreover, trade and production levels are endogenous variables, which can move in response to many stimuli. Without further information, correlations between them and relatives wages are uninterpretable.

Using the framework just outlined we can consider a few of the contributions to the literature. Evidence on relative price changes for the US economy is mixed, largely because of empirical uncertainties about how to define importables, exportables and non-tradeables. If US exportables are defined as investment goods, prices move the wrong way to explain the decline of low-skill wages: that is, the prices of low-skilled imports generally fall by less than those of investment goods – *e.g.*, Lawrence and Slaughter (1993).[17] But if one separates out computers, other investment goods prices have risen relatively – *e.g.*, Sachs and Shatz (1994) – and if one focuses on imports of clothing, in which US production is relatively *very* low-skill, import prices have fallen sharply – Leamer (1995). Related empirical difficulties bedevil the definition of skilled workers which is currently based either on the production/non-production split or, more appropriately, length of education with 12 years as the dividing line.

A question that is frequently posed is how can shifts in manufactured imports from developing countries, which account for only 1.5 per cent of OECD countries' GDP (UNCTAD, 1995; data exclude China), cause such large changes in the relative wages of unskilled workers? The answer is that they can because nearly everything of interest in economics happens on the margin and 1.5 per cent is potentially quite a thick margin. Indeed, prices can change even if imports remain constant (even constant at zero) if industrial country producers respond to the introduction of potential competitors by matching their prices. On the other hand, however, if goods are not perfect substitutes, such extreme responses will not occur and there is some presumption that impacts on the margin are positively correlated with the average sizes of flows.[18] In addition, once we enter the realms of complete special-isation such that the OECD has no unskilled workers remaining in import-competing sectors, unskilled wages will essentially be independent of imports being determined just by market clearing in non-tradeables (Freeman, 1995). Clearly this is a very extreme outcome, but coupled with the differentiated good model it does start to rehabilitate the view that changes in imports of manufactures from develop-ing countries are just too small to have major effects on the relative wages of skilled and unskilled workers.

A further empirical challenge to the "trade causes inequality" thesis is that if unskilled wages had been driven down by trade changes, every industry would have shifted its technique of production to use relatively more unskilled workers.[19] In fact, the opposite appears to occur, with most industries showing rising shares of skilled to unskilled workers, Sachs and Shatz (1994). Moreover, these authors also find that the shift towards skills is stronger in skill-intense sectors, which is the opposite of what would have occurred if measured sectors included ranges of sub-sectors with differing intensities. In this "aggregation story", the greater the number of unskilled-intensive sub-sectors included in a sector, the greater the proportion of the latter that would be squeezed by imports and hence the more extensive its subsequent adjustment. Leamer (1995) observes that if regions differ in their endowments (which are immobile across regions), unskilled-abundant regions could lose from opening developing country trade, even while the country as a whole gains.

Extensions

The theoretical analysis discussed so far and which has been used to interpret the data has mostly been based on an extremely simple and pure Heckscher-Ohlin model – frequently the $2 \times 2 \times 2$ model, always a "square" model with equal numbers of factors of production and goods, and rarely formally recognising prod-uct differentiation. This model predicts factor price equalisation under free trade (at least subject to well-known caveats). Even in this context, however, it has been recognised that quantitative analysis is required to identify the magnitude of the effect of trade on relative wages for trade is never perfectly free and the relative sizes of trade and technology shocks is not known *a priori*. Once the model is extended, this requirement becomes even more pressing. This sub-section, therefore, briefly introduces some research conducted for the World Bank that generalises the theo-retical model and tries to offer plausible quantifications based on actual data.

Falvey (1996) explores the theory of non-square factor endowment models of trade in which the number of factors exceeds the number of goods and in which comparative advantage might depend on technology differences as well as on factor endowments. Either of these modifications would be sufficient to exclude factor price equalisation under free trade let alone partial liberalisations such as those we have actually experienced. Falvey asks, therefore, whether in these circumstances his model predicts even the convergence of factor rewards across countries. The answer is that it depends.

First, one has to characterise the initial protection or trade frictions and the nature of the liberalisation undertaken. Falvey assumes that protection was designed to fix the vector of domestic prices somewhere between its free trade and autarchy values and that the liberalisation is a radial reduction in the wedges between domestic and border prices. If comparative advantage is based only on factor endowments, then such liberalisation tends to generate international wage convergence, but only in a rather weak sense. The most powerful result is that if endowments differ in only one factor, e.g., unskilled labour, liberalisation will cause international convergence in that factor's rewards. No prediction is possible for other factors, however.

Where comparative advantage stems from technological differences the tendency is, if anything, away from factor price convergence. This is especially true if the technology differences are factor augmenting. These reduce factor returns per efficiency unit of the "favoured" factor, but generally increase them per physical unit. Protection enhances the former effect (i.e., reduces the return to abundant factors), pulling physical rewards downwards, and so liberalisation allows these returns to grow; that is, liberalisation raises the returns of "favoured" factors, increasing international dispersion. Overall, therefore, it is not at all clear that in the real world we should expect a great deal of factor price convergence. Convergence is not ruled out, of course, but neither is trade liberalisation left holding a smoking gun beside the corpse of narrow skill differentials in wages.

A second paper – Falvey, Tyers and McDougall (1996) – introduces differentiated products into the analysis and, by simulating a very simple general equilibrium model, asks what features of the economy – parameters – encourage endowment and technology shocks in one region to have large effects on factor rewards in both regions. Essentially this is asking what are the critical parameters that we should devote most effort to understanding if we want to explain the effects of trade shocks on relative wages if the former arise either from factor accumulation or technological change. Two important features are identified.

First, the wider the dispersion of factor intensities *across industries*, the greater the effects of endowment changes on relative factor rewards.[20] The more different are different industries' intensities, the less able is one industry to absorb factors in the proportions in which they are released by another in response to a shock, and thus the greater is the excess supply or demand of factors that must be accommodated by factor reward changes. The importance of this observation is that we currently have only very crude information on factor intensities (few factors are distinguished) and that we tend to work with rather aggregate industries. Both will lead current data to understate variation across industries and thus to understate the impact of shocks. This is essentially the point made above that certain sub-factors or regions could be hit hard by trade.

Second, and more obviously, the greater the substitutability between home and foreign goods, the greater the effects of trade shocks. Substitutability means that quantities change more in response to a given shock; this implies larger output changes, which translate into larger factor demand changes and hence larger changes in rewards. As so often, the issue is: do OECD and developing countries produce very similar goods. Most evidence suggests not, on average, but again in specific sectors the effects could be significant.

I turn now to quantification, focusing on a "back-cast" of the period 1970-92. Tyers and Yang (1996) work with small-scale general equilibrium models of the world economy which distinguishes three sorts of labour (production, professional and farm) as well as capital and land. They distinguish six regions, of which "rapidly developing economies" (RDEs) is the principal source of disturbance. It comprises China, Indonesia, Hong Kong, Malaysia, Singapore, Korea, Taiwan and Thailand and the principal disturbance it generates is a disproportionately rapid rate of capital accumulation and total factor productivity growth – see Table 3.

Tyers and Yang conduct three backward-looking exercises, which suggest rather modest effects on OECD wage differentials from the emergence of the RDEs. The first, "RDE trade and growth", asks how the world would have looked in 1992 had there been neither growth nor opening of the RDEs since 1970. Starting with the 1992 database, RDE factor use is reduced by proportions consistent with row 5 of Table 3, while endogenous tariffs are applied to ensure that RDE openness is held at 1970 levels. The second, "OIE technical change", asks how the world would have

Table 3. **Measures of growth, 1970 to 1990, per cent**[1]

	Labour use	Capital stock	Total factor productivity	Real GDP
North America	22	82	30	79
European Union	7	101	42	69
Australasia	33	114	19	74
Japan	18	320	61	134
Rapidly Developing Economies (RDEs)	41	554	75	303

1. Because their sources are disparate, there is no necessary consistency between the four columns of this table and any particular GDP function. Complete statistics on all columns are unavailable for the slow-growing developing group economies.
Source: Tyers and Yang (1996).

looked in 1992 had there been no technical change in OIE production since 1970. The shares of different types of labour and total factor productivity in the old industrial areas are returned to 1970 levels. This entails declines of 19 to 40 per cent in output relative to 1992 plus switches from professional to farm and production labour's shares of output ranging up to 15 percentage points. The final simulation combines the first and second.

Table 4 reports the changes in factor rewards in North America stemming from these three experiments. Those in Europe and Australasia are basically similar. The principal effect of the growth and increased openness of the RDEs is agricultural. As these land-scarce economies open up, resources move out of agriculture into manufacturing and services while the opposite occurs elsewhere in the world. Farm labour and land experience a large boost, but the relative rewards of production and professional labour are basically unchanged. Note, *inter alia*, that no North American factor loses from the RDEs' growth and integration.

Technical change in the old industrial areas has much bigger effects. The change in TFP over 1970-92 boosts all wages and returns to capital, but just as significant is the differential effect on professional and production labour. The differential widens by over 20 per cent (25.6/121.0). Recalling that these shocks are based on historical data, the relative magnitudes in Table 4 suggest rather strongly that it is technology rather than trade that is driving wage dispersion in OECD countries. It is true that a finer industrial classification (Tyers and Yang have "only" 37 sectors) would probably increase the wage dispersion effects of both shocks and that at least some of the apparently neutral technical progress observed over 1970-92 was stimulated by import competition. Thus these results may understate the relative importance of trade for wage differentials somewhat. Nonetheless, it

Table 4. **Changes in real unit factor rewards in North America, per cent**

	North America		
	RDE[1] trade and growth	OIE[2] technological change	Combined trade and technological change
Professional labour	0.2	46.6	47.0
Production labour	0.0	21.0	21.8
Farm labour	10.4	11.4	15.6
Land	18.2	−3.6	15.7
Capital	0.2	30.1	30.6

1. Rapidly Developing Economies.
2. Old Industrial Economies.
Source: Tyers and Yang (1996).

seems clear that trade has not been the major cause. Moreover, in a separate, forward-looking exercise, Tyers and Yang show that protection is likely to exacerbate not relieve skill differentials in the future.

What now?

Whatever the cause of changes in relative factor rewards, economists are nearly unanimous that restricting international trade is not the way to deal with the problem. All our theory and experience and a good deal of quantitative analysis suggests that such a response will be costly in aggregate terms. Rather, what is required is compensation in the short run to shelter existing low-skill workers from unacceptable burdens (however these are defined) and adequate facilities to try to ensure that fewer new unskilled workers are created. In the long term transfers to the poor in the form of cash or the public provision of goods and services face the possibility that, if borders are open to migrants, the supply of unskilled workers is fairly elastic at any rate of reward materially above subsistence. If so, subsidies are almost inevitably coupled with immigration restrictions. The latter reduce the scope for adjusting to changes in the world economy and arguably reduce world welfare. It may be feasible to restrict benefits to nationals or citizens in the short run – *i.e.*, to exclude temporary migrants – but in the long run such discrimination is not desirable.

NOTES

1. The views expressed in this paper are those of the author. They should not be attributed to the World Bank or its member governments. This paper draws freely on the work of colleagues of the International Economics Department of the World Bank and I am grateful to them all. I am also grateful to Will Martin and Maurice Schiff for comments on an earlier draft, to Francis Ng for help with certain data, and to Audrey Kitson-Walters and Sarah Lipscomb for excellent logistical support.

2. The new rules agreed to will facilitate future liberalisation, but not without the will to negotiate lower tariffs.

3. Its distribution over destinations is largely determined by this factor.

4. Fiscal deficits in OECD countries increased by 3 per cent of GDP between 1989 and 1993, with a little under half the increase being structural (OECD, 1994). The OECD-wide structural deficit is estimated to have fallen by 0.3 percentage points of GDP in 1994 as a result of fiscal consolidation in the United States, Germany, and the United Kingdom. Given current fiscal reform plans, the bulk of future fiscal consolidation will be in the EU, where the Maastricht deficit-reduction targets for 1997 are expected to be substantially, though not fully, met.

5. Other than in the short term, the effects of OECD growth on commodity prices are relatively minor.

6. For example, Röger (1996) suggest that fiscal reforms will allow tax cuts which in turn increase incentives for production in OECD.

7. It seems safe to assume that substitution effects dominate income effects in these circumstances.

8. This bias declines as networks make it easier for poorer and less experienced people to move, but it still appears to rule overall.

9. In my view, this absence of harm is less persuasive for Eastern Europe than for other developing countries.

10. Estimates of the degree of pressure vary, but few economists identify immigration as the principal cause of changes in differentials in low- and high-skilled wages.

11. This section is closely based on Chapter 4 of *Global Economic Prospects*, 1995, The World Bank, the principal authors of which were Uri Dadush and Zia Qureshi.

12. In 1985, the latest year for which the most complete set of data from the UN International Comparison Program are available, the coefficient of variation of consumer prices across industrial countries was 0.21; it was 0.54 when developing countries were added to the sample.

13. The Sharpe ratios (ratio of mean return to standard deviation) in emerging markets have, in general, been improving over time (Bekaert, 1993). For many emerging markets the ratio is higher than that for industrial countries, indicating a better risk-return trade-off for emerging markets. Over January 1989-December 1994, the Sharpe ratio for the IFC composite Emerging Market Index was 0.92, compared to 0.85 for the Standard and Poor's index.

14. Since the gains consist of an improvement in the risk-return trade-off, they need to be evaluated in terms of utility to industrial country savers. The gains are expressed here as the increase in GDP required to yield savers the same level of utility as the improvement in the risk-return trade-off (or "utility equivalent" gains). The gains are calculated by applying a 1 percentage point higher risk-adjusted mean rate of return (associated with a portfolio mix of 11 per cent in emerging markets, which would be the optimal mix if correlations between emerging market and industrial country returns increased to 0.65) to industrial country financial wealth as measured by stock market capitalisation. For FDI flows the gains are calculated by applying a 3 percentage point higher risk-adjusted mean rate of return to the inward FDI stock of developing countries.

15. The correlation between emerging market and industrial country expected returns is likely to increase in the future and the differential in risk-adjusted returns to narrow. Therefore, it is assumed that the correlation of returns is 0.65 (compared to an estimated 0.44 for recent years) and that risk-adjusted rate of return in emerging markets falls to 0.87 (from 0.92 over January 1989-December 1994) – the comparable risk-adjusted rate of return on the Standard and Poor's index was 0.85 over January 1989-December 1994. Since Obstfeld's framework assumes that both financial and capital assets (physical and human) are perfectly mobile globally – and without cost – the estimated gains represent an upper bound that is unlikely to be reached. Nonetheless, the estimate suggests that dynamic gains from financial integration could potentially be significant.

16. There has also been concern expressed about employment in general, but I think it is now widely accepted that to the extent that this is related to trade at all it is a transitional issue, not one of long-term relevance.

17. Richardson (1995) gives fuller sets of references.

18. Essentially each of the myriad differentiated goods has a margin and the share of the overall margin impacted by developing countries' trade depends on the latter's share of the total number of varieties which is, at least roughly, given by their share of sales.

19. Aggregate employment of the unskilled remains unchanged in the simple model, of course, increasing intensity in each industry being offset by a shift in the composition of output away from unskilled-intensive sectors.

20. The model contains two large regions; thus endowment changes are global in scale even if geographically restricted.

BIBLIOGRAPHY

Bekaert, G. (1995), "Market integration and investment barriers in emerging markets", *World Bank Economic Review*, Vol. 9, pp. 75-107.

Bhagwati, J. and M. Kosters (1994), *Trade and Wages*, American Enterprise Institute, Washington, DC.

Borjas, G.J. (1995), "The economic benefits from immigration", *Journal of Economic Perspectives*, Vol. 9-2, pp. 3-22.

Burtless, G. (1995), "International trade and the rise in earnings inequality", *Journal of Economic Literature*, Vol. 33, pp. 800-816.

Coe, D., E. Helpman A.W. and Hoffmaister (1995), "North-South R&D spillovers", *CEPR Discussion Paper*, No. 1133, London.

de Melo, J. and L.A. Winters (1993), "Do exporters gain from VERs?", *European Economic Review*, Vol. 37, pp. 1331-1350.

Falvey, R. and R. Tyers (1989), "Border price changes and domestic welfare in the presence of subsidised exports", *Oxford Economic Papers*, Vol. 41, pp. 434-451.

Falvey, R. (1996), "Factor price convergence", mimeo, The World Bank.

Falvey, R. and R. Tyers (1996), "Trade shocks and the magnitude of transmitted wage adjustments", mimeo, The World Bank.

Finger, J.M. (1993), *Anti-dumping: How it Works and Who Gets Hurt*, University of Michigan Press, Ann Arbor, MI.

Freeman, R.B. (1995), "Are your wages being set in Beijing?", *Journal of Economic Perspectives*, Vol. 9-3, pp. 15-32.

Friedberg, R.M. and J. Hunt (1995), "The impact of immigrants on host country wages, employment and growth", *Journal of Economic Perspectives*, Vol. 9-2, pp. 23-44.

Lawrence, R.Z. and M. Slaughter (1993), "Trade and US wages: Giant sucking sound or small hiccup?", *Brookings Papers in Economic Activity, Microeconomics*, Brookings Institution, Washington, DC, pp. 161-226.

Leamer E.E. (1995), "A trade economist's view of US wages and globalisation", mimeo, University of California.

Low, P. and A. Yeats (1995), "Non-tariff measures and developing countries: Has the Uruguay Round leveled the playing field?", *The World Economy*, Vol. 18, pp. 51-70.

Mansfield, E., D. Teece, and A. Romeo (1979), "Overseas research and development by US-based firms", *Economics*, Vol. 46, pp. 187-96.

Martin, W. and L.A. Winters (1995), "The Uruguay Round: Widening and Deepening the World Trading System", The World Bank, Washington, DC.

McDougall, R. and R. Tyers (1995), "East Asian expansion and factor markets in industrial countries", mimeo, The World Bank.

Nehru, V. and A. Dhareshwar (1993), "New estimates of total factor productivity growth for eighty-three industrial and developing countries", Policy Research Working Paper, No. 1128, The World Bank, Washington, DC.

Obstfeld, M. (1992), "Risk taking, global diversification and growth", *NBER Working Paper*, No. 4093.

OECD (1994), *Economic Outlook*, December, OECD, Paris.

Revenga, A. (1995), *The Employment Crisis in Industrial Countries: Is International Integration to Blame?*, Regional Perspectives on the World Development Report, 1995, The World Bank, Washington, DC.

Richardson, J.D. (1995), "Income inequality and trade: how to think, what to conclude", *Journal of Economic Perspectives*, Vol. 9-3, pp. 33-55.

Röger, W. (1996), "Macroeconomic effects of fiscal consolidation and competition in Europe", prepared for conference on "Interactions between structural reform, macroeconomic policies and economic performance", OECD, January.

Romer, P. (1994), "New goods, old theory and the welfare costs of trade restrictions", *Journal of Development Economics*, Vol. 43, pp. 5-38.

Sachs, J.D. and H. Shatz (1994), "Trade and jobs in US manufacturing", *Brookings Papers in Economic Activity*, No. 1, pp. 1-84.

Summers, R. and A. Heston (1991) "The Penn World Tables (Mark 5): An expanded set of international comparisons, 1950-1988", *Quarterly Journal of Economics*, Vol. 106, pp. 327-368.

Tyers, R. and K. Anderson (1991), *Disarray in World Food Markets: A Quantitative Assessment*, Cambridge University Press, Sydney.

Tyers, R. and Y. Yang (1996), "Trade with Asia and skill upgrading: the effects on factor markets in the older industrial countries", mimeo, The World Bank.

UNCTAD (1995), *Trade and Development Report*, 1995, UNCTAD, Geneva.

Wadhwani, S. and M. Shah (1994), "Emerging giants, globalisation and equities", *Portfolio Strategy*, Goldman Sachs, New York.

Zimmermann, K.F. (1995) "Tackling the European migration problem", *Journal of Economic Perspectives*, Vol. 9-2, pp. 45-62.

CONCLUDING DISCUSSION

The last round of discussion before the end of the Conference covered a wide range of issues: first those arising from the presentation of three further papers, addressing international and country-specific aspects of structural reform, and then a winding-up and wrapping-up of all previous discussions. In order to ensure that contributions to the debate would be geared as closely as possible to the title of the final session, the Chairman had suggested at the close of the previous session three sets of questions:

– How can structural reform and macroeconomic policy best be combined to enhance economic performance and welfare?

– Are there structural reforms which can be introduced either individually or collectively in combination, whose benefits are so straightforward and evident, and perhaps so immediate, that everybody should move ahead and introduce them without delay?

– Are there other cases where structural reforms will best work if they are combined with supportive macroeconomic policies, and if this is the case, how should one proceed there?

An underlying assumption of most discusssants was that structural reform, widely defined, would improve the allocation of resources, thereby raising productivity and easing the unemployment-inflation trade-off. Against this background, it was argued that the scope for monetary expansion has been increased. However, it is important to distinguish between structural reforms which tend to stimulate demand and those which involve major adjustment costs in terms of job losses and weaker short-term demand. It is only in the latter case that demand-supporting macro policy action might usefully be considered for some time. An issue here was the timing of supportive macroeconomic policy measures with respect to the introduction of structural reform. A clear majority view emerged in favour of support to be given as a "reward" after the event rather than as a "bribe" before the event.

Referring to the high share of structural unemployment in Europe, there was widely-shared scepticism about the possibilities on the macro policy side to bring relief to the unemployment problem. A more promising avenue was felt to be changes in tax wedges, notably in favour of "risk groups" in the labour market. An important point was made in this context, namely that budget consolidation is going to be extremely hard to achieve without better labour market performance. As long as countries have to live with high structural unemployment, the overall burden on the public sector was bound to remain high. Also, without clear signs of an improved labour market there would be severe political constraints to take discretionary measures towards fiscal consolidation.

Apart from lowering taxes on employment and labour income, another subject for discussion on the fiscal side was reform of the unemployment benefit system. Concern was expressed about the negative effects on job search intensity and, more generally, the willingness to work as a result of unconditional unemployment benefits but also about guarantees of automatic renewal of eligibility for benefits after a spell on an active labour market programme. It was suggested that activation strategies towards the long-term unemployed should include "sticks" as well as "carrots". Otherwise, the balance between savings on passive income support and extra costs of financing "activity" may well turn out negative. Nobody who participated in this debate opposed the view that the duration of unemployment benefits is one of the key determinants of the level of unemployment. There was also consensus that in many countries increased efforts need to be made to raise the quality of the labour force as part of the solution to the unemployment problem which typically hits unskilled workers particularly hard. Finally, nobody contradicted the view that deregulation in the service industry could make an important contribution to the creation of new job opportunities.

MAIN SALES OUTLETS OF OECD PUBLICATIONS
PRINCIPAUX POINTS DE VENTE DES PUBLICATIONS DE L'OCDE

AUSTRALIA – AUSTRALIE
D.A. Information Services
648 Whitehorse Road, P.O.B 163
Mitcham, Victoria 3132   Tel. (03) 9210.7777
Fax: (03) 9210.7788

AUSTRIA – AUTRICHE
Gerold & Co.
Graben 31
Wien I   Tel. (0222) 533.50.14
                         Fax: (0222) 512.47.31.29

BELGIUM – BELGIQUE
Jean De Lannoy
Avenue du Roi, Koningslaan 202
B-1060 Bruxelles
                   Tel. (02) 538.51.69/538.08.41
                         Fax: (02) 538.08.41

CANADA
Renouf Publishing Company Ltd.
1294 Algoma Road
Ottawa, ON K1B 3W8   Tel. (613) 741.4333
                     Fax: (613) 741.5439
Stores:
61 Sparks Street
Ottawa, ON K1P 5R1   Tel. (613) 238.8985

12 Adelaide Street West
Toronto, ON M5H 1L6   Tel. (416) 363.3171
                      Fax: (416)363.59.63

Les Éditions La Liberté Inc.
3020 Chemin Sainte-Foy
Sainte-Foy, PQ G1X 3V6 Tel. (418) 658.3763
                       Fax: (418) 658.3763

Federal Publications Inc.
165 University Avenue, Suite 701
Toronto, ON M5H 3B8   Tel. (416) 860.1611
                      Fax: (416) 860.1608

Les Publications Fédérales
1185 Université
Montréal, QC H3B 3A7   Tel. (514) 954.1633
                       Fax: (514) 954.1635

CHINA – CHINE
China National Publications Import
Export Corporation (CNPIEC)
16 Gongti E. Road, Chaoyang District
P.O. Box 88 or 50
Beijing 100704 PR   Tel. (01) 506.6688
                      Fax: (01) 506.3101

CHINESE TAIPEI – TAIPEI CHINOIS
Good Faith Worldwide Int'l. Co. Ltd.
9th Floor, No. 118, Sec. 2
Chung Hsiao E. Road
Taipei   Tel. (02) 391.7396/391.7397
                      Fax: (02) 394.9176

CZECH REPUBLIC – RÉPUBLIQUE TCHÈQUE
National Information Centre
NIS – prodejna
Konviktská 5
Praha 1 – 113 57   Tel. (02) 24.23.09.07
                   Fax: (02) 24.22.94.33
(*Contact* Ms Jana Pospisilova,
nkposp@dec.niz.cz)

DENMARK – DANEMARK
Munksgaard Book and Subscription Service
35, Nørre Søgade, P.O. Box 2148
DK-1016 København K   Tel. (33) 12.85.70
                      Fax: (33) 12.93.87

J. H. Schultz Information A/S,
Herstedvang 12,
DK – 2620 Albertslung   Tel. 43 63 23 00
                        Fax: 43 63 19 69
Internet: s-info@inet.uni-c.dk

EGYPT – ÉGYPTE
The Middle East Observer
41 Sherif Street
Cairo   Tel. 392.6919
                        Fax: 360-6804

FINLAND – FINLANDE
Akateeminen Kirjakauppa
Keskuskatu 1, P.O. Box 128
00100 Helsinki
Subscription Services/Agence d'abonnements :
P.O. Box 23
00371 Helsinki   Tel. (358 0) 121 4416
                      Fax: (358 0) 121.4450

FRANCE
OECD/OCDE
Mail Orders/Commandes par correspondance :
2, rue André-Pascal
75775 Paris Cedex 16 Tel. (33-1) 45.24.82.00
                     Fax: (33-1) 49.10.42.76
                     Telex: 640048 OCDE
Internet: Compte.PUBSINQ@oecd.org

Orders via Minitel, France only/
Commandes par Minitel, France exclusive-
ment :
36 15 OCDE

OECD Bookshop/Librairie de l'OCDE :
33, rue Octave-Feuillet
75016 Paris   Tél. (33-1) 45.24.81.81
                           (33-1) 45.24.81.67

Dawson
B.P. 40
91121 Palaiseau Cedex   Tel. 69.10.47.00
                        Fax: 64.54.83.26

Documentation Française
29, quai Voltaire
75007 Paris   Tel. 40.15.70.00

Economica
49, rue Héricart
75015 Paris   Tel. 45.75.05.67
                        Fax: 40.58.15.70

Gibert Jeune (Droit-Économie)
6, place Saint-Michel
75006 Paris   Tel. 43.25.91.19

Librairie du Commerce International
10, avenue d'Iéna
75016 Paris   Tel. 40.73.34.60

Librairie Dunod
Université Paris-Dauphine
Place du Maréchal-de-Lattre-de-Tassigny
75016 Paris   Tel. 44.05.40.13

Librairie Lavoisier
11, rue Lavoisier
75008 Paris   Tel. 42.65.39.95

Librairie des Sciences Politiques
30, rue Saint-Guillaume
75007 Paris   Tel. 45.48.36.02

P.U.F.
49, boulevard Saint-Michel
75005 Paris   Tel. 43.25.83.40

Librairie de l'Université
12a, rue Nazareth
13100 Aix-en-Provence Tel. (16) 42.26.18.08

Documentation Française
165, rue Garibaldi
69003 Lyon   Tel. (16) 78.63.32.23

Librairie Decitre
29, place Bellecour
69002 Lyon   Tel. (16) 72.40.54.54

Librairie Sauramps
Le Triangle
34967 Montpellier Cedex 2
                        Tel. (16) 67.58.85.15
                        Fax: (16) 67.58.27.36

A la Sorbonne Actual
23, rue de l'Hôtel-des-Postes
06000 Nice   Tel. (16) 93.13.77.75
                        Fax: (16) 93.80.75.69

GERMANY – ALLEMAGNE
OECD Bonn Centre
August-Bebel-Allee 6
D-53175 Bonn   Tel. (0228) 959.120
                        Fax: (0228) 959.12.17

GREECE – GRÈCE
Librairie Kauffmann
Stadiou 28
10564 Athens   Tel. (01) 32.55.321
                        Fax: (01) 32.30.320

HONG-KONG
Swindon Book Co. Ltd.
Astoria Bldg. 3F
34 Ashley Road, Tsimshatsui
Kowloon, Hong Kong   Tel. 2376.2062
                        Fax: 2376.0685

HUNGARY – HONGRIE
Euro Info Service
Margitsziget, Európa Ház
1138 Budapest   Tel. (1) 111.62.16
                        Fax: (1) 111.60.61

ICELAND – ISLANDE
Mál Mog Menning
Laugavegi 18, Pósthólf 392
121 Reykjavik   Tel. (1) 552.4240
                        Fax: (1) 562.3523

INDIA – INDE
Oxford Book and Stationery Co.
Scindia House
New Delhi 110001   Tel. (11) 331.5896/5308
                        Fax: (11) 371.8275

17 Park Street
Calcutta 700016   Tel. 240832

INDONESIA – INDONÉSIE
Pdii-Lipi
P.O. Box 4298
Jakarta 12042   Tel. (21) 573.34.67
                        Fax: (21) 573.34.67

IRELAND – IRLANDE
Government Supplies Agency
Publications Section
4/5 Harcourt Road
Dublin 2   Tel. 661.31.11
                        Fax: 475.27.60

ISRAEL – ISRAËL
Praedicta
5 Shatner Street
P.O. Box 34030
Jerusalem 91430   Tel. (2) 52.84.90/1/2
                        Fax: (2) 52.84.93

R.O.Y. International
P.O. Box 13056
Tel Aviv 61130   Tel. (3) 546 1423
                        Fax: (3) 546 1442

Palestinian Authority/Middle East:
INDEX Information Services
P.O.B. 19502
Jerusalem   Tel. (2) 27.12.19
                        Fax: (2) 27.16.34

ITALY – ITALIE
Libreria Commissionaria Sansoni
Via Duca di Calabria 1/1
50125 Firenze   Tel. (055) 64.54.15
                        Fax: (055) 64.12.57

Via Bartolini 29
20155 Milano   Tel. (02) 36.50.83

Editrice e Libreria Herder
Piazza Montecitorio 120
00186 Roma   Tel. 679.46.28
                        Fax: 678.47.51

Libreria Hoepli
Via Hoepli 5
20121 Milano   Tel. (02) 86.54.46
                      Fax: (02) 805.28.86
Libreria Scientifica
Dott. Lucio de Biasio 'Aeiou'
Via Coronelli, 6
20146 Milano   Tel. (02) 48.95.45.52
                      Fax: (02) 48.95.45.48

JAPAN – JAPON
OECD Tokyo Centre
Landic Akasaka Building
2-3-4 Akasaka, Minato-ku
Tokyo 107   Tel. (81.3) 3586.2016
                      Fax: (81.3) 3584.7929

KOREA – CORÉE
Kyobo Book Centre Co. Ltd.
P.O. Box 1658, Kwang Hwa Moon
Seoul   Tel. 730.78.91
                      Fax: 735.00.30

MALAYSIA – MALAISIE
University of Malaya Bookshop
University of Malaya
P.O. Box 1127, Jalan Pantai Baru
59700 Kuala Lumpur
Malaysia   Tel. 756.5000/756.5425
                      Fax: 756.3246

MEXICO – MEXIQUE
OECD Mexico Centre
Edificio INFOTEC
Av. San Fernando no. 37
Col. Toriello Guerra
Tlalpan C.P. 14050
Mexico D.F.   Tel. (525) 665 47 99
                      Fax: (525) 606 13 07

NETHERLANDS – PAYS-BAS
SDU Uitgeverij Plantijnstraat
Externe Fondsen
Postbus 20014
2500 EA's-Gravenhage Tel. (070) 37.89.880
Voor bestellingen: Fax: (070) 34.75.778

Subscription Agency/Agence d'abonnements :
SWETS & ZEITLINGER BV
Heereweg 347B
P.O. Box 830
2160 SZ Lisse   Tel. 252.435.111
                      Fax: 252.415.888

**NEW ZEALAND –
NOUVELLE-ZÉLANDE**
GPLegislation Services
P.O. Box 12418
Thorndon, Wellington Tel. (04) 496.5655
                      Fax: (04) 496.5698

NORWAY – NORVÈGE
NIC INFO A/S
Ostensjoveien 18
P.O. Box 6512 Etterstad
0606 Oslo   Tel. (22) 97.45.00
                      Fax: (22) 97.45.45

PAKISTAN
Mirza Book Agency
65 Shahrah Quaid-E-Azam
Lahore 54000   Tel. (42) 735.36.01
                      Fax: (42) 576.37.14

PHILIPPINE – PHILIPPINES
International Booksource Center Inc.
Rm 179/920 Cityland 10 Condo Tower 2
HV dela Costa Ext cor Valero St.
Makati Metro Manila   Tel. (632) 817 9676
                      Fax: (632) 817 1741

POLAND – POLOGNE
Ars Polona
00-950 Warszawa
Krakowskie Prezdmiescie 7 Tel. (22) 264760
                           Fax: (22) 265334

PORTUGAL
Livraria Portugal
Rua do Carmo 70-74
Apart. 2681
1200 Lisboa   Tel. (01) 347.49.82/5
                      Fax: (01) 347.02.64

SINGAPORE – SINGAPOUR
Ashgate Publishing
Asia Pacific Pte. Ltd
Golden Wheel Building, 04-03
41, Kallang Pudding Road
Singapore 349316   Tel. 741.5166
                      Fax: 742.9356

SPAIN – ESPAGNE
Mundi-Prensa Libros S.A.
Castelló 37, Apartado 1223
Madrid 28001   Tel. (91) 431.33.99
                      Fax: (91) 575.39.98

Mundi-Prensa Barcelona
Consell de Cent No. 391
08009 – Barcelona   Tel. (93) 488.34.92
                      Fax: (93) 487.76.59

Llibreria de la Generalitat
Palau Moja
Rambla dels Estudis, 118
08002 – Barcelona
          (Subscripcions) Tel. (93) 318.80.12
          (Publicacions) Tel. (93) 302.67.23
                         Fax: (93) 412.18.54

SRI LANKA
Centre for Policy Research
c/o Colombo Agencies Ltd.
No. 300-304, Galle Road
Colombo 3   Tel. (1) 574240, 573551-2
                      Fax: (1) 575394, 510711

SWEDEN – SUÈDE
CE Fritzes AB
S–106 47 Stockholm   Tel. (08) 690.90.90
                      Fax: (08) 20.50.21

For electronic publications only/
Publications électroniques seulement
STATISTICS SWEDEN
Informationsservice
S-115 81 Stockholm   Tel. 8 783 5066
                      Fax: 8 783 4045

Subscription Agency/Agence d'abonnements :
Wennergren-Williams Info AB
P.O. Box 1305
171 25 Solna   Tel. (08) 705.97.50
                      Fax: (08) 27.00.71

SWITZERLAND – SUISSE
Maditec S.A. (Books and Periodicals/Livres
et périodiques)
Chemin des Palettes 4
Case postale 266
1020 Renens VD 1   Tel. (021) 635.08.65
                      Fax: (021) 635.07.80

Librairie Payot S.A.
4, place Pépinet
CP 3212
1002 Lausanne   Tel. (021) 320.25.11
                      Fax: (021) 320.25.14

Librairie Unilivres
6, rue de Candolle
1205 Genève   Tel. (022) 320.26.23
                      Fax: (022) 329.73.18

Subscription Agency/Agence d'abonnements :
Dynapresse Marketing S.A.
38, avenue Vibert
1227 Carouge   Tel. (022) 308.08.70
                      Fax: (022) 308.07.99

See also – Voir aussi :
OECD Bonn Centre
August-Bebel-Allee 6
D-53175 Bonn (Germany)
                      Tel. (0228) 959.120
                      Fax: (0228) 959.12.17

THAILAND – THAÏLANDE
Suksit Siam Co. Ltd.
113, 115 Fuang Nakhon Rd.
Opp. Wat Rajbopith
Bangkok 10200   Tel. (662) 225.9531/2
                      Fax: (662) 222.5188

**TRINIDAD & TOBAGO, CARIBBEAN
TRINITÉ-ET-TOBAGO, CARAÏBES**
SSL Systematics Studies Limited
9 Watts Street
Curepe, Trinadad & Tobago, W.I.
                      Tel. (1809) 645.3475
                      Fax: (1809) 662.5654

TUNISIA – TUNISIE
Grande Librairie Spécialisée
Fendri Ali
Avenue Haffouz Imm El-Intilaka
Bloc B 1 Sfax 3000   Tel. (216-4) 296 855
                      Fax: (216-4) 298.270

TURKEY – TURQUIE
Kültür Yayinlari Is-Türk Ltd. Sti.
Atatürk Bulvari No. 191/Kat 13
06684 Kavaklidere/Ankara
                      Tél. (312) 428.11.40 Ext. 2458
                      Fax : (312) 417.24.90
                      et 425.07.50-51-52-53
Dolmabahce Cad. No. 29
Besiktas/Istanbul   Tel. (212) 260 7188

UNITED KINGDOM – ROYAUME-UNI
HMSO
Gen. enquiries   Tel. (0171) 873 0011
                      Fax: (0171) 873 8463
Postal orders only:
P.O. Box 276, London SW8 5DT
Personal Callers HMSO Bookshop
49 High Holborn, London WC1V 6HB
Branches at: Belfast, Birmingham, Bristol,
Edinburgh, Manchester

UNITED STATES – ÉTATS-UNIS
OECD Washington Center
2001 L Street N.W., Suite 650
Washington, D.C. 20036-4922
                      Tel. (202) 785.6323
                      Fax: (202) 785.0350
Internet: washcont@oecd.org
Subscriptions to OECD periodicals may also
be placed through main subscription agencies.

Les abonnements aux publications périodiques
de l'OCDE peuvent être souscrits auprès des
principales agences d'abonnement.

Orders and inquiries from countries where Dis-
tributors have not yet been appointed should be
sent to: OECD Publications, 2, rue André-Pascal, 75775 Paris Cedex 16, France.

Les commandes provenant de pays où l'OCDE
n'a pas encore désigné de distributeur peuvent
être adressées aux Éditions de l'OCDE, 2, rue
André-Pascal, 75775 Paris Cedex 16, France.

8-1996

OECD PUBLICATIONS, 2, rue André-Pascal, 75775 PARIS CEDEX 16
PRINTED IN FRANCE
(11 96 04 1) ISBN 92-64-15326-8 – No. 49057 1996